PRINTMAKING

Off the Beaten Track

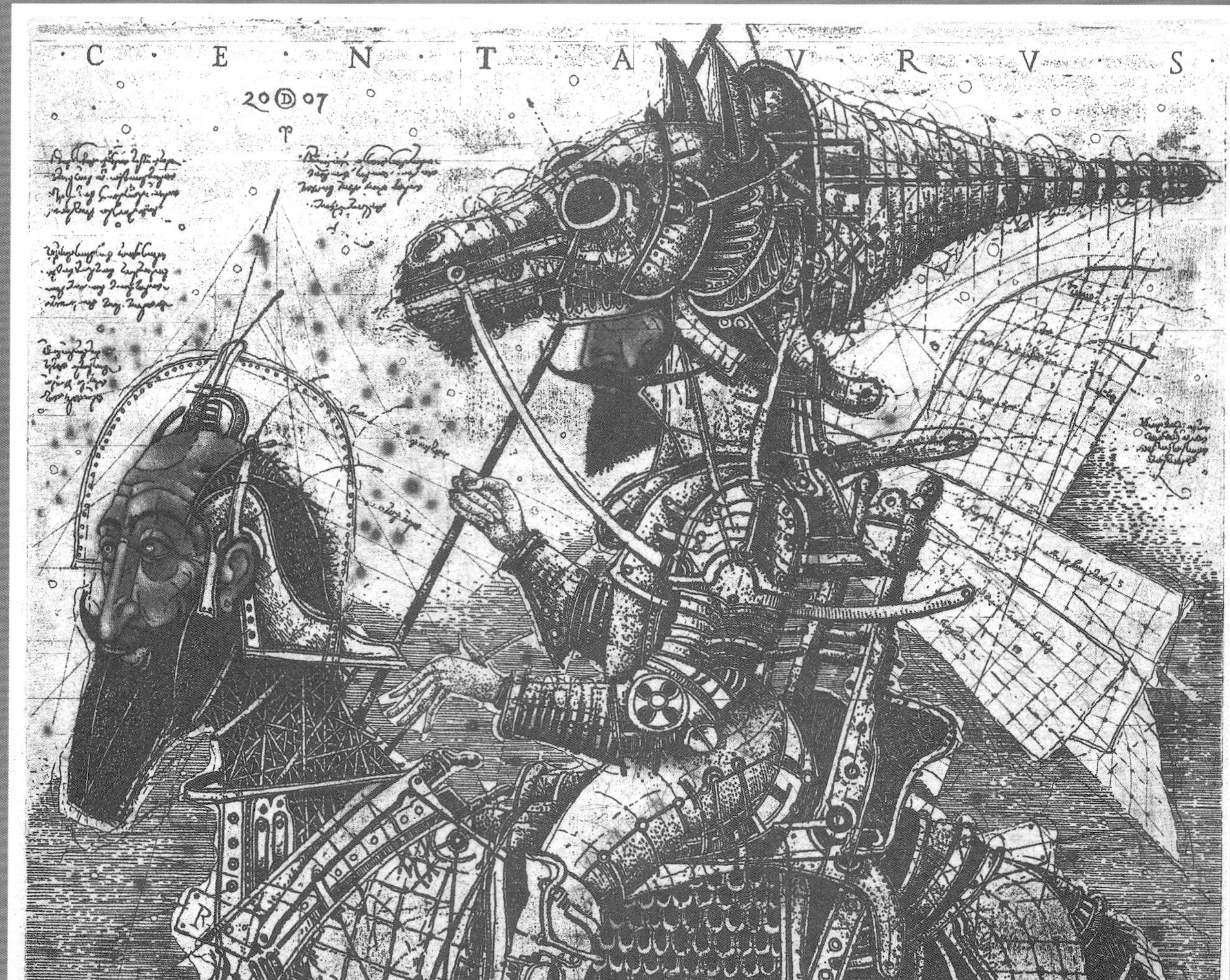
C · E · N · T · A · V · R · V · S

PRINTMAKING
Off the Beaten Track

RICHARD NOYCE

BLOOMSBURY
LONDON • NEW DELHI • NEW YORK • SYDNEY

First published in Great Britain 2013
Bloomsbury Publishing Plc
50 Bedford Square
London WC1B 3DP
www.bloomsbury.com

ISBN: 9781 4081 5672 8

A CIP catalogue record for this book is available from the British Library

Commissioning editor: Susan Kelly
Project manager: Davida Forbes
Copy editor: Julian Beecroft
Page design: Susan McIntyre
Cover design: Eleanor Rose

Typeset in 9.75 on 12.5pt Adobe Caslon Pro

This book is produced using paper that is made from wood grown in managed, sustainable forests. It is natural, renewable and recyclable. The logging and manufacturing processes conform to the environmental regulations of the country of origin.

Printed and bound in China

Half title: Nan Mulder, *Starting the Journey*, detail, 2011. See page 38.

Frontispiece: Oleg Denysenko, *Centaurus*, 2007. See page 149.

Contents page: Gil & Moti, *Future Line Tours – Old in Tel Aviv*, 2009. See page 76.

CONTENTS

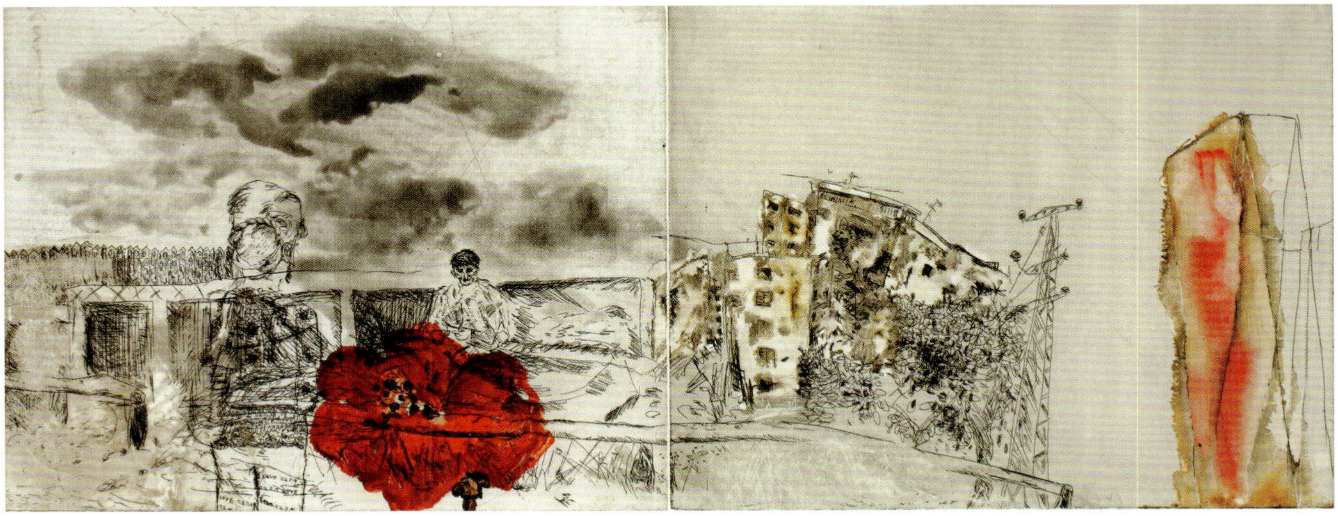

ACKNOWLEDGEMENTS

The work I did in researching and then writing this book began in June 2011 and was completed in November 2012. The ideas I explore in the book had been emerging some years before that during the writing of my two previous books on international contemporary printmaking. In the course of producing this book I received help and advice from many people in the international printmaking community, and am grateful to all of them. Their advice, suggestions and critical friendship have been, as always, of great value in this work.

I would like to thank all the artists whose work is included in this book for their faith in my desire to pursue what turned out to be a complex project. Their willingness to provide catalogues, information, texts and images has been much appreciated and I thank them warmly for their professionalism and their time.

The journeys I made in researching the book took me to many places, and the support and friendship I received are gratefully acknowledged. In particular I wish to thank Professor Rahman Mohamed at the Universiti Sains Malaysia in Penang; Ms Izan Tahir in Kuala Lumpur for her generous assistance in Malaysia; Esther Attar-Machanek in Vienna for her helpful suggestions of directions for research; Johannes Aldrian and the staff of the K&K Hotel Elisabeta in Bucharest for their hospitality; Olivia Niţiś and her colleagues at the International Experimental Engraving Biennial in Bucharest; Gönül Nuhoğlu and her colleagues at the Resim Ve Heykel Müzeleri Derneği in Istanbul; Mrs Slava Ivanova, Executive Director of the National Art Gallery in Sofia; Emil Mirazchiev of the Art Today Association in Plovdiv; Antonia Dimitrova of the Resonance Art Gallery in Plovdiv; Robert Baramov and Nevena Valcheva for their hospitality in Sofia; Mary Hood at Arizona State University; and all the other people who made my journeys and visits so interesting.

The professional assistance of Susan Kelly, and of Davida Forbes and her colleagues at Bloomsbury Publishing, during the research, writing and production of this book has been much appreciated.

Finally, I thank my family, especially Fiona, for their support and tolerance during my work on this book, and for their understanding and assistance.

Wales, November 2012

All quotations used in the book are from correspondence between the author and the artist, unless otherwise noted.

Right: Zulkifli Yusoff, *Peace III*, 2010. See page 30.

PART 1

CONTEXTS

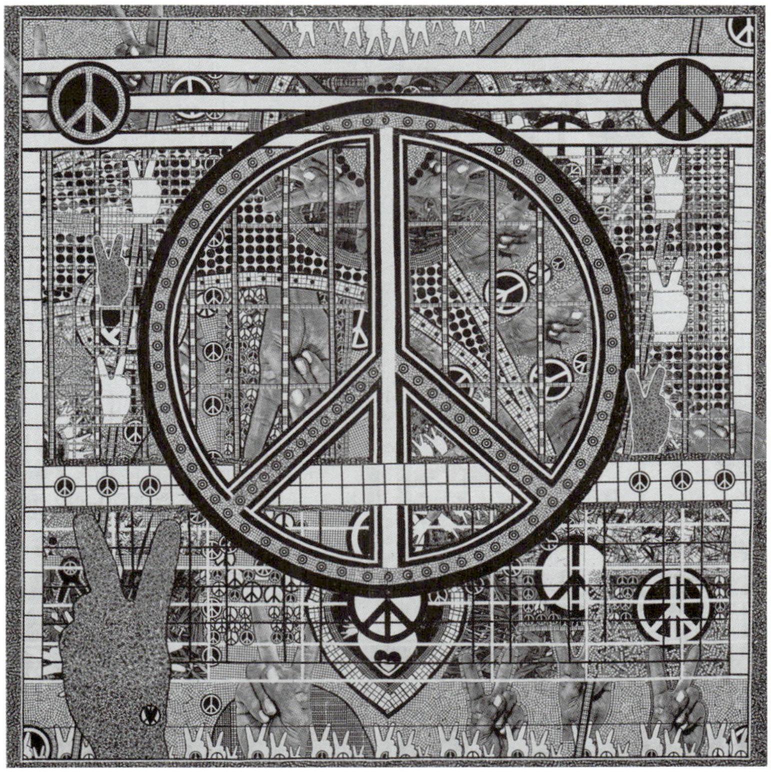

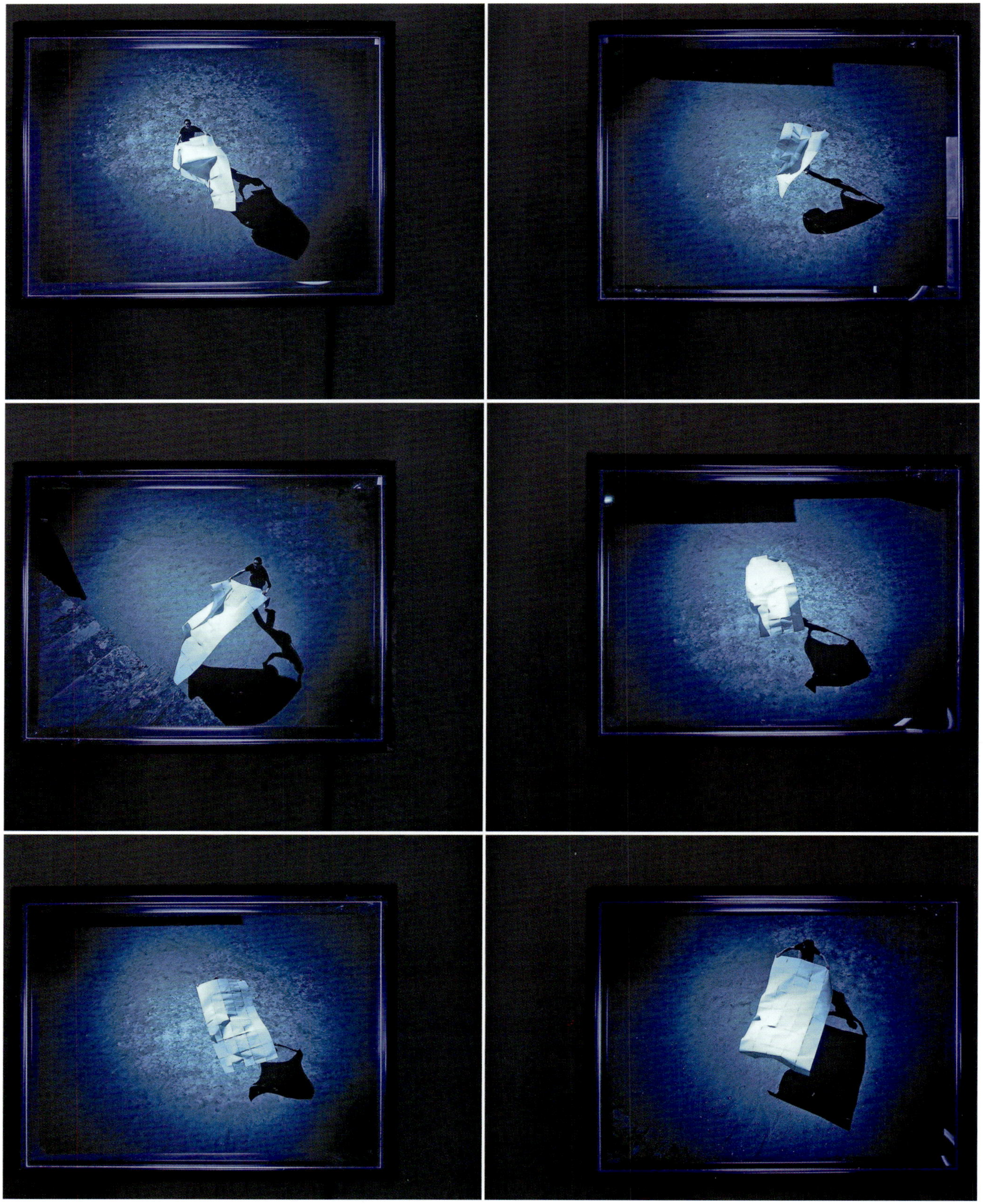

Ciprian Ciuclea, *Apparent Silence, Movement 1–6*, 2011 See page 100.

INTRODUCTION

Printmaking Off the Beaten Track follows on from *Printmaking at the Edge* (A&C Black, 2006, reprinted 2008) and *Critical Mass: Printmaking Beyond the Edge* (A&C Black, 2010). Those two books considered aspects of the multiplicity of new developments in international printmaking at the beginning of the 21st century, and sought to widen the understanding of the possibilities of printmaking among academics, students and art lovers. This third book seeks to achieve a different, although connected, end.

During the writing of the previous two books, through the journeys and activities that I undertook during the research for those books, and subsequently through participation in conferences and juries as a result of them, it became apparent to me that there are many aspects of printmaking that are too little appreciated, if at all, within printmaking and art circles in Western Europe, North America, Australasia and Japan – the mainstream centres of the contemporary arts. It seems that many critics and gallerists in that particular art world are too little aware of the work and ideas of artists pursuing printmaking as an active art form in the wider world. The lack of readily available information is one factor, but there is also the still persistent problem of how printmaking is perceived, and how printmakers position themselves, within the contemporary visual arts in general.

Printmaking techniques have played an important role in the development of the visual arts in most of the countries and cultures of the world. Some of the earliest forms of visual art and communication were made using printmaking, or related, techniques. Despite this, in the upper echelons of the contemporary gallery and museum world – at least in what can broadly be termed 'the West' – printmaking (and its connected mediums) is still for the most part considered to be something of a poor relation, even a second-class medium, and not as interesting or important as the current mainstream fashions for video, performance, and installation art, or for the new variants of painting and sculpture. This is despite the historic and continuing inclusion of printmaking as part of their practice by a large number of the world's most celebrated artists, as has been the case since the early 19th century. Little wonder then that the printmaking (and print-related art) of countries that are considered by the art world to be 'off the beaten track', and therefore of little if any interest or value, is largely unknown and unacknowledged.

It is from this initial position that *Printmaking Off the Beaten Track* has been conceived and created. It aims to celebrate the achievements of artists who include printmaking as part of their practice, either as a continuation of the traditions in the countries in which they live or from which they originate, or as a reaction to those traditions. These countries fall in something of a crescent reaching from the equatorial tropics in the south and east of Asia to the temperate forests and lakes in the north and east of Europe, together with a few other parts of the world that have their place in the book for other and connected reasons. A number of the featured countries have in the recent past suffered from internal violence and political or social disruption, or from conflict with neighbouring countries. Within such countries the making of art of any kind (if it is made at all) takes on a different set of imperatives and a different rationale. Some aspects of the sociopolitical function of contemporary art in such situations will be explored. At the same time the book will look at the broad range of printmaking mediums and approaches undertaken by artists from those countries – everything from strictly traditional forms to experimental forms in which the connection to printmaking may seem at best to be peripheral.

There is an old English joke: A chauffeur-driven Rolls-Royce glides to a halt outside a village inn somewhere off the beaten track in a remote part of the country, where a couple of countrymen are sitting on a bench, enjoying their beer in the sunshine. The rear window of the limousine whispers down. 'I say, you there,' calls out one of the rich people sitting in the back, 'How do we get to London?' The countrymen fall about laughing, and the voice from inside the Rolls-Royce repeats the question, more demandingly this time. The two countrymen continue to laugh and point at the large shiny car. Exasperated, the voice from within shouts, 'You're stupid!', to which one of the countrymen shouts back, 'We may be stupid, but we ain't lost!'

The definition of 'off the beaten track' depends on the perspective from which it is defined. In the same way, just as the street markets of Penang may seem exotic to someone living in Britain, the suburbs of London or New York may seem equally exotic to someone living in a small village in the Carpathian mountains. 'Exotic' is, after all, defined in the Concise Oxford Dictionary as, 'introduced from abroad' and 'attractively strange or unusual': and 'abroad' is defined as 'in or to foreign lands'. It all depends on where you start from and in which direction you are looking.

For the purposes of this book, 'off the beaten track' does not mean a specific place, or places, but rather some of those countries in which printmaking is being pursued as a contemporary art form, but which are unknown or too little recognised in the mainstream of the printmaking world. Of course, there are parts within those mainstream locations that are, in their own local sense, 'off the beaten track', and little known or appreciated further afield, even within the countries in which they are to be found. Such is the nature of the Western nations in which the primary focus of the media and arts funding bodies is on the big cities; this is a 'metro-centric' view of the world that pays little heed to the wider picture. It is a curious fact that the capital cities of a number of major countries are situated far from the geographical centre, sometimes towards the bottom right hand-corner of the map . Until fairly recently it was the case in many countries that the primary focus for artists was on the capitals, where the major public and private art galleries and the attendant media have tended to be concentrated.

London was once a prime example of this phenomenon. Artists who worked outside the capital cities had for a very long time struggled for recognition and acceptance. It was widely acknowledged that, in order to build a career, an ambitious artist had either to live and work in London, or at the very least to have major gallery representation there. To choose to live and work outside the capital was, and to some extent still is, something of a brave decision, and for this reason capital cities, including London, continue to act as a magnet for young artists. And yet there is an encouraging and stimulating renaissance of art galleries and initiatives in places beyond the capital, a development that brings its own curious results. For example, a prominent British art critic, speaking on a radio programme some years ago, questioned why a major exhibition was being staged at the Baltic Centre for Contemporary Art in Gateshead, some 250 miles (400 km) north of London, complaining that in order to see the exhibition he would be forced to make a long journey by train. Indeed, how dreadful to be dragged out of his metropolitan comfort zone! Since then other cities in the UK – Liverpool, Manchester, Glasgow and Edinburgh among them – have developed and continue to develop as major centres, and London no longer holds quite the same sway as the centre. There are similar initiatives in cities in other countries, and some architecturally exciting new galleries have been built, engendering a new impetus for artists along with new locations in which the public can experience their work. The focus is shifting and expanding, with the contemporary arts and their audiences the beneficiaries.

This book seeks neither to present a complete overview of the work being made using print techniques in places off the beaten track, nor to present a complete view of the work in any of the countries featured. Such is the proliferation of printmaking as a vital contemporary art form that either of these aims would require a much larger book. Instead it offers a selection of work from artists living in, or originating from, some of those places. Beyond that selection there is, without question, a lot more printmaking out there, equally interesting and equally worthy of attention, as well as many more artists making work that is challenging and original. It is hoped that those reading and looking at this book, and who share my sense of being intrigued by what can be found in the wider reaches of the international printmaking community, will make their own explorations and discoveries in that expanding world.

JOURNEYS & DESTINATIONS

I investigated a large number of countries while researching this book. It will be noted by readers that there are omissions among the featured countries: this is inevitable, since printmaking has continued to emerge as one of the most widespread and popularly supported of the contemporary visual arts mediums. This can been seen as indicating a vitality in the pursuit of creative expression that deserves further study. For example, for this book I have not chosen any work from the countries of Africa: it is certain that this vast continent deserves a dedicated book of its own. The emergence of new democracies, including those in North Africa following the Arab Spring of 2012, and the maturation of the art scenes in the postcolonial countries to the south, coupled with a rich and varied visual arts heritage, offers a great deal of work of interest and importance, and it is to be hoped that a writer will rise to the not inconsiderable challenge of exploring the contemporary African printmaking scene in all its complexity. The same may be said of the printmaking scene in South America: there is certainly much to discover in this complex continent, with its own particular blend of postcolonial and indigenous cultures, and often intense sociopolitical scenes.

It gradually occurred to me during the course of my research that the countries that are home to, or otherwise the places of origin of, artists to whose work I found myself drawn, form a broad crescent across the surface of the planet. The home countries of artists featured in this book cover a range from Indonesia and Malaysia in the tropical Far East, via Bhutan, India, Nepal and Pakistan, and eastwards through Iran, Iraq and the United Arab Emirates, then onwards north and east through Israel, Lebanon and Palestine, then through Turkey, Bulgaria, Romania and Ukraine, before heading north through the Balkans – Bosnia-Herzegovina, Croatia and Serbia, with a detour to Belarus and Russia, on the way to Finland in the north-east of Europe. Beyond this broad crescent there are artists from Venezuela, Japan and Alaska whose works have particular stories to tell.

The variety of work from the featured countries is about as wide as it could be. There is everything from ex-libris prints in strictly traditional techniques, through digital prints, to installations incorporating printmaking techniques, and on to experimental techniques that do not yet have a settled name. Some of the works belong in and stem from the traditions of the countries from which they come, while others provide a stark challenge to the national orthodoxies. As with my other books, there are artists from every generation, from new graduates to established masters, because I believe that all art made with passion and meaning is valid and that artists from all generations have something to say and share. The selection of work collectively represents a wide-ranging exploration of the ways in which ideas can be described and communicated, and in which the visual arts, in this case through the medium of printmaking, can seek to tell the world about itself. And that, in essence, is what the arts are about, and where the visual arts have a particular potential for success.

The printmaking community is spread across the world, so it is inevitable that, in researching the books I have written on the phenomenon, I have made journeys to a number of countries. While the ideal for this book would have been to be able to visit all the countries and to meet all the artists, it was not possible given that the 54 artists included currently live and work in 32 countries. Instead much of the research was conducted through e-mail correspondence and questionnaires, Skype calls and letters. Many of the artists were generous in sending catalogues of their work, and all sent images and personal texts by disc or electronic file transfer. The increased accessibility to people and places simply through communicating by computer made the task of research so much easier than it was when I wrote my first book in 1993-4: at that time I was reliant on conventional post and the occasional fax, and the accumulated research material resulted in several large boxes of information!

In researching this book I did, however, make a number of journeys, which, together with my records of earlier journeys, proved invaluable in forming a bank of impressions and information, as well as a set of personal contexts. Short travel diary excerpts are included at appropriate places within Part 2 of the book.

CONFLICT & RESOLUTION

Conflict has been a constant ingredient in international and national politics for millennia, and the impacts of such conflicts can be traced in the visual art of the countries involved. Images of military triumph can be found in early Egyptian art and continue through the Greek and Roman periods, to be revived and extended in the Renaissance and later to become a major constituent of the grand painting tradition of the 18th and 19th centuries in depictions of battles and in history paintings. The consequences of war formed a major part of the output of Goya, and his *Disasters of War* suite of etchings remains one of the most powerful artistic responses to man's inhumanity to man. Following Goya, many artists have expressed their feelings towards war and injustice through the medium of print, a noble tradition that continues to this day. The use of photography as a medium for recording conflict and its consequences goes back to the powerful images made by Mathew Brady and others during the American Civil War, and photography is still recognised as a powerful medium for both propaganda and protest. Through such means the knowledge of conflicts – and also the propaganda connected with them – has increased greatly during the past century and a half. The development of movie film and then video led to the expanding influence of visual news, and the subsequent evolution of 24-hour rolling news on satellite television and the internet has since then made visual and verbal reports of world events of all kinds a permanent and pervasive part of the lives of many people.

Television can heighten awareness or deaden it, and constant battering with words and images can lead to people losing their deep initial concern as one new news story rolls along to displace another, leading to a cynicism among many towards the truth of television broadcasting, and a mistrust of the authorities behind the media, together with the suspicion of news manipulation or censorship of one kind or another. However, and at the same time, the widening of access to personal internet technology and the social media played a crucial part in the events of the Arab Spring, and undoubtedly will to do so in other countries. The ability of a witness to an atrocity to shoot short pieces of video, and then to post them immediately on the internet, has had a profound effect on the widening of international public knowledge of the crimes committed by despotic regimes, which before the rise of technology they were able to keep secret for much longer. However, such a large number of international events being shared instantly on television has led to a cynical backlash, with more and more people finding themselves unwilling to devote sufficient time to current events, and increasingly dismissive of soundbites and political spin. For some people, news of another disaster or atrocity is just yet more yatter, and the news is switched off in favour of another dose of so-called 'reality' television.

Many of the artists in this book come from countries in which there has been, or continues to be, significant conflict of one kind or another. Some of them still live in those countries, while others have moved away, but in both cases their knowledge and awareness of what is happening continue to have an effect, often a profound one, on their work. In some places the conflict has been in the form of civil or international war, in others as a result of the ending of communist rule and the changes that have come about since then, while in some others the conflict comes from the friction between the growing influence of fundamentalist faiths and a conflicting desire for modernity. The range of impacts varies according to the causes of the conflicts: in some countries there have been mass killings or deaths in battle or in terrorist attacks; in others less fatal civil unrest, injuries and human-rights abuses; in still others repression and censorship.

The ways in which artists in general react in their work to their experience of conflict varies from extreme protest to more subtle techniques, but in all cases it is clear that their work becomes an important vehicle for responding to the events that affect their own lives. What is also clear, as you'd expect, is that artists within a particular country or region react in different ways and with different means to the same events. Whether or not the work of an artist in response to a situation of conflict ever changes anything is uncertain. Picasso's epic painting *Guernica* was painted in response to an atrocity during the Spanish Civil War: despite its being shown in major galleries in New York, and more recently following its return to Spain, permanently in Madrid, and regardless of the painting being the subject of countless reproductions in books and posters, wars and atrocities have continued. Such works do not on their own bring about a major shift in public consciousness and conscience, nor the ending of atrocities such as the bombing of Guernica, but they do perhaps increase the willingness among some people to protest against war and to work for peace, though one cannot be certain even of this.

A number of the artists in this book provided answers to questions that I sent them about their experiences of conflict, and selected responses are included within Part 2.

DIASPORA & EXILE

As well as being, for the most part, a gregarious part of the human community, for many years printmakers have also been travellers, willing to go to other countries to learn techniques or to work, or indeed to attend one of the many conferences and events at which printmakers and print lovers gather to share ideas and work. I have in the past compared this phenomenon to the medieval world in which scholars would travel to distant universities or monasteries to learn from great teachers or to study in celebrated libraries. The rich cross-fertilisation of influences and approaches that this willingness to travel brings to the international printmaking community has become one of its important strengths.

However, travelling to work or live in another country is not always such a simple matter, nor is it always entirely voluntary. The often violent political, social or sectarian upheavals of the 20th century have spilled over into the 21st and show no immediate sign of ceasing. Because of this, it is not always viable for people, artists included, to think of remaining in their homeland among the roots of their heritage. There have been and continue to be extensive population movements away from troubled countries into the safer and more economically and culturally attractive countries of Europe, North America and elsewhere.

Some population shifts involve large numbers of groups of people, and the cultural effect of such shifts can have profound implications for the host countries. One of the most often referred to is the Jewish diaspora of the 20th century that resulted from the persecution and genocide at the hands of the Nazis. This in turn, through a series of politically motivated agreements, resulted in the creation of the modern state of Israel, and then to the ongoing conflict between Israel and Palestine. Less well-known is the Palestinian diaspora outside the Middle East, as large numbers of people have left their native country during the last 100 years or so to seek refuge elsewhere, many of them in Central and South America. It is estimated that the numbers of Palestinians permanently resident in that part of the world total over 600,000.

Notable forced mass dispersions also occurred as a result of the slave trade and the consequent forced movement of large numbers of African peoples to North America; other historical events include the forced movements of Poles and Germans following the ending of World War II and the realignment of national boundaries of the countries of Central Europe; and the interchange of peoples between India and Pakistan following Partition in 1947. More recently, there have been considerable movements of people from the countries comprising the former Yugoslavia as a result of the consequences of years of war and civil unrest, as well as the relocation of considerable numbers of people from the former Communist countries of Eastern Europe as their homelands were welcomed into the European Union. All such mass migrations have had profound social and cultural implications for those undertaking the move and also for the destination countries. At the same time, the cultural heritage that people take with them has helped to enrich the cultural life of their adopted countries.

Not all movements from one country to another can be defined as diasporas; in some cases it is a matter of exile, whether forced or self-imposed. There are many instances of people leaving their homeland to seek a better life elsewhere, away from the persecution – whether personal, political, racial, religious or sectarian – to which they had been subjected, or otherwise feared might happen. While there are inevitably tensions in some cases, in others there can be a sense of a new start, and better opportunities to make a living, as well as better ways to express opinions in the manner of protests, without the fear of reprisals such activities would have incurred in their native countries. Some people have sought self-imposed exile because of dissatisfaction with life and conditions in their native countries and the perceived attractions of life elsewhere.

Yet again, however, this is nothing new, as can be demonstrated through an examination of the cultural history of Britain and the influences brought to the country through successive waves of immigration, particularly from the mid-20th century onwards as former colonies gained independence. These have played a big part in shaping the contemporary national character. Likewise, the multicultural nature of the population of the United States is even more the result of successive human waves, first of conquest and then of immigration; the arrival of many European artists in the United States in the years leading up to World War II can be shown to have had a profound effect on painting and sculpture and, eventually, the rise of Abstract Expressionism and, later, Pop Art. There are many other instances of population movements caused by colonisation and its aftermath. While the effects of immigration on countries around the world are not always welcomed by the indigenous peoples, they are nonetheless usually absorbed into the complex fabric of the national culture, bringing greater diversity and new cultural opportunities.

Artists will continue, as they have done for centuries, to be wanderers, explorers and travellers, to move around the world in order to experience different cultures and environments, or to learn skills that are indigenous to other places, and thereby to enrich the sources of their inspiration. Printmakers are frequently travellers: the continuing evolution and growth of the calendar of annual and periodic international competitions and exhibitions, including specialised as well as general themes, provides ample evidence of their collaborative nature and their inherent desire to learn and share skills and approaches to the making of their art. Every year newly established printmaking workshops and studios add their opportunities and attractions to those already available to artists, both those in their immediate communities and those willing to travel and learn. To the physical possibilities of travelling and sharing must be added the continually evolving opportunities for sharing works and ideas in the virtual world via the internet. The artist in the garret, isolated and even detached from the people far below, is no longer a tenable concept, now that all but the most remote of locations can be linked to the world by a thin copper or fibre-optic cable.

A number of the artists included in this book now live in countries far from their homelands. Their reasons for leaving are as various as they are, and each has a personal story to tell. Where appropriate, parts of their stories are included in their profiles in Part 2.

Right: Parastou Forouhar, *Ashura*, 2012. See page 57.

PART 2

A PARTIAL ATLAS OF WORLD PRINTMAKING

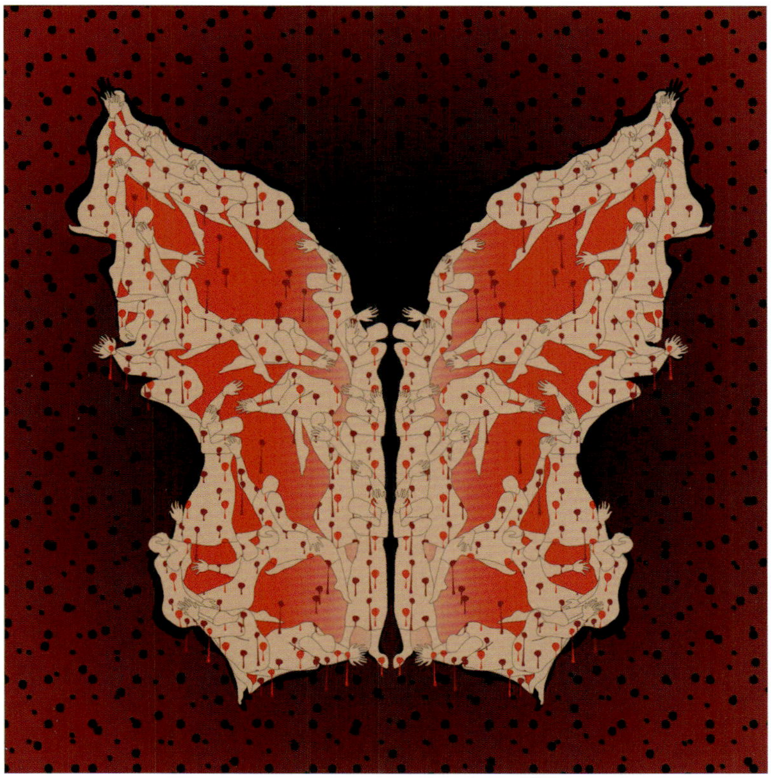

54 ARTISTS, 24 COUNTRIES

INDONESIA
Tromarama .... http://tromarama.blogspot.com

MALAYSIA
Juhari Said .... www.juharisaid.com
Kim Ng .... http://ngkimpeow.arts.com.my
Zulkifli Yusoff .... www.zulkifliyusoff.com

INDIA
Aditi Pande

BHUTAN
Tenzin Dorji www.drukpa.bt/bhutan/886/etching-art/

NEPAL
Nan Mulder .... www.nanmulder.com
Ragini Upadhyay .... http://ragini-art.blogspot.com/

PAKISTAN
David Alesworth .... www.davidalesworth.com/
Huma Mulji .... www.humamulji.com/
Mehreen Murtaza .... http://mehreenmurtaza.com/

IRAN
Fahimeh Vahdat .... www.fahimehvahdat.com/
Parastou Forouhar .... www.parastou-forouhar.de/english/
Tarlan Rafiee .... www.tarlan-rafiee.com
Yashar Samimi Mofakham .... www.yashar-samimi.com

IRAQ
Nedim Kufi
Talal Refit .... http://www.talalrefit.com/

UNITED ARAB EMIRATES
Maitha Demithan .... http://maitha-d.blogspot.com/
Shamsa Al Omaira .... http://shamsaalomaira.com/web/

ISRAEL
Gil & Moti .... www.gilandmoti.nl
Lihie Talmor .... www.talmorlihie.com/
Orit Hofshi .... www.orithofshi.com/

LEBANON
Alfred Tarazi .... www.beirutexhibitioncenter.com/learn/artist/alfred-tarazi

PALESTINE
Alexandra Handal .... http://alexandrahandal.org/
Leena Nammari .... www.leenanammari.co.uk

TURKEY
Asli Türkeli
Irem Sevgör .... www.iremsevgor.com

ROMANIA
Ciprian Ciuclea .... www.ciuclea.ro/
Ortansa Moraru .... www.ortansa.com/
Suzana Fântanâriu .... http://geocentral.net/suzana/
Valeriu Schiau .... http://www.youtube.com/watch?v=P9lNw L5LIGw

BULGARIA
Onnik Karanfilian .... www.rakursi.com/artistsonnik_karanfilian_en.htm
Peter Lazarov .... http://peterlazarov.wordpress.com/
Robert Baramov

SERBIA/MONTENEGRO
Dana Tosić http://vimeo.com/29453574

SERBIA
Ana Milosavljević .... http://anamilosavljevic.webs.com/
Aleksandar Mladenović Leka .... www.amleka.com
Lidija Bogdanović .... www.arte.rs/en/umetnici/lidija_bogdanovic-4118/ukratko/
Zeljko Skribić .... www.zeljkoskrbicphoto.com/
Zoran Todovic .... www.arte.rs/sr/umetnicizoran_todovic-4086/

BOSNIA-HERZEGOVINA
Endi Poskovic .... www.endiposkovic.com
Jelena Milesić .... http://jelenamilesic.blogspot.com/

CROATIA
Karen Oremus
Melinda Kostelac .... http://free-ri.htnet.hr/melinda/index.html

UKRAINE
Konstantin Kalynovych .... www.kalynovych.net
Oleg Denysenko .... www.olden.com.ua

BELARUS
Alexandr Grigoriev .... www.grigart.brest.by/index_eng.htm
Juri Jakovenko .... http://beautiful-grotesque.posterous.com/the-art-of-juri-jakovenko

RUSSIA
Anna Ceeh .... www.annaceeh.com

FINLAND
Annu Vertanen .... www.annuvertanen.com

VENEZUELA
Irene Furlan

ALASKA
Allie High .... www.alliehigh.com

ALASKA/POLAND
Christopher Nowicki .... www.chrisnowicki.com

JAPAN
Yoko Hattori .... www.yokohattori.com

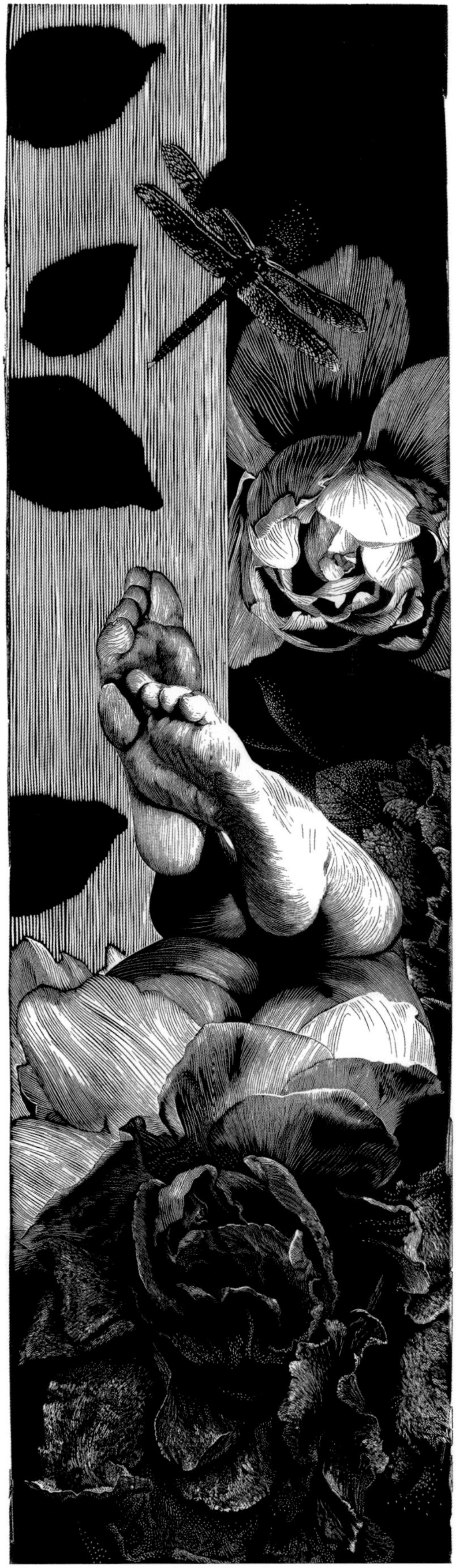

Peter Lazarov, *Hakka Dragonfly*, 2010. see page 116.

INDONESIA

TROMARAMA

TROMARAMA is a collective, formed in 2004 by Febie Babyrose (b. 1985, Jakarta), Herbert Hans (b. 1985, Jakarta) and Ruddy Hatumena (b. 1984, Bahrain), who met at the Bandung Institute of Technology, where Babyrose was studying printmaking and Hans and Hatumena were studying visual communication design. Indonesia is a large archipelago of more than 17,500 islands, with 238 million people from hundreds of distinct ethnic and linguistic groups, renowned for its traditional woodblock batik printing, *wayang kulit* shadow puppets and gamelan orchestras. It is also one of the largest and most vibrant economies in the world. This diverse background has given Indonesia a rich gamut of influences from the religions of its peoples and its trading history due to its position on many sea routes, as well as the enthusiastic adoption of Western cultural ideas in science, technology and entertainment. There is much poverty remaining in the overcrowded cities and, as the devastating tsunami of 26th December 2004 demonstrated, an uncomfortable proximity to one of the world's seismic hotspots.

Tromarama's name originates from the first joint project they undertook together, when in 2006 they were commissioned by the thrash-metal band Seringai to make a video clip for their song 'Serigala Militia'. Rather than following the more familiar approach of MTV videos they decided to create a stop-frame video using woodblocks, eventually ending up with 450 blocks produced over a six-week period. They were traumatised by this experience, according to Hans, who remarked (to the writer Cristina Sanchez Kozyreva) that they came across the Greek word *rama*, meaning 'view', and so combined the two parts to create their name. The installation derived from this video work, with the blocks creating the walls of the enclosure in which the video was shown on a 4-minute continuous loop, was one of the highlights of the Philagrafika festival of printmaking in Philadelphia in 2010. The making of the video led to commissions for other bands, and in 2008 the trio quit their day jobs to work together on art and mixed-media projects. Their innovative work has since been shown with success and to critical acclaim in exhibitions and festivals in many parts of the world across the full range of art, music, new media and video-based contexts. It is a curious reflection that two of Marshall McLuhan's more celebrated quotations coincide in the work of Tromarama: *'the Balinese say "we have no art, we do everything as well as we can"'* and, *'The new electronic interdependence recreates the world in the image of a global village'.*

Tromarama's work has been described as being playful, and this seems quite correct in the sense that many aspects of their work require a high degree of complicity from those who see it, as well as a preparedness to interact. This is not to say that their work lacks seriousness, as it is increasingly linked to issues that are of daily concern in their, and other peoples', lives. Their approach to concepts in which there is a distinct 'play' element is as serious as that taken by those who play chess, or football, of whom a British team manager, when asked if football was *'a matter of life or death'*, replied that it was *'far more serious than that'*. As many printmakers will recognise, it is often the case that the most satisfying results arise when the artist thinks, *'I wonder what happens if I do this…'*, reflecting the need for an element of serious play if the evolution that has characterised printmaking throughout its millennia-long existence is to continue.

In *Nothing is What it Seems*, a 3-minute 50-second stop-motion animation with sound by Bagus Mandega, made in 2012, Tromarama created a large collage of live flowers with their stems threaded through the mesh of a supporting grid, and with the letters forming the title of the piece made from shredded paper. The video was made using the stop-frame technique as the flowers, deprived of water, gradually faded to reveal the paper words. The simplicity of the concept is built on a complex meditation on the notions of life, death and immortality, with the final punchline offering a succinct comment on the fallibility of all things and the impossibility of any living thing remaining in a constant steady form. The use of flowers refers in different ways to Buddhist, Hindu, Confucian and Christian rituals surrounding birth, existence

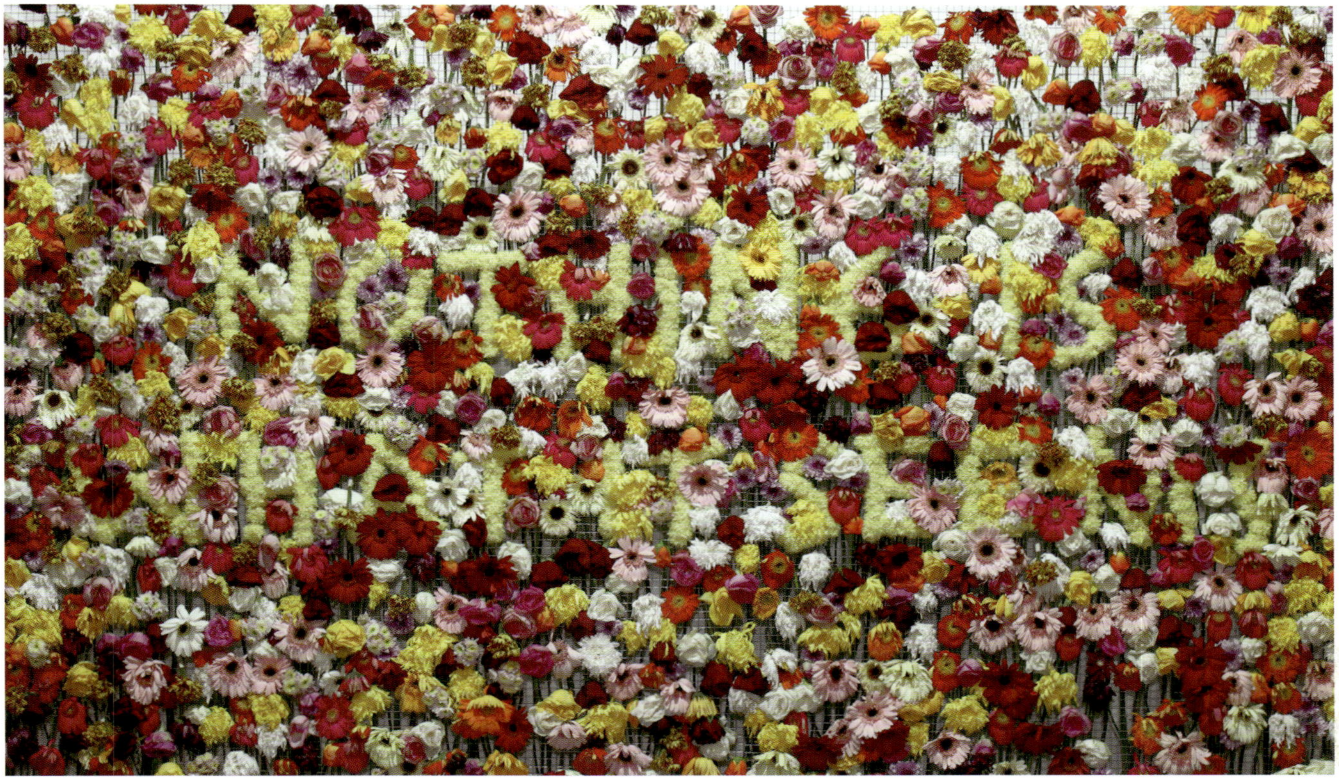

Tromarama, *Nothing Is What It Seems*, 2012. Stills from stop-frame animation, with flowers and paper, 3m 50s. Private collection.

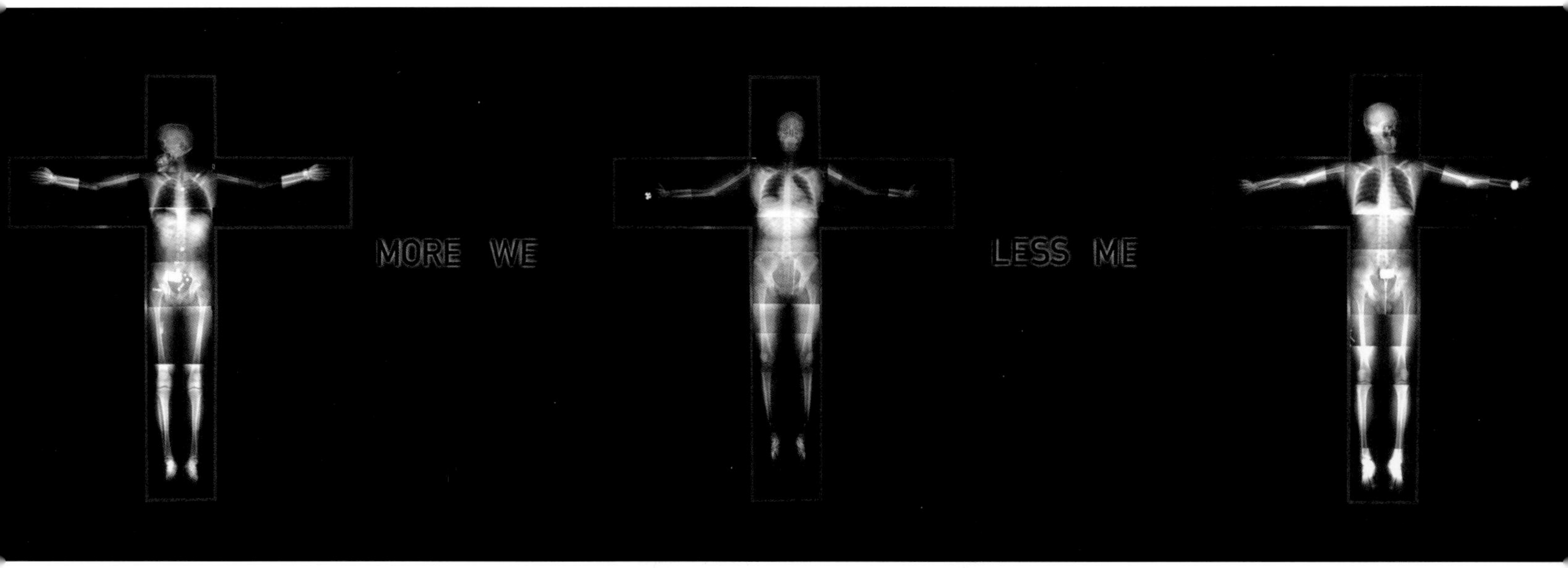

Tromarama, *More We Less Me*, 2011. X-ray films, stainless steel, Plexiglas, LED lighting, variable dimensions. Private collection.

and death. While not incorporating printmaking in the conventional sense, the work does include the element of reproducibility through the way in which it can be transmitted in the form of a DVD, or as digital video.

More We Less Me was created for the Asia One presentation at the 2011 Hong Kong International Art Fair. Unusually for Tromarama this work does not involve animation, but is instead an installation in which the figures are over life size. It is made from X-ray images of the three artists, combined together behind Plexiglas within a stainless-steel-framed light box. The work has complex layers of meaning and relevance, based on the principle that the group is stronger than the individuals within it, which is true of Tromarama but equally true when applied to society at large. The use of the cross is not primarily intended to signify crucifixion in the Christian sense, but to suggest the wider relevance of the symbol across the world. Other possible readings of the work are that it signifies alienation, that it criticises the use of intrusive technology in airport security, or that it is about the impossibility of achieving the aim of the title: the heads of the outer figures face away from each other, while the central figure looks straight at the viewer. Complexity and simplicity meet head on in the work of Tromarama.

MALAYSIA: KUALA LUMPUR & PENANG

MALAYSIA occupies a range of latitudes from two to six degrees north of the Equator, and as a consequence is very hot with high humidity. The climate affects everything, from narrow streets bathed in moist heat, to air-conditioned public buildings, hotels and vehicles, to the dense profusion of vegetation outside the built-up areas. The country is multi-ethnic and multicultural, and the state religion is Islam, with other faith systems being protected in law. There is a varied contemporary arts scene, with state museums and galleries and private galleries, and the visual arts are taught at the universities and at private colleges. I visited Kuala Lumpur, the capital, and Penang during September 2010 and these are some impressions of that time.

Kuala Lumpur is a modern world capital city, mixing clusters of high-rise buildings in the business district, including the twin Petronas Towers (until fairly recently the highest buildings in the world), with remnants of colonial architecture, some remaining traditional shophouses (shops at street level with residential rooms above), and a sprinkling of eclectic religious buildings reflecting the multi-faith nature of the populations, including Kuala Lumpur's oldest Hindu building, the Sri Mahamariamman Temple. The National Art Gallery, built in a blend of contemporary and traditional Malay styles, is the major centre for Malaysian visual art. This is complemented by the Petronas Gallery, showing national and international contemporary art, which is situated in the lower part of the twin towers, as well as the magnificent privately owned Islamic Arts Museum of Malaysia. I saw an excellent exhibition of paintings by Anurendra Jegadeva at the Wei-Ling Gallery, which is situated in a former colonial factory in the Brickfields district.

Kuala Lumpur has to be one of the only city centres in the world where it is possible to climb from traffic-filled streets and up the narrow paths through a large area of virgin tropical forest, the Bukit Nanas Forest Reserve. You emerge at the top of a hill, from where an elevator takes you to the viewing platform of the Telekom Tower, from which a full panorama of the city can be seen. The Chinatown district centred on Pataling Street is extensive and fascinating, with bright lights, jumbles of signs in many languages, piles of fruit and vegetables and goods of all sorts, and some of the best street food in the city: I ate an excellent and cheap meal while being observed by a glass tank full of frogs. At night the city lights, particularly those of the Petronas Towers, provide a vivid spectacle, and at dawn, as the call to prayer sounds throughout the city, the sky turns from darkness through pale shades of blue to the deeper blues of another hot day.

Between Kuala Lumpur and the northern city of Penang the modern highway winds its way through areas of tropical forest and palm nut plantations, curving through some spectacular hills. Off the highway and bypassed by progress are small traditional towns and villages, such as Kuala Khansar, where it is still possible to gain an impression of how the country was in the early 20th century when it was still colonial Malaya. The plateau of the Cameron Highlands district, an extensive hill station, rises to the south and east of Ipoh. The road reaches the coast of the Malacca Strait near Butterworth from which the impressive Penang Bridge crosses the Strait to Penang Island. Apart from being a major industrialised and economically important region on both sides of the Strait, Penang is also a major tourist destination with an extensive and fascinating historic centre and some world-class beaches. There are also two important institutions, the Universiti Sains Malaysia (USM) and the Penang State Museum and Art Gallery, organisers of the very successful Penang International Print Exhibition, which at the last event brought together contemporary prints from 40 countries. Outside the printmaking department at USM there are banana trees: the students eat the fruit and the leaves are used to make paper – a source of materials that is not available to printmakers in most other countries.

The colonial history of the island stretches back to the 15th century and in the late 18th century it became a major centre for the East India Company, and a legendary place for trading and business, including the notorious trade in opium. Proud Malaysians now insist that the street food on the island is the best in the world, and it is hard to argue with that assertion. I walked along the beach at Batu Ferringhi at sunset, with dark clouds looming over the sea, then retreated to the shelter of a café to drink coconut milk as a spectacular tropical rainstorm thundered on the tin roof, defeating conversation, and rolling thunder shattered the night as forked lightning lit up the sea and surrounding hills. The silence as the storm departed was broken only by the loud dripping of water from the leaves of the trees.

JUHARI SAID

OUTSIDE the glittering high-rises of Kuala Lumpur and beyond the encircling suburbs lies the jungle – a dense complexity of trees, foliage and flowers that is, to the Western eye at least, exotic in its richness and diversity and hot humid air: the contrast between the urban and rural parts of Malaysia is extreme. Juhari Said has a house and a separate studio in a cleared area of land surrounded by the jungle of Selangor, some distance outside the capital. It is there that he works, raises his family and has a plantation of vanilla, a high-value crop through which he aims to sustain his work/lifestyle without recourse to state aid, while continuing to encourage other younger artists in the development of their art and careers. Born in 1961, he graduated from the Universiti Teknologi MARA in Shah Alam, Selangor in 1983. Since then he has pursued a successful career in Malaysia, and has travelled widely, including lengthy visits to Tunisia, Jordan and Japan – with more than ten visits to the latter country, including a visit in 1994 to study traditional woodcut techniques with Yoshisake Funusaka in Tokyo. His exhibition history includes solo exhibitions in Malaysia, Japan and Austria, and participation in numerous national and international group exhibitions. He has received a number of awards, including being appointed Creative Fellow at the School of Art, Universiti Sains Malaysia (USM) in Penang, and receiving the Malaysian Artist Award in the two-dimensional category from the Ministry of Arts, Culture and Heritage of Malaysia in 2009.

His practice has been largely based on printmaking, with an emphasis on woodblock and silkscreen, but he has also made works using linocut, mixed printmaking mediums (including a series incorporating coffee), drawings and wood sculpture. Said's works are predominantly abstract, but with underlying figurative references in some of the earlier work, and indications from the mid-1990s onwards of an exploration of the nature of art and its making that led him towards experimenting with mixed mediums and the incorporation of three-dimensional objects in some of his works. The prints made in the years immediately after his graduation are typified by their use of strong colour and the references to vegetation – elements that can be traced in much of his work. The *Spilled Coffee* series (1991–94) shows a more experimental streak in which random spills of coffee are incorporated with other mediums and drawing techniques, including woodblock print in the later part of the series. Although he has since then returned to the use of colour in most of his work, one series, *Kilimanjaro in Nagasaki* (1994–95), made following his Japanese experience, is based on formal woodcuts printed either in black on white or with the addition of red. Looking through a selection of his work makes it clear that Said has an emphatic visual sensitivity to shape, form and colour, coupled with an imaginative curiosity about the ways in which these basic threads can be woven together to create images of integrity and haunting mystery. An unusually large woodblock print with added watercolour from 1998, *Berunding Dengan Tunggul* (*Wrestling with a Tree Stump*) (90 x 189cm/35 x 75 inches), demonstrates a masterly skill in both the physical carving of

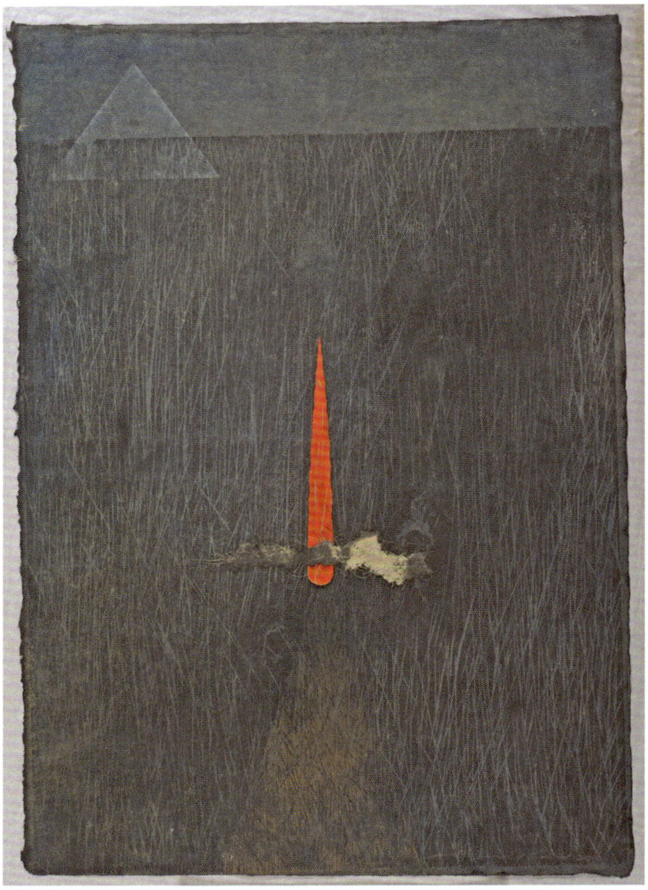

Juhari Said, *Peak*, 2010. Woodcut, bamboo, on handmade paper, 76 x 53cm (30 x 20¾in.). Private collection.

Right: Juhari Said, *Staircase*, 2010. Woodcut, bamboo, on handmade paper, 76 x 53cm (30 x 20¾in.). Private collection.

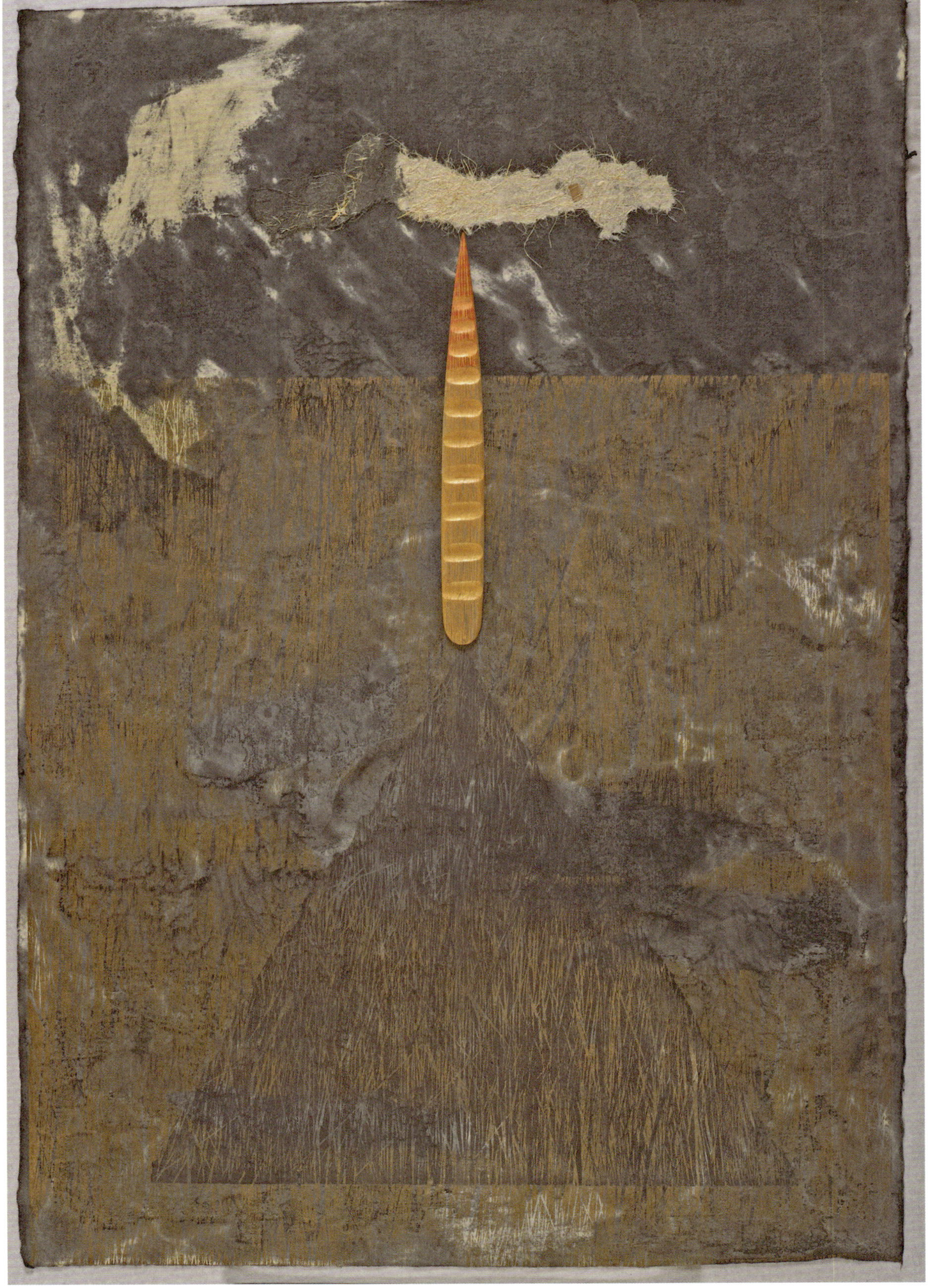

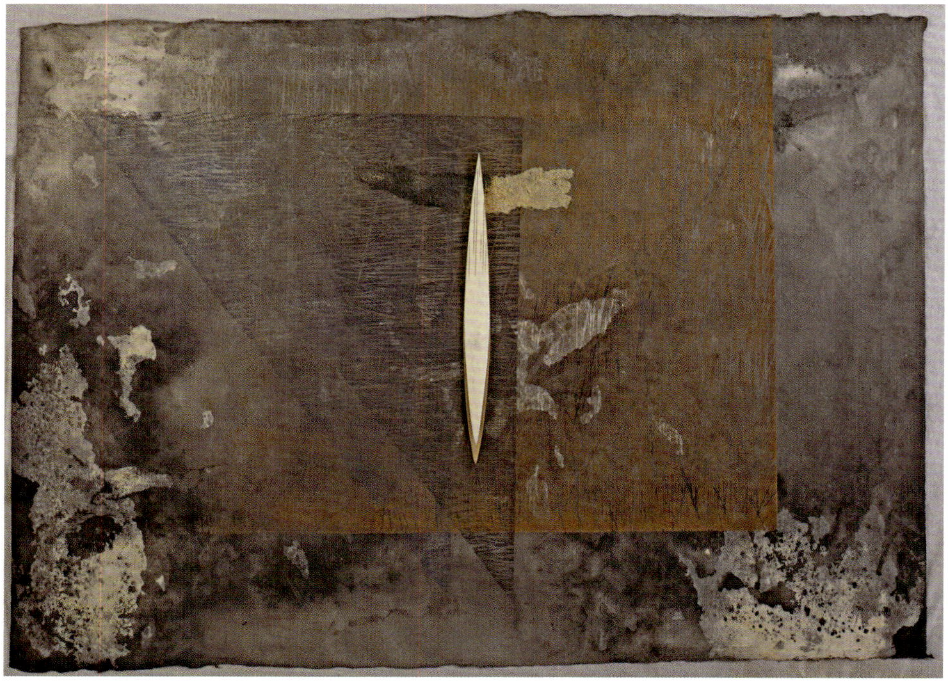

Juhari Said, *White Infinity*, 2010. Woodcut, bamboo, on handmade paper 53 x 76cm (20¾ x 30in.). Private collection.

the wood and the creative rigour of the composition. Other large prints made around the same time indicate high levels of both physical and conceptual ability that he has used with even greater effect in his more recent work.

In an interview with Dr Tony Donaldson of Monash University in Australia (published in the catalogue for Said's 2011 solo exhibition Yes or No at the MOMA Gallery in Kuala Lumpur) the artist talked at length about the development of his art. He recalled how in 2005 he realised that having been a printmaker for twenty-three years had brought him to the point at which it was no longer exciting. After a year or so of making no art, he was invited to participate in a workshop in Kelantan and was given a large piece of jambu laut wood, a rare hardwood tree that grows along the beaches in that area, which can be carved deeply and in many directions without splitting. This experience led Said to creating a series of large sculptures in jambu laut, the *Okir* series, shown in a solo exhibition at the Wei Ling Gallery in Kuala Lumpur in 2007. The surfaces of these pieces are deeply carved using the repertoire of the mark-making techniques familiar in woodcut prints, and then coloured, as if for producing prints, using oil paint and rollers, mostly in black but with some accents in colours such as red or ochre. This new technique released Said's creative block and was continued with further series, *Samudra* (2009) and *Imagine* (2011). Asked by Donaldson about the defining characteristics of his art, Said replied, 'It is the use of black and white. When an artist produces a black and white work, it is the pure natural expression of the artist. In black and white, the artist cannot be pretentious or conceal anything.' Nevertheless, some of the works in the *Samudra* series incorporate vivid colours, applied by hands, fingers and rags.

In 2010, between the two sculptural series, Said returned to making prints with a new series of woodcuts on handmade paper, incorporating small elements of carved and painted bamboo. These are austere, almost minimalist, prints in which varied textures and a reduced palette of colours are used with collaged elements such as bamboo and fragments of paper to create powerful images in which those elements create a sculptural reference, but also assume a presence akin to abstract icons, indications that Juhari Said's artistic explorations into print and sculpture are far from over.

KIM NG

KIM NG produces art works with hybrid techniques combining those more normally associated with the fine arts of painting and drawing and those more generally found in printmaking. This positions his work in what is a new but expanding territory, one that is likely to become clearer in years to come. But in short it adds considerable weight to my belief that printmaking is an integral part of contemporary art and not something other, or belonging in another niche – one in which some traditionally minded printmakers have been content to let it remain. It is, in fact, entirely appropriate to consider the question of hybridity in considering Ng's work, in that it derives from his continuing observations of life on the streets of Malaysia, primarily those of Kuala Lumpur; it's a city in which much of daily life takes place on the streets, which in turn become an interim space between private and public.

Born in Malaysia, Ng studied in Kuala Lumpur before moving to England to study for his BA and subsequent MA in Fine Art. Following this period, he returned to Kuala Lumpur to teach at a private university, and he has since had a series of successful exhibitions in the city. Of his background he writes, 'Being an artist of Chinese origin in Malaysia there is always a sense of belonging that I try to search for in my perception and my work – the identity of "Malaysian" – and yet without losing the perspective of the origin. Therefore there is always a search for balance in both visual representation and its significance of meaning.' He adds that, although the population of Malaysia has a Muslim majority, the majority of the private and commercial galleries are run by Chinese people and offer equality of opportunity for exhibitions to all ethnic groups. In a statement about his work he writes, 'My art is "making ideas" rather than having a consistent routine. Consistency refers to persisting in making one singular subject matter constantly, like landscape or figure; I don't follow the rules with conventional indulgence. The visual outcome of my artwork changes according to situation, environment, experience, observation and perception, and of course forms and materials will be varied as well. But the main concern to me is the thought and the techniques involved. The final

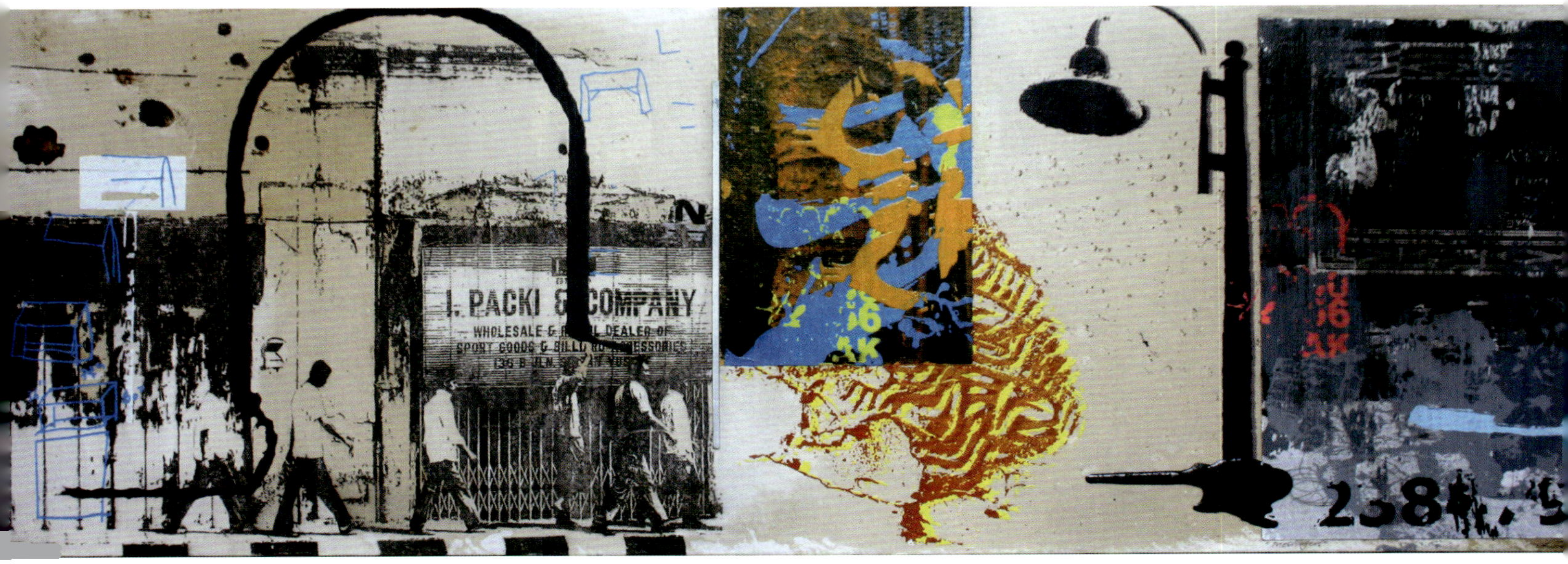

Kim Ng, *Messengers*, 2011. Silkscreen print, transfer-print collage, pencil drawing and graphite powder with varnish. 30.5 x 91.2cm (12 x 36in.).

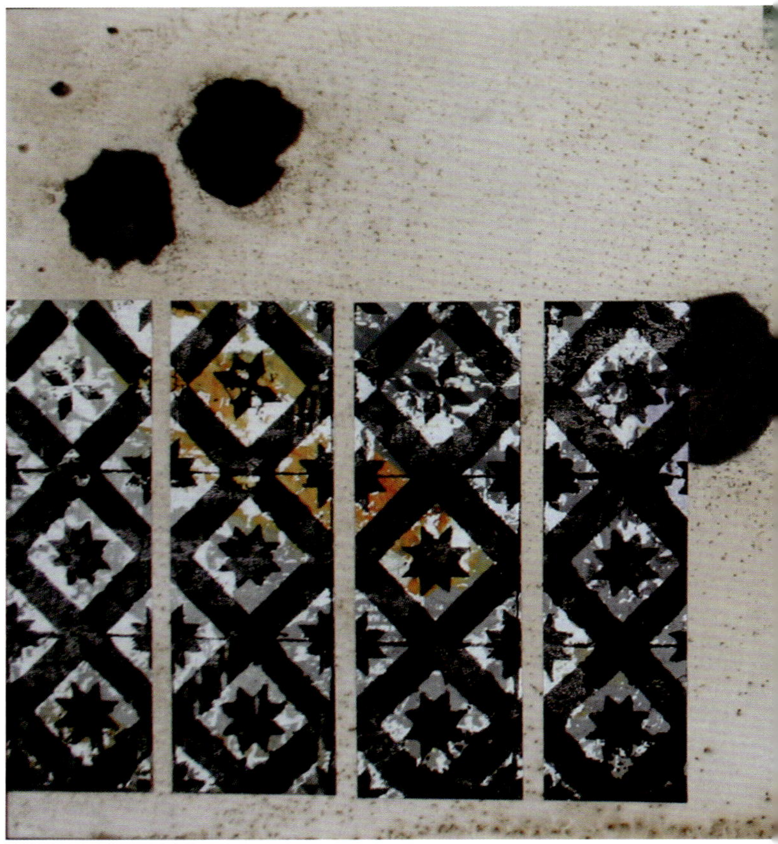

outcome of the artwork has to be "print"-related in its usual physical way, or abstract in concept.'

With reference to his work *Just Around the Corner* Ng writes, 'Through multiple disciplines and various mediums, I try to depict the complexity of my society and environment. I use images that repeatedly confront me as I move around, scenes and structures that keep appearing in my line of vision as I walk down the street.' This work is not a topographical record, but rather a synthesis of numerous individual images, combined to produce a multi-faceted impression of parts of the city with which he is familiar on a daily basis. These streets are crowded, noisy, full of colour and movement, along which pedestrians pass in close proximity to each other during their daily lives, looking to one side and the other, keeping an eye out for scooters and other vehicles, taking in a kaleidoscopic series of images that create an effect that is at the same time both exciting and exhausting. Given the size of this work it can either be read from a distance, in which case a general impression can be gained, or, by approaching the work, sequentially from one side to the other, in which the details emerge and can be synthesised into an overall picture. These different modes of viewing need to be considered in the case of all such works of this nature.

Issues of a different variety are contained within *Messengers*, which concerns Malaysia's vaunted multicultural policy and its open-door policy towards the introduction of migrant workers from other countries to undertake the jobs that were formerly handled by local people. As with such policies in other countries, there are advantages and also tensions that are not always open to easy resolution and can be politically contentious. As far as the incoming workers are concerned, they have to contend with the additional problems associated with being away from their homes, without the support in Malaysia of family and friends, and being housed in substandard accommodation away from the bright lights of the city centre. There are echoes in this of similar migrant worker communities elsewhere in the world, and indeed in the historic situation that faced the colonial masters in the former Malaya. The print shows a group of workers walking past shops with their shutters down, and a cluster of fragments of images from their daily life and cultural background. It is a sad, reflective image rather than a politically critical one, one that would recognisable to others in their own communities.

Much of Ng's work does have a sociopolitical component, as the issues of his culturally mixed and intensely vibrant country provide many causes for producing such works, but he is also an artist who is closely aware of the light and colour of Malaysia, and the exuberance of its plant life. *Where it All Begins* is another large-scale mixed-medium work, with an accompanying note, 'From outer space to life on earth, a kind of formation begins.' Fragments of a meteor at the left lead the eye towards the right across the work via the blaze of colour of a scarlet flower and brightly coloured patterns to the abstraction of the contrast of flowers against lush green leaves that typifies the landscapes and gardens of his tropical country. It is a work that contrasts with the previously described works and their clear social comment, but which is equally part of the landscape within which he lives.

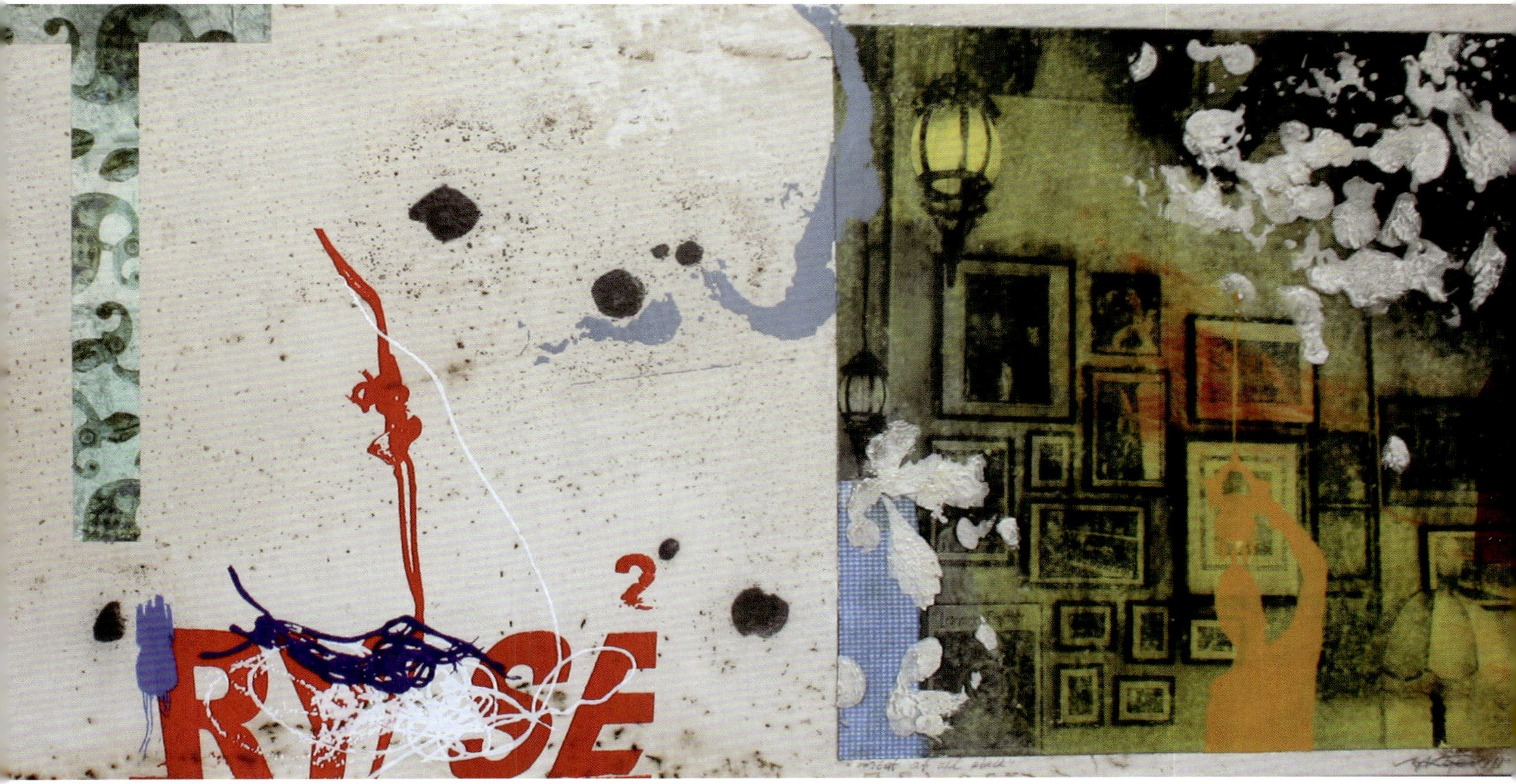

Kim Ng, *Meet at the Old Place*, 2011. Silkscreen print, transfer-print collage, screenprint-embossed paste, pencil drawing and found inkjet collage, 30.5 x 91.2cm (12¼ x 36in.).

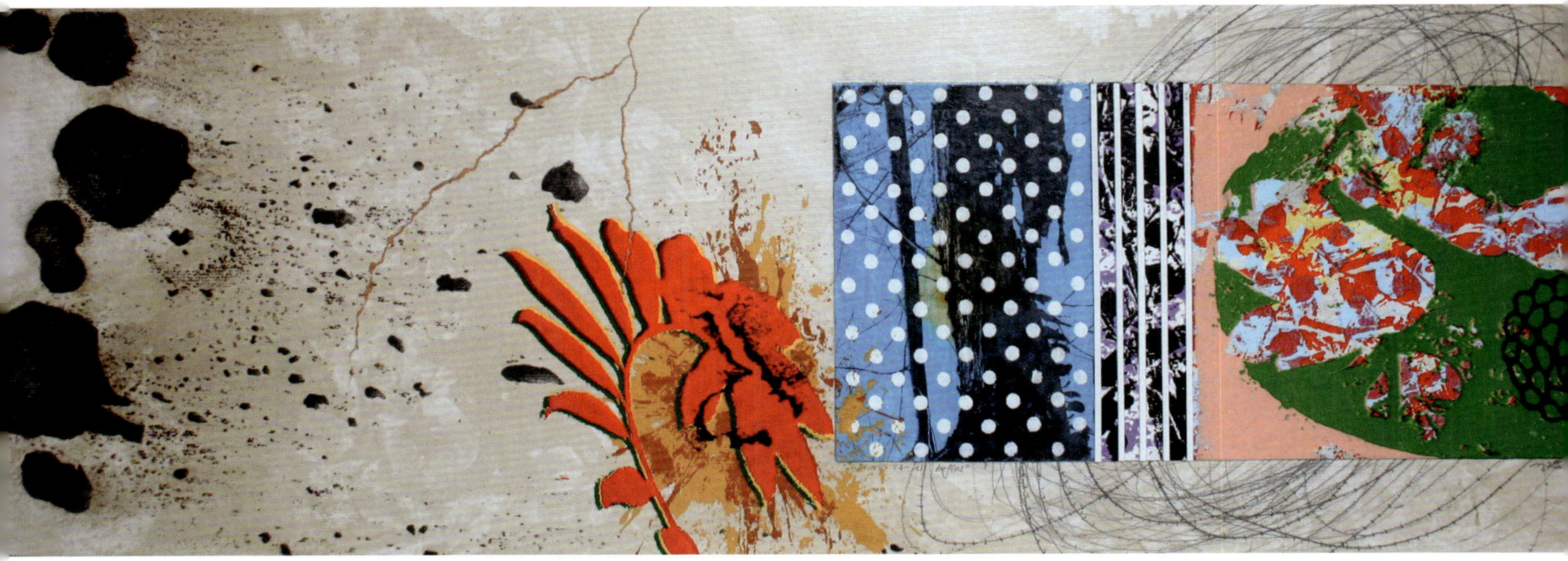

Kim Ng, *Where It All Begins*, 2001. Silkscreen print, transfer-print collage, bitumen, pencil drawing and collage, 30.5 x 91.2cm (12¼ x 36in.).

ZULKIFLI YUSOFF

A MAJOR EXHIBITION at the National Art Gallery of Malaysia in Kuala Lumpur in the autumn of 2010 featured the work of Zulkifli Yusoff, a major figure in contemporary Malaysian culture with a high national and international reputation. The exhibition was titled Negaraku, meaning 'My Country', which is also the title of the country's national anthem. Yusoff is a prolific artist, whose work defies easy categorisation, as he is equally at home with the making of small-scale work or large installations, and with the use of a wide range of painting, print and construction mediums, often in combination in mixed-media work. In short he is an artist who has a profound connection not only with contemporary art but also with his country, its history and complexity, its past, present and future. The exhibition gave an insight into the work of this artist whose imaginative abilities are harnessed in the creation of works that puzzle, intrigue, inform and, ultimately, remain unforgettable and mysterious.

In the catalogue for the exhibition of work by the 'Go Block' group of artists, of which he is part, Yusoff wrote, 'My latest works touch on issues that arose during the British colonial era, such as the position of the three ethnic groups in Malaya, as well as their socioeconomic situation, their ideologies and their feelings.' He describes the various positions occupied by the Malay, Chinese and Indian peoples during the colonial period, and how 'Colonisation represented a burden to them and they wanted to be independent and free to choose a profession … they kept their feelings bottled up, hoping for a new life without oppression.' While some artists in other countries have followed a similar theme in their work, and have ended up with didactic works that in some cases veer into pomposity, Yusoff takes a calmer and more complex approach, producing works that require and repay careful viewing and consideration. At the same time, he has been described (by Seah Tzi Yan, on the artist's own website) as 'Malaysia's ruling enfant terrible … his work is sharp and fast, often making deeply critical statements about personal, social and historical situations.'

Zulkifli Yusoff was born in Kedah state in 1962, and graduated in fine art from the MARA Institute of Technology in Shah Alam in 1989, before studying in England and graduating as master of arts from Manchester Polytechnic in 1991. He has shown his work internationally and within Malaysia in an extensive range of solo and group exhibitions, has been the recipient of a number of prestigious awards and honours, and his work is held in the major public collections in Malaysia as well as in private collections. In 1997 he represented Malaysia at the Venice Biennale, and in 2007 received the Anugherah Akademik Negara (National Academic Award), the highest award of the Malaysian government, for his achievements in the visual arts. He pursues an extensive personal practice, for which he has recently built a new studio, and in addition is Associate Professor in the Faculty of Art at Universiti Pendidikan Sultan Idris in Tanjong Malim, Perak. His work has for many years been predicated on a deep reading of literature and historical texts, especially those concerned with Malaysia and its former incarnation, Malaya. His installation work (see *Pendita* (*'Ecclesiastic'*) and *Merdeka* (*'Independence, Freedom'*)) juxtaposes quotations from a disparate variety of sources, together with photographs and printed and painted elements, to create both two- and three-dimensional forms that are placed together, often symmetrically, to create visionary spaces that can, literally, be read as a critical, interpretive whole. Contrasting different ideas and themes, placing them in such a way as to create critical and contextual dialogues, with elements from colonial sources set against elements from native sources, allows them the space to work against, or with, each other. Much of the source material is, necessarily, in Malay, and this does prevent non-Malay readers from receiving the full charge from the quotations. This lack of full understanding is a problem and yet not one that prevents an appreciation of the formal elements that Yusoff employs, in which shape, form and texture, and their relative placement against each other, are employed to arrive at a situation which he refers to as, 'I needed to come up with my own "hukum" or "order", so to speak, and even at times break with it.' In this there is a clue to the artist's intention to create both order and disorder to make his ideas positive, and as Shabbir Hussein Mustafa, curator of the gallery of the National University of Singapore, wrote in his essay for Yusoff's exhibition there in

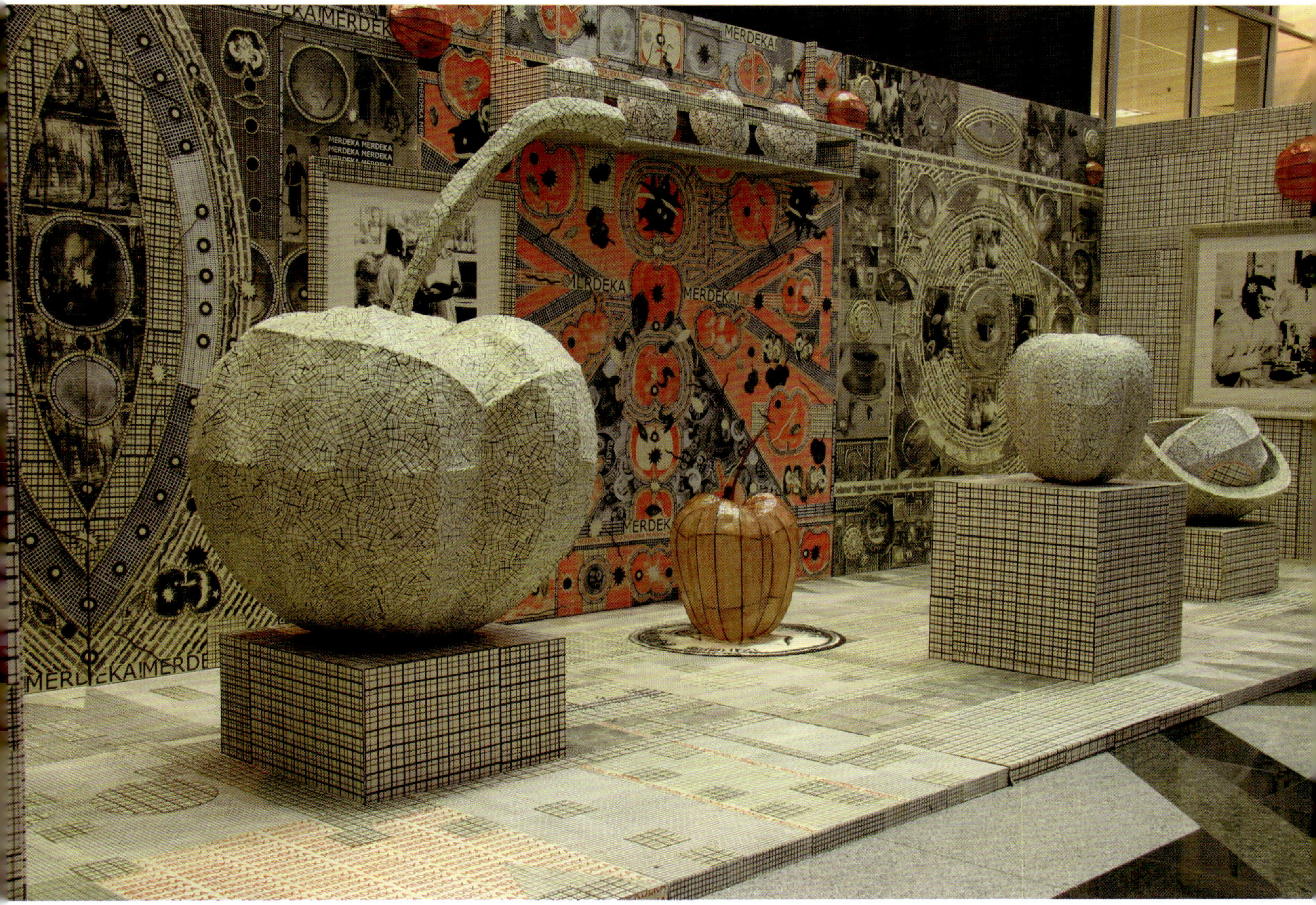

Zulkifli Yusoff, *Merdeka*, 2010. Mixed-media installation, variable dimensions.

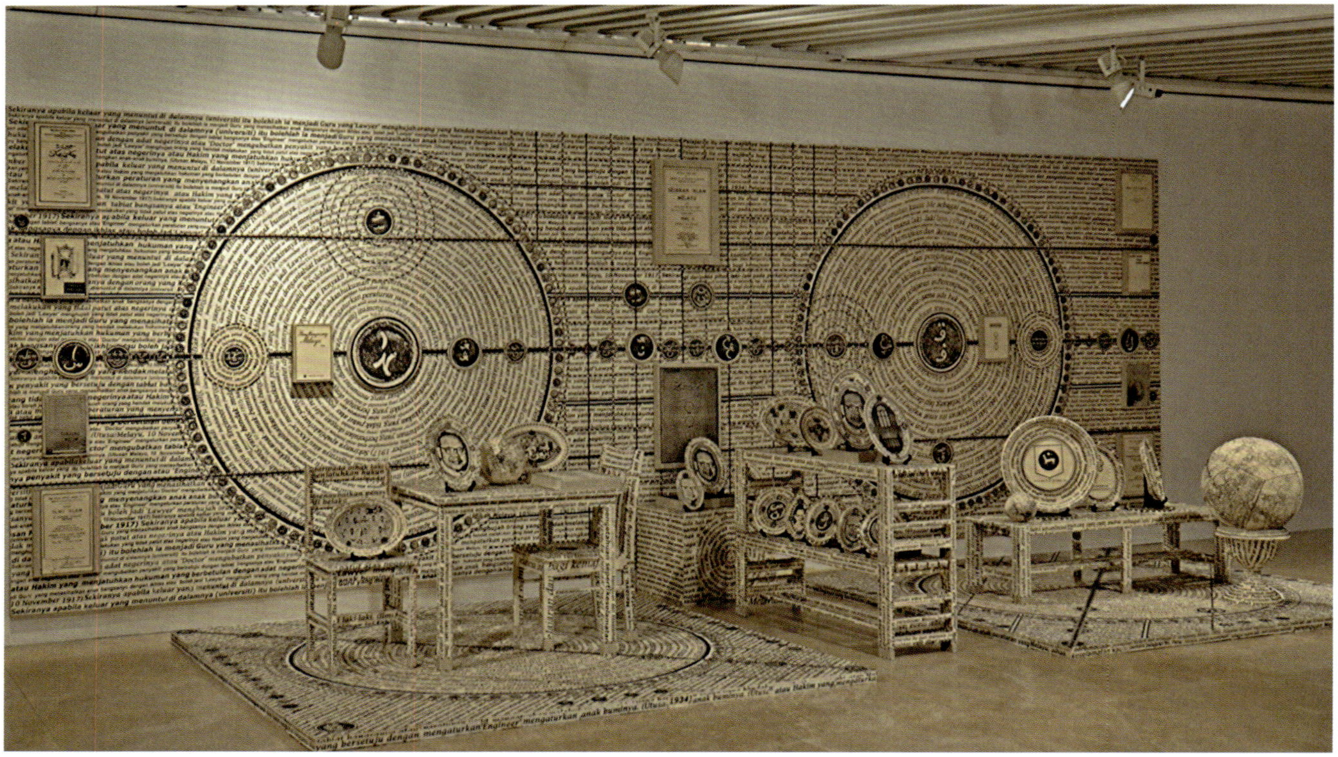

Zulkifli Yusoff, *Pendita*, 2011. Installation, collage, embossed dye-printed canvas, variable dimensions.

the autumn of 2011, '... if it matters not knowing what these traces mean, who made it, when and why, where do we place them, or how to approach them?'

Not all Yusoff's work is in the form of three-dimensional installation: in the 2010 exhibition in the National Art Gallery he showed a series of conventionally made etchings from metal matrices with the title *Bunga Raya* (the national flower of Malaysia, also known as the hibiscus), with the series exhibited in formal symmetrical arrangements on three walls at right angles to each other, creating a room within which the 54 prints could seen as a celebration of the structure, colour and exuberance of the flower, and through this that of the nation. In the same exhibition was shown *Peace I*, comprising a set of four international peace symbols formed from circular thick metal rods, painted with delicate patterns in colours echoing those of the hibiscus. The peace element recurs in *Peace III*, together with the international hand sign, in which densely packed elements are printed on embossed canvas mounted on wood panels. The message resembles the complexity of batik-printed fabric but is unmistakable in its intent.

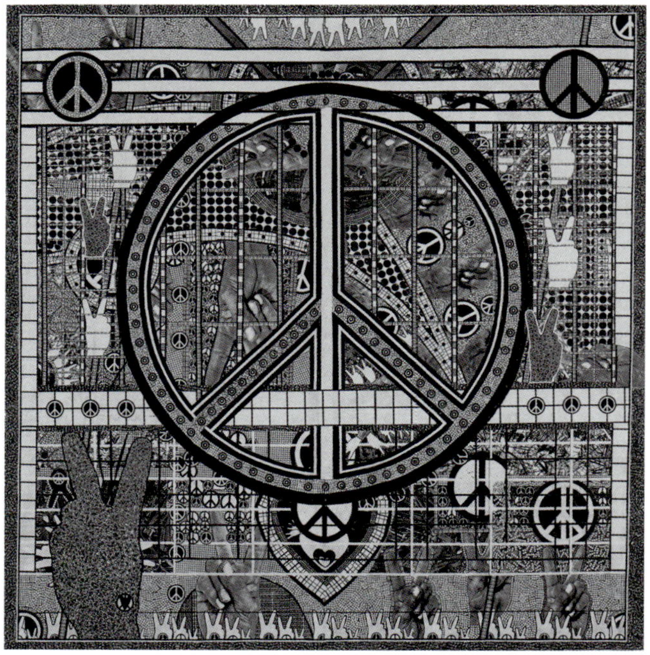

Zulkifli Yusoff, *Peace III*, 2010. Canvas, embossed dye print, wood panels, 244 x 244cm (96 x 96in.).

INDIA

ADITI PANDE

PRINTMAKING has deep roots in India, with a tradition of block prints that extends as far back as the introduction of printing presses for books in the late 18th century, when it comprised mainly woodblock prints. British artists with a taste for what was, for them, exotic became part of the Indian Raj and created engravings for books illustrating aspects of Indian life for the British market. This trend was short-lived as more technologically advanced commercial printing methods were introduced, and there was in the end no great impact on the Indian fine-art scene. Then, in the mid-20th century, a number of Indian artists made strong efforts to introduce fine-art printmaking, one of whom, Krishna Reddy, had learned his craft in the studios of William Hayter. There is now a proliferation of artists who use printmaking techniques, and a growing market in the country for their work. Despite India's rapidly evolving technological and commercial life the work of such artists has yet to make a substantial impact on the established printmaking scene in Western Europe and North America. Printmaking is taught at a number of Indian universities and art academies – not only the traditional techniques but also the new digital techniques. It can only be a matter of time before a wider interchange of artists and prints between India and other countries increases the level of knowledge of what is being achieved there.

Aditi Pande was born in 1984 and graduated in 2009 with a Master in Visual Art (Printmaking) qualification from Maharaja Sayajirao University in Vadodara (formerly Baroda) in the northwestern Indian State of Gujarat. She has worked in a primary school and is currently a freelance artist and studio coordinator for the CHHAAP Foundation for Printmaking Trust in Vadodara. She has had work included in many exhibitions in India over the last six years. While still in the early stages of her artistic career, she has achieved a body of work with considerable interest and potential which encapsulates some of the links between traditional and digital approaches to printmaking. She writes of her involvement with primary teaching, 'I have been dealing with children of age group five to twelve as their teacher, familiarising them

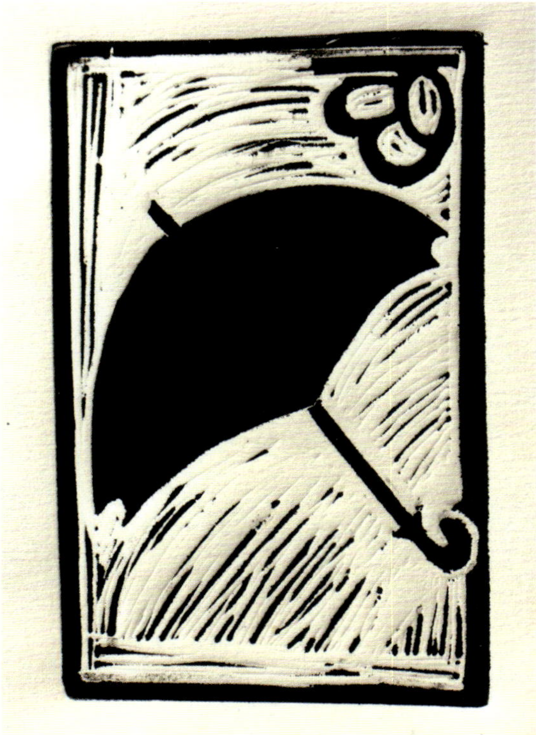

Aditi Pande, *Ch se chatri* (from the *Varanmala* series), 2012. Linocut, 14.5 x 9.5cm (5¾ x 3¾in.).

with the means and mediums which would help them to express themselves better, and in return they opened a whole new world of possibilities for me. My interaction with them started showing its reflexes in my work. I moved towards newer language.'

In particular she was struck by the fact that the children used very simple but liberated forms and figures in their work. She adds that her involvement in teaching helped her to move away from the art language that she had learned and developed and into new spheres of interest. This process, by which a teacher can learn from those she (or he) teaches raises the interesting question of reciprocity, whereby teaching and learning are mutually enriching. The combination of roles, those of artist and teacher, has been a central factor in the lives of many artists for centuries. One is essentially introspective and meditative, while the other has by necessity to be outward-looking, predicated on active communication and the sharing of ideas. The balancing trick is to be able to keep the two roles separate while still allowing the experiences gained in one to influence the other.

Pande understands the complexity of the two roles – the essential differences and the commonalities – and that both call upon her ability to increase public engagement with her work. She considers that her personal work contains an undercurrent of nostalgia and melancholy and that translating complex ideas into picture or visual form is a challenge. Her classroom experience showed her that the ways in which children found simple visual solutions to ideas became for her the key to simplifying all that she thought was complicated, resulting in her more recent work in an interesting play of complex and effortless. This, however, does not mean that she chose to reduce her work to a bare minimum of simple signs, but rather to seek ways in which her use of materials and techniques – linocut, paper cutting, silk screen and photopolymer – can form a synergistic whole with her conceptual thinking and imagination. She writes of her work that it is, 'not strictly printmaking; however, it often involves reproducible images either through techniques of printmaking or casting. My work results in objects and images.'

Her work at present forms two series. In the *Varanmala* series she is creating a set of 40 linocut prints based on characters of the Hindi alphabet in the Devanāgarī script. Each of the images is a simple graphic representation of a common object, such as an umbrella, a plant, a rabbit, a chili, with its relevant initial character in a range of single colours. The completed work will be presented in the form of an accordion-folded book that can be looked through or displayed, forming what Pande refers to as a 'garland of stories'. This work can be compared with the familiar nursery presentation of the alphabet in book or wall-chart form – A is for apple, B is for ball, etc. – but given a twist that positions it within contemporary Indian society, offering potential interpretation on a number of levels. By contrast, her work in the *Parivar* (family) series is both more personal and more complex, technically and conceptually. Using a range of techniques, including photopolymer, Pande is creating a series of unique prints with images of members of her family taken from photographs and placed within graphic frames incorporating text. Being away from her family during her eleven years of studying and working in Vadodara not unnaturally created a sense of longing, and in making this series she honours the tradition of family bonds, and bridges the distance between her and them.

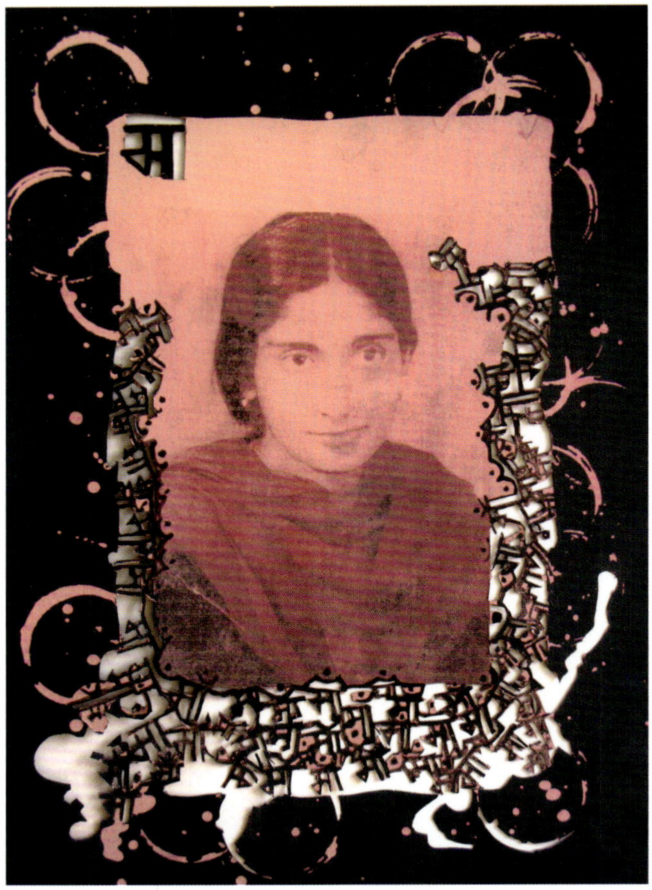

Aditi Pande, *Relation 2*, 2012. Unique print, 30 x 21cm (11¾ x 8¼in.).

Right: Aditi Pande, *Relation 1*, 2012. Unique print, 30 x 21cm (11¾ x 8¼in.).

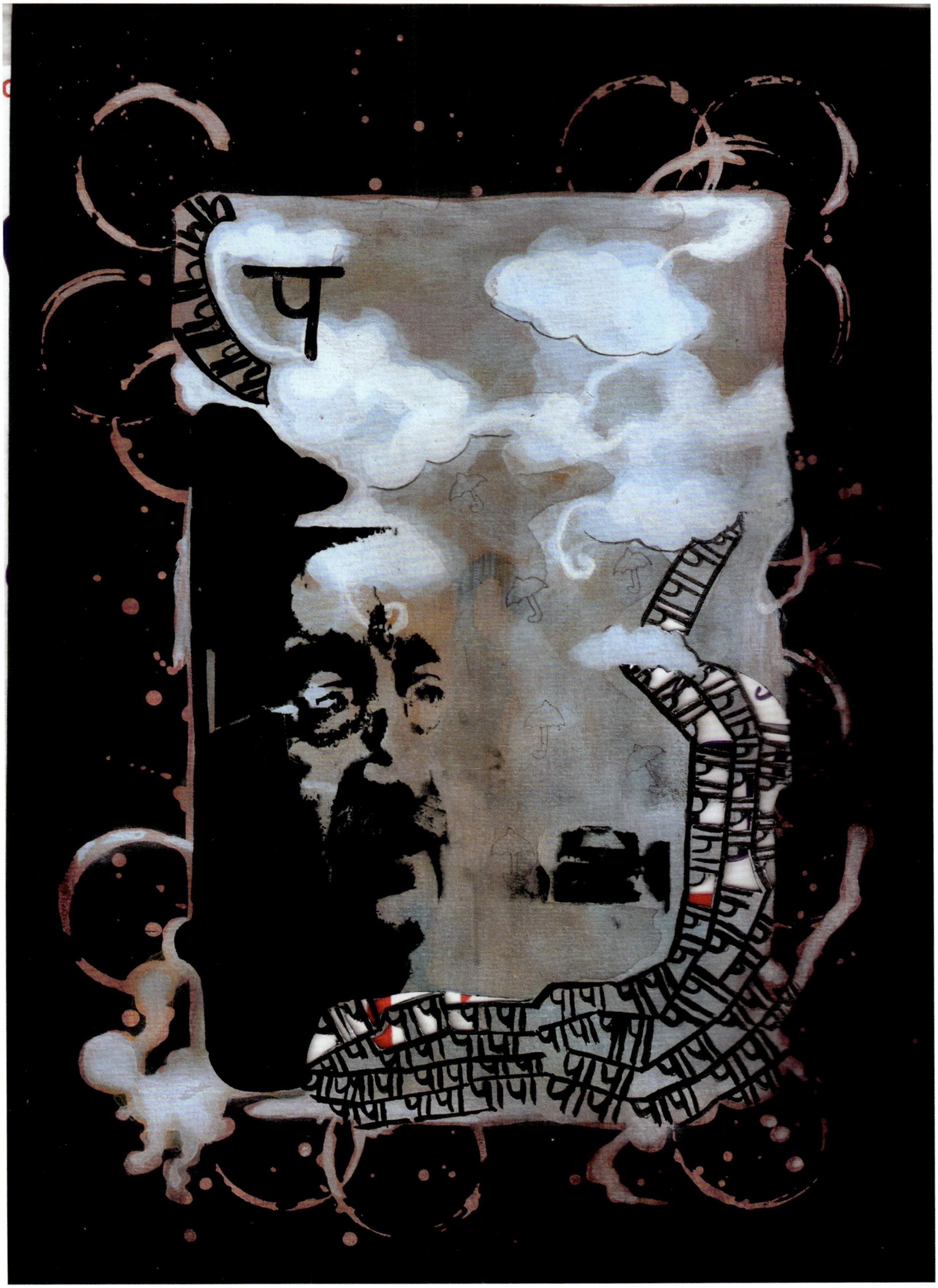
प

BHUTAN

TENZIN DORJI

THE HIMALAYAN KINGDOM of Bhutan is a culture based on deeply revered Buddhist traditions nowadays combined with an increasing acceptance of the globalised technological world. Following centuries in which the rulers of the country chose policies of isolation, with little or no connection to the world outside its mountainous borders, there is now an increasing openness to modernisation, with a cola bottling plant opening in 1997 and, in 1999, 60 channels of satellite television (excluding MTV) becoming available. In addition, access to the internet is now good, and mobile telephone networks have increasing numbers of users. At the same time there are prohibitions on Western-style advertising billboards, plastic bags and the sale of tobacco. The traditional arts in Bhutan are taught and practised with strict adherence to Buddhist principles, and artistic freedom in these arts is limited to minor details in the backgrounds. These restrictions are based on the concept that art serves a spiritual purpose, in which each element of the iconography has special attributes that combine to transmit Buddhist teaching and wisdom. The evidence of the strength of this approach can be seen in the continuity of excellence from ancient works to contemporary works that follow these traditions.

The contemporary arts, however, are also being practised in the country, and are not discouraged by the traditional authorities. Karma Singey, a journalist in the capital, Thimphu, offers this observation, 'If Western art promises change, excitement and vitality, Bhutanese art strives for peace, serenity and grace,' and suggests that Bhutanese artists can tap into the creative yin-yang energy of East and West. In a similar manner artists taught in the Western traditions can learn much from the traditions of countries such as Bhutan. Thimphu is also the base for Voluntary Artists' Studio, Thimphu (VAST), an informal and non-profit organisation set up by a group of professional artists in 1998 with manifold aims, including promoting the importance and value of visual art, and providing guidance and assistance to young artists in developing their full creative potential, as well as encouraging their participation in national and international events.

Tenzin Dorji was born in 1979, and following his early education in Bhutan studied Western, Indian and Far Eastern art at the Visva-Bharati University at Santiniketan in West Bengal, India, graduating in printmaking in 2007. He has exhibited his work in India, Bangladesh and Japan, and is the recipient of a number of scholarships. In addition, he has participated in art camps and workshops in Bhutan, India and Thailand. While at university in India he studied intaglio, lithographic, silkscreen and woodcut techniques, and developed a preference for etching. As one of the first Bhutanese artists to study printmaking using what are, to Bhutan, distinctly non-traditional techniques, Dorji is in the rare position of being able to appreciate both the historical approaches to the making of art within his own country and the wider possibilities offered in the world beyond its borders. He writes, in response to some questions I put to him, 'It's true that there is a lack of facilities for printmaking techniques like etching or lithography, as they have never entered Bhutan. The only printmaking technique that has been followed is woodblock, which has been used mostly in printing ancient Buddhist texts and images. It has never been used by artists to experiment and explore its potentialities.' He goes on to explain that he isn't enthusiastic about introducing etching and other similar techniques into Bhutan, since they require the use of toxic chemicals, although he would be interested if suitable non-toxic and ecologically friendly methods could be found that would be acceptable in his country.

At the time of writing (2012) Dorji remains interested in exploring the ways in which woodblock methods can be used in a contemporary manner, as suitable materials are already available in the country: he is working on a series of prints inspired by the masks that have traditionally played an archetypal role in Bhutanese rituals. Dorji intends that this series will not only reflect the way masks relate to the natural world, but also to the emotional nature of humans, and intends that they should become a satirical portrayal of the decadence of the present global situation. In this way, he writes, 'I am displaying traditional "physical metaphors" in

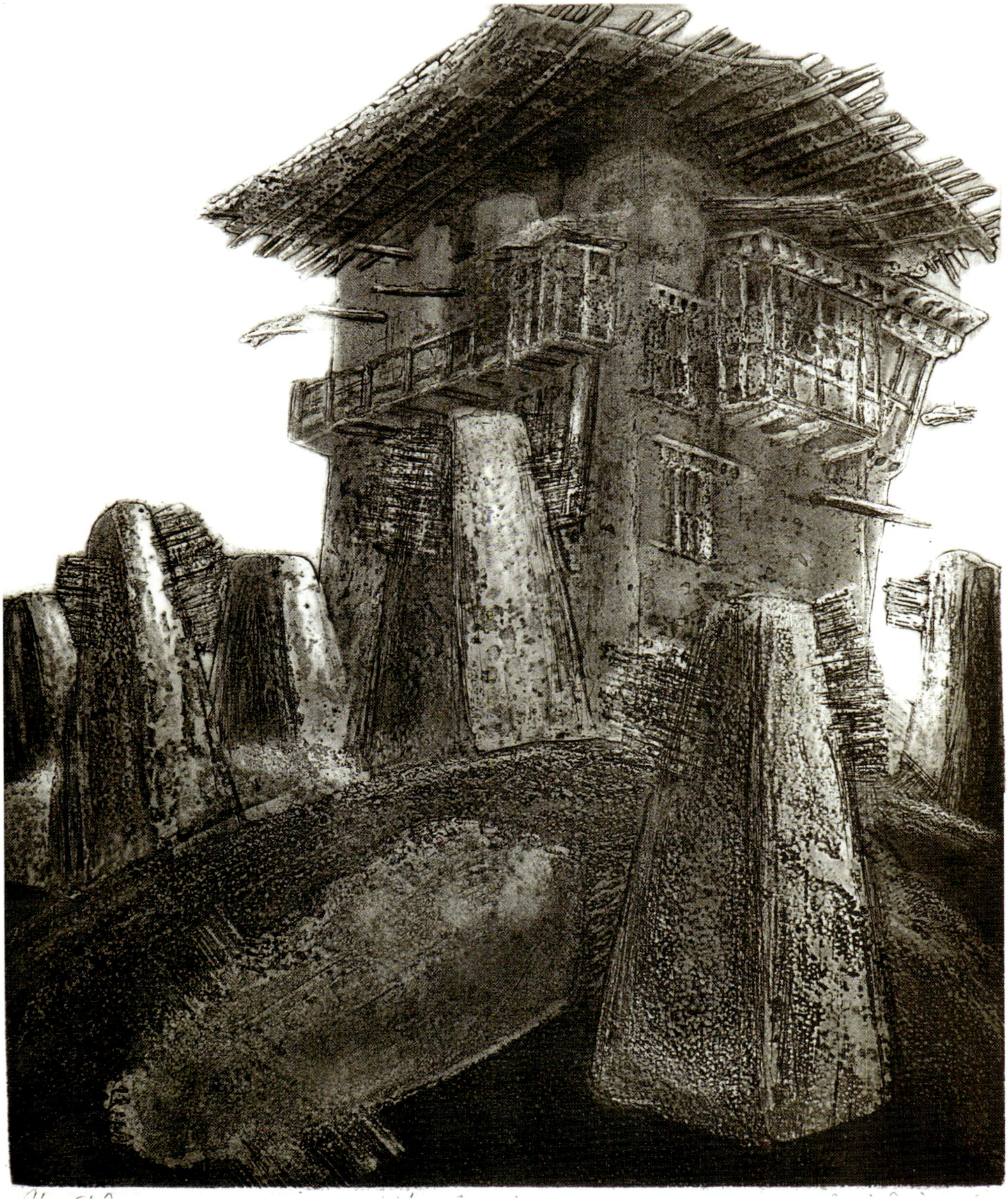

Tenzin Dorji, *My Ruins*, 2007. Etching, 70 x 29cm (27½ x 11½in.).

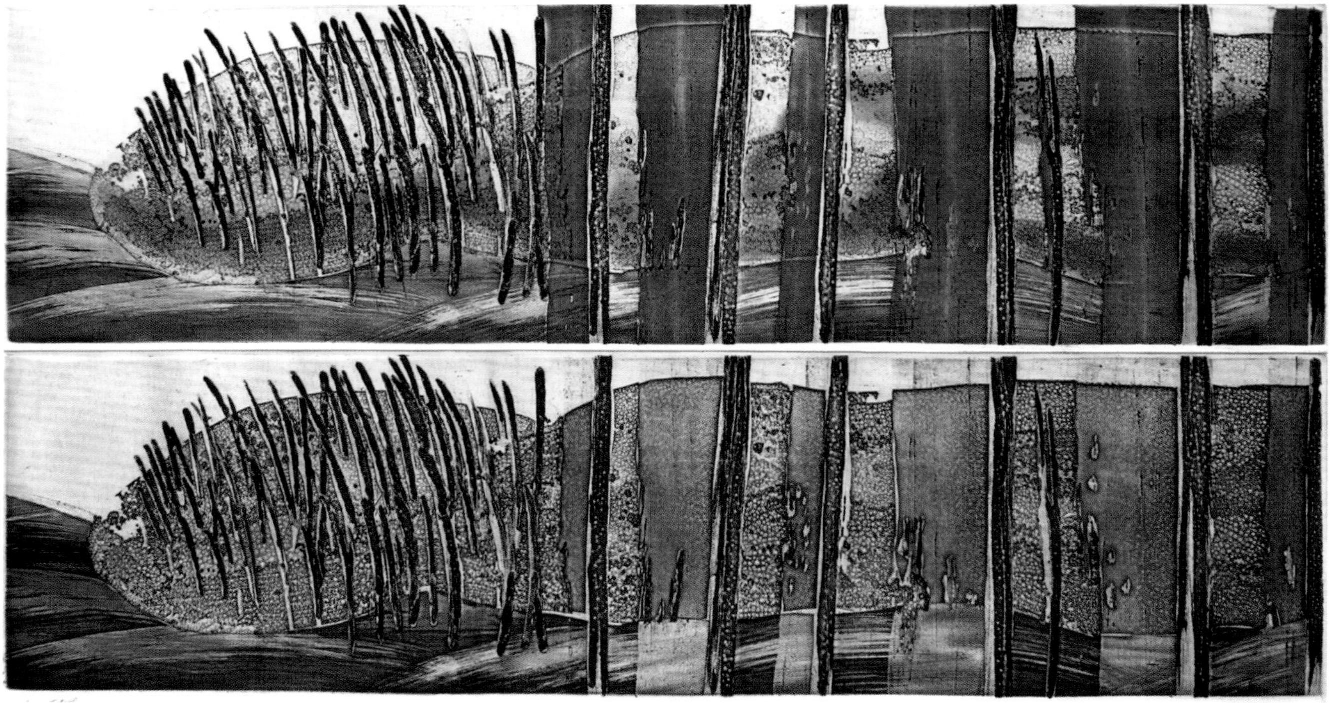

Tenzin Dorji, *Prayer Flags*, 2007. Etching, 48 x 24cm (19 x 9½in.).

a non-conventional manner, to reinstate the modern'. These attitudes are very much in line with the underlying philosophy that guides much of contemporary life in Bhutan, and which creates a situation for printmaking that is very different from most other countries in the world.

The three etchings from 2007 can be seen as transitional works, from which Dorji's new work will develop. *My Ruins* is his reaction to the traditional houses built of mud and wood that have survived for at least 300 years, symbolising the impermanence of all things, as the organic structures of the past, now falling into ruin, give way to modern construction. *Prayer Flags* is a semi-abstract approach to depicting the prayer flags that are a central part of daily life, which in their gradual disintegration disperse the prayers printed on them into the atmosphere, to become part of the universe; in their turn they are replaced by new flags. The repetition within each half of the print, and the doubling of the image itself, play their part in this belief. *When I Met You* incorporates a fragment of a traditional wooden structure, and two elemental forms, one of which bears the structural pattern of a traditional mandala. For Dorji this shows, 'Impermanence in our existence, like a dew drop on grass. The moment it is there it disappears.' These etchings are the evidence of an artist from a culture outside the usual parameters of the contemporary world, one who is clearly aware of both past and future.

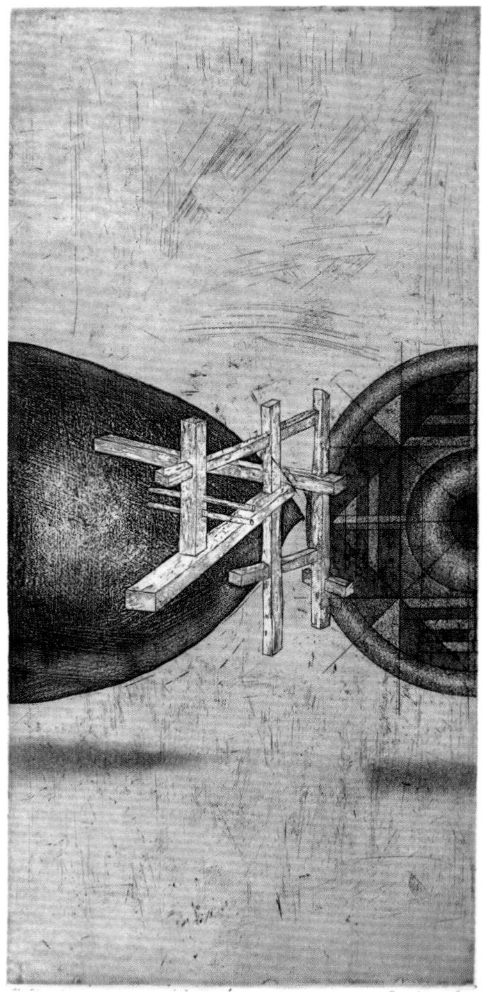

Tenzin Dorji, *When I Met You*, 2006. Etching, 48 x 24cm (19 x 9½in.).

NEPAL

NAN MULDER

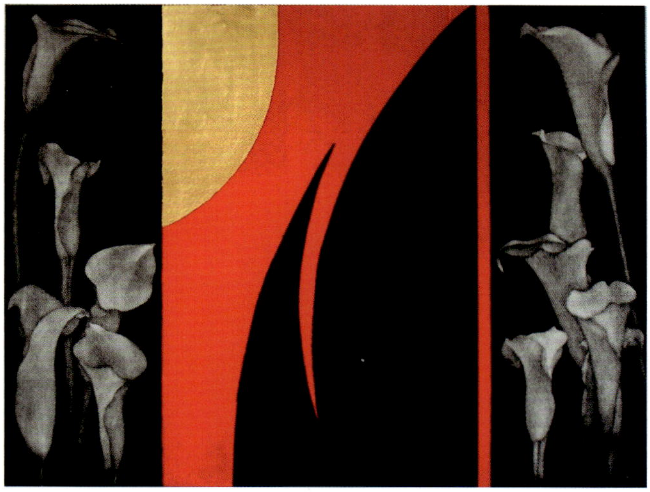

Nan Mulder, *Red Nights,* 2006. Mezzotint and gold leaf, 30 x 40cm (11¾ x 15¾in.).

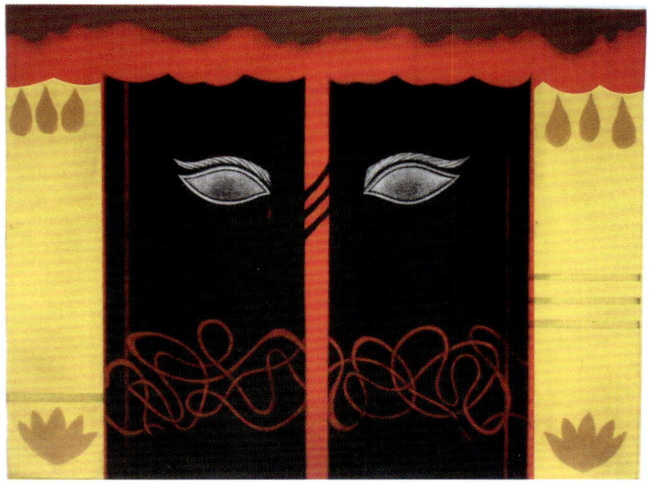

Nan Mulder, *Temple Doors*, 2007. Mezzotint, 30 x 40cm (11¾ x 15¾in.).

'WE LIVE in two worlds: the external and the internal world. The approach I have to my work is driven by a desire to express the hidden, inner world. As this world seems often mysterious it asks for an indirect approach or language to explore and express. Other cultures, and particularly Asia, offer a rich visual kaleidoscope, which, because the symbolic meaning is not obviously revealed to an outsider, can become a source of transferable imagery.' So writes Nan Mulder in a statement about her work, which is the product of a long career as an artist, teacher and – importantly for her work – a traveller. Born in Leiden, the Netherlands, she graduated in drawing and printmaking, with a postgraduate study in painting, from the Gerrit Rietveld Academie in Amsterdam in 1974, having also spent a year on a printmaking scholarship at the Academy of Fine Arts in Krakow from 1973–74. She also holds an MA in English Literature from the University of Edinburgh, in which city she has lived for many years. In addition to her work as a practising artist she also taught Printmaking at the Edinburgh College of Art, as well as teaching in Ireland and elsewhere in Europe. Mulder's record of exhibitions, both solo and group, is extensive and international, with her work being held in many international public and private collections, and she has also been the recipient of numerous awards.

Her work in both printmaking and painting is characterised by a deep appreciation of the subtleties of technique, her love of colour and, especially in recent years, her attraction to the imagery derived from her travels in many countries, including a deep appreciation for the arts of India, Nepal and Bhutan. It is not coincidental that many European artists, particularly since the mid-20th century, have found themselves drawn to the arts of the Indian subcontinent, not only to the visual arts, but also to music, dance and theatre. This can be explained not only by the exotic differences that the cultures of Southeast Asia offer to Westerners but also by an expanding awareness of the visual vocabulary of the global multicultural society. Having travelled with Gea Karhof, a fellow printmaker from the Netherlands, to Central America and a number of countries in Asia, she found herself in Nepal in 2004, stranded in the capital due to the activities of Maoist-instigated strikes. As a result of this she came across the Siddhartha Gallery in Kathmandu, and through them met a number of Nepalese printmakers, in particular Ragini Upadhyay and Seema Sharma Shah. These meetings led to a joint exhibition of work by the two Nepalese and two Dutch artists that has been shown in Edinburgh, Antwerp, Haarlem and Eefde (the Netherlands), Kathmandu and, in 2013 (as planned at the time of writing), in Lahore and Islamabad in Pakistan.

Mulder's paintings are figurative and intricately composed, and contain narratives that are hinted at rather than described, with saturated colours and often a single perspective point, combined with faint echoes of de Chirico, Hopper and Mughal miniature paintings. Her recent work in printmaking continues this rich mix of influences and

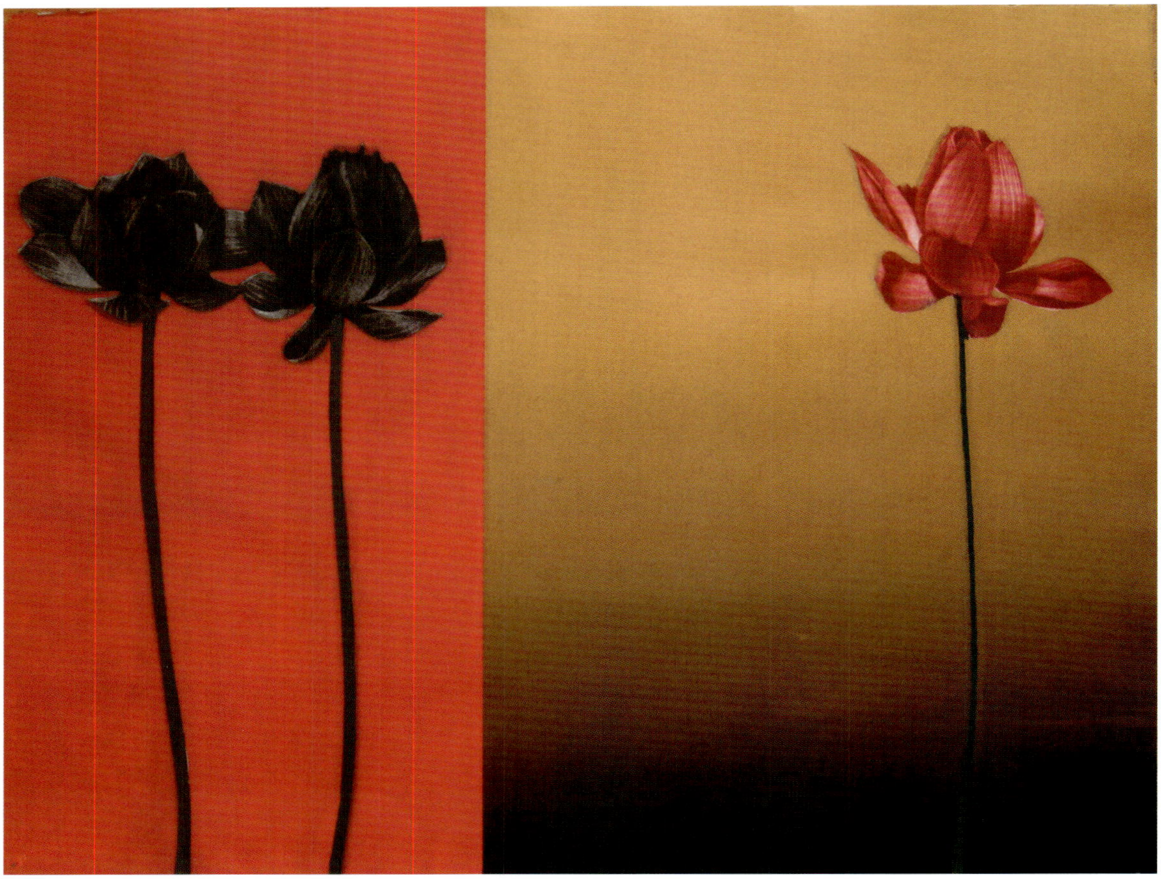

Nan Mulder, *Starting the Journey*, 2011. Mezzotint and screenprint, 56 x 76cm (22 x 30in.).

styles, but with a greater degree of formality and a reduction in detail, while imagery from her travels has made its way into the narratives of her paintings, giving them a mysterious presence and the familiarity of a fading dream.

Before embarking on a long and ambitious series of paintings Nan Mulder had worked mainly as a printmaker, and has in the past decade returned to the challenges of this medium. She is skilled in a number of printmaking techniques, among them silkscreen, intaglio and mezzotint, often combining two or more mediums in one print and also adding elements in chine collé and gold leaf. The richness of this approach, and her predilection for strong colour, gives her printmaking a painterly feel that is particularly evident in the work she has made since she travelled in Southeast Asia. This unique work is clearly connected with her experiences in countries such as Cambodia, Thailand, India, Bhutan and Nepal, having an exotic breadth of imagery and composition that relates her refined and hybrid style to the intricate and highly evolved colour and content of miniature paintings, the intricacies of temple architecture and the colourful tumult of the markets.

One source of imagery that has been important for Mulder is the lotus flower, with its deep significance for the Buddhist and Hindu faiths, as it had for the religious iconography of Ancient Egypt. For Mulder the lotus became a personal symbol as a result of a dark period in her life, from which she emerged stronger, echoing the symbolism in Eastern faiths that comes from the manner in which the lotus emerges pristine from the mud beneath deep waters to bloom in the light. In *Red Nights* (2006), the two side panels are in mezzotint, with grey lilies emerging from the dense black, flanking a central panel in black and red with gold leaf, a stylised abstraction of foliage and a rising sun – optimism emerging from between the curtains of pessimism, indicating a new beginning. *Temple Doors* (2007) has a similar composition of formal elements, derived from Nepalese art but simplified through a more Western approach to pattern and composition. There is in this work a sense of drama and an implied silence, suggesting a different and more chaotic world behind the doors. *Starting the Journey* (2011) takes the reduction and compression of themes a stage further. The paper is divided into two sections, with two black lotus flowers against red and a single red lotus against shaded gold. Lotus flowers were symbolic of rebirth to the Ancient Egyptians, in Buddhism they symbolise spiritual awakening, and in Hinduism beauty, fertility, prosperity, spirituality and eternity. These meanings resonate powerfully in Mulder's work.

RAGINI UPADHYAY

NEPAL is a landlocked country sandwiched between India and the Tibet Autonomous Region of China, and has a geography that reaches from the subtropical south to the Himalayan peaks in the north. Formerly a monarchy, and closed to outsiders until the 1950s, the country has since 1990 been a republic, with a recent history of political instability, including the civil war from 1996 to 2006 that followed the Maoist-led insurgency. At the time of writing, there is some doubt about the elections planned for November 2012. Despite the political uncertainty, the country retains a vibrant and ancient culture based largely on the Hindu faith practised by over 80 per cent of the population, but with important connections to Buddhist art, including that from Tibet. The multiplicity of ethnic groups within the country gives a richness to the culture, and this is one of the factors that has made Nepal a major tourist destination for many years, in addition to its attractions as a climbers' paradise and, more recently, a destination for white-knuckle sports.

Ragini Upadhyay was born in the capital, Kathmandu, in 1959 and graduated in Fine Arts from the Arts and Crafts College in Lucknow, India, in 1982. She followed this with further studies at the Lalit Kala Academy in New Delhi (1983–85), with subsequent fellowships at Peacock Printmakers in Aberdeen, Scotland, and Oxford Printmakers in England, together with a course at the art academy in Stuttgart. Upadhyay has a long history of solo and group exhibitions in many countries, her work is included in many international collections, and she has received a number of awards. She has also been a guest artist at institutions in a number of countries including Germany, Finland, Sweden and Pakistan. Her work includes both painting and printmaking, with some mixed-media works. Although printing from woodblocks has long been a prevalent technique in Nepal, it has until very recently been used to print fabrics for clothing rather than for the making of art. It is for this reason that this artist, like many others, had to travel outside Nepal – mostly to India – to learn about printmaking. That situation is now changing, and since the early 21st century printmaking has been included in the curricula of further education institutions in the country, with a master's degree being available since 2010.

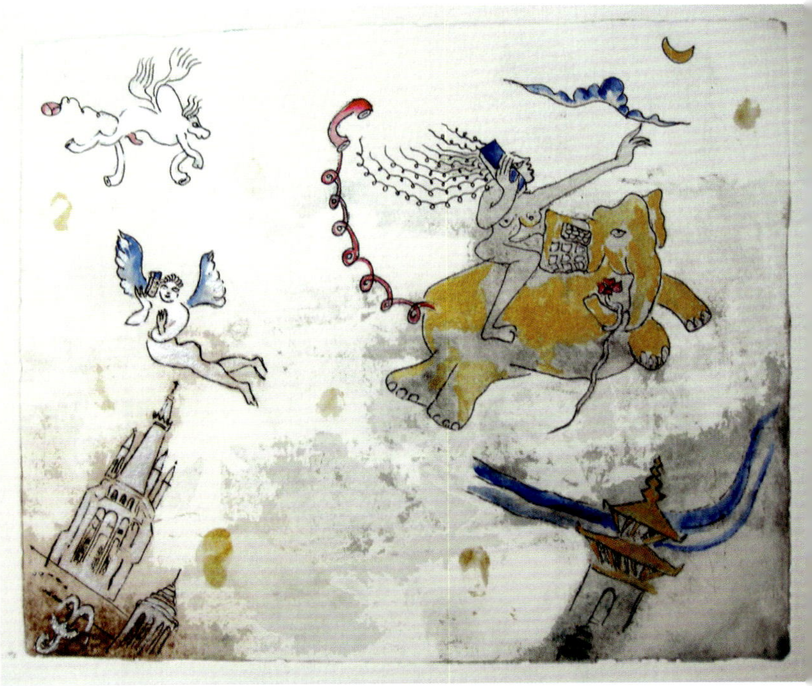

Ragini Upadhyay, *Love in the Air 02*, 2008. Etching and mixed media, 24 x 30cm (9½ x 11¾in.).

With a strong commitment to both the visual arts and to her country's cultural development, Upadhyay has in recent years continued to work on her own practice, but also to provide opportunities for other artists. This has included the development of the Ragini Art Village in Balkot, on the outskirts of Kathmandu, where she has her home, a studio and a gallery, and also a guesthouse to accommodate artists and students from all over the world, giving them access to both the studio and the gallery, as well as opportunities for immersion in the local culture. Her desire to improve the position of printmaking among the contemporary visual arts in Nepal led her, in 2011, to open the Artist Proof Print Gallery in Kathmandu, the first such gallery in the country, and associated with the gallery of the same name in Antwerp, Belgium; her husband is Belgian. The aim of the

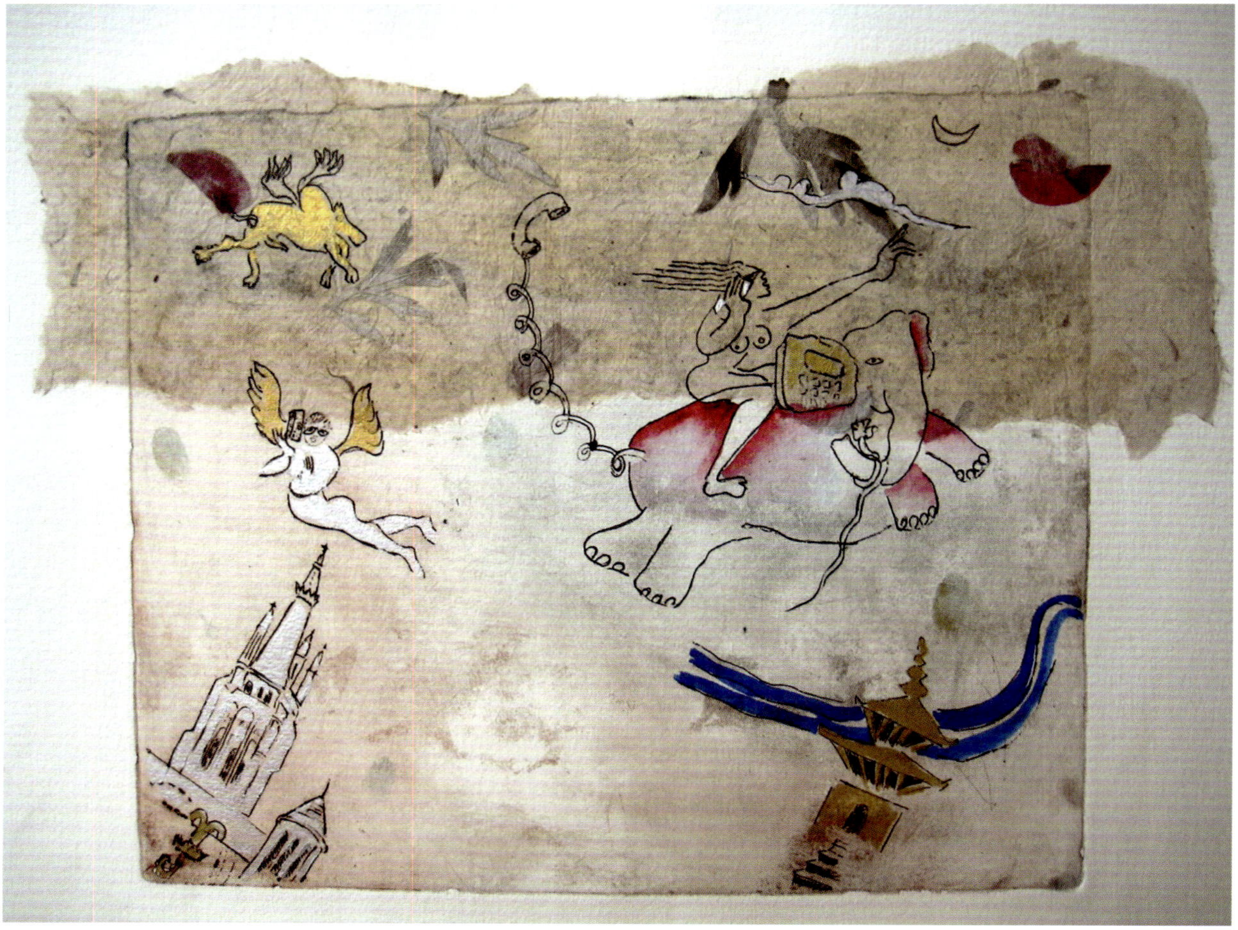

Ragini Upadhyay, *Love in the Air 04*, 2008. Etching and mixed media, 24 x 30cm (9½ x 11¾in.).

gallery is to encourage Nepali artists to consider printmaking or to be inspired by it, and for those already active in the medium to show their work together with exhibitions of work by international artists visiting the country. The exhibition programme since the opening has been welcomed by the art-loving community in Nepal, and has been supplemented by talks and other activities.

Upadhyay's own work in both painting and printmaking follows concerns and themes derived from her own background and experience. Growing up in Nepal in the 1960s gave her the experience of the depth of influence of Hindu culture, in particular the traditional emphasis given to sons in preference to daughters and, despite her own father being very supportive of her, the ways in which society in general was repressive, even aggressive, towards notions such as equality of opportunity regardless of gender. As a consequence, feminist themes played an important part in the development of her art in the 1980s and early 1990s, which included a series of works on the theme of the Kumari, the Living Goddess, seen as being a symbol of the repression of women. A later series, *Woman in Love*, shows a shift in direction that coincided with her own marriage, and also with the changes that began to be seen in Nepali society following the ending of the monarchy and the troubled steps towards the country becoming a federal democratic republic. The shift has been considerable and while there is still much to be achieved, the role of women and the need for greater equality is being more widely recognised. In recent years, as Upadhyay has travelled and shown her work more widely, it has developed still further, both stylistically and thematically, showing the influences brought about by her experience of cultures beyond Nepal and India.

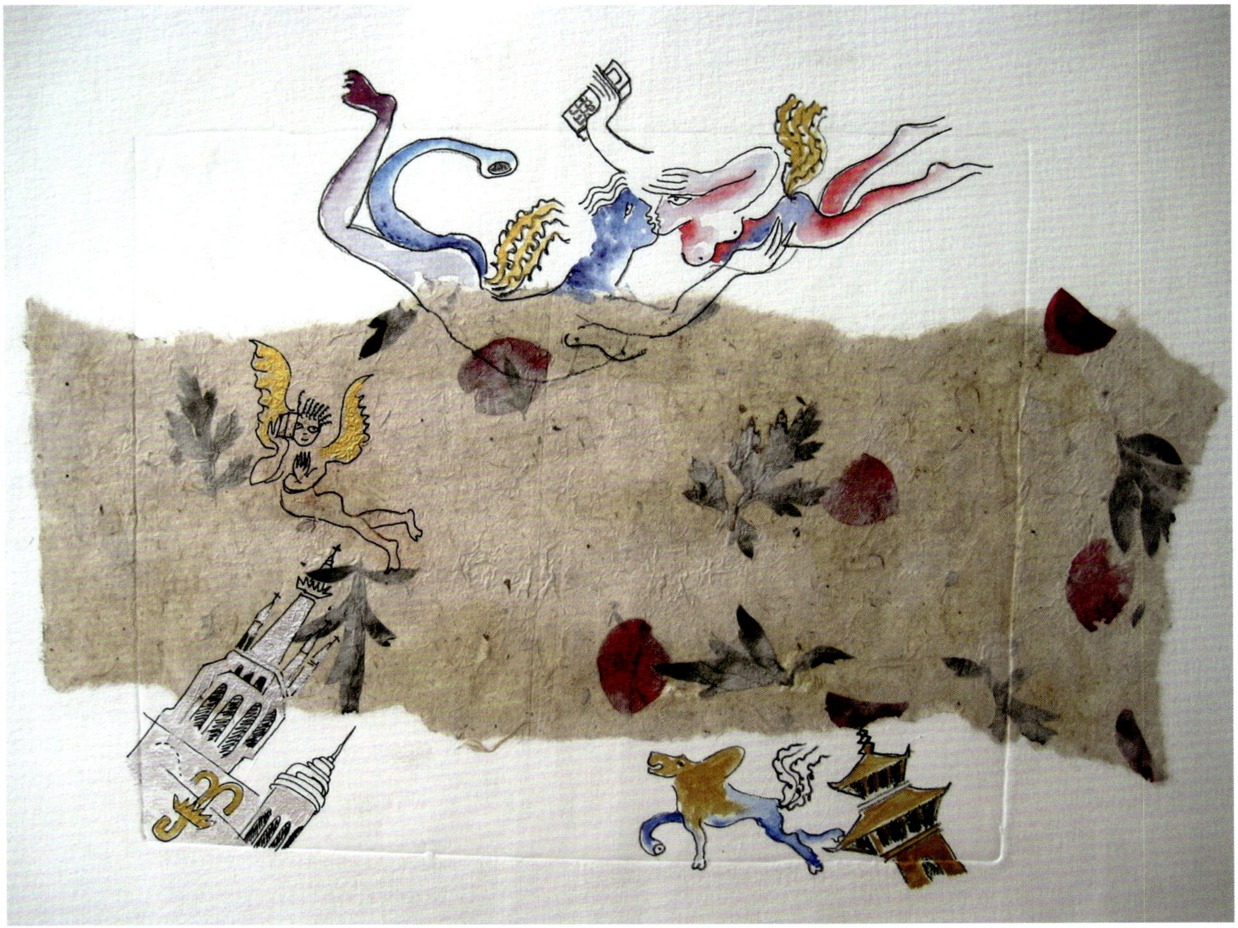

Ragini Upadhyay, *Love in the Air 06*, 2008. Etching and mixed media, 24 x 30cm (9½ x 11¾in.).

The images from a continuing series of works in both painting and print, under the title *Love in the Air*, show a greater sense of lightness and openness than some of her previous work, and the influence of Western art, including that of Chagall, is evident. Using etching and mixed media this series of small prints presents a more liberated vision that includes visual references to the Nepali and Western worlds and cultures, in which European church spires meet Nepali temple towers, flying angels hold mobile phones, bulls sprout wings, and airborne elephants bear naked women. All of this imagery is presented with a sense of joy and celebration of the freedoms beginning to spread thanks to the growing use of mobile technology, while still paying a degree of respect to traditional beliefs.

PAKISTAN

AS PART OF the research for this book I asked a number of artists and others from Pakistan a series of questions in an attempt to gain a broader picture of a country that I have not visited but which I know something of from a distance. Their answers, edited as anonymous comments, provide a context for this part of the book. They are not, nor are they intended to be, definitive, but do raise some matters of interest. One interesting initial comment was, '... Pakistan might be said to be in a state of low-grade civil war, with all that this implies. It's not just the terrible acts of urban terror, it's the growing division of public opinion into positions of absolute extreme, defined by their mutual opposition'; and also, 'Like every country, the population is layered, politically, economically, culturally, but with such huge disparities of any broader exposure, education, wealth and all that goes with it. However, almost anyone I have known to visit Pakistan has come away inspired by the land, its culture and its people, and especially, its hospitality.'

The first question asked about the current position of contemporary visual art in Pakistan's cultural life, and responses included: 'As Pakistan has gained access to the international map of countries producing edgy contemporary art, it has drawn the attention of collectors, writers, television channels and the layperson. I would say there is more curiosity than ever before, more tolerance for what artists do, and more art schools producing more artists ...'; 'The fine arts sector is mostly marginalised due to its "bourgeoisie" status. Private individuals run galleries where expenses are incurred on an individual basis'; 'Artists from within Pakistan and the diaspora are exhibiting in prestigious museums and fairs the world over'; 'It's marginal. If it were more mainstream it would be targeted by attention-seeking extremist organisations or even the government itself; occasionally it is';

'Art is more of an elite activity ... for the most part in Pakistan today. Though is that so very different from "the west"?'

The second question concerned the importance of printmaking in Pakistan, and responses included: 'Printmaking itself has been replaced by the digital copy due to its convenience. Printmaking is a laborious time-consuming method that, ironically, requires materials – inks, papers, presses – that are not easily available resources. Therefore it is a medium rarely chosen by younger artists, although more senior artists and professors have not only been teaching the craft but practising it'; 'Many if not most artists here today make prints, albeit digital editions from large-format printers'; 'Traditionally, all art schools had a printmaking department, and most continue to have one. As photography and printmaking possibilities go digital, the work produced is far ahead of the processes art-school departments offer. More and more, digital art work and work that can be editioned is understood as "real" art.'

The third question asked if artists in Pakistan occupied an anti-establishment position and, if so, to what degree their work could be said to be political. The responses included:

'The "political" in the world of art today is also an "aesthetic". An easy path to visibility, especially if you come from Pakistan or any of the developing nations, or countries at war. Having said that, artists and everyone else in Pakistan are very political, and, because of where we live, art and literature cannot NOT be edgy and political'; 'Just being an artist in a society like this is a quite anti-establishment position, though in a genteel sort of way. Poetry is the work of subversion in this culture much more so than the visual'; 'The undercurrent amongst the artists is not that of an anti-establishment but rather one of reconciling, redefining and articulating affective forces of working in a complicated political and psychological terrain.'

The fourth question asked what opportunities there are to show in galleries in which discourse is encouraged, and the responses included: 'The gallery scene is small, but it's there. There may be just three or four good galleries whose agenda is not only commercial, but they do exist. The bigger gap in Pakistan is that of historical, critical and insightful writing, critique and philosophy in the areas of art and culture'; 'There are some good galleries; many of the better ones don't last very long'; 'Most art practices in Pakistan involve a discourse very dissimilar to the model of the international art world, or in most cases oblivious to the current theories'; '... the Grey Noise gallery has begun to bridge a gap between the international art world [and Pakistan] and therefore to help initiate a dialogue that insists on redefining the current

DAVID ALESWORTH

image and expectations of art being produced from this region.'

The fifth question asked how magazines and journals covered the art world and if there were any good and reputable arts journals, and the responses included:

'There have been several over the years and the most recent, *Sobhet*, is an extremely sound journal of international standing, All journals and magazines, however, have had very short lives. Very recently (mid-2012) *Sobhet* had to close down'; '*Sobhet* is a new journal that is facing attack at present. Someone is trying to force a blasphemy case upon them. That's not the usual way of things. *Nukta* is another art magazine. There is art criticism in the *Herald*, *The Friday Times* and *Newsline* magazines, also *Dawn* and *The News* newspaper. The Urdu press also carries some reviews. The quality is very variable.'

The sixth question asked about the attitude of the Islamic establishment to contemporary visual art, and the responses included: 'It would be against it, if it had to face it; as it's a marginal activity, it mostly ignores it. It's more concerned that women should be covered on TV'; 'The art world, because of its small scale, is quite invisible in Pakistan! Artists get away with a lot. If anything there is more self-censorship than state censorship. The views of the Islamic establishment are probably pro-calligraphy and anti-nudity, but beyond that they do not have a manifesto of wrong and right.'

A final question asked about the state of art education in schools and at university level in Pakistan, and whether or not it was or can be progressive, and the responses included: 'Art schools in Pakistan are strangely the most progressive of teaching environments. I don't think they are very different from art schools abroad. If anything, the discussions are liberal, broader and unbiased'; 'Art education is excellent here, surprisingly much better than our larger neighbour, India. That's about money too; less art market money means more good artists in teaching. We travel, lecture, mentor groups all over ... so we know what the broader context and standard is like internationally, and Pakistan is a good place, art-education wise, at least'; 'Vasl Artists' Collective is a significant organisation that has helped many artists connect with the international art world, meet artists from around the globe and access residency/workshop-based opportunities.'

THE DEFINING of species in the natural world (taxonomy), or objects in the manmade world (cataloguing, indexing), has been an obsession in civilised society for centuries. Attempts at defining what a person is or does are entirely another matter, one that is seldom successful. In a world in which systems of definition run counter to the natural tendency towards anarchy – evidenced by the chaos of urbanisation or the overgrown garden running wild – attempts to define people accurately are seldom straightforward. David Alesworth defines himself as, 'a visual artist, landscape designer and art educator who has lived and worked in Karachi and Lahore for more than twenty years.' Born and educated to first degree level in Wimbledon, in southwest London, he was the Picker Fellow in Sculpture at Kingston University before completing his MFA in New Media at the Transart Institute in Berlin; he has lived and worked in Pakistan since 1988, and has held Pakistani citizenship for most of that time. He has an extensive record of international exhibitions, considerable teaching experience in a number of countries, and has

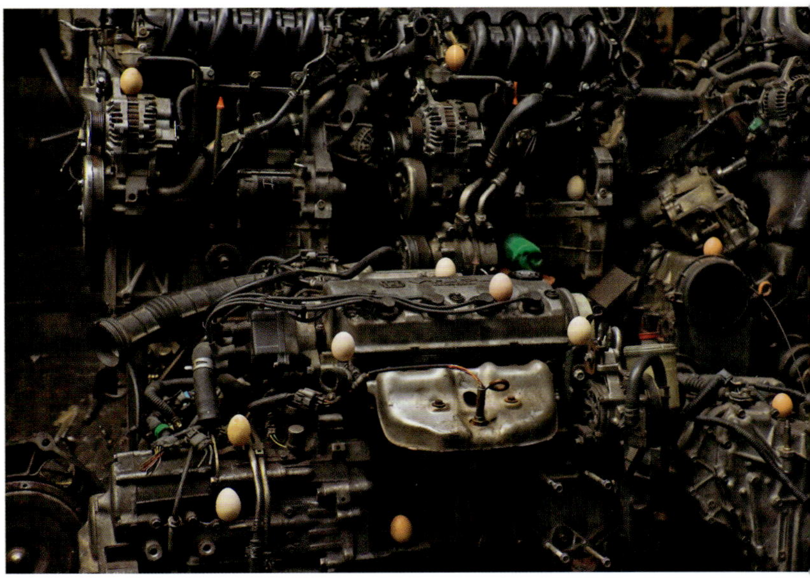

David Alesworth, *Desi Unday (Bilal Gunj Market, Lahore)*, 2010. C-Print, 114.3 x 76.2cm (45 x 30in.).

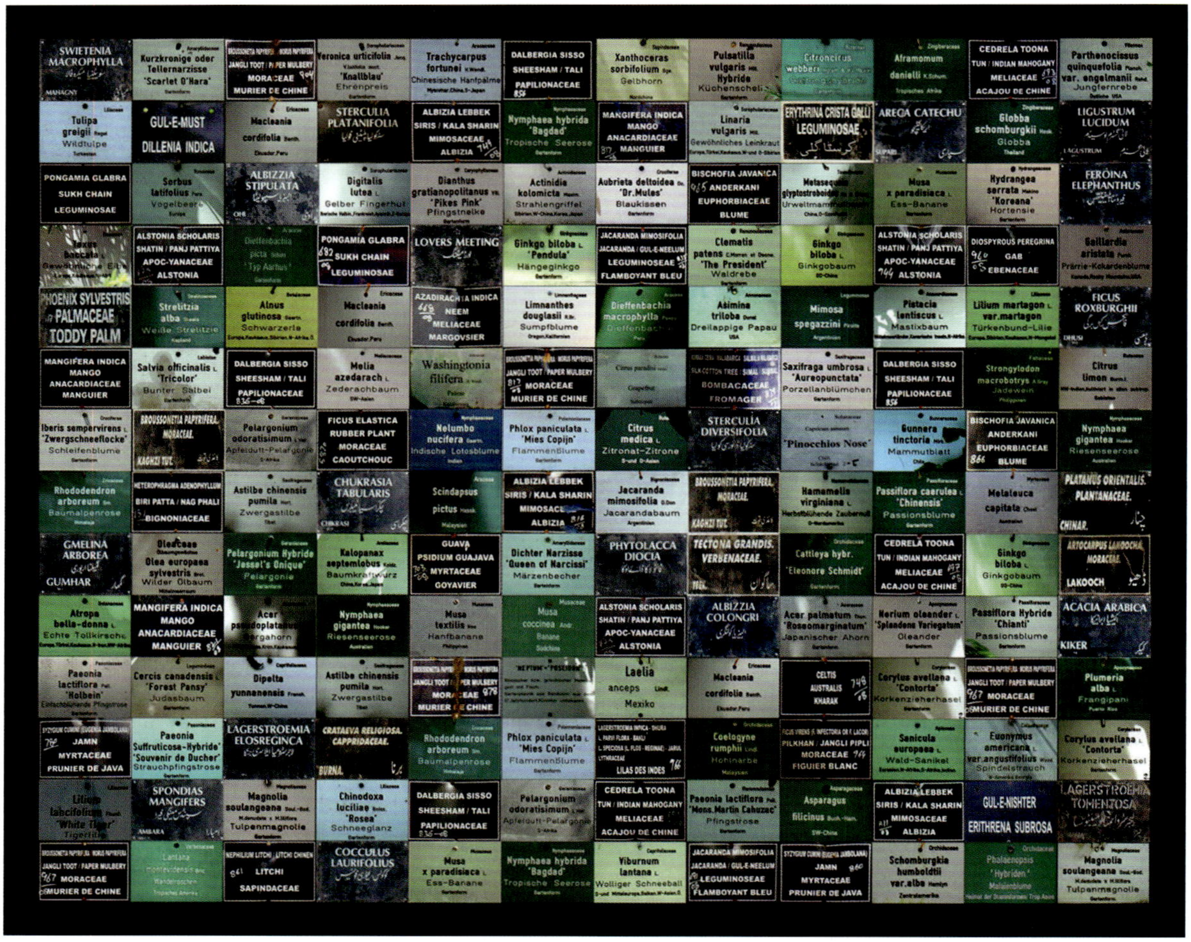

curated exhibitions in Pakistan and Europe. His working experience, as suggested by the terms in his self-definition, has been an eclectic one, combining a close involvement with the contemporary visual arts and craft culture of his adopted country with a parallel career as a horticultural consultant and landscape designer. He writes, 'I neither fit neatly into the role of the ex-pat European artist (of which there are almost none in Pakistan) nor am I the "expected" Pakistani artist abroad.' He also contrasts the manic energy of the mega-city of Karachi with Lahore, where he now lives, and where 'the slower, more agrarian, pace of life and its very evident historical depth also led me to greater introspection and a renewed consideration of the postcolonial.'

Alesworth's approach to his work is broad and inclusive, with each aspect of his work informing the others. In a statement to accompany *A Taxonomy of Eden* he outlines how he subscribes to the Darwinian approach in both gardening and art production, linked through their survival being dependent on how relevantly they fit their environmental niche. In Pakistan, as in other non-Western countries with rapidly developing economies in which large and expanding populations are to be found in huge cities, the natural and social environment is under constant threat. This is exacerbated in his adopted country by the presence of simmering conflicts and terrorism which impinge on daily routines, and in which survival – whether of the fittest, or otherwise by mere chance – is an ever-present motivation to adapt to those dynamic and shifting circumstances. He writes of how in his life in Pakistan he has been struck, 'by the intense profusion of everything. Vegetables, fruits, animals, often in stages of dismemberment, eyes in a pile to this side, next to engines also being dismantled and parts stacked according to type. The profusion of people in the mega-city of Karachi, the "horror vacui" that pervades all aspects of Pakistani popular culture and design including such as the henna on a bride's body, painted animals, painted trees, intricately decorated vehicles; that all speak of the energy of the multiple'. It is within these contexts that he makes his art, and from which he derives inspiration.

In *The Garden of Babel*, he assembles images of plant identification labels in a formal grid that, on close inspection

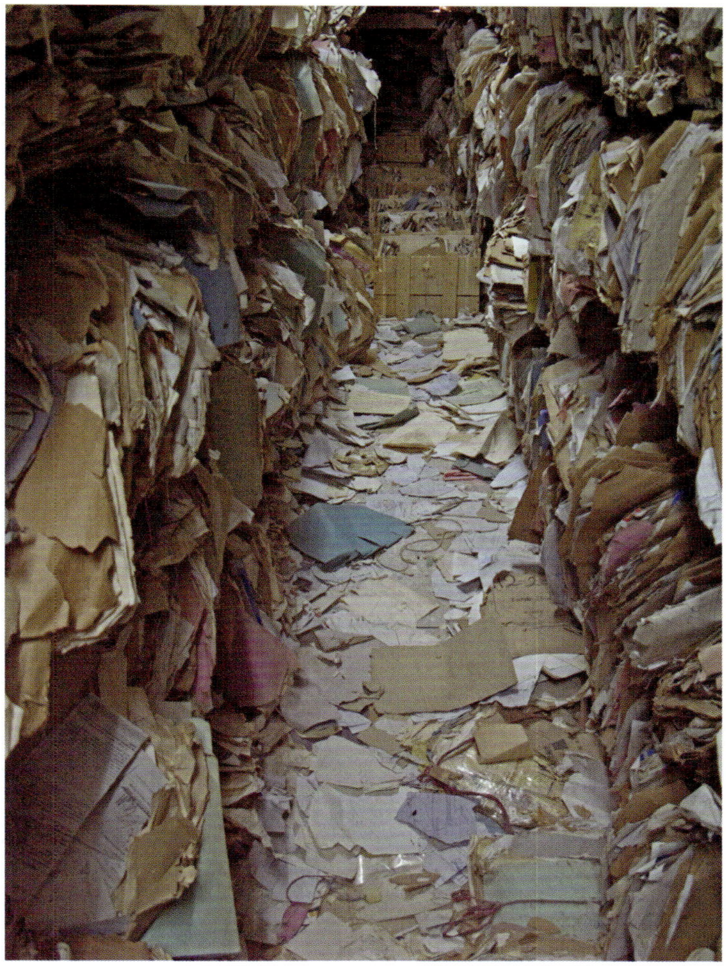

Left: David Alesworth, *The Garden of Babel*, 2009. Archival giclée print, 137 x 114cm (54 x 45in.).

Right: David Alesworth, *Record Room* (from the *Record Room* series), 2008-present. C-Print, variable dimensions.

and consideration, reveals the complexity of languages, text fonts, type conventions, colours and layout that have been used to define the exact position of a plant or tree in a horticultural classification. Deprived of their true function through being detached from the plant to which they belong, and instead marooned within a frame and subsequently recorded as a digital image, they serve to point out the confusions of nomenclature that exist in the plant world, and also our complicity with the assumption that the label is attached to the correct plant. Taken away from such an association, they approach meaninglessness. By extension, they refer also to any and all human attempts to impose order on the profusion of urban life and the natural environment. *Desi Unday* is a digital print that records two contrasting images from the Bilal Gunj market, the local wild chicken eggs of the title superimposed and apparently floating in front of neatly cleaned and stacked vehicle engines, bound for recycling either as functioning machinery or through scrap. The purity of the eggs is set against the apparent chaos of bits of machinery, but an alternative reading of the image could be that both elements within the print are destined to lead to either new life or the maintenance of the present; both feed the needs of society, and both are designed for specific functions.

One of the enduring legacies of the British Raj that was imposed on the Indian subcontinent during the days of empire is the civil service, which attempted to enforce British rule through a bureaucracy of byzantine complexity. That legacy can be seen in the continuing series of digital prints, *Record Room*, which Alesworth began in 2008. The images portray what appears to be, and perhaps is, complete chaos, with folders full of paper stuffed into shelves and spilling some of the contents onto the floor to gather dust. Whatever the system of classification was, it is now lost to all but the most experienced and assiduous filing clerk who, it may be supposed, could still find a certain file or document if it was required. Other than that, the files, as with the plant labels, eggs, and engine parts, are destined for recycling and yet remain captured in the form of digital prints which themselves can be subject to further classification in an endless cycle.

HUMA MULJI

THE CONCEPT, described by Baudelaire in the 19th century, of the artist as 'flâneur', wandering through the streets and arcades of Paris, absorbing the atmosphere and thinking great thoughts, can now be seen in retrospect as being excessively romantic – a notion that was rapidly overtaken and trampled by history. Huma Mulji (in an interview in *Platform* in 2010) mentions this before going on to compare it with driving around Pakistani cities, never at a significant speed, which gives her the space and time for her mind to wander, 'the visual feasting and consuming of the city, without literally thinking about it'. This attitude, of allowing a sort of interior free fall into which drift images and ideas, to be processed and thought about later, or to be forgotten, is not uncommon in the artistic experience of the age in which we live, surrounded almost to the point of being overpowered by a welter of information and imagery. To attempt the making of art with depth and meaning in such circumstances is considered by some to be a futile activity. Fortunately, there are many artists who accept the challenge that is offered, making work that presents carefully considered reflections on contemporary society – in other words, a long way from the production of decorative space-filling objects posing as 'art'.

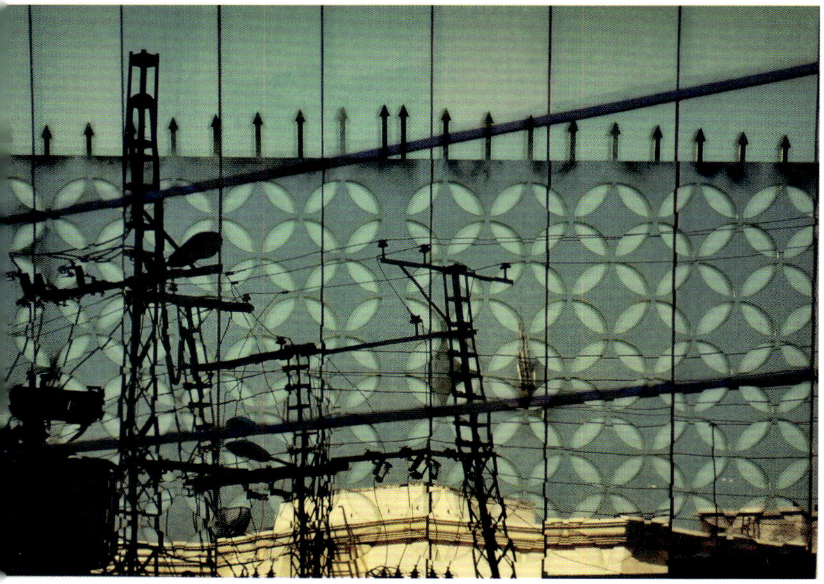

Huma Mulji, *Tinted Viewpoint*, 2011. Inkjet print on Hahnemühle paper, inkjet print on vinyl, laser-cut acrylic. 35.6 x 50.8cm (14 x 20in).

In notes on her work she writes, 'Looking at the absurdities and conflicts of living in an urban society in transition, of "living 200 years in the past and 30 years in the future", simultaneously, my works broadly address the visual and cultural overlaps of language, image and taste that create the most fantastic collisions.' She also refers to 'the unacceptable, forced Arabisation of a South Asian country like Pakistan, away from its regional identity to a deliberate religious one with the Middle East', another conflict that has a strong and powerful bearing on the society and politics of both her country and the wider world.

Huma Mulji was born in Karachi and completed her BFA (Sculpture and Printmaking) at the Indus Valley School of Art and Architecture in 1995, following this with a master's degree from the Transart Institut in Berlin in 2010. She lives in Lahore and, in addition to her art practice, teaches at the School of Visual Arts and Design at Beaconhouse National University. She has exhibited her work widely in Pakistan and internationally and was a recipient of the prestigious 2013 Abraaj Capital Art Prize. These awards are for artists from the Middle East, North Africa and South Asia, and are for projects to be completed for showing at the Art Dubai fair before being exhibited elsewhere. Her current and recent work has primarily been in the form of sculpture, and it is unsurprising therefore that her work in printmaking has a distinct sculptural quality. Mulji has used mirror in her sculpture, making reference not only to the use of fragments of mirror in the traditional Multani style of decorative objects and fabrics, but also to the wider metaphysical attributes of mirrors and reflections. It is also significant that the use of reflective glass for the façades of high-rise buildings is prevalent in many Pakistani cities, the outward display of an aspiration for international credentials but also, as with other cities around the world, providing a mirror for whatever else is in front of these new buildings.

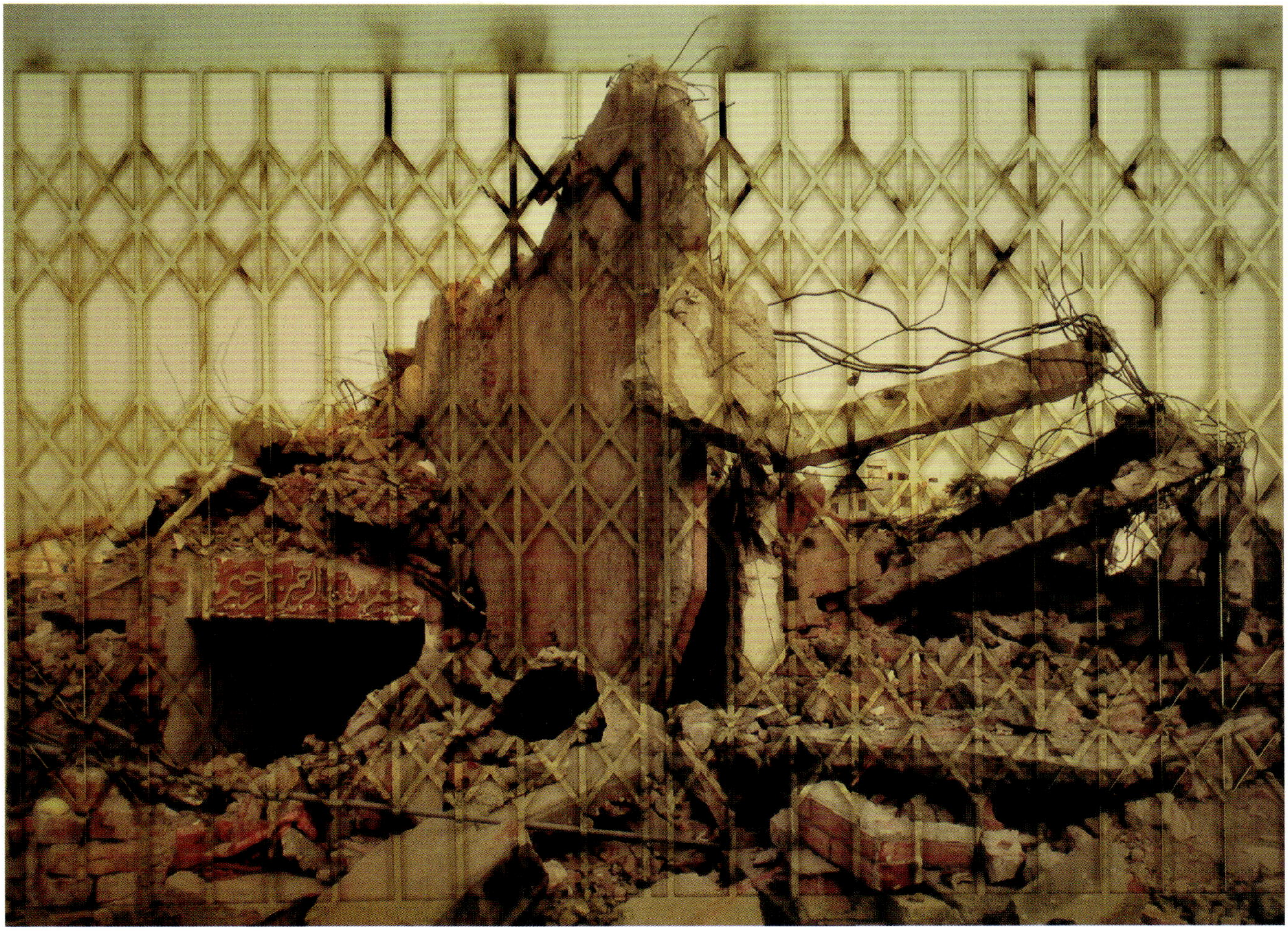

Huma Mulji, *Obscured Horizon*, 2011. Inkjet print on Hahnemühle paper, inkjet print on vinyl, laser-cut acrylic, 35.6 x 50.8cm (14 x 20in).

In *Tinted Viewpoint*, the artist combines inkjet prints on paper and on vinyl with a laser-cut acrylic sheet that adds its own reflectivity to the already complex series of surfaces within the print. The image of a high-rise façade, with its strongly geometric mirrored fenestration, reflects with some distortion the older building opposite, the street lamps and the tangle of wires and metal lattice towers of the power supply: and, in front of all these layers there is the acrylic sheet, cut precisely by a laser to create what could be a traditional screen pattern. This adds its own distortions and interior reflections that change the colours behind, and the image is distorted further as the viewer moves in front of the print, taking the place of the person in the street, excluded from the building, a metaphor for deracination in the urban jungle.

In a similar manner, *Obscured Horizon*, composed of the same combination of techniques, provides an alternative view of urban change and regeneration. The image shows a building, a shop perhaps, that has been demolished or otherwise destroyed in an area awaiting regeneration – a jumble of concrete and wires – with fragments of an Urdu text, the former building sign, and remnants of the belongings of the departed inhabitants left tangled in the rubble. In the background there are parts of other buildings, newer developments that indicate the process of continual change. In front of these images there is a laser-cut sheet of acrylic in the form of the sliding steel barriers that bar access to an entrance, or in this case perhaps symbolise the impossibility of the former occupants of the destroyed building gaining access to the newer buildings behind.

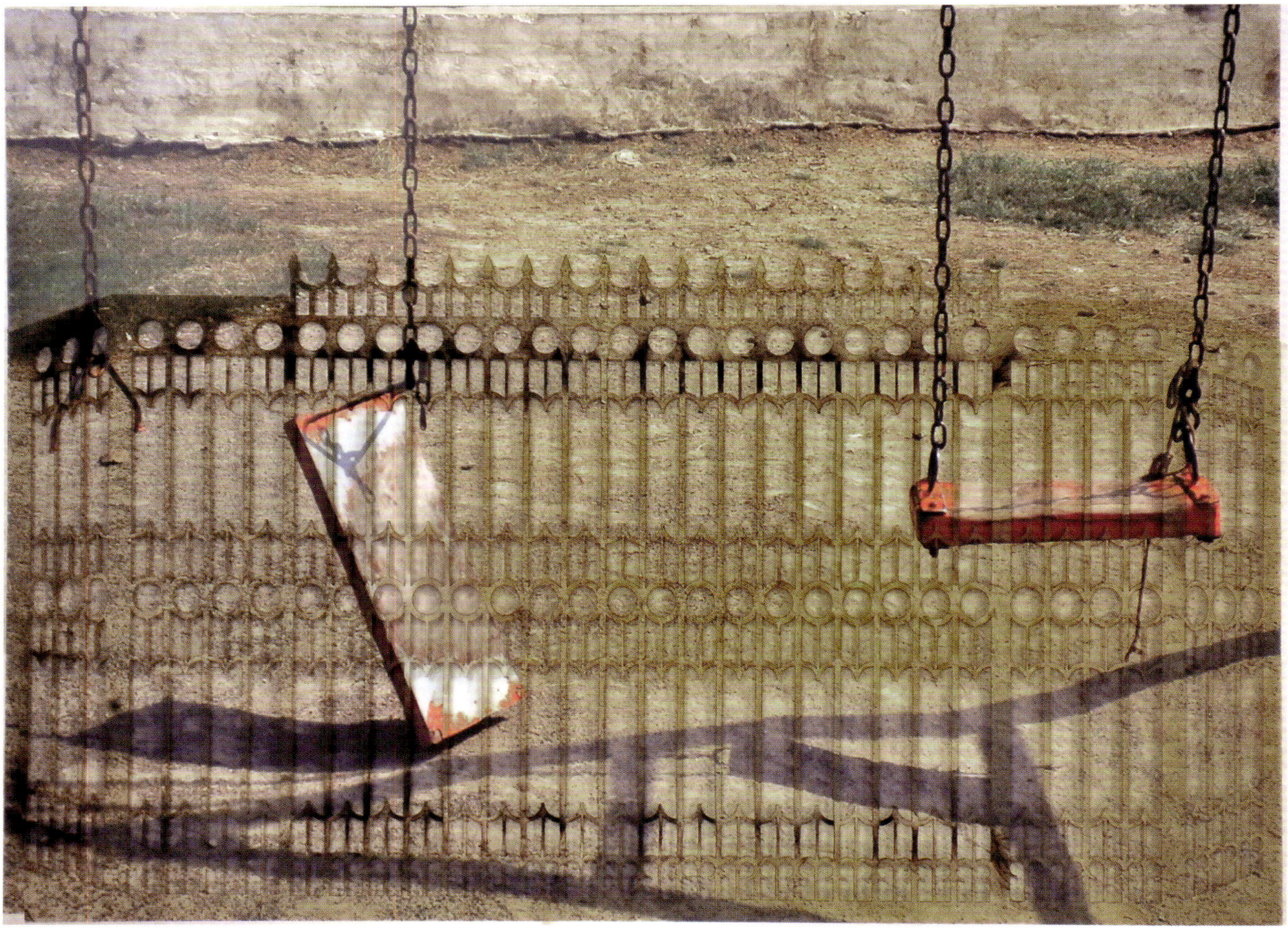

The third image, *When the Boys Came Out to Play*, offers a different range of alternative interpretations: is this simply an image of a broken playground swing awaiting repair or replacement, or does it symbolise the destruction of young lives caused by terrorism and violence? In either case the design of the laser-cut acrylic sheet represents the complex decorative fences erected around expensive houses and developments, signifying not only the wealth of the owners, but also their desire to exclude all but the elite. All these images are small in size, requiring viewing from close to, and bringing the viewer into close complicity with their layered meanings, and with the evocation of displacement in a changing city.

Huma Mulji, *When the Boys Came Out to Play*, 2011. Inkjet print on Hahnemühle paper, inkjet print on vinyl, laser-cut acrylic, 35.6 x 50.8cm (14 x 20in).

MEHREEN MURTAZA

CHARACTERISED by its precision of execution and complexity of underlying ideas, the work of Mehreen Murtaza defies easy definition, and in fact would not benefit from it. Instead it offers a wide range of possibilities for interpretation, and in the meantime is fascinating and original in its initial visual appeal. It is not, even in the most subtle of ways, the type of visual art that people would expect to emerge from contemporary Pakistan unless they had a close personal knowledge of the contemporary art scene in that country. But, upon deeper investigation, it takes its place in the long succession of cultural developments in a country that, before Indian independence, Partition and the formation of Pakistan in 1947, extended back millennia into the distant past. Murtaza was born in Riyadh in Saudi Arabia in 1989 and graduated from the Beaconhouse National University in Lahore, Pakistan, in 2008, gaining her teaching diploma there a year later. She currently lives, and has established her practice, in Lahore, and despite being at the start of her career has already established a good record of international exhibitions and activities. Of her approach to making art she writes, 'In fact, my creative approach has utilised appropriating mundane archival objects and imbuing them with a radical affective force of fabulated narratives to understand the remnants of the past in the present; narratives can ultimately critique cross-cultural representation and geopolitics through the retelling of the mundane as it intersects with the imaginary'; and 'My work does not come with political or artistic manifestos. I am searching to find a transnational position beyond Orientalism, Futurism, consumerism and propaganda.'

Her work encompasses digital printmaking, sculpture, video and installation, and, as her statements suggest, contains a symbolism that cannot be easily untangled. It is provocative, seeming to suggest one direction for interpretation but, with further consideration, suggesting another. There are elements from many disciplines, including organised religion, spirituality and science or (as she prefers to call it) 'speculative' fiction. These threads are in fact coherent, given that the work of many science fiction writers has embraced or reinvented religious and spiritual practices, among them Robert A. Heinlein (in *Stranger in a Strange Land*) and Walter M. Miller Jr. (in *A Canticle for Leibowitz*). Her approach may at first sight appear to be light, with familiar items being combined in a way that gives them a humorous twist. But there are darker resonances, suggestions of a dystopian future in which the superficialities of civilisation are subverted into subtle forms of control, by which everyday life is altered forever by forces beyond the understanding of all by a small elite. This also is a familiar theme in science fiction, particularly in films. Unlike the combative and overtly political approach of some artists dealing with complex themes such as these, Murtaza instead chooses to maintain what Somak Ghoshal, the writer and critic, describes as '... a bemused distance from the turmoil and treachery of politics, happy to be an aloof but involved observer'.

The selected images are from a series dating from 2011, *Tastes like Futurism*, in which the artist explores aspects of what she calls 'gastroculture', that heady mix of cooking and technology that has become pervasive in a number of TV cookery programmes that present a bizarre and somewhat confusing blend of alchemy, culinary expertise and flashy science unlikely to be replicated in most kitchens. Instead the viewer is presented with technological showmanship that positions the preparation and presentation of food beyond the reach of the average home cook.

Alphabet Soup is devised for the irrepressible bookworm, enabling each consumer/reader to (literally) feed on the biographies of those famous people they admire. Specially editioned books are prepared using squid ink blended with brown sugar and dried fig extract at low temperatures and then pressed into the pages for precisely three seconds and left to dry for another three seconds, making a ready snack for the erudite. Impossible and nonsense perhaps, and clearly a messy process to use. The *Hoverphonic* is a machine devised to enable 'an endless endoscopic gaze and draw in the stimulating aroma of an aesthetic freedom from terror'. Over a period of time this device is intended to allay such unhealthy emotions as fear and paranoia, enabling the consumer (for whom the device is positioned at a usable height) to gain mastery over their emotions. For the artist, living in a society in which threats of terrorism and militant action are a daily reality,

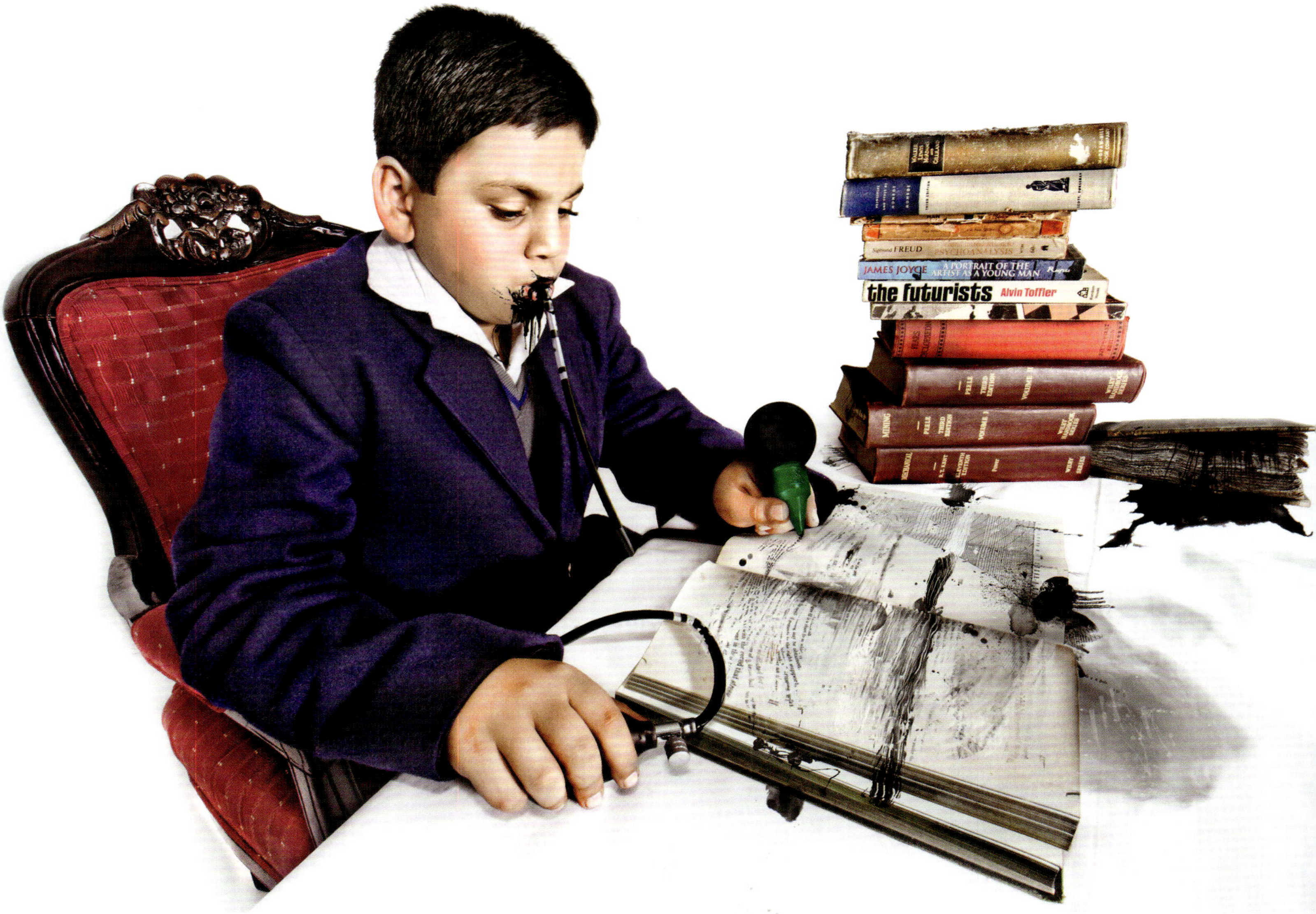

Mehreen Murtaza, *Alphabet Soup* (from the series *Tastes like Futurism*), 2011. 3D imaging and photomontage, inkjet on Epson glossy paper, 83.8 x 127cm (33 x 50in.).

Right: Mehreen Murtaza, *Fuva Fuva* (from the series *Tastes like Futurism*), 2011. 3D imaging and photomontage, inkjet on Epson glossy paper, 127 x 83.8cm (50 x 33in.).

Bottom right: Mehreen Murtaza, *Hoverphonic Parts I and II*, 2011. 3D imaging and photomontage, inkjet on Epson glossy paper, 83.8 x 127cm (33 x 50in.) (*Part I*), 55.9 x 127cm (22 x 50in.) (*Part II*).

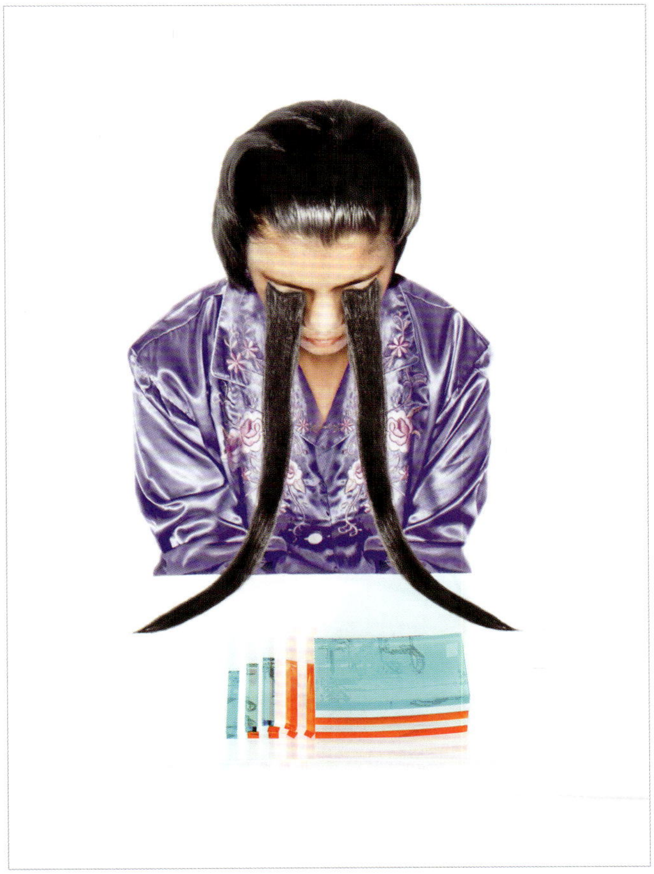

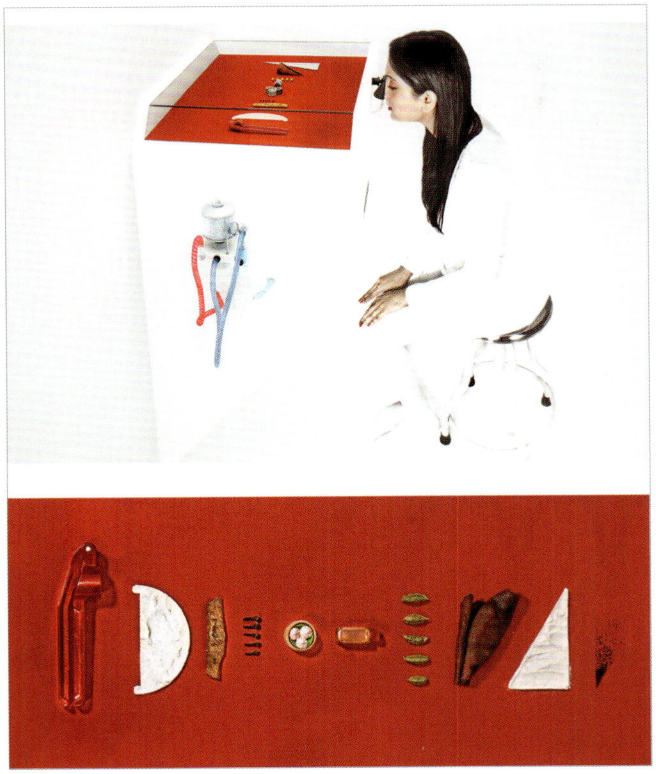

the devising of such a device is presented both as a sardonic commentary on extremism in society and one that is wholly impossible to realise.

Fuva Fuva takes molecular cuisine to a new height of absurdity, in which a delicious dessert may be prepared to curb the worst aspects of bashfulness; it is described in following terms: 'Seated on top of the raspberry liquid lava jelly, a special aqua-flavoured jelly contains a mix of two parts oceanic air essence and one part coconut extract, all fortified with two tablespoons of electrolytes.' The result of ingesting the electrolytes is, apparently, that the eyelashes of the consumer suddenly grow between one and three metres a day. The shy consumer can then hide behind her or his eyelashes and be immune from having actually to look at what is going on beyond the curtain.

In all these works, as in other works by Murtaza, there is a dark humour that conceals a sharp intelligence, not only in the ways in which the techniques of technologically driven art practices (at which she excels) can be mobilised, but also in arriving at an idiosyncratic critique of the society in which she lives – not only that of contemporary Pakistan but also the world in general. When direct opposition fails, surreal satire might perhaps stand a better chance.

IRAN

IT WAS NOT possible to visit Iran during the research for this book, so I sent a series of questions to a number of Iranian artists in order to gain a fuller understanding of the circumstances under which they work and their views on the place of contemporary art in Iran. An edited selection of their anonymous responses is given. I was also sent a copy of *Tehran Art, A Popular Revolution*, compiled by Ehsan Lajevardi, and published by Contemporary Art Publications. I am grateful to Yashar Samimi Mofakham for this and the selection of other catalogues that he sent, as they have broadened my knowledge and understanding of Iran and its contemporary art scene. The current (Autumn 2012) situation regarding the UN embargos and the political situation in the country does not permit as open an access to facts as I'd like, and exchange of electronic information is sometimes slowed down by the Iranian authorities. However, the information I have been able to obtain from the artists has been very helpful.

The first question concerned whether the news media, in Iran or internationally, present a clear and honest account of events in Iran. Responses included: 'I think any news media controlled by big powers like governments, parties, rich and large companies, etc., never tell the truth about what is going on anywhere, and they are always geared towards the benefits of their supporters, whether it is ideological (as in Iran or past Soviet countries) or it is politically/capitalist oriented'; 'Hopefully there are some amateur and/or professional news media growing, especially in this information age. Without those cell phones with cameras and internet it would have been impossible to inform the world about what was going on during the Green Movement, exactly like the Arab Spring or Syria or Russia';

'The media in Iran are subject to the strict control of the ruling power. This control is focused on political news. The culture and art scene always manages to create discrete spaces that the leaders overlooked or tolerated. And that's where the cultural sector succeeds over and over again in making visible their criticism'; 'Outside of Iran, the media often have a very one-sided picture of Iranian society. The diversity of society and the everyday struggle of the population to emancipate themselves from the regime is often left aside'; 'I believe there have been many differences between the true stories that are happening to the people of Iran, and the news that the media publish ... all media publish the kind of news that helps them reach their goals and their advantages. The true stories would be found in people's lives, in their art works, literature, movies and other media that are close to people or other media which common people can use easily like the internet'; 'The media from any country has its own agenda and they only cover the parts of an event or story as they have been told to do, more or less. I believe many forms of self-censorship take place in any country, such as the USA by artists, curators, galleries and museum directors, various corporations, media, film industry, radio and in some cases the blogs on the web.'

The second question asked if the work of Iranian artists can help make news and events better known, and if so what problems arise. Responses included: 'Yes. I believe any artist living in any country that deals with current social and political issues through their art work will affect the public opinion and will bring awareness to a much larger audience. At the same time, these kinds of art work will present many problems for the artists and their careers'; 'I believe in the important effects that contemporary Iranian artists make by producing art works. But there have been many problems about producing art without boundaries; even showing them in an exhibition would be impossible in Iran, and then if they were to be shown outside of Iran there would be many problems for the artist from the government of Iran'; 'There are different forbidden matters for the regime – political, ideological, traditional society taboos and religious matters. The worst and most dangerous part is religious and ideological, because they have the power to punish without any kind of trial (like the inquisition in the Middle Ages); after that is political, and then social taboos'; 'Many Iranian artists deal within their work with social and political issues. Even though very often a direct criticism is avoided, this type of work again reflects the current situation. In this sense, art opens lots of windows to the soul of a society that the ruling regime tries fiercely to hush up.'

The third question asked if it is inevitable that art made in or about Iran will be politically or socially critical, or whether non-critical art can have any credibility, other than being merely decorative. Responses included: 'From my point of view, I am an artist interested in art that interferes and does not avoid political issues. In Iran, all subjects are political. The state has regulations for almost all facets of the life of citizens, rules for dressing up, reading, writing, loving, social behaviour …'; 'I believe any Iranian artist who is serious about his or her work, no matter where he/she lives, is political by the nature of the long and intense tension and negative interaction between Iran and other countries, especially the USA'; 'Calling an artwork politically or socially critical is not just about telling it in obvious ways; sometimes there is only the title that makes people consider it as a political work. There can always be many layers of political and critical views in some art works that only the artist can make it possible to consider by pointing to it'; 'But I think that even if they do not believe in making this kind of (non-critical) art, they are doing much more since we are living in a political and very traditional society and being an artist is against society's taboos and beliefs'; 'I know myself as a socially critical artist and I prefer this kind of orientation in art. Being an artist is a socially critical job, whether doing political or critical art, or something else.'

The fourth question asked whether art with a socially or politically critical content can make any difference to a country such as Iran. Responses included: 'Collecting art work is something of a luxury in Iran and the Middle East ... and that is why most buyers and new collectors are people who want to change their class. So I think art at first is some kind of dialogue between these parts of society, some kind of discussion to challenge their beliefs'; 'Iranian artists trying to show the world that there is a voice of protest from inside Iran that is trying to say something different from the regime, are calling the world to hear their voices about the reality of Iran, and the Iranian people, culture and heritage'; 'Leaders are always afraid of artists, who are the voice of their own people. They (the artists) tolerate (the risk of) torture, exile, death and destruction for the power their art may have on society as an agent of change'; 'As artists we try to break the boundaries of ignorance and to bring awareness through art to the public'; 'Art can open spaces for perception, sensation and reflection.'

FAHIMEH VAHDAT

'I AM AN Iranian-American, Baha'i woman artist, who lives in exile in the USA after the revolution of 1979 in Iran, rather than just simply being part of the mainstream art world: an artist.' This statement by Fahimeh Vahdat crystallises one of the common problems faced by artists who, whether by necessity or their own choice, leave the country of their birth to seek a new and better life elsewhere. As a young college student in Dallas, Texas, she faced the sorts of problems of prejudice that are faced by exiles and immigrants alike, who encounter difficulties that the indigenous populations find hard to comprehend. Such problems are, however, often made more difficult when faced by an artist, even more so when the artist is a printmaker rather than a painter or sculptor; the layers of ignorance or misunderstanding become more confusing to many non-artists. The complexity of the

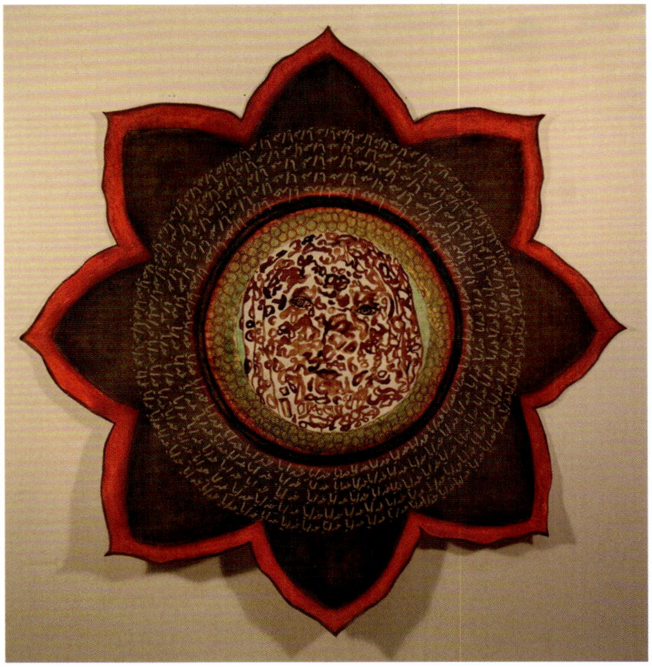

Fahimeh Vahdat, from the *Freedom* series: *Protest*, 2012. Charcoal drawing, collage, block print, ink, oil pastel, watercolour and acrylic on Rives BFK paper, 132cm (52in.) diameter. Photo: Larry Chatman.

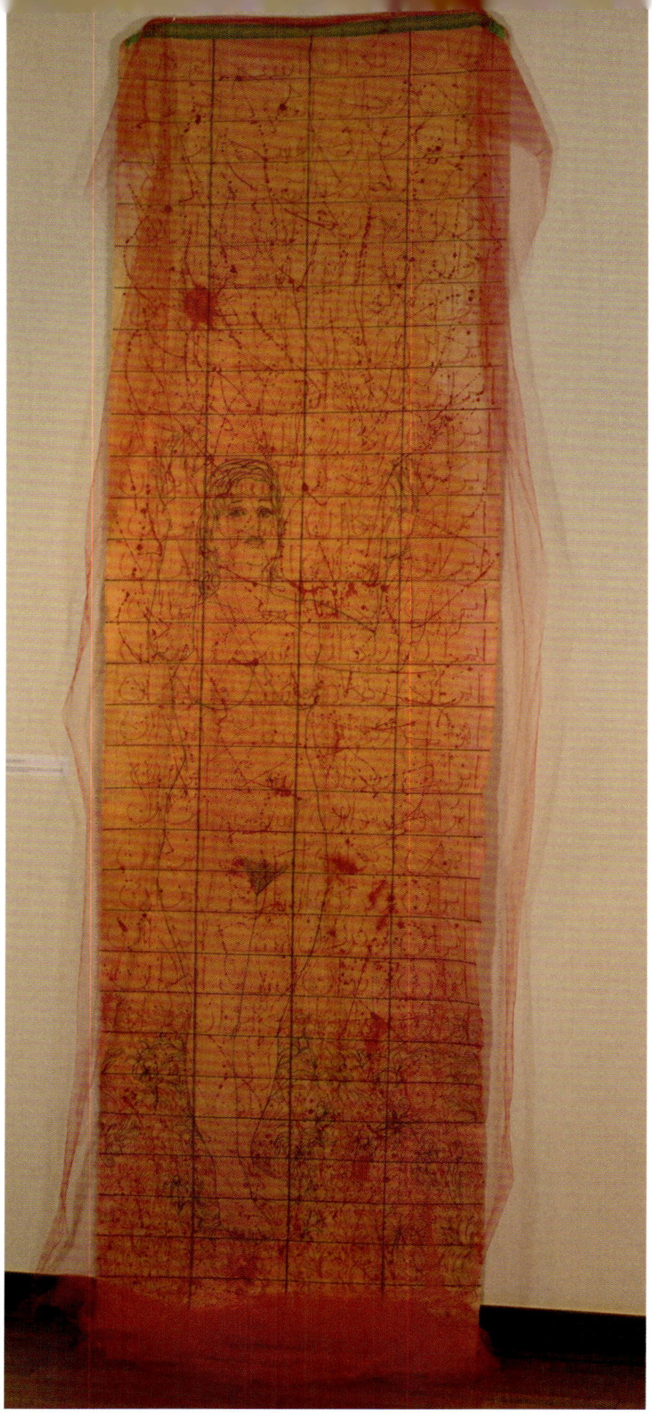

Fahimeh Vahdat, from the *Freedom* series: *A Prison Called Iran*, 2011. Charcoal drawing, monotype, ink, acrylic, sewing, lace and fabric on hand-dyed canvas, 216 x 130cm (85 x 51¼in.). Photo: Scott Gara.

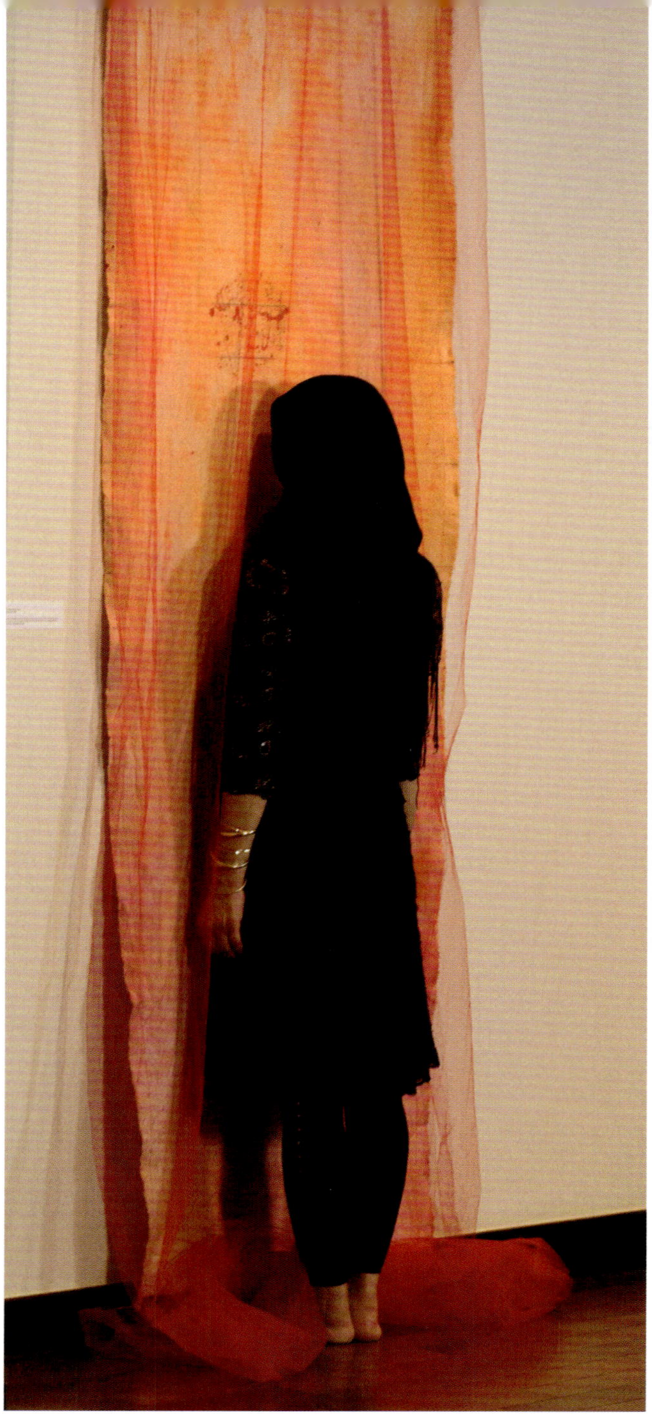

Fahimeh Vahdat, from the *Freedom* series: *Facing the Wall*, 2011. Documentation of silent performance facing censored work entitled *A Prison Called Iran*, 2011. Variable dimensions. Photo: Scott Gara.

personal situation in which she found herself was made more complex by her membership of the Baha'i faith, adherents of which are persecuted in her native Iran and little understood elsewhere. This essentially peaceful and conciliatory faith has been persecuted since its beginnings in the early part of the 19th century, and successive regimes in Persia, later Iran, have treated them with extreme hostility, with many being tortured or executed, and with many forced into exile. She has written, 'I am an artist who was born in Iran and living in the west in exile for the past 30 years. Three of my relatives were executed in the early 80s for their faith as Baha'is. For the last 20 years as an artist, I have devoted my art to dealing with social injustice and human rights issues, especially women and human rights abuses in Iran.'

When asked whether she considers herself a printmaker or an artist who uses print techniques, Vahdat replied, 'I am

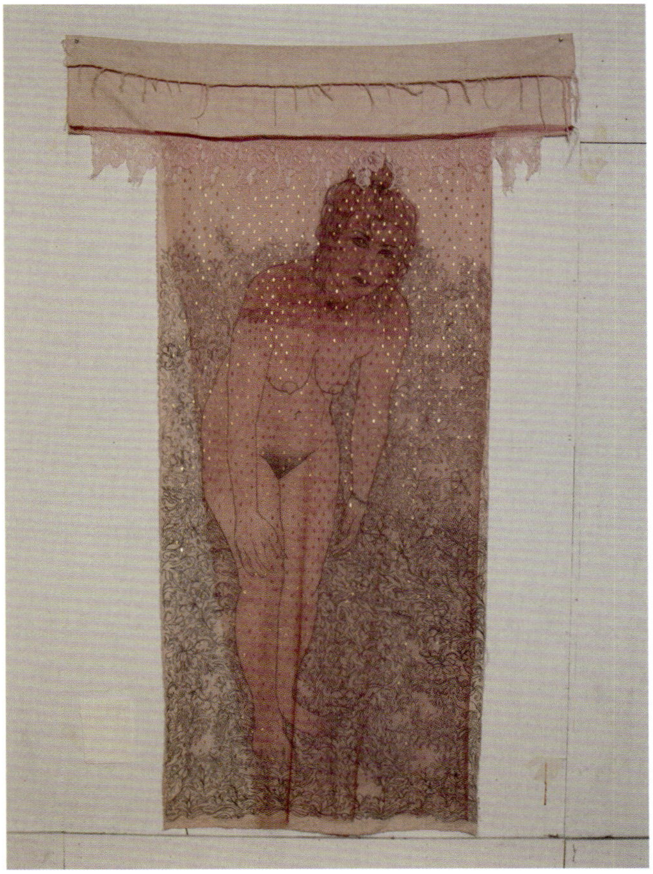

Fahimeh Vahdat, from the *Object of Violence* series: *Woman*, 2009-12. Monotype, charcoal drawing, sewing, lace and fabric on hand-dyed canvas, 350 x 142.2cm (137¾ x 56in.). Photo: Scott Gara.

a printmaker/painter by training who uses traditional and non-traditional methods of printmaking with any materials or surfaces ... A printmaker/painter's work has a very distinct artistic characteristic, and sensibilities that do not apply to a painter or sculptor who is not a printmaker. It is all about layering and scraping away the surfaces of things, adding and subtracting from those surfaces and reaching beneath them to rebuild again and again.'

In the case of much of Fahimeh Vahdat's work, this description of the essence of printmaking is particularly apt. Her work, much of which takes the form of installations in which printed elements play the primary part, seeks to illuminate the issues surrounding the oppression in her native Iran. The contrasting use of materials such as rope and stones – both used in punishment and torture – with fabrics that are more usually associated with clothing and home furnishings, makes for an additional level of comment and critique. In some of the works there are drawings of naked female bodies, often of young women, vulnerable and isolated, as if about to be subjected to the abuse and restrictions on freedom that persist in some traditional societies. A major work, shown in Milwaukee in 2004, *Sacred Crossings: A Memorial*, was based on her interpretation of the killing of 218 Baha'is in Iran following the 1979 revolution, including her great-uncle and a cousin, together with others – women and men, teachers, nurses and other workers in society – all of whom followed a peaceful faith to which the regime was violently opposed. This work, in which a series of individual panels in the form of a memorial stone showed each of the victims, incorporated her early use of digital printmaking.

In *I am Iran, I am America*, shown at the Milwaukee Art Museum in 2012, two semicircular white tables face each other with translucent curtains printed with Farsi text behind them and a low painted platform in traditional decorative form on the floor between them, bearing an image of naked feet. Quiet and dignified in its silence, this work depicts emphatically the failure of two opposing ideologies to begin to understand each other and to coexist in peace.

The artist's work has caused controversy in some of the places in which it has been exhibited: in one case four paintings were slashed by a man wielding a knife, in others there have been hostile comments relating to the artist's origins. More recently, in June 2011 in Milwaukee, Vahdat's mixed-media work *From the Freedom Series: A Prison Called Iran*, incorporating a length of fabric hung over a painted canvas bearing the outline of the figure of a naked woman holding out her hands in supplication, with flower motifs on her feet symbolising hope and freedom, became the subject of considerable criticism. The exhibition was staged in Gallerie M, an exhibition space within the Intercontinental Hotel through which the public could pass. The organisers deemed the work 'inappropriate' for its location, and asked for it to be shortened to exclude most of the figure. Believing this to be a form of censorship of a work which itself represented the fate of women imprisoned in Iran for their beliefs, Vahdat staged a performance at the opening in which she took the work down, rehung it facing the wall, and then stood silently immediately in front of the work, veiled in black. Of this she wrote, 'Censorship takes place in all levels of society, but not mostly by the public. Rather, censorship takes place by those who make decisions about what kind of art should be seen or not. I believe the public should not be deprived of the opportunity to have exchange of ideas over issues that are current and urgent, and to see works of art that can open the dialogue and lead to new awareness.' Uncomfortable truths are often found close to home.

PARASTOU FOROUHAR

ARTISTS have for many years chosen to move from one country to another to seek further inspiration and to develop their work, and the migrations of printmakers during the past three decades have led to a strengthening of the international printmaking community. But it is an entirely different matter for an artist to be forced into choosing exile because of intolerable social and political conditions in their homeland. Parastou Forouhar was born in Tehran and graduated from the University of Tehran in 1990. The Iranian Revolution of 1979 that overthrew the failing regime of the Shah established a theocracy under which there was a brutal suppression of dissent and the imposition of strict Islamic codes of social behaviour. During her youth and her time at university, Forouhar experienced for herself the widespread private and public terror, and the restrictions on the freedom of behaviour and thought imposed by the regime that had become commonplace in her homeland. In 1991 she moved to Germany, where she has lived ever since, and studied for her MA at the College of Art and Design (Hochschule für Gestaltung) in Offenbach, graduating in 1994. As a young Iranian woman living in Germany, she was able to compare her own experience of living in a country in which human rights and natural justice were denied with accounts of the horrors perpetrated by the Nazis and her own observations of their consequences. Her parents, Dariush and Parvaneh Forouhar, were well-known activists and intellectuals engaged in the struggle to maintain the separation of state and religion; in 1998 they were murdered in their home by secret agents of the regime. This traumatic event hardened her resolve to become politically active and to make art that is directly concerned with human rights and open justice.

Forouhar writes of her work: 'Printing is often an unavoidable part of my artistic practice. A lot of my work is digital and only by printing them do they materialise. The search for the appropriate printing technique and paper is this part of my work.' Her work takes the form of sculpture, installation and printmaking, often exhibited in combination. The themes that she follows are clearly defined and the nature of her imagery is closely allied to the formalism of Islamic art, with its strong emphasis on calligraphy and abstract patterns. However, while the Islamic roots are apparent, there are other aspects of her art that link it to Western traditions, including an emphasis on the repetition of clearly defined forms and the use of flat areas of colour as found in Pop Art. In addition there are connections with the optical pattern-making of artists such as M.C. Escher, and the formalism of Oriental art. The resulting work, however, is idiosyncratic and establishes an approach that is entirely the artist's own, resulting in works that reveal the political commitment slowly at first and then with emphatic impact.

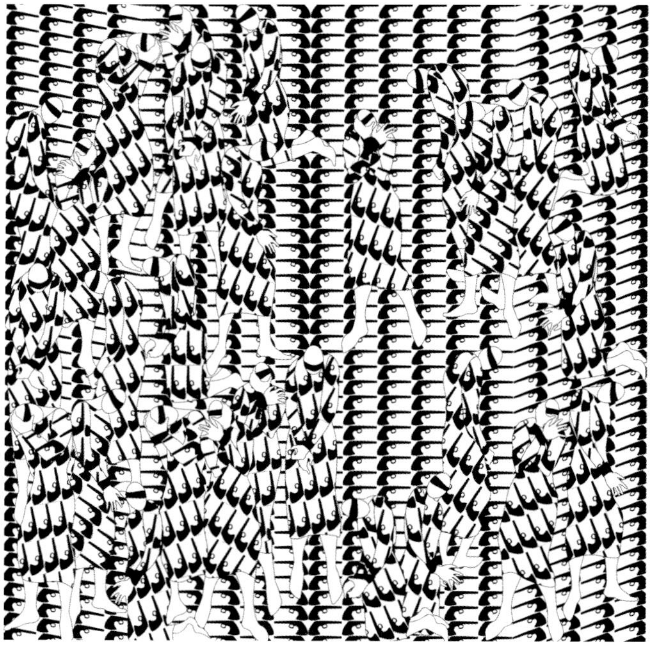

Parastou Forouhar, *Black is My Name/White is My Name II*, 2010. Digital print, 100 x 100cm (39¼ x 39¼in.).

Under the generic heading, 'digital drawings', Forouhar has embarked on several series of works grouped around broad themes. In *The Colour of my Name* series, dating from 2008 onwards, she takes a single element – an eye, a stylised representation of male genitals, a revolver, a dagger – and then repeats the element across the whole work, creating a regular background against which figures can be discerned, their heads bowed, or their hands tied, or crouching in positions of punishment or torture. To begin with, the eye does not fully resolve the figures against the background: confusion arises from the controlled use of the figure/ground illusion, from

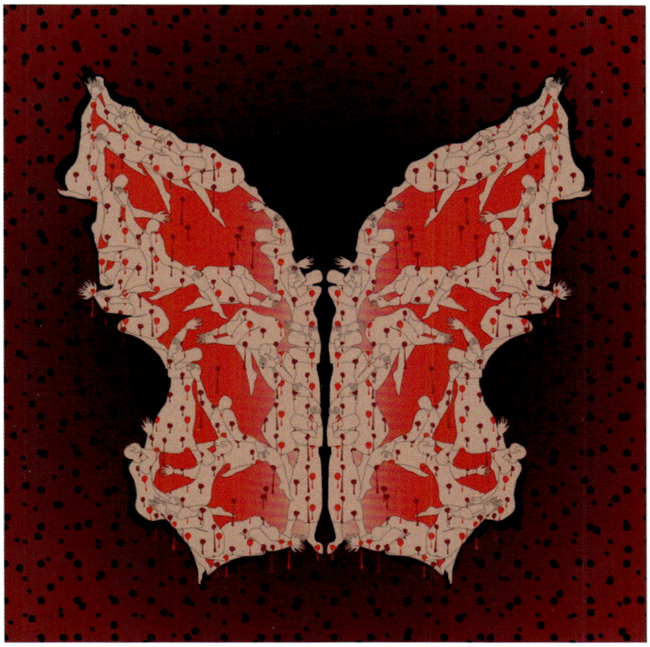

Parastou Forouhar, *Ashura* (from the *Papillon* series), 2012. Digital print, 100 x 100cm (39¼ x 39¼in.).

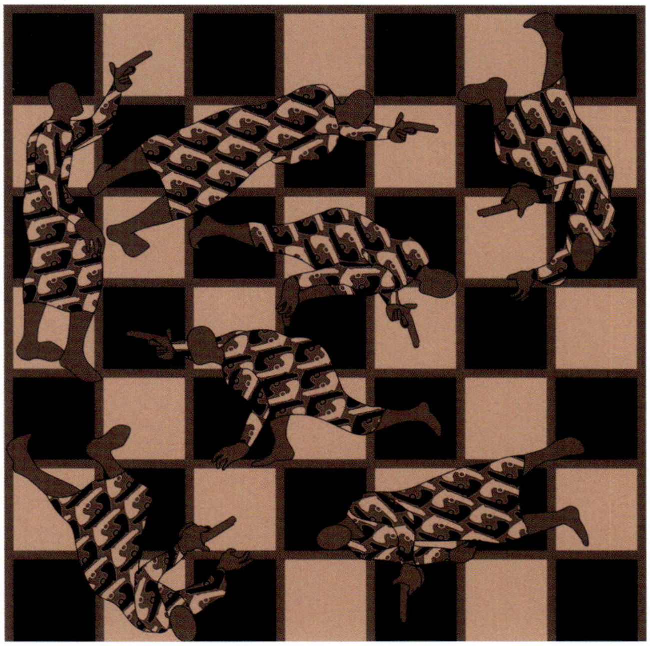

Parastou Forouhar, *Board Games 3*, 2010. Digital print, 100 x 100cm (39¼ x 39¼in.).

which eventually the figures emerge, one by one, in a manner that is unsettling and clinical. *Black is my Name, White is my Name – Revolvers* is from this ongoing series of works. The *Papillon* series, from 2010 onwards, operates in a similar way, except that in this series the figures shown in postures of anguish or despair, or with superimposed targets, or behind bars, are repeated, used as drawing elements to create the outline of a butterfly, each symmetrical half arranged with its opposite in a mirrored pair. The figures are featureless, each image set against a simple background colour, each butterfly form stilled, as if pinned down in a collector's display.

Within the broader group of the series *He Kills Me, He Kills Me Not* is the *Board Games* series, also from 2010 onwards, which takes the approach further, setting figures clad in robes on which the pattern of the chosen element – knuckledusters, revolvers, grenades, knives – is repeated in two or three colours to create something akin to camouflage fabric, with the figures in aggressive postures against the background of a stylised chessboard. The implication is clear: games of war and domination, played out literally as if a grim board game, in which the losers are the suffering population and the victors the forces of the regime.

In a video interview made at the time of her solo exhibition at the Leighton House Museum in London in 2010, Parastou Forouhar spoke about her work and its genesis and nature. She told of how, following the murder of her parents, she made journeys back to Iran in a fruitless attempt to persuade the judicial system to investigate who the killers were and to bring them to justice, and of how the failure of those attempts led to her taking her work in an increasingly political direction. In speaking of her digital drawings and the construction of patterns within them, she referred to her liking for empty spaces within a work, and of how she attempts to create works that have at the same time both beauty and horror, where the feeling behind her ideas leads her to the construction of the patterns. The work of this artist is undeniably beautiful, but at the same time emits a silent scream of pain.

YASHAR SAMIMI MOFAKHAM & TARLAN RAFIEE

AS YOUNG ARTISTS living and working in Tehran, Yashar Samimi Mofakham and Tarlan Rafiee belong to an elite and intellectual group in Iranian society, not because of any conscious or elitist decision on their part but because of the manner in which the regime either ignores the work of contemporary artists or pushes it to the margins. Considering that Iran has a very long and sophisticated cultural tradition that reaches back to the period of Xerxes, king of the Persian Empire in the 5th century BCE, and beyond, its current isolation can been seen as a retrograde development. However, unless there is a radical change in the nature of the ruling regime, it seems unlikely that there will be any major shift, whereby the arts become more widely shared and appreciated. Artists of Mofakham and Rafiee's generation who have chosen to remain in Iran rather than seeking, or being forced into, exile understand the limits within which they must make and show their work. Despite all the problems that those in more liberal and open countries might find hard to comprehend, the contemporary visual arts do survive and grow, and international contacts are established.

For example, in 2012 these artists worked closely with the London Print Studio in hosting the exhibition London Calling: Tehran in the 7Samar Gallery in Tehran. This exhibition, being the first part of what will be an exchange of exhibitions, was curated by John Phillips of LPS and Liz Sullivan, and showed a selection of mostly digital works and drawings by artists living and working in London, who produced pieces representing the social, political and dominant cultural aspects of this capital city. Of this exhibition, Mofakham said (in an interview for Iranian.com), 'This exchange is a symbolic act of creating dialogue between Iranian and British artists ... a platform for continuous artistic/intellectual dialogue in the future'; and, 'We want to act independently of official decisions, and we need to keep pace with the rest of the world. However, we don't want this to be a one-sided connection – we also want them to see what is going on in Iran, and this project will help achieve this, if only just a bit.' Rafiee added, 'The best answer is to make connections against all the borders and limitations, of course. In my opinion this small scale project is a very big step for both parties in learning more about themselves. In our experience in collecting works from Tehran, we have noticed that it is not just about showing some works to the British artists and audience, but also a self-exploration to determine what we are going to present to show a real "us" – not just the beauties and what we are proud of. It's a review, and time to talk about ourselves.' The complementary exhibition, Tehran Calling: London, was shown at the London Print Studio in March 2013.

Yashar Samimi Mofakham

Yashar Samimi Mofakham was born in Tehran in 1979 and studied Fine Art at Tehran University. He teaches printmaking at a number of workshops in Tehran, has worked as stage designer for theatres and puppet theatres since 2000, and in addition has designed medals, winning the award for the Best Abstract Art Medal in the British Museum exhibition of the British Art Medal Society in 2008. He has had numerous solo exhibitions, and has participated in group shows, in Iran and internationally, with work in a number of international public and private collections. In defining his work he writes, 'I find printmaking techniques suitable for me to create and bring my ideas to paper, or canvas or other surfaces, beside other mediums for making art ... so I usually call myself a visual artist who uses printmaking techniques ... But this distinction is not important at all, the important thing is creation and making art.' His paintings, in acrylic on canvas, are essentially abstract, derived from Farsi calligraphic forms; this approach is closely in line with the strict Islamic prohibition on the depiction of living things but is also a way of honouring the long tradition and intellectual elegance of calligraphy.

Mofakham followed this theme in a series of screenprints entitled *Existence* (2008), in which he explores the importance of literature in Persian culture. The prints are based on words and phrases from poets, including Khayyam, Rumi and Hafiz, whose mystical works continue to inspire people in many countries. By repeating the words over and over,

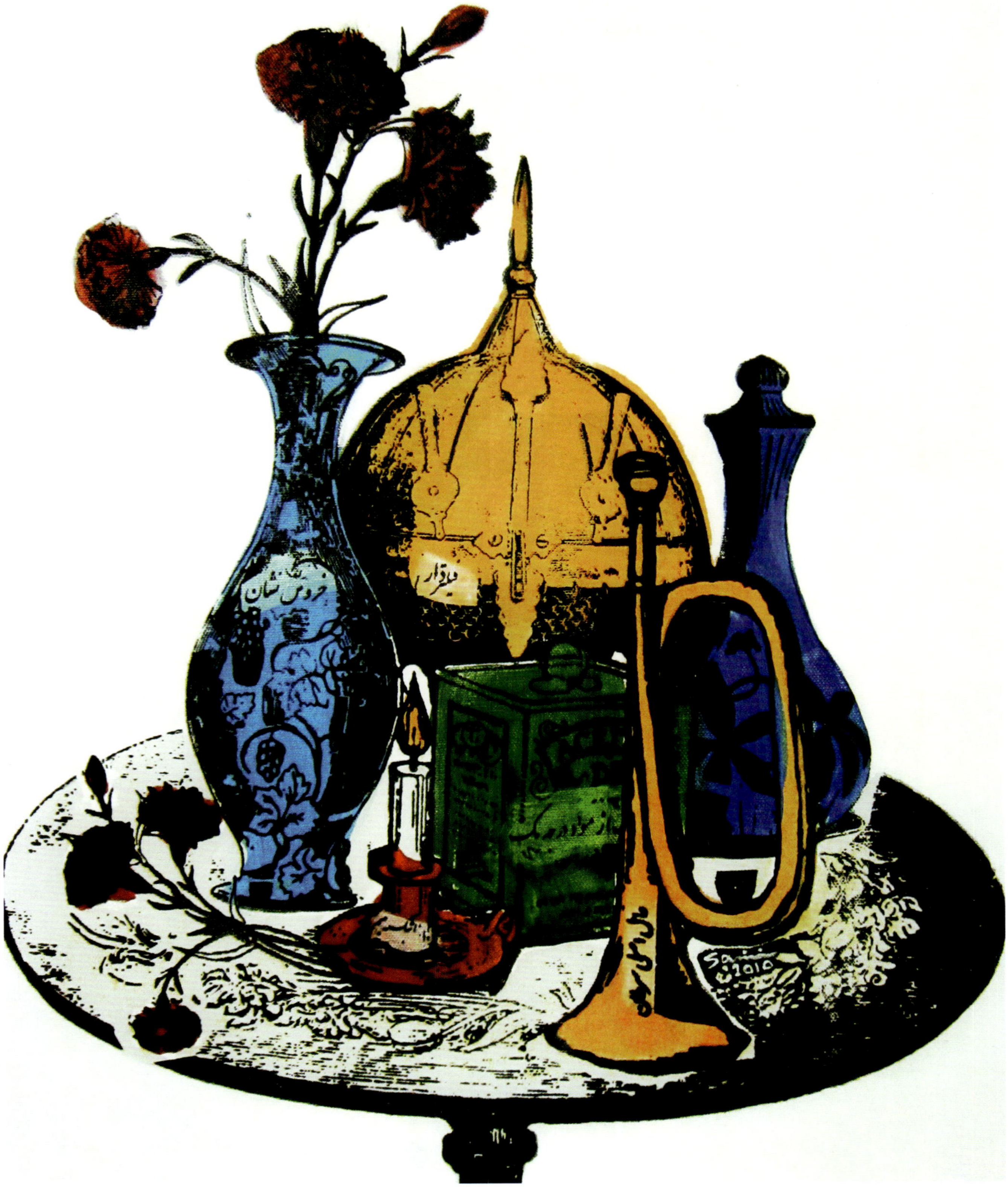

Yashar Samimi Mofakham, *Untitled* (from the *Stilled Life* series), 2011. Screenprint on canvas, 70 x 50cm (27½ x 19¾in.).

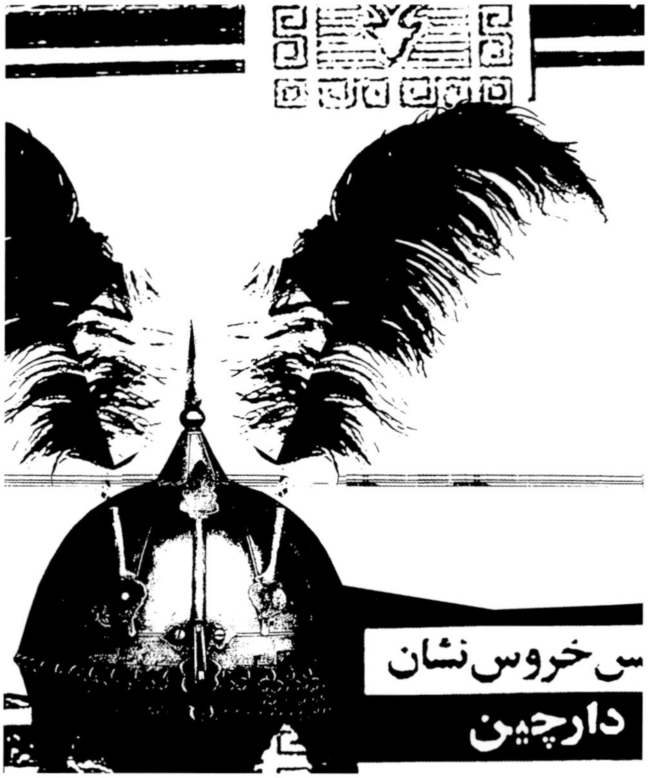

Yashar Samimi Mofakham, *Untitled* (from the *Stilled Life* series), 2011. Photo-etching, aquatint, copper etching, on Fabriano Rosaspina paper, 40 x 35cm (15¾ x 13¾in.).

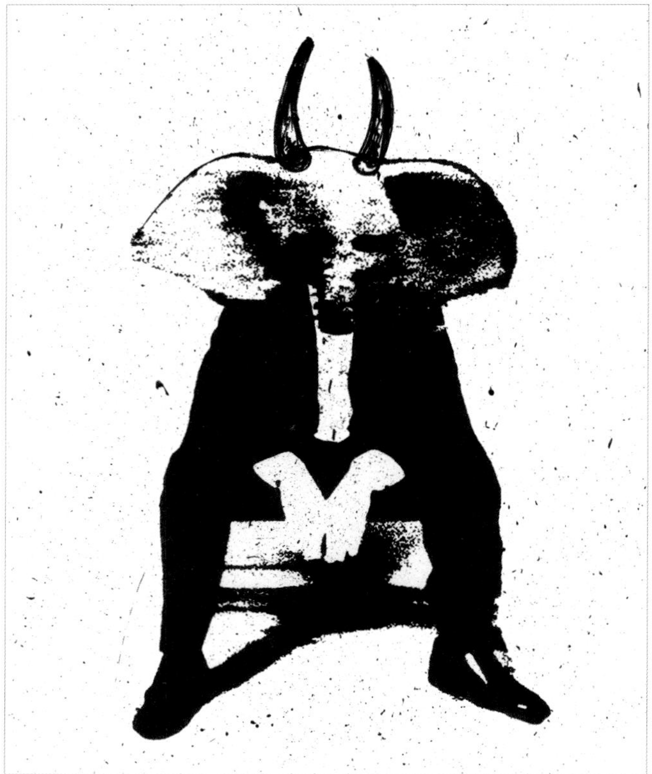

Yashar Samimi Mofakham, *Manouchehr* (from the *Manouchehr* series), 2012. Photo-etching, aquatint, drypoint on copper, on Fabriano Rosaspina paper. 40 x 30cm (15¾ x 11¾in.).

building up dense clouds of black through which parts of the words can be discerned, the artist creates images that remind viewers of the important role of literature in inspiring future generations, but also that such concentrated clouds of philosophy and religion from past traditions can prevent new thoughts from emerging in the present. After the Green Movement protests that followed the disputed 2009 elections in Iran, Mofakham made a series of works, *Paperballs*, in which he intentionally censored the past to demonstrate that the government cannot turn precious intellectual matters into rubbish by throwing them away, and reminding people that what were taken away from them were their democratic rights. The large screenprints on Plexiglas are of balls of screwed up paper on which have been written phrases from the poets, so that what were legible have become illegible symbols on a hard surface.

The theme of language, its power and its misuse, is pursued in his *Stilled Lives* series, in which familiar objects from Iranian life are shown in the style of 19th-century illustrations, subverted by the added texts. In *Untitled 5*, the helmet is named 'Cock Signed', referring to the cheapest brand of chewing gum in Iran, with the additional comment, 'Cinnamon Flavoured'. The presence of the trumpet in *Untitled 3* refers to the newspaper *Suri Israfil* (named after the angel that blows its horn on the day of judgement), which Mofakham considers the most important intellectual and democratic newspaper in Iranian history, but which has been persecuted by the regime. The text on the trumpet reads, 'the main cause of cancer', while that on the candle reads, 'Tears of the Orphan', recalling the sanctity and purity of fire in the pre-Islamic Zoroastrian beliefs. Manouchehr is a character from a much admired play, *City of Tales* by Bijan Mofid, in which people take the form of animals. An elephant, Manouchehr, comes to the city and breaks a tusk, so the other animals break off his other tusk and fix the pair to his head as horns. After doing this they are confused about the animal, and all but the Monkey (the intellectual) and the Mouse (the lover) cut up his trunk (because it is disproportionate) and share out the pieces. Thus deformed, the elephant needs a new identity and becomes Manouchehr; he has since become an icon in Iran, being a character that everybody can identify with – deformed by society, and in need of a new identity. The artist says of this work, 'This series is still in progress and continuing very slowly because I am afraid of him, and also it is a very responsible work to do, with such an important character.' In choosing the themes and motifs for his work, Mofakham selects elements that are familiar to Iranians, but reuses them in ways that subvert them and add new resonances.

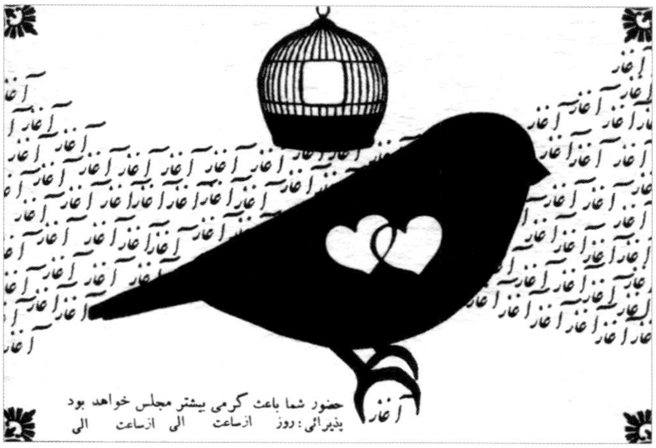

Tarlan Rafiee, *Card 8* (from the *Invitations* series), 2011. Silkscreen print 10 x 15cm (4 x 6in.).

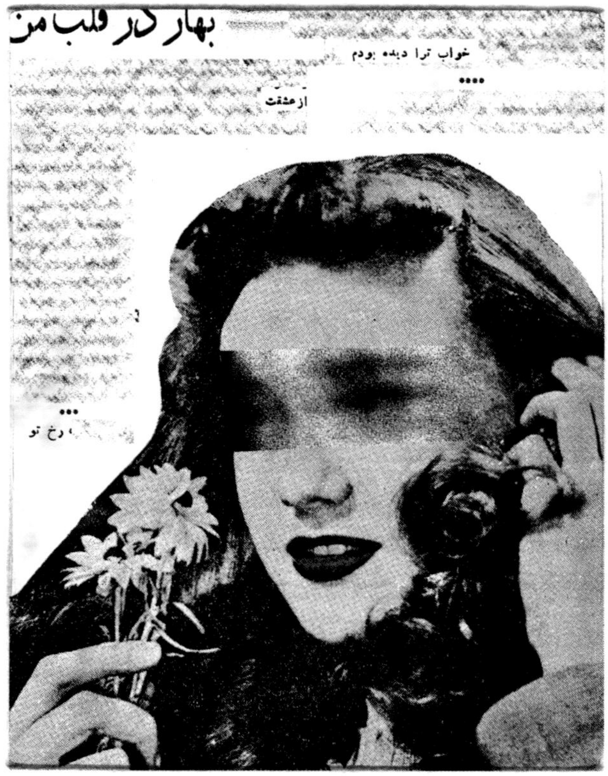

Tarlan Rafiee, *News 4* (from the *News* series), 2012. Photogravure, 30 x 25cm (11¾ x 9¾in.).

Tarlan Rafiee

Tarlan Rafiee was born in Tehran in 1980, and graduated in industrial design from the city's Azad Art University. She started printmaking in 2004 and since then has worked as a visual artist and printmaker, starting her own workshop in which she has also taught classes, just as she has at other art institutes. She writes, 'I consider myself as an artist who mostly uses printmaking techniques; it is not really an important distinction for me, but as I believe that there is a special spirit in printmaking media, I always consider mentioning my job as a visual artist/printmaker.' Her work has been shown in numerous group and solo exhibitions, both in Iran and internationally. She also works as a book illustrator, notably for *The Black Goat and the Palm Tree* by Mohammad Reza Yousefi. Her work is deceptively simple, much of it in black and white and often at small scale. Rafiee has chosen to work this way as it allows her to create series of works that appear innocuous at first sight but that, on closer consideration, carry a greater degree of contextual and conceptual power. Working as a woman artist in a society in which fundamental Islam plays a major role has the potential to create problems, and this awareness does place constraints on full expression, requiring strategies that are not necessary in more liberal, Western countries.

The Wedding Collection offers a new approach to the traditions of the wedding and the view of women in society, and of marriage as a rite of passage. Rafiee chooses to present images that are factual, rather than offering a critical view, to suggest the ways in which a marriage can take its place in memories and fantasies. The series (in two parts, photography and photogravure) presents the wedding dress, rings, shoes, some with parts of old rhymes and sayings, and some with written 'sound effects' such as the traditional cheers that greet the bride. In highlighting these traditions and symbols, the artist both respects their continuation, and perhaps also marks the beginning of their decline as even the strictest of societies undergoes change. In an innovative public art event, Rafiee presented the *Invitation Project* at the 3rd Contemporary Printmaking Exhibition in Tehran, which consisted of a large colour screenprint and a set of ten different postcard-sized screenprints produced in large numbers that visitors to the exhibition could take away as they wished. The concept was a memorial in the form of invitations to the protests of the Green Movement, the Arab Spring, the Prague Spring and other public uprisings, as well as simpler invitations to a party or a wedding. The texts are partial, stating dates or locations or, in one case, 'from 3pm to have a tear gas party', conflating private and public events. The artist notes that

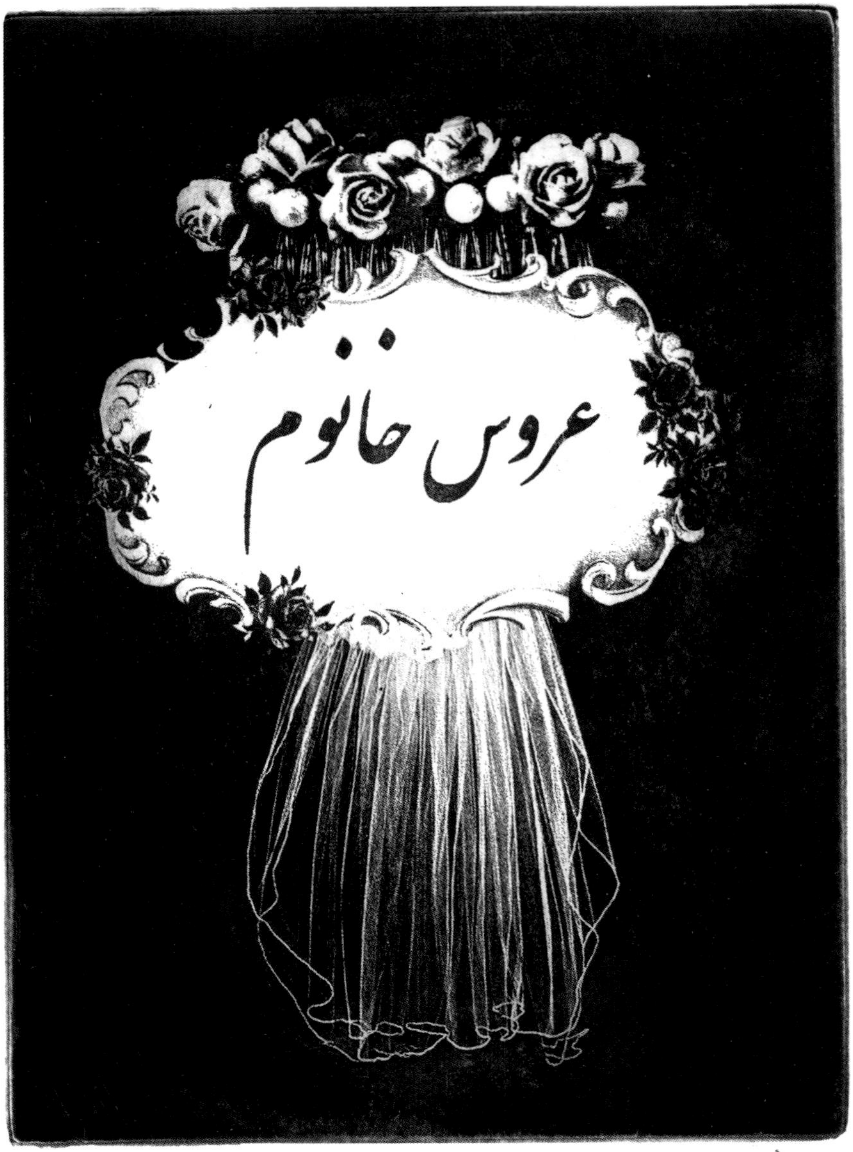

Tarlan Rafiee, *Wedding 10* (from the *Wedding* series), 2010. Photogravure, 21 x 15cm (8¼ x 6in.).

about 1000 postcards were taken during the opening day of the exhibition.

More recently, Rafiee has started work on a series entitled *News*, which is still in progress, the first part of which is *Woman, Art, Love, Beauty*. She has not specified the precise subjects of the news, but the pieces are based on newspaper layouts, with some of the texts emboldened and others blurred, depending on the emphasis she wishes to give. The series will gradually accumulate to present a puzzling overall image of the ways in which newspapers convey stories and images of society to their readers. While far from being stated, there are implications of selective reporting, at best, and state control, at worst; but neither is comfortable, and the prints will raise questions about the nature of the news media rather than offering answers. In a recent (late 2012) series, *Treasures*, of digital prints with gold leaf, mounted on red and in gilded wood frames, the artist presents a view of puberty and its implications. Each print shows part of the torso of a white female shop-display figure, with pubis or breast discretely covered by a coloured and gilded section from a traditional textile. In a note referring to the precious nature of the onset of maturity, the artist comments that, 'Due to the evolution of society, these (traditional) meanings are changing so fast, now puberty and sex mean something different, especially in younger generations.' The approaches taken by this artist in making art are subtle, but powerful – determination enclosed in a soft glove, steering a careful course between honesty and taboo.

IRAQ

NEDIM KUFI

IRAQ is a country that has suffered war and unrest for much of the past forty years, leading many artists and intellectuals to seek exile elsewhere in the world. While this is entirely understandable it is also regrettable, though it does not mean that the long threads of Iraqi art history have been broken, simply that they have spread more widely in the world. Iraq is the site of the ancient Mesopotamian civilisation, reaching back millennia and forming one of the cradles of world culture. The role of artists from that part of the world – in music, literature, poetry and architecture as well as in painting and sculpture – has long been respected, not only in Iraq but in many other countries. Being an artist in exile does add layers of complexity to the work they are doing, and the feelings of deracination become part of that work; it is more a matter of continuation than disruption. But, while it is to be hoped that as the political and security situation in Iraq improves, artists at present in exile may wish to return, sadly this is not likely to happen in the near future.

BORN IN Baghdad in 1962 where he graduated in printmaking, Nedim Kufi has lived and worked in the Netherlands, where he studied graphic and multimedia design for more than two decades, and has exhibited his work in many countries since 2003, receiving a number of awards. These are the bald facts, but as with all experiences of exile they conceal a great deal more. Kufi is, in one sense, an unusual artist in that he expresses himself with equal facility not only through visual objects, but also through words, sometimes in the forms of stories from his childhood. With both mediums he is striving through his art to come to terms with memories of his life in Iraq, and at the same time to rationalise his life in the Netherlands. The two countries have widely contrasting climates – the wide cool skies of Northern Europe are very different from the hot desert skies of his homeland – and equally different cultures and histories. The adaptation to one will inevitably lead to a deep nostalgia for the other. Iraq, in common with other Islamic cultures, has a long tradition of

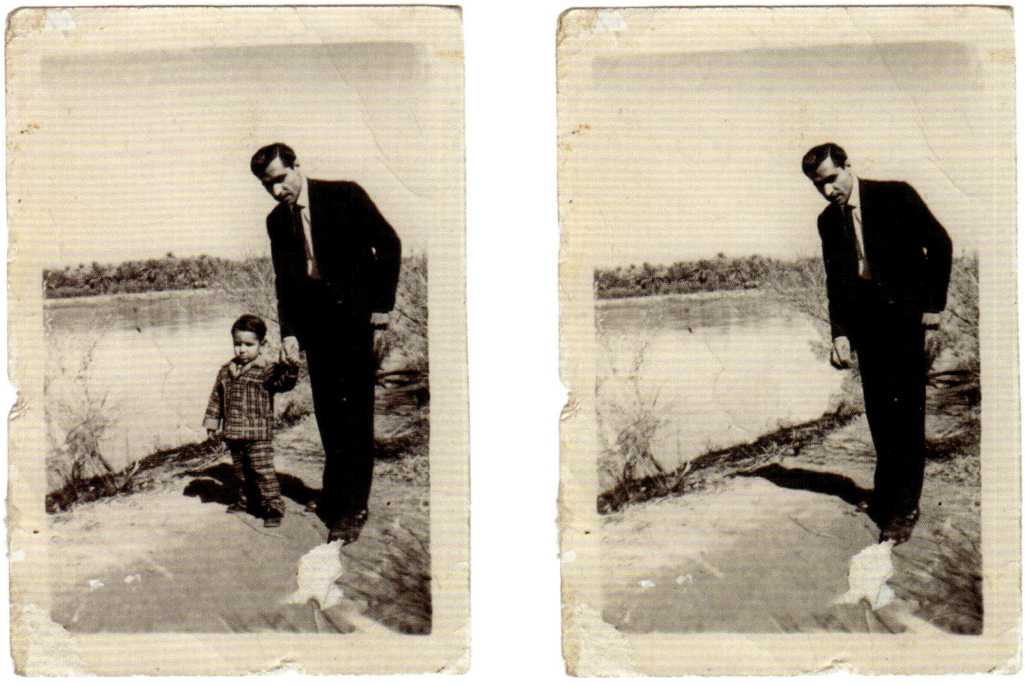

Nedim Kufi, *Absence (Diptych)*, 2011. Digital print on canvas, 150 x 110cm (59 x 43¼in.) (each part).

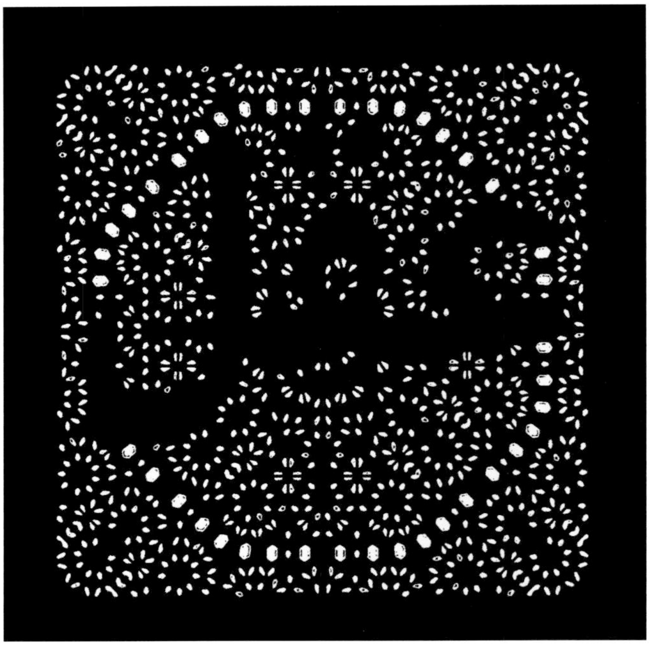

Nedim Kufi, *Aqil*, 2011. Silkscreen on canvas, 180 x 180cm (70¾ x 70¾in.).

poetry in which the observational powers of the writer are threaded through with mystical insights that infuse simple words with added depths. When written in Arabic calligraphy the words do not simply stand for objects, ideas, emotions and so on, but are expressed through the forms of the individual characters, which in themselves are works of art. It is as if, in addition to understanding the meanings of the words of a poem in English, the reader sought to appreciate the fluency of line and the white spaces between individual printed letters. This perhaps offers a clue to the work of Kufi for those viewers educated in the Western tradition.

In *An 'attar' from Baghdad* (2005), Kufi writes, 'I have not yet been back to Baghdad. I know that everything there has changed, including my old postal address, but my dark restless shadow still roams the streets to this day. My continuing relationship with Baghdad, "the city of war and peace", closely resembles my quarrel and suffering with her'; and also, 'My vision developed in Baghdad's earthen culture: it was surprised, it struggled, feared, was refreshed, loved and hated, left and returned, rebelled at the end and went into exile.'

An 'attar' is a vendor of herbs, spices and perfumes, those valuable essences that enrich the senses of sight, taste and smell: for Kufi the comparison with his work as an artist is apt, in that he too blends the different elements of images and memories, seeking the balance that will convey his intentions clearly and without compromise. It is significant that, when creating his paintings, he chooses not to use brushes, preferring to use his hands and fingertips, or his feet, sticks and brooms, and to incorporate twigs, seeds, leaves, mud and henna with pigments. His installations, likewise, are made from a variety of materials, including pierced canvases hung away from walls, with the solidity and permanence of the canvas creating shifting, ephemeral constellations of coloured light. His work has been described as 'enigmatic' and it is certainly open to poetic interpretations, but at its core is a strong sense of identification with the past, respect for the present, and hope for the future.

Nedim Kufi's prints are generally at a large scale, which takes them beyond the conventional concept of a print as being a work to be framed for display in a home or office, and into the realm of works for galleries or museums. *Aqil* ('Mind') is in silkscreen on canvas, one of a series called *Haqq* (meaning 'Truth' in Arabic and also, in the Islamic context, 'Right' and 'Reality') that show a single word in Arabic within a formal pattern, of white against a black background, recalling the pierced screens and mosaics of Islamic architecture; the calligraphy of the word remains in darkness until illuminated by the myriad points of light around it.

Arab Mirror is a tantalising image of blurred shadows of leaves on a wall, as if seen from a passing car. The original image was a photograph taken by Kufi on a visit to Kuwait, and the text is from the inscription in Arabic on the rearview mirror of a Japanese car that translates, roughly, as, 'Measurements and the dimensions of the image appearing in the mirror are not real'. The print is a metaphor for the way in which reality is presented to society. *Absence 11* is one of a series of paired digital prints based on photographs from Kufi's childhood, many taken by his father (shown in this image), the first of the

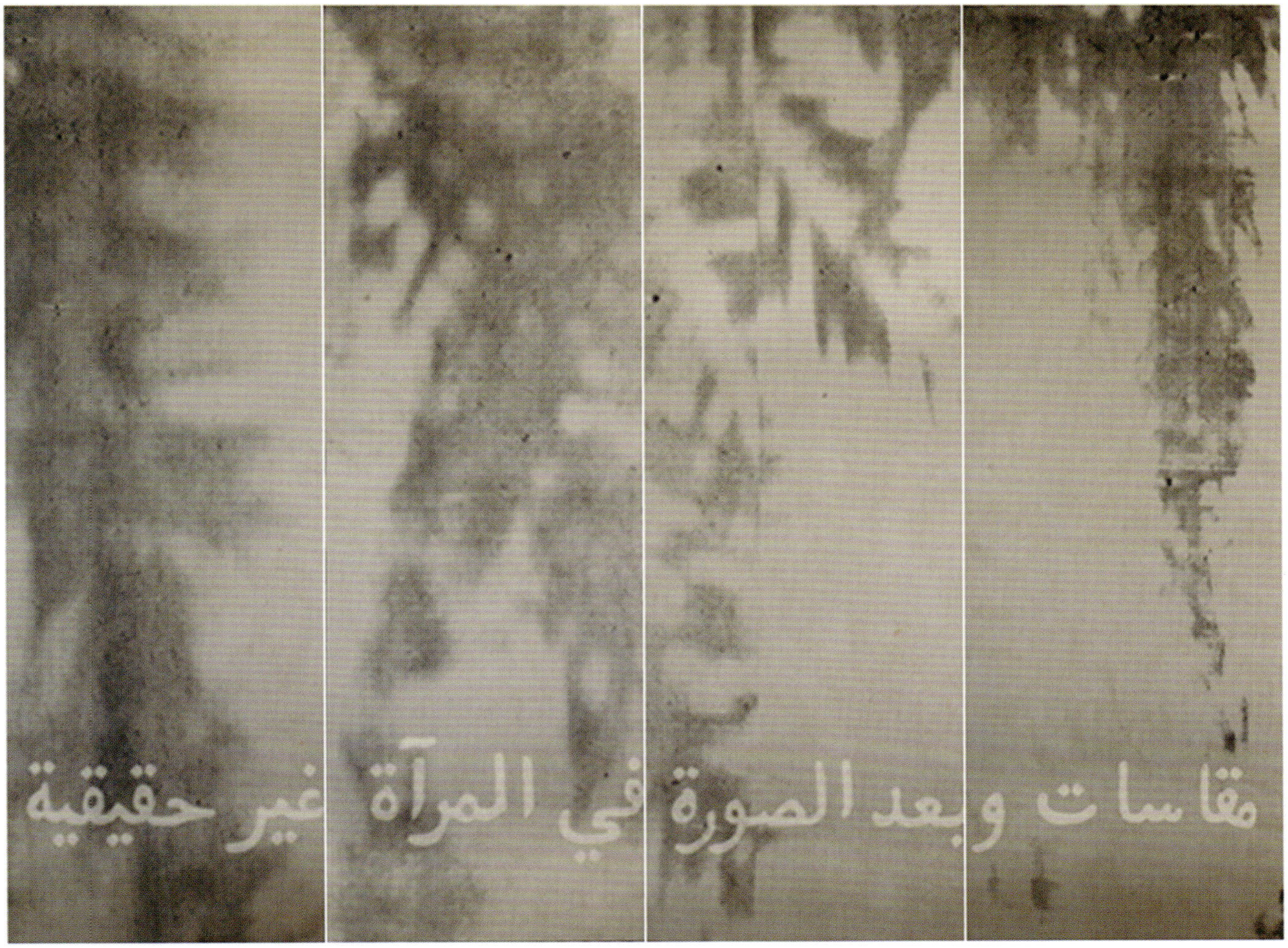

pair being as taken, the second with the figure of Kufi edited out using Photoshop. In this series the artist is addressing his feelings of being away from his homeland by erasing himself symbolically from the evidence of his childhood as shown in photographs taken, mostly by his father (shown in this image) in the 1960s. For Kufi the photographs also bring back the smells and sounds of that time, but for the viewer there is only the echo of an elegiac silence.

Nedim Kufi, *Arab Mirror*, 2011. Silkscreen on canvas, 180 x 280cm (70¾ x 110in.).

TALAL REFIT

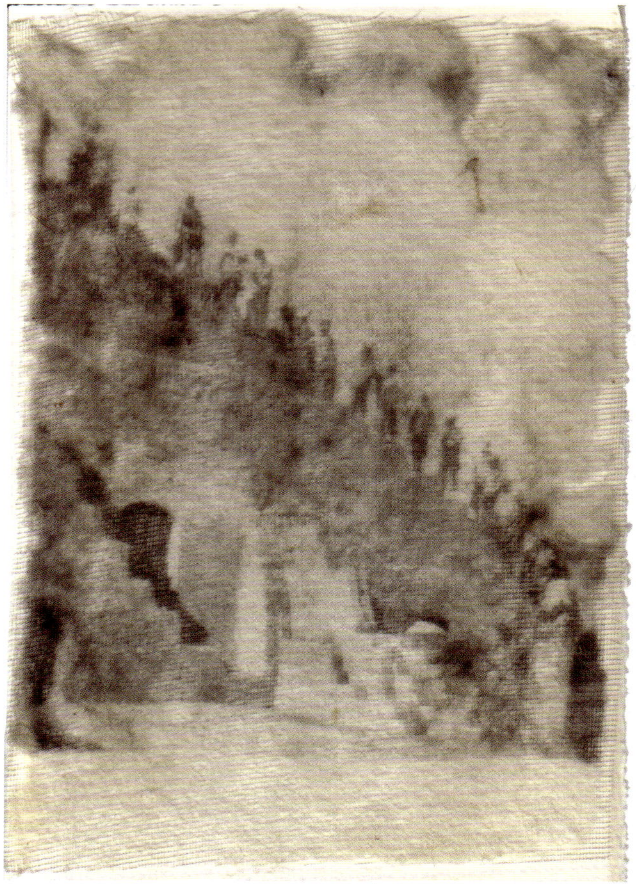

Talal Refit, *Zigurat*, 2005. Woolprint, 30 x 21cm (11¾ x 8¼in.).

TALAL REFIT was born in 1957 in Kirkuk, a major city in Northern Iraq, 236 km (147 miles) north of Baghdad. It is built on the site of the Ancient Assyrian capital Arrapha, which rose to prominence in the 10th/11th centuries BCE and is the site of a citadel built on an artificial mound in the reign of King Ashurnasirpal II between 884 and 858 BCE. Its strategic position has given the city an important role for centuries (especially since the discovery of the biggest oil field in Iraq in the early 20th century), and it is home to a mixture of Iraqi, Kurdish and Turkmen peoples. The region remains unstable following the invasion of Iraq in 2003 and its aftermath, with multiple bomb attacks in September 2012. Refit left Iraq to study in Turkey, graduating in architecture from the Middle East Technical University in Ankara, where he lived and worked as an architect and urban planner until 1985, before settling in Germany, where he now lives and teaches painting and printmaking. He describes himself as, 'A painter and passionate printmaker', but his personal work also encompasses drawing, video and sculpture; his work has been shown in many international exhibitions.

With the background of his art education and experience, Refit approaches his work with a specific aim, which is the new challenge offered by computers, and in particular the possibilities of interactivity that come from a thorough understanding of the writing of computer code. He admits that the main problem for many artists comes through lack of knowledge of mathematics, but that with perseverance this can be overcome to the point that works can be created in which the spectator becomes the third intimate participant (following the artist and the computer) in the art experience. Some of the results of his ten-year exploration of what was for him a new direction can be found in his short movies. The measure of interactivity is limited in this early work to moving the cursor of the computer across various parts of the image on the screen.

In the first of these, *Babel*, a scrolling text reads, '... I remember my Grandma: early in the morning whispering to a running tap, she believed that bad dreams ought to be told to streaming water, and that all bad influences will flow away ...', beneath a sepia image of a rural landscape containing palm trees and an Assyrian lion statue: the image is divided into thin vertical slices and moving the cursor to right or left causes the panning of the camera to change speed and direction. This image can never quite be held still, only delayed. Meanwhile the scrolling text continually repeats. The mismatch, between the clarity and insistence of the text and the indeterminacy of what appears as a memory captured in a fading photograph, is an encapsulation of the nature of memory. Others in the *Movie* series include the effect of the movement of the cursor creating a bubble across an image, or causing one drawing in sand to crossfade into another. A more recent 3.25 minute animation project from 2005, *Epilog*, is created from pencil drawings. Refit writes that he originally intended to record his memories of his homeland as single drawings but that these memories also included gestures and events in motion, resulting in the first episode of the animation, which took six months of work and was shown with success at exhibitions in Berlin and Barcelona.

Another project that absorbed Refit's attention from 1995 to 2005 was a print project, *Pixel Absorber*, based on his wish to express the feelings of a visually aware person living with electronic screens in which everything is becoming increasingly virtual, emphasising the longing to touch real things. In a series of experimental prints, firstly using a

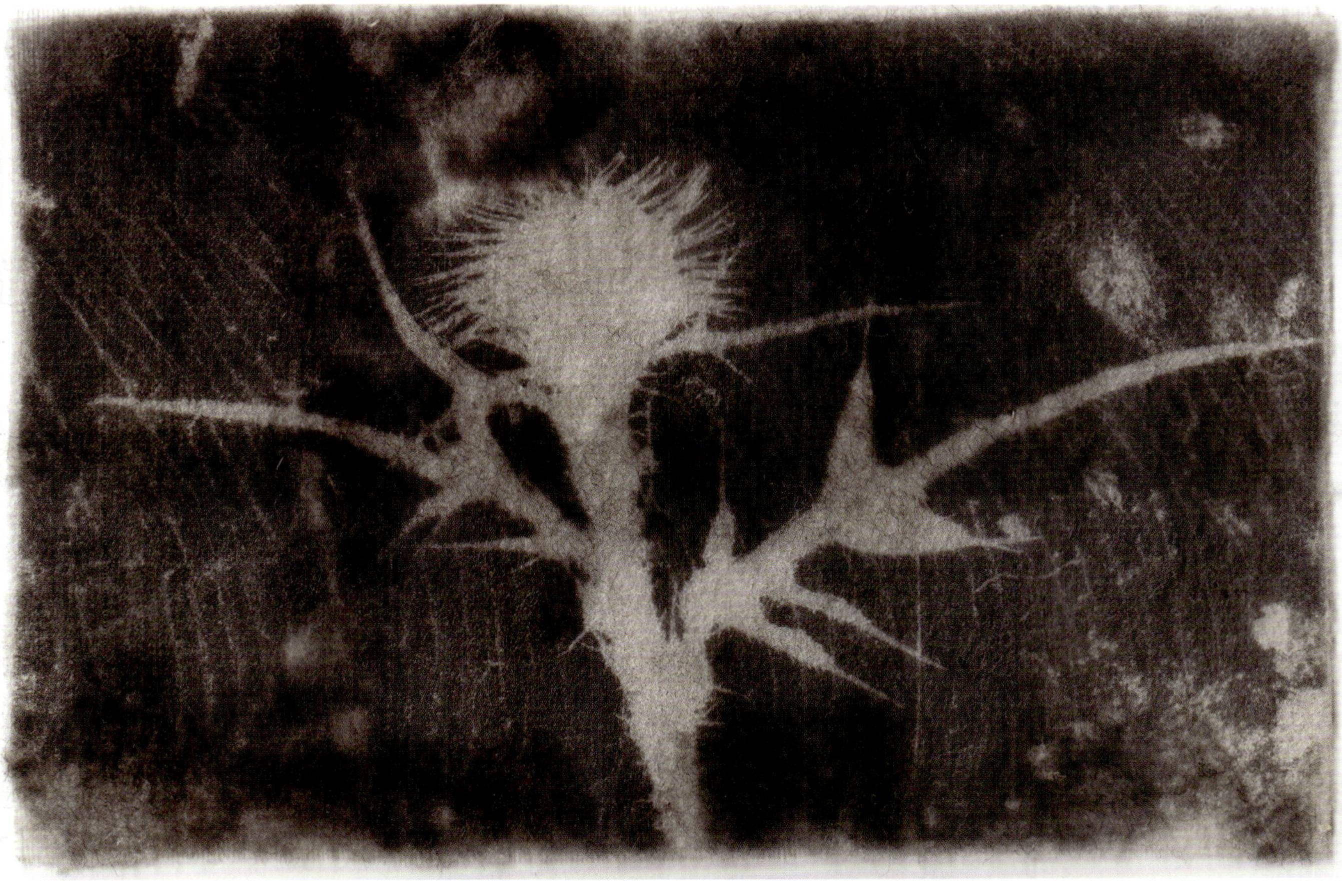

Talal Refit, *Thistle*, 2004. Woolprint, 21 x 30cm (8¼ x 11¾in.).

simple home inkjet printer and later a large-format printer, he explored the ways in which a computer-based image could be transferred onto pieces of open-weave woollen fabric that he had prepared, so that the virtual pixels on the screen could be converted into pixel-sized real drops of ink floating on the threads within the open mesh of the fabric. The three featured images of Refit's work, *Zegurat*, *Thistle* and *Time*, are from this series. They are taken from photographic images that would in conventional printing methods be rendered as prints with a higher degree of sharpness. By discarding glossy paper, the normal substrate for prints, and substituting a soft fabric, the images are rendered in a much less obvious, much more mysterious form. The figures on the ziggurat become blurry outlines and the sense of depth is subverted into an indeterminate pattern of tones; the outline of the thistle is changed into something more like a photogram printed on a soft surface and the nature of the very familiar prickly plant is changed; while the image of the clock mechanism becomes a soft machine incapable of functioning as a device for indicating the time. All these images, like the others in the series, are open to a range of interpretations pointing to memory, the passage of chronological time and the uncertainty of the period in which we live.

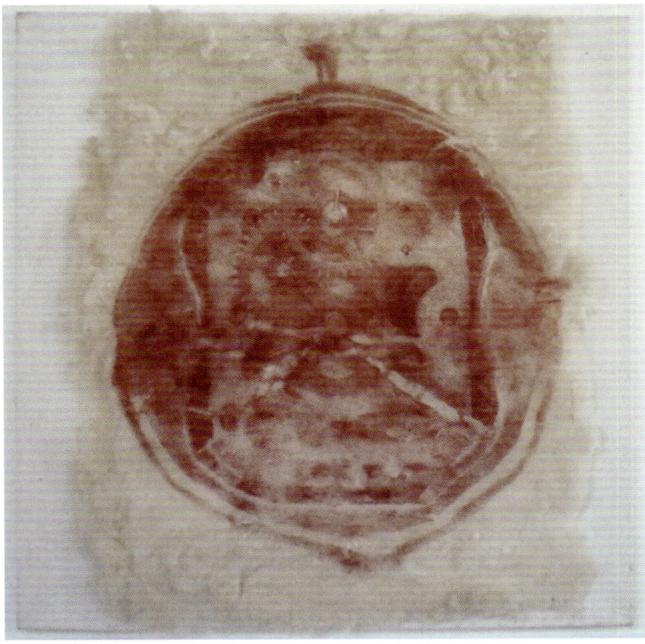

Talal Refit, *Time*, 2004. Woolprint, 80 x 80 cm (31½ x 31½in.).

THE UNITED ARAB EMIRATES

THE UNITED ARAB EMIRATES is a young country, founded in 1971 as a federation of seven absolute monarchies occupying a crescent of land along 650 km (403 miles) of the southern coast of the Persian Gulf. Dubai and Abu Dhabi airports have become major international business and tourist airline hubs. With a thriving economy based largely on oil, the Emirate states are considered by some to be relatively progressive and diverse multicultural societies which, in addition to having major urban development and infrastructure programmes, are establishing museums and galleries of international standard and repute. The annual Art Dubai fair is becoming one of the major events in the international arts calendar, while Abu Dhabi, the largest of the Emirates, is developing a major culture district on Saadiyat Island. When completed it will include a National Museum, the Guggenheim Abu Dhabi, the Louvre Abu Dhabi, a maritime museum and a performing arts centre, all designed by celebrated international architects, together with the Biennale Park with its sixteen pavilions.

Admirable though these initiatives are, there have been criticisms to the effect that wealth alone does not build an instant culture, even if it can buy works of art and install them in prestigious buildings. The UAE, however, has a large expatriate population whose expectations have to be considered, and while artists from beyond the Middle East may seem at times to be given priority in these ventures, the work produced by artists from the immediate region is gaining in respect and popularity. Moreover, it is to be hoped that a broadening of education and a wide dissemination of information about the achievements of these artists will in time be effective in encouraging progress in this direction. Zayed University, bearing the name of the founder of the nation, Sheikh Zayed bin Sultan Al Nahyan, is based in Abu Dhabi, its stated vision to become the leading university in the region. The university offers a very wide range of undergraduate and graduate degree programmes, including art and design, multimedia design, and museum studies.

Karen Oremuš, Chair of the College of the Arts and Creative Enterprises at the university, and her colleague Janet Bellotto noted in their paper, 'The Nomadic Resolution: Multiple Making in the United Arab Emirates', at the IMPACT Conference in Melbourne in 2011, that, 'In the last decade, artists based in the UAE have been successful in creating cross-cultural intersections and counterpoints through various projects including the printed multiple. The notion of the printed multiple in printmaking and photography has facilitated the wide exposure of the works of indigenous UAE artists to the international art community. Participation at prestigious events such as the Venice Biennale is a particularly notable example of this.

'The printed form, through multiple identities and manifestations, has provided an instantaneous venue to narrate histories, investigate cultural identity, and to further develop artistic practices and conversations in the UAE. Photography, primarily in digital form is one of the most commonly explored mediums with emerging artists in the UAE due to its availability/feasibility and its potential for dissemination. It is not only explored in print but also electronically through mobile cameras, social networking and other online facilities. Printmaking, which embodies a rich relationship between photography, drawing and mechanical image making, also has a strong presence due to its synchronism with storytelling and history of exchange, a traditional element that continues within Emirati culture.'

These well-informed observations give a sense of optimism that rapid progress is likely, and that the position of the visual arts within the wider culture of the UAE is likely to become more prominent in the future. The work of two young artists who graduated from the department of art and design at Zayed University, both of whom have already shown their work nationally and internationally, illustrates the progress that has been made and the potential for its future development.

MAITHA DEMITHAN

MAITHA DEMITHAN, born in the UAE in 1989, has developed an unusual method of recording digital images, which complements her work in painting, drawing and with more conventional methods of photography. Her technique, which she calls 'scanography', involves the use of an A4 flatbed scanner as the recording device through which she registers multiple images of her subjects, before compositing them using her computer and printing them out as very large-scale archival digital prints. She will make in excess of one hundred scans for each print before editing them down to around fifty for processing via software to the final high-resolution image. Some of the scans are made with the subject lying on the scanner on the floor, while others are made by holding the scanner against successive parts of the standing subject. Demithan states that, 'My scanography, like all art, reflects the ideologies of my own culture – the Emirati culture – including the exploration of women's roles, the rituals performed and the dress worn'; and also, 'Some art is seen to be a public event, a thought to stir social conscience. My art seeks to invite people into the private space of a ritual, a very real yet surreal theatrical experience.' She is inspired by the manner in which photography can suspend time, and also culture, thoughts and feelings, so that something from the past can be brought into the present, capturing both life and death. Among her influences are Frida Kahlo, Lucien Freud and Paula Rego and, particularly, the photographs of Julia Margaret Cameron.

To the Moon (2009) depicts the artist's niece and nephew, eyes closed as if dreaming and floating against the darkness of space. The niece has a cut-out silver figure in her outstretched hand, emphasising both the transitory nature of childhood and the importance of dreaming the future, as well as the crucial value of family ties in traditional society. This is taken further in *Ajyal* (2012), in which a young man in white holds a hooded falcon on his wrist and a young bird in his other hand, which in turn is being guided by the hand of an older man – perhaps his father. Quietly reflective, this image refers not only to the sport of falconry but also to the way that it provides an antidote to modern life and celebrates the heritage of the Emirati people.

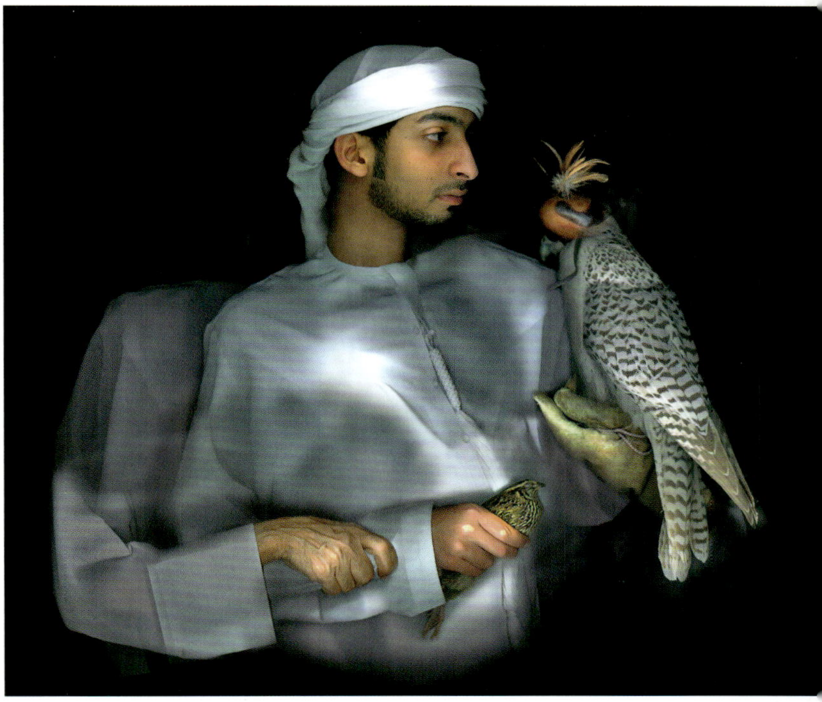

Maitha Demithan, *Ajyal*, 2012. Scanography, 142 x 170cm (56 x 67in.).

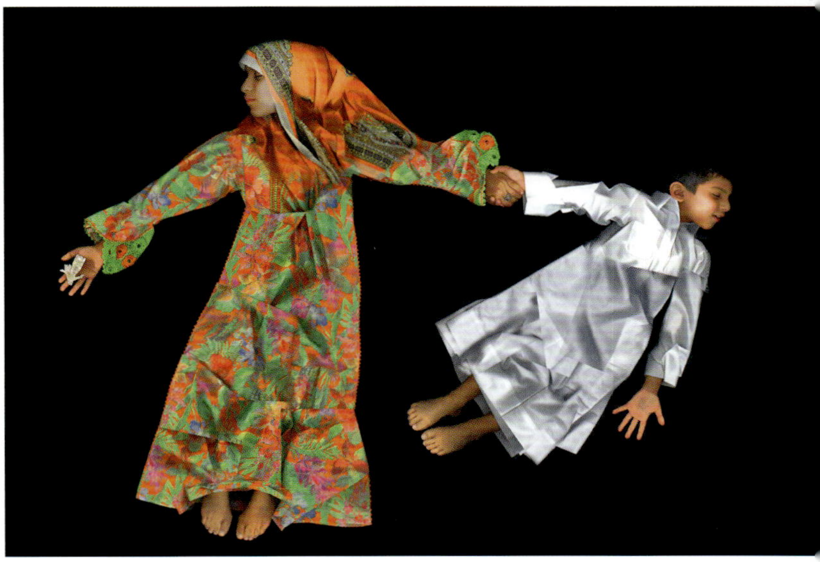

Maitha Demithan, *To the Moon*, 2012. Scanography, 122 x 180cm (48 x 70¾in.).

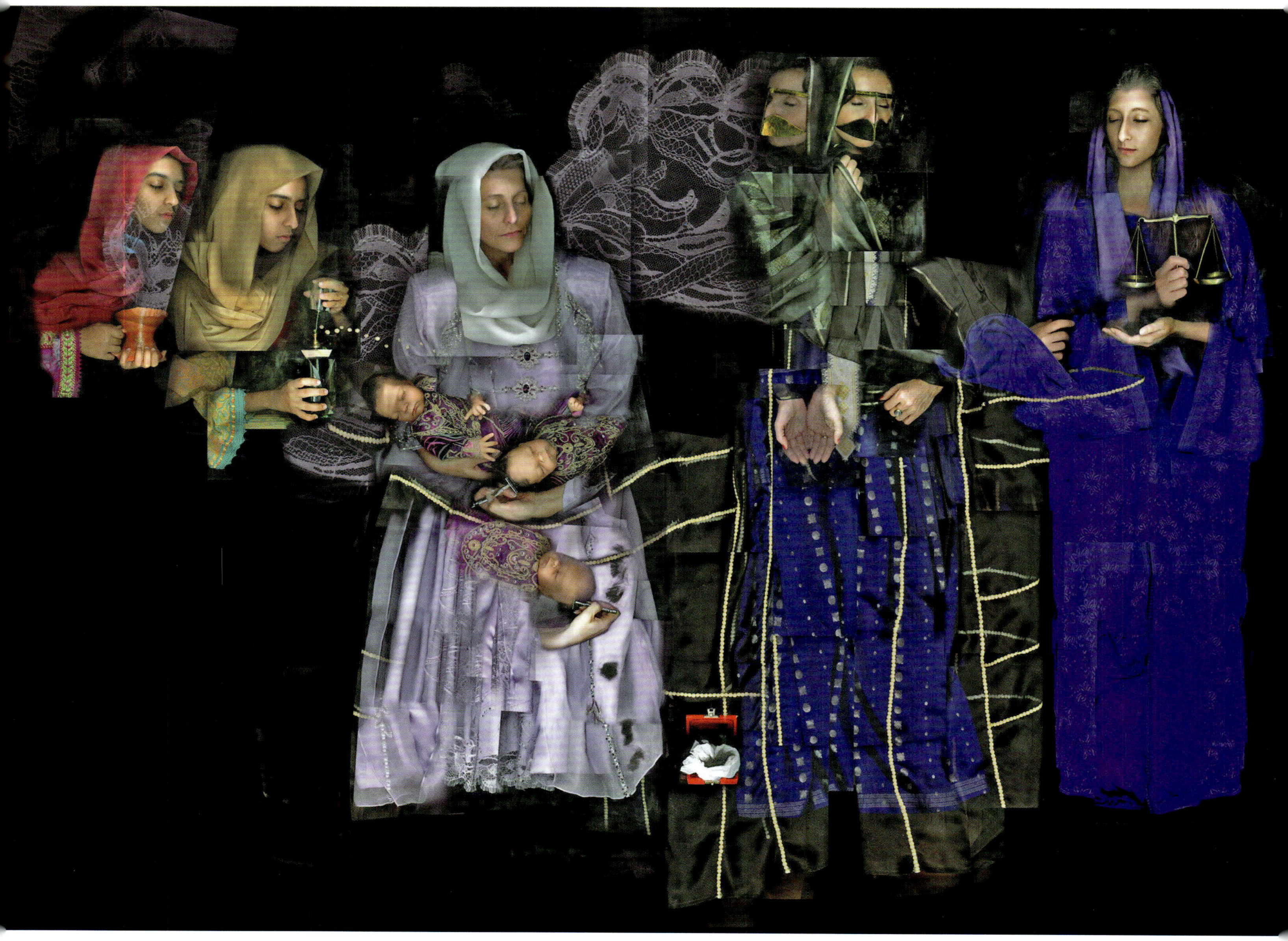

Maitha Demithan, *The 40th Day*, 2012. Scanography, 187 x 268cm (73½ x 105½in.).

In her most ambitious work to date, *The 40th Day*, Demithan has created a haunting and moving image of the ritual known as Aqiqah. It is customary in Islamic society for a baby's head to be shaved on the seventh day of its life, an act generally carried out by the women of the family. In accordance with Quranic practice, a ritual offering is made of a sheep or goat, following which the hair is gently shaved from the baby's head in a prescribed manner, and then weighed, with an equivalent weight of silver or gold being given to charity. The ritual concludes with prayers and celebration, and the baby's head is rubbed with perfume or saffron. Making the print required a long process of selecting the appropriate garments and props and also the commissioning of a 'reborn doll' – a doll that has been carefully painted to provide precisely the right skin tone and appearance – as the artist did not wish to subject a real baby to the scanning process. The scanning of the various participants was time-consuming and involved variations of pose and lighting before the artist could complete the tableau on her computer. In capturing this ritual, albeit through a staged and theatrical performance, Demithan is honouring the importance of the rituals and the relationships among women in her culture. At the same time, her images are made using cutting-edge technology, bridging a vast gap between the timeless origin of these images and the future into which she and her country will grow.

SHAMSA AL OMAIRA

'AS A YOUNG FEMALE artist from the United Arab Emirates, one might think we are surrounded by limitations that can curb our creativity, and restrain our professional growth as artists. All these are just false notions that have no realistic ground, and I found that it has nothing to do with being a female or an Emirati. As opportunities started to arise I found that the only thing that matters was proving myself as an artist. Being an emerging artist from the United Arab Emirates in this stage of artistic growth put me in the right spot, at the right time. The fact that I graduated as a visual artist from Zayed University was the start of many doors opening to me. In conclusion, being a female Emirati artist is a blessing.'

In this statement, Shamsa Al Omaira offers an optimistic view of the position that a young woman artist can occupy in a young and dynamic Arab country, a view that might surprise some critics. Her work is based on her fascination for the details in the world around her, threads in a textile, the history behind certain objects, anything that gives a clue about the stories and ideas that led to its existence. She writes of the emotional rollercoaster that she goes through in creating a new piece of work and adds, 'To build an object inspired by a thought, an idea, or a form, provoked by emotions and holding a strong message, is in my belief the sturdiest and greatest method of creation.'

The range of her work encompasses sculpture and three-dimensional paintings as well as printmaking, and there is a unity of concept and approach to making that unites them as the expression of her fascination with philosophy and 'the machinations of the mind'. In her first solo exhibition, Deer in the Headlights, at the Ghaf Art Gallery in Abu Dhabi in 2012, she produced a sculpture entitled *Deranged*, comprising classical-style chairs, a sofa, a standard lamp and a table all mounted on rockers, some of which were actuated by motors, together with wall plaques bearing miniature pieces of furniture, with paintings of chairs on fabric beneath them, and small painted jars – all of which created the illusion of being a logical arrangement that didn't quite resolve itself, leaving lingering questions about reality.

This sense of disruption is found to have deeply personal resonances in a more recent series of print-based works, derived from her experience of the death of her very young niece. She writes of the sense of loss and sadness that this child will never grow to fulfil the Emirati saying, 'Every

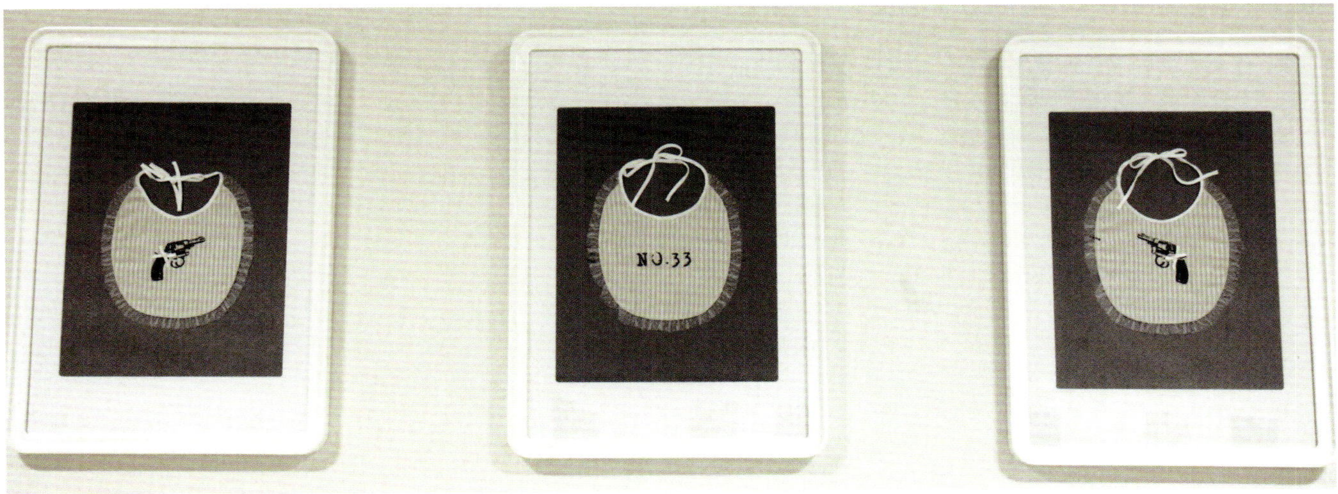

Shamsa Al Omaira, *I-Feminism*,1975. Woodcut, hand-printed on Japanese washi, 100 x 125cm (39¼ x 49¼in.). Private collection.

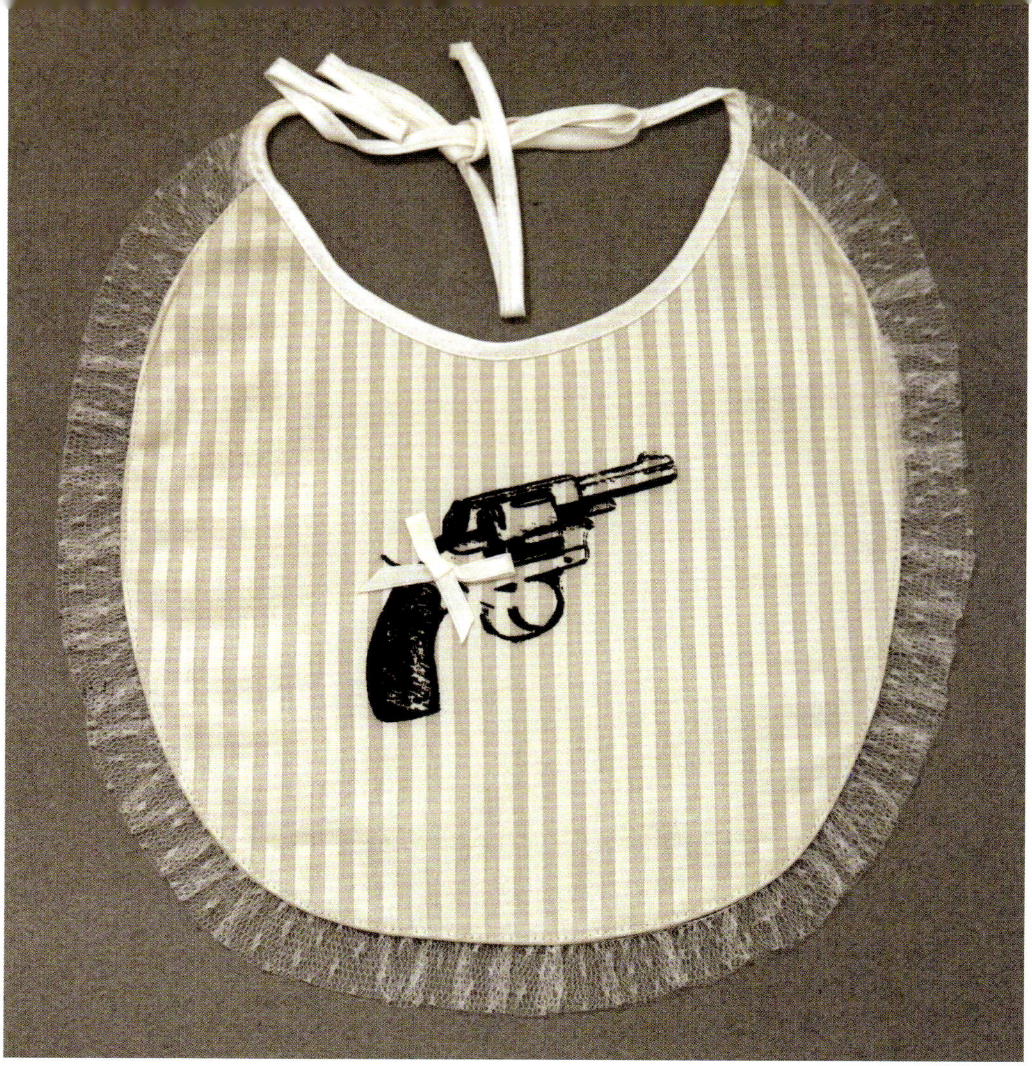

Left: Shamsa Al Omaira, *Dragon +1*, 2001. Woodcut, hand-printed on Japanese washi, 125 x 100cm (49¼ x 39¼in.). Private collection.

Below: Shamsa Al Omaira, *The Shadow of the Book*, 2003. Object: wood, paper, acrylic, 21 x 30 x 7cm (8¼ x 11¾ x 2¾in.). Private collection.

girl has seven different looks in her lifetime'. Al Omaira has a considerable interest in working with fabrics and using them in her own designs for objects and garments, which she manipulates further in the creation of her art works. In this instance, seeking to highlight the fragility of a young life, she created seven small dresses in her niece's size, each screen-printed with part of a lullaby whose words are beginning to fade. While a lullaby is intended to soothe a baby and lull her or him into a deep sleep, in this instance the silent words have associations with vulnerability and loss, this further layer of meaning juddering against the more conventional and romantic notions of a small child's world. The installation also included a series of delicate bibs screen-printed with images, such as a gun or a serial number, which would normally not be associated with these delicate childhood items, triggering associations with the loss of other young lives through violence, parental carelessness or child abuse. These unsettling works deal with the loss of innocence, the unpredictability of life, and the failure of responsibility. While they were created by the artist as a direct response to a personal tragedy, they resonate with the tragic news of world events.

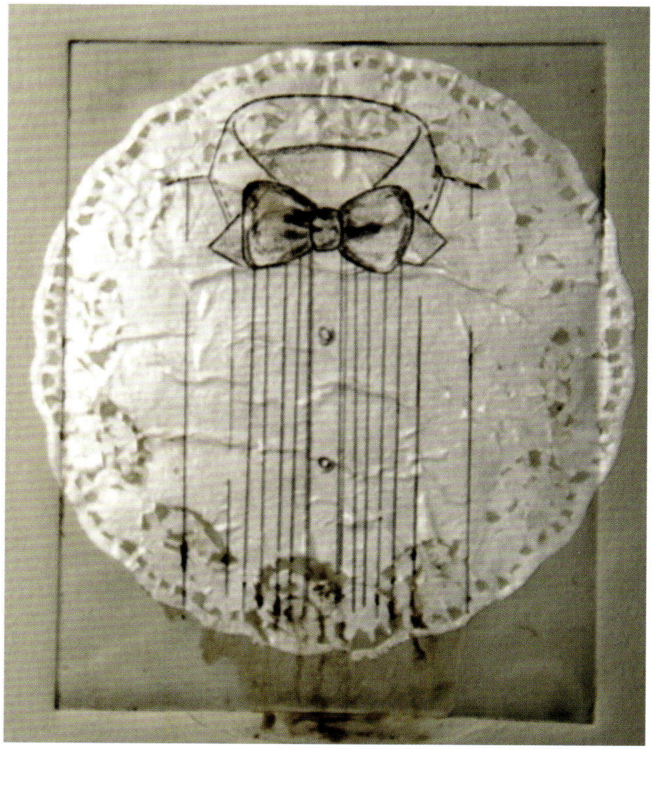

THE MIDDLE EAST

FEW OTHER REGIONS on Earth have been so disputed and for so long as the Middle East. Disagreements over borders and religious faiths have spilled over into insurrection, skirmishes and war at many stages of the region's long history, especially since the collapse of the Ottoman Empire after WW1. As with other zones of conflict, the news and information that emerge from this region are prone to modification through anything from editorial bias to blatant propaganda. As ever the people who suffer the most are those who live in the region, and their stories, if told at all, are open to manipulation in the interests of those who broadcast them. Artists are active in all parts of the Middle East, and some of them align themselves with one side or another in a given argument, while others prefer to take a subtler and more neutral position. Both approaches, however, present opportunities for understanding that are greatly different from reports in the news media. As part of my research for the book I sent a series of questions to artists in and from the Middle East, and excerpts from their responses, presented here anonymously, offer a range of views on the issues that provide a context within which they work.

The first question concerned the extent to which the local and international news media present a clear and honest account of news and events in that region. Responses included: 'I do feel the media are neither clear nor honest. It is hard to find news that is unbiased'; 'Israel is known internationally for the freedom of its press, except for censorship by the state as a security measure relating to military issues. However, the boundaries that divide details that threaten the security of the state from other information are not always transparent'; 'The news media for the most part rarely give a full or complete objective picture of circumstances and events, so it seems most news would need to be taken in context and with the awareness of possible biased circumstances. There is an inherent difference between local news in any country vs. international news reporting the very same events'; 'There is also free access to international networks and TV stations, including ones from the Arab and more widely the Islamic worlds. What these show is that despite freedom of the press in the country, Israeli accounts of Israeli–Palestinian contact differ from those of international sources'; 'The reality and tragedy is that many times there are casualties on both sides, frequently civilians who are not directly engaged in warfare, and that for long periods of time one violent round leads to another without succeeding in achieving any significant progress towards the reduction of violence and future two-states solution.'

The second question asked whether or not the work of artists can help to make news and events better known, and if so what problems might arise. Responses included: 'I do not know whether my work would help make news or events better known. What I represent is the personal, immediate and direct result of my own experience, memory and belief. I use subtle politically infused images that are loaded when prodded gently, but on the surface are quietly thought-provoking and aesthetically melancholic'; 'I do feel that some of my works can help change foreign perceptions of and conversation about the situation, largely through edification. People often hold stereotypical views that do not reflect the complexity, ambiguity and multiplicity that define Israel/Palestine'; 'I feel for the most part my work or the work of other artists has a limited effect on mass-media news. Art work might facilitate or stir discussion over a period of time, addressing dramatic events or significant ongoing public discussions. But the fact of the matter is that art is usually not part of the public dialogue or agenda.'

The third question asked whether or not art made in or about the Middle East would inevitably be political, or socially critical. Responses included: 'I feel that the assumption that living in an area where there is ongoing conflict would drive "meaningful art" as critical and politically oriented is exaggerated … the situation in the Middle East, while being an ongoing conflict, is far from being a continuous intense crisis'; 'Art work from the Middle East is always saturated with social commentary and will always be politically flavoured'; 'There are no "apolitical artworks", but the work does not necessarily have to reflect only the occupation and/or Israel. The political can be social, about Islamic symbolism, calligraphy, architecture or film'; 'I would not draw a clear line between art as a statement and art as aesthetic expression, nor would

I find it easy to name areas of the world which do not have social and political problems that art can address. The burden of representation put upon artists from so-called "troubled regions", whereby everything they make needs to "represent" their place in limited form, is a problem in the international art world'; 'My work emanates from my personal journey and introspection. It is the outcome of images and news I am aware of, my own photographs and imagination. My focus and mindset are life as I experience it directly and indirectly, and the human condition.'

The fourth question asked if art with a socially or politically focused content and meaning can make a difference to regions such as the Middle East. Responses included: 'It is important to keep the political situation at the forefront, and to keep the dialogue alive. It provides a "myth-breaking" situation for the viewer, breaking the myth of "lack of culture or refinement" of the savage uncultured philistine Palestinian Arab'; 'I believe that art can make people more conscious of social and political situations. Unfortunately I am quite sceptical as to its ability to effect real change. It might, however, allow people to reconsider their attitudes and to become more tolerant'; 'I think that art is for the most part not a significant part of the mainstream mass population dialogue, therefore possessing a limited effect on the general political discussion'; '... over a longer period of time I feel art work would have very tough "competition" with current events, historical perspectives (subjective or objective), as well as public opinion leaders with access to mass media platforms'.

The fifth question asked if the artist considered her or his work actively political or made in the role of the artist as an observer. Responses included: 'My work is not actively political. It is subtle. I deal with the everyday political, and I can only reflect the immediately personal take on this ... I do see myself also as an observer, especially as I do not live "at home". I record with film and photography the changing places and times. I do see the changes more vividly, as my visits are not frequent. Even in a year, the changes are tangible and sometimes overwhelming'; 'I prefer to see myself as an observer, as one who presents a view that is open to others to interpret as they choose. However, in recent years, my preliminary image source is of a political and social nature, associated with the socio-political realities of the Middle East and the transnational conditions of the modern world more largely'; 'As I see my works as my individual journey and expression of my own sense of events and realities, I would hesitate to label my work as actively political. Furthermore, as most of my work can rarely be associated directly with specific events or places and is not symbolic in any manner, it would hardly be commonly "qualified" as politically active. This does not contradict the sense that much of my work is quite pensive and unsettling. I think my work reflects the emotional turmoil I experience, and my struggling with the realities of life in our region, and in many other areas of the globe.'

ISRAEL

GIL & MOTI

GIL & MOTI occupy a unique niche in the contemporary arts: in their introduction to themselves they write, 'In our multimedia work, we, the artist duo Gil & Moti, negate the existence of boundaries separating life and art, and performance and social intervention. As Jewish Israelis and homosexual immigrants living in Rotterdam, we contribute to discourses about being different and about sets of rules that are supposed to regulate social existence.'

Born in Israel in 1968 (Gil) and 1971 (Moti), the pair studied first in Israel and later in the UK, Rotterdam and New York. They have lived and worked together since 1994 and, since 1998, have based themselves in Rotterdam. They have a considerable record of showing their work in solo and group exhibitions in many countries, and have undertaken a number of international residencies. Their shared concern for creating works of art together led to their decision to dress identically, and to live and work together to the extent that they have narrowed the gap between art and life. This has resulted in the development of a body of work that extends many normal definitions, resulting in projects that cannot easily be categorised. They tell stories '... about our experiences in the form of diary-like videos, drawings, photographs and paintings. On the border of the public and the private domain, of art and life, of the individual and the collective, and the art institute and the street.'

Their concerns, while being focused on their own shared identity and relationship, are extended into the wider community through a variety of media, from traditional painting and drawing to printmaking and video. For example, in a series of video diaries they documented attitudes to the conflicted relationship between Israelis and Palestinians in Israel, through encounters and discussions with Arab immigrants in Rotterdam and Copenhagen. In a linked installation, *Dreamers and Storytellers* (2011) they used paintings, etchings and texts as tools for their analysis of some of the sociopolitical problems of their native country. They

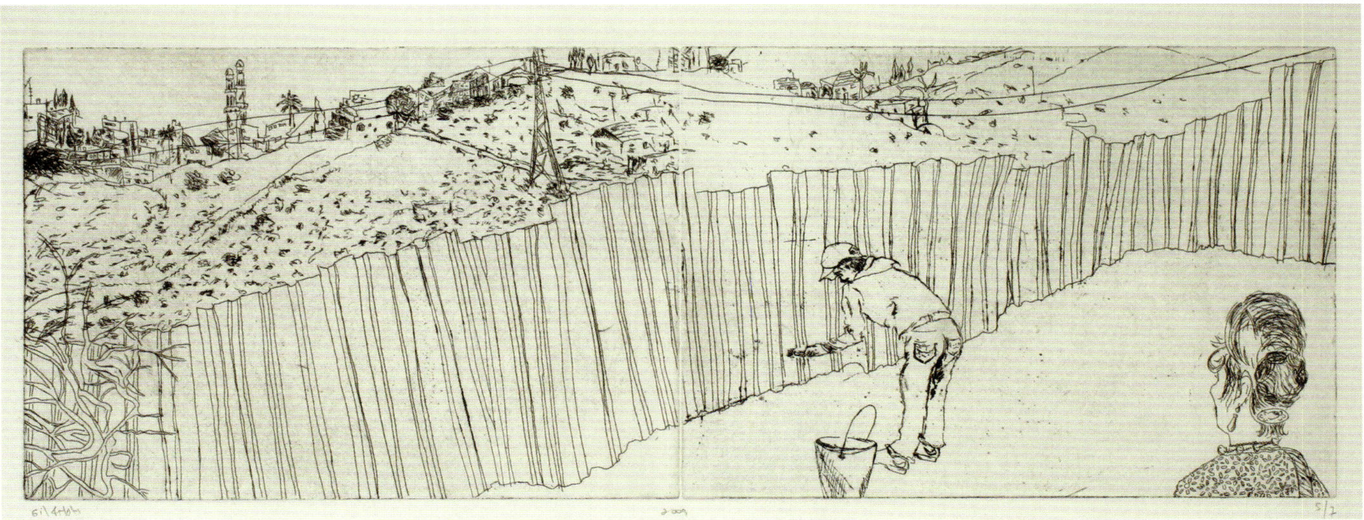

Gil & Moti, *Future Line Tours – Painter in Jerusalem*, 2009. Etching, 38 x 81cm (15 x 32in.). Courtesy of the Gottesman Etching Centre, Kibbutz Cabri. Photo: Avraham Hay.

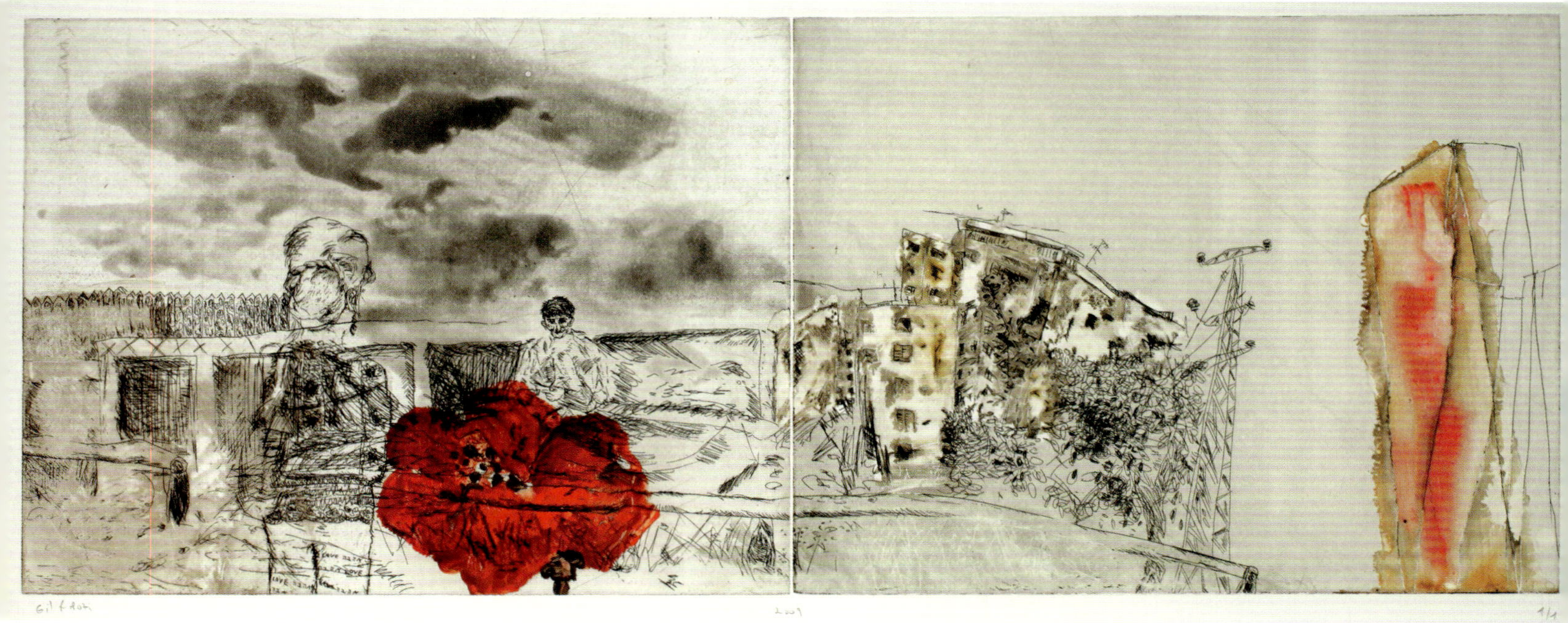

Gil & Moti, *Future Line Tours – Old in Tel Aviv*, 2009. Etching, aquatint, monoprints, 37 x 88cm (14½ x 34¾in.). Courtesy of the Gottesman Etching Centre, Kibbutz Cabri. Photo: Avraham Hay.

write, 'These artworks present innovative ways to produce art which is itself a political gesture and that challenges audiences. We are strongly motivated to develop new perceptions on the way to a better society.'

They recount how, when in art school in Israel, they were taught to think about a final product with a 'signature' – that is, some factor that made the work clearly identifiable with the artist. They add that, sadly, they were not taught about the need for and value of communication, their own view being that art that is another tool to communicate with people. In addition they consider that a work of art can be successful if it enlightens people and makes a positive change in their thinking, adding, 'We get excited when we see something that makes us change our thinking. We are part of a problematic society. We are not so much looking from a superior view. We want to change others, but meanwhile we change ourselves.'

Examples of this unusual approach can be seen in their extensive record of projects. In *The Gil & Moti Wedding Project*, they focused on their wedding, one of the first for a gay couple in the Netherlands, which was conducted by the Mayor of Rotterdam on the balcony of Rotterdam's City Hall. The ceremony was conceived as a fully documented art project and has since then been the subject of a number of exhibitions in Europe. In a series of three linked projects, *Letters to Laylah*, they explored the ramifications of establishing an imaginary love relationship with an Arab man, highlighting as they did so a range of social and political issues. The project resulted in a set of 13 letters, each painted on several large panels, together with texts, a video and, for successive exhibitions, an installation of furniture including a triple bed. Other works have included a complex ongoing project, *Gil & Moti's Homegallery*, which has involved a large number of installations, exhibitions and collaborations with other artists since 1998, and which continues to evolve.

While Gil & Moti happily define themselves as 'conceptual artists', their work is a long way from the highly intellectual approach, padded out with endless dense texts, that characterises the work of some others in this genre. They quote with pleasure the words of Marina Abramovich in an interview with the Israeli newspaper *Haaretz*: '... I dislike phoney or too intellectual emotionless artworks. People do not have to learn and read complicated theories in order to understand an art piece. Art should be emotional and touch first the stomach and only later should we seek for the various meanings ...' This is precisely, they say, what they are aiming at, as they hope that most of the people who experience their

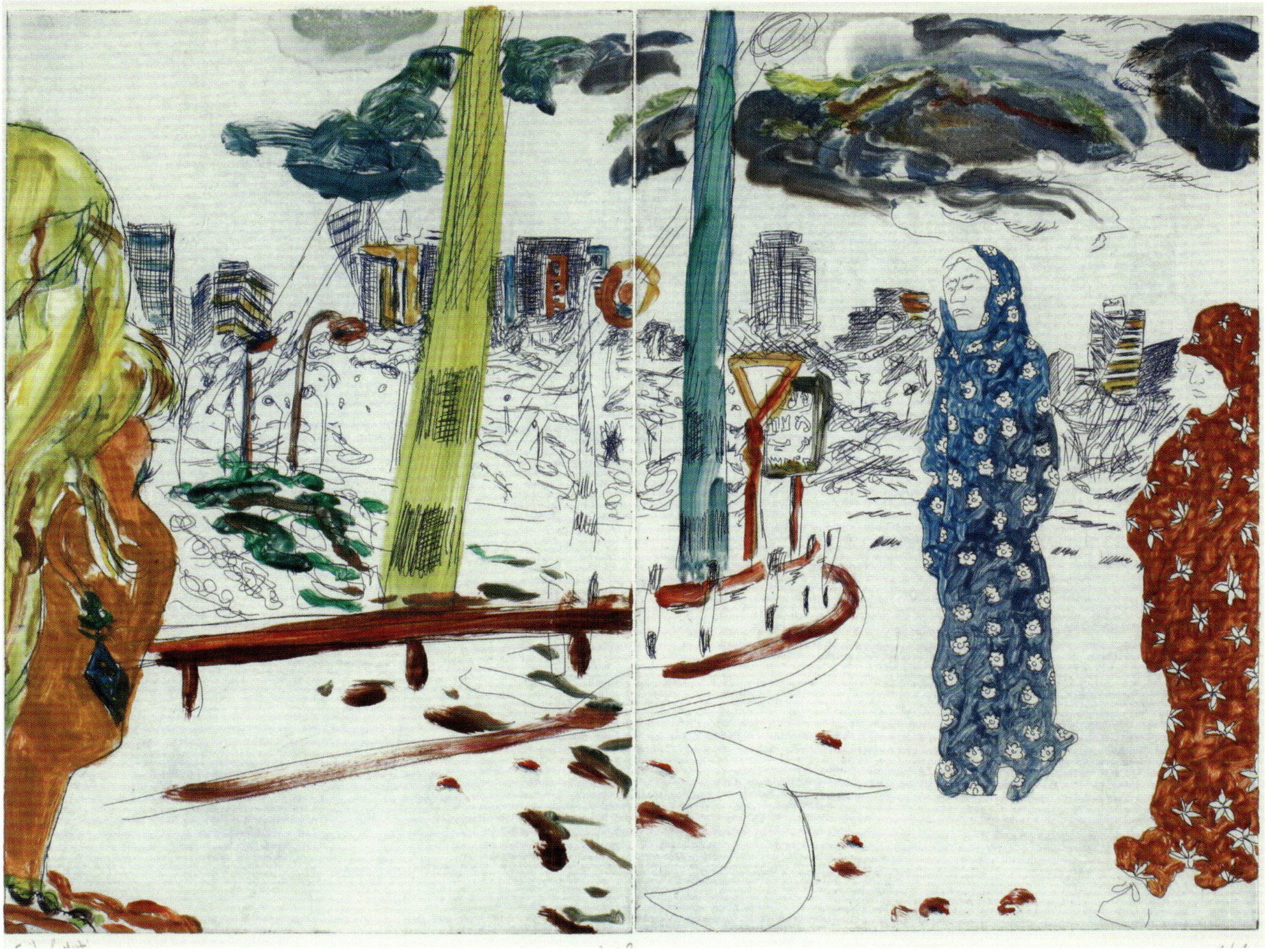

Gil & Moti, *Future Line Tours – West*, 2009. Etching, monoprints, 40 x 47cm (15¾ x 18½in.). Courtesy of the Gottesman Etching Centre, Kibbutz Cabri. Photo: Avraham Hay.

work will see behind the façade of apparent sweetness and recognise the conflict or the question raised.

In a printmaking-based project, *Future Line Tours*, which was shown at the City Art Gallery in Herzliya, Israel in 2009–10, they chose to use a classical medium, etching. Unusually in this case they chose not to feature in the works in their usual way, but instead replaced their presence with that of a fictional character, an eccentric well-dressed lady, perhaps a tourist, an investor, an inspector – her role is not defined. They observe an aspect of Israeli reality with a critical eye, looking at sociopolitical problems by directing their gaze through the works at the town of Jaffa on the outskirts of Tel Aviv. Based on the photographs they took during their exploration of the area, they worked with a range of etching techniques, some incorporating modifications of their photographs. The figure of the anonymous female becomes a sort of archetype, the witness, the searcher, the migrant, wandering in an area occupied by Palestinian migrants on the fringe of society, illuminating the uncertainty and the risk of conflict in this microcosm of Israeli society.

LIHIE TALMOR

THE NOTION of place is central to the work of Lihie Talmor, both in the literal and topographical sense and in the extended sense that links real places to places in the imagination, in history and geography, as symbolic locations for myth and memory. Much of her work is based on the photographs she takes of places that are important to her, in which a fraction of time in a specific location is captured through the lens of a camera and registered as an electronic record in a computer file. This first encounter is then revived and modified through a second encounter as she looks again at the images she has made and processes them to become digital prints or photo-etchings. The complexity built up through a continuing series of closed loops such as these creates a bank of memories of real and imagined places, which in turn leads to the complex nexus from which her art is derived. This experience is becoming more common as people devour and record the incidents and places that comprise their lives with digital cameras. The accessibility and the ease with which excessive numbers of images can be captured with these increasingly sophisticated devices encourages a profligacy of image-taking which vastly exceeds that of the analogue era, in which a greater degree of selectivity was ensured due to the limits of length of film rolls and the subsequent need for costly processing. The need to recognise and understand this phenomenon is generally ignored, and such a collecting of images is for many people becoming a substitute for actually seeing what is going on and subsequently remembering it.

Talmor was born in Israel, and studied architecture and urban planning, and then poetics and comparative literature, achieving degrees in both. She also studied painting and, following her move to Caracas, Venezuela, studied painting at the Center of Studies for the Graphic Arts. Since then she has taught and participated in courses at cultural centres and workshops in the Americas, Israel and Europe, has had numerous exhibitions and received various awards, and has worked with writers on the creation of artists' books. This range of experiences has brought her into contact with the experience of a wide variety of landscapes, added to substantially by a recent period spent living in India. Her focus, in recording these landscape experiences, transcends mere recording. As she writes, 'My etchings stem from photographs taken in very precise moments in order to document experiences, the images become the specific, referential, springboard for the development and evolution of thematic series of works.' In some instances these photographs become only the 'preliminary image source' because, '... usually, the images I start with, which reference specific places, are so transformed in the working process that they become metaphors for larger social conditions.' In other instances the photographs are taken with a view to being more literal and direct, as in a series of photographs of the high wall, erected between Israel and the territories of the Palestinian Authority, for her project, *While we can, we cross.*

The places in which Talmor leads her life could not be more different: the Venezuelan capital city of Caracas, on the Caribbean coast, chaotic and constantly reshaping itself; and Israel, a country rooted in ancient histories and religious texts, cleaving to the certainties of the past while expanding as a modern nation with powerful ambitions: residing in two countries with very different but equally distinct political regimes. She is, in a sense not so different from her Hebrew ancestors, a nomad, moving from place to place, creating memories as she passes. These factors have given her a clear vision of the wider implications of global politics. As she has written, '... my view of the political expresses itself in the following dualities. I am interested in the opposition between distance and proximity, inside and outside, the embraceable and the unreachable, represented by alternate spaces, cohesion of scales, topographic reminiscences, and the superimposition of contradictory angles and perspective. My constant moving forces and enables me to view the world in these terms.'

The selected images are informed by this quotation. Two come from the *Track Before Detect* series of photo-polymer etchings based on images taken during a guided excursion in Jerusalem that was sponsored by an organisation for coexistence geared towards finding a just solution to the Israeli–Palestinian conflict. In these images her recordings of the hidden and secret places between the two communities are combined with images of parts of her sculptures, redefining them so as to form new images

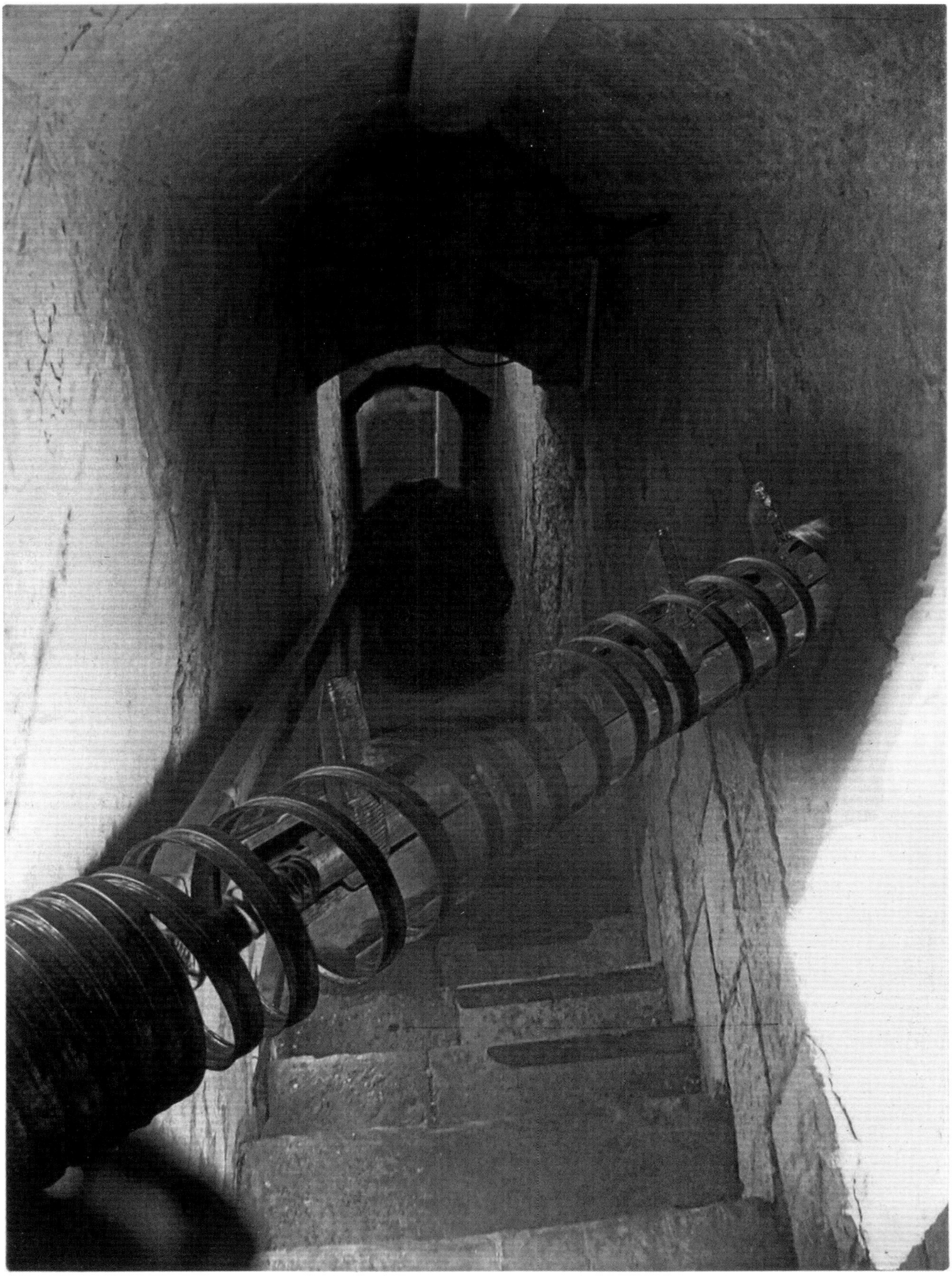

Lihie Talmor, *Track before Detect 1*, 2009. Photo-etching, 49.5 x 37.8cm (19½ x 15in.) (plate).

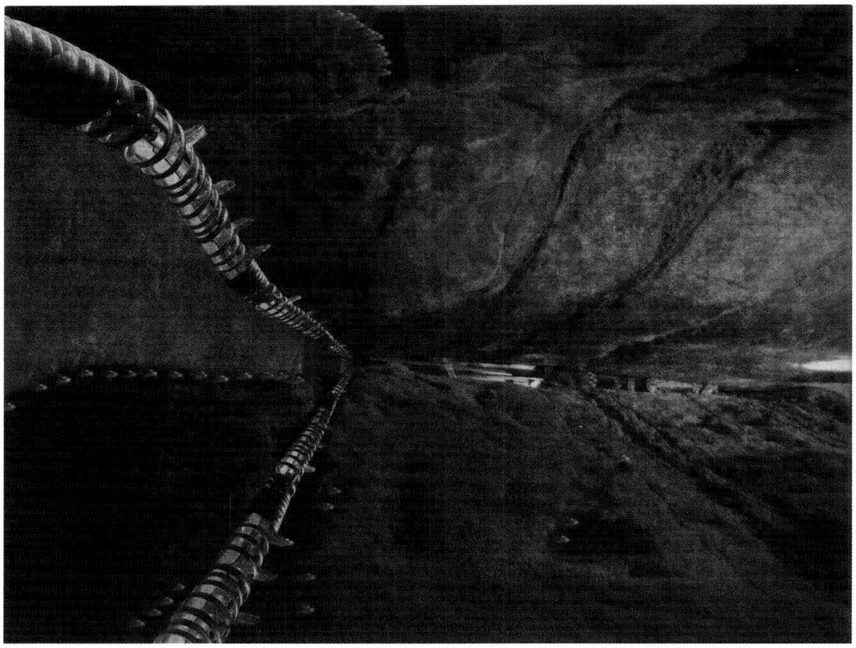

Lihie Talmor, *Track before Detect 5*, 2009. Photo-etching, 37.8 x 49.5cm (15 x 19½in.) (plate).

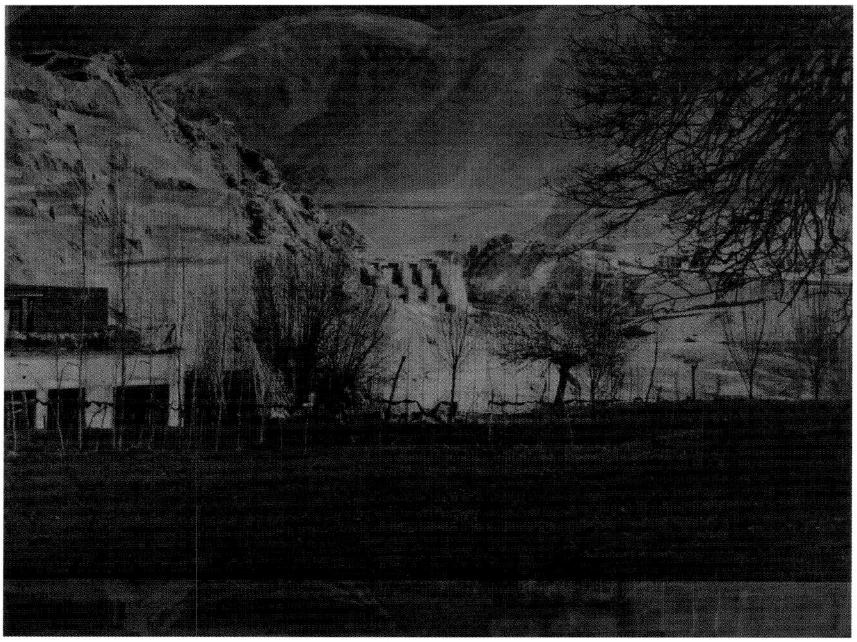

Lihie Talmor, *Makom, Place 1*, 2012. Photo-etching and aquatint from two colour plates, 30 x 40cm (11¾ x 15¾in.) (plate).

that create a lingering sense of unease and claustrophobia. Images of the narrow spaces, built or tunnelled through and beneath the city, are evidence of man's exploration of, and work to impose his will on, what is for many people of different faiths the most important city on Earth. These images are combined with tubular sections of some unknown machinery that in turn suggests channels for communication that interpenetrate and cross the narrow spaces. The prints themselves have been reworked by the artist, who added paint, and scratched and otherwise made alterations, to the pristine etchings to enhance the mystery of the combined images. Made and dominated by Man, they are nonetheless devoid of human presence, except through implication.

Makom, Place 1 is a photo-etching with aquatint, derived from images Lihie Talmor made in the remote region of Ladakh during a lengthy stay in India. The Hebrew word *Makom* can be interpreted as 'place', 'space' or, through the meaning of 'presence', God. It is the sense of presence that is most powerfully conveyed in this image, in which the efforts of man to tame and exist in a hostile and dominant environment are subject to an external force beyond his control.

ORIT HOFSHI

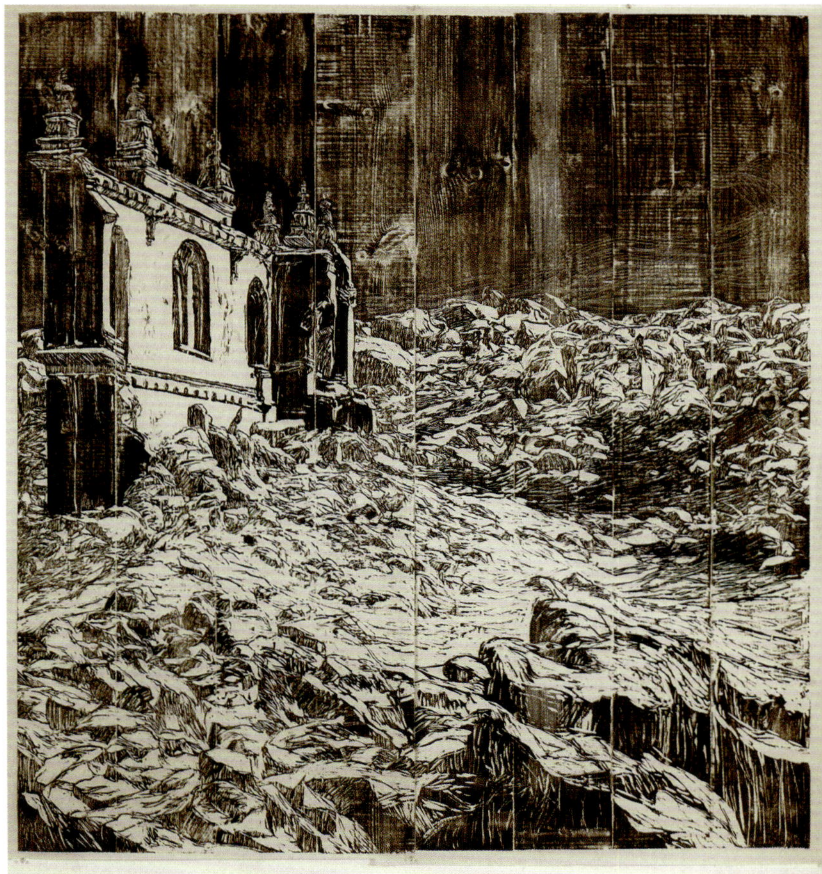

Orit Hofshi, *Resilience (Holešov 1944)*, 2008. Spoon-printed woodcut on Okawara washi, 180 x 172cm (70¾ x 67¾in.). Collection: The Open Museum, Tefen. Photo: Avraham Hay.

WOODCUT is a time-honoured printmaking technique that reaches across the globe and through centuries of time and development. It is essentially a straightforward technique in which a smooth, flat piece of wood is carved with tools to remove the areas not intended to be printed, leaving raised areas to be coated with ink, whereupon the image is transferred to a sheet of paper by means of a press or by hand pressure using a baren (the traditional Japanese pad) or the back of a wooden spoon. That said, it is a technique that is capable of extreme subtlety and sophistication, as the classic prints of Dürer attest. By limiting the material demands to wood, ink and paper, the technique is also available to those artists who lack access to a fully equipped print shop, requiring nothing other than the three simple materials and sufficient space in which to work. That said, given the right equipment, colours and papers, woodcut is also capable of producing extremely sophisticated and complex prints. For Orit Hofshi, however, the simple and very basic approach has proven the best; her skilful and idiosyncratic art has gained her an international reputation and a long history of exhibitions and awards, with her work being held in numerous prestigious collections.

Born in Israel on the Matzuva kibbutz that was founded by her parents, who were Holocaust survivors, she later studied art in Haifa, Israel, then subsequently at the Pennsylvania Academy of Fine Arts in Philadelphia, and at the University of Leeds, where she gained an MA. She currently lives in Herzliya, Israel, and travels widely. Her work is typified by its graphic strength, its large scale, and its figurative directness. Often monumental in approach it is nonetheless produced in a relatively small studio, requiring that the works are built up from a number of modules. Her vision and inspiration are wide, the works often depicting large-scale landscapes and events, and yet are reduced in the working process to smaller sections, before being combined into the final exhibited work. She writes that '… much of my own work stems from my personal deep concern and preoccupation with the state of affairs in Israel and the surrounding countries. While the work does not depict specific locations, nor does it strive to document particular events, my main motivation and emotional drivers are my reactions to the atmosphere, lack of prospects for normalisation and the human condition in the region. … I am troubled by the seeming dead end we exist in, with the Palestinians having to face so many hardships in their daily routines and in emergency situations as well.' The humanity of this approach fits well with the essentially organic and low-tech character of her chosen technique, in which the main effort of making comes through devotion to hours of hand-crafting in the cutting of the block and the subsequent lengthy process of printing by hand – a process from which emerge prints of exceptional sensitivity.

While some of her prints are produced in the familiar form of ink on paper, others are combined with ink drawings on wood, with watercolour, and in some cases are built out into the third dimension to create print installations. One of the significant elements in Hofshi's recent work is the creation of larger blocks made by gluing a number of pine boards together, edge to edge; she favours this wood for its pronounced grain and figuring. In combining both print and wood panels the artist allows for multiple interpretations, and also for the textural complexity that comes not only from the

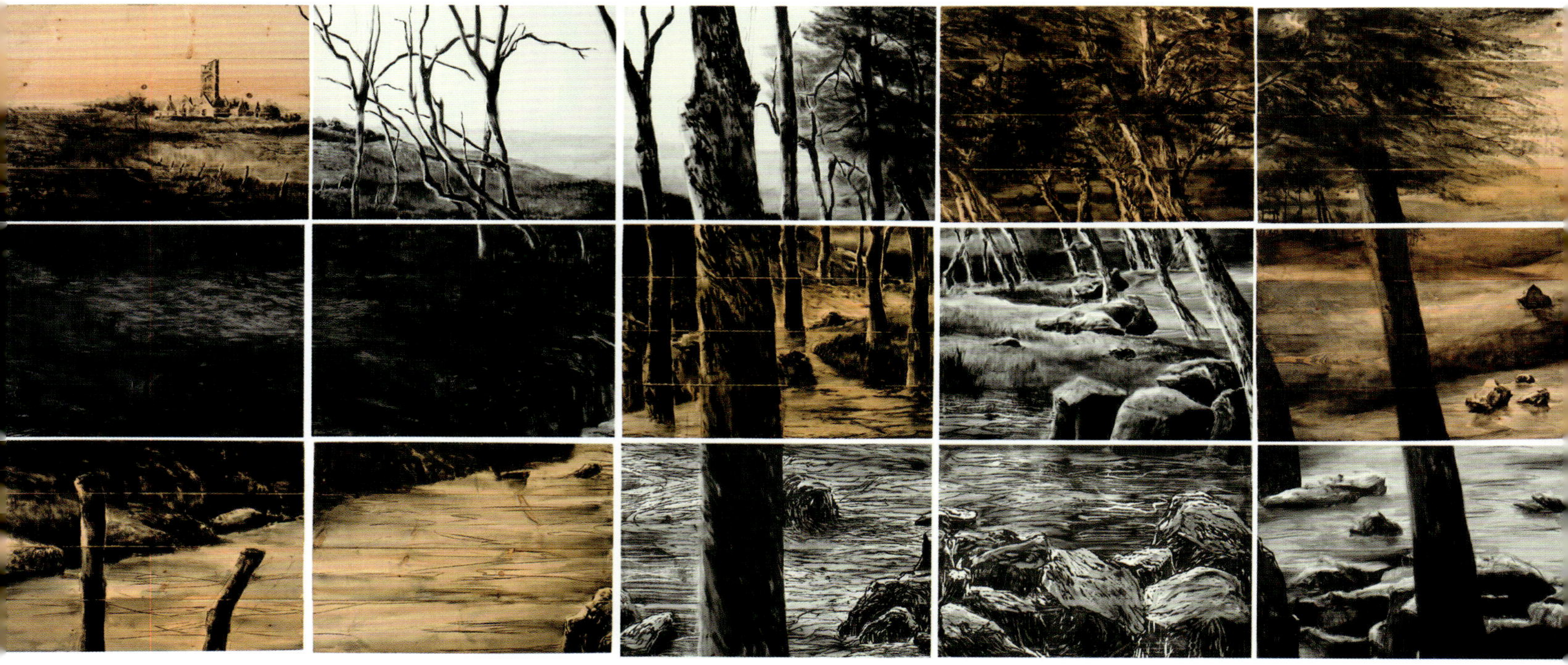

grain but from the combination of vertical bands caused by the abutting of the pine panels, and the horizontal emphasis in the carving of the image. This creates an additional layer of tension and the potential for viewers to contemplate not only the visual contrast in forms but also the philosophical implications of passing time that are inherent in that combination. The attention to detail that is shown in the making of both block and print takes away any suggestion of roughness and instead offers a clear view of the sophistication of this artist's approach.

Upon this Bank and Shoal of Time is a major work from 2006 that incorporates woodcut on horizontally planked boards, ink drawings and watercolour to form an image measuring 259 x 1016cm (102 x 400 in.). A middle-aged man in a suit stands in the water at the edge of a stream, apparently pondering his fate. The stream flows through an idyllic landscape with grass and trees, and all appears calm. But the conjunction of panels of drawing and others of inked, carved wood subverts what could at a much smaller scale in either print or drawing be seen very differently. At the scale of this work it becomes unsettling and poses other questions. *Resilience (Holešov 1944)* was inspired by a 1944 photograph of the synagogue of Holešov (in what is now the Czech Republic), which was burned down by the Nazis in 1942. Hofshi's mother was the only Jewish child to escape the fate in which all but a few of the Jews in that town were murdered. This large woodcut print reveals the manner of its making through the clearly evident vertical boards upon which the image of a fragment of the building is surrounded by utter chaos. Created in 2008, this print became the central part of the 2010 triptych, *Steadfastness*, which is not only an act of remembrance but also a mark of human resilience. *Amassment* (2012) combines a three-part woodcut print on paper, with ink on carved pine boards in a form resembling that of an altarpiece with predella, in which the chaos of destruction rises towards the resemblance of a peak against a dark sky. These works are epic in both their scale and the depth of their intent.

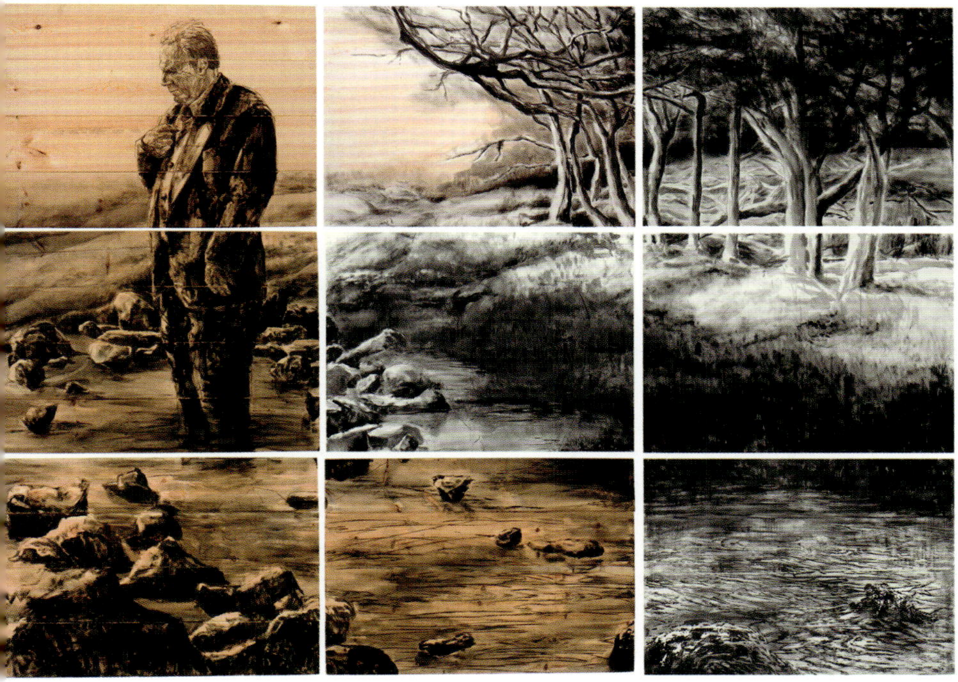

Orit Hofshi, *Upon this Bank and Shoal of Time*, 2006. Ink drawing, woodcut and watercolour, on paper and pine wood panels, 259 x 1016cm (102 x 400in.). Private collection. Photo: Avraham Hay.

Below: **Orit Hofshi**, *Amassment*, 2012. Ink, carved pine panels, framed woodcut on Fabriano paper, 168 x 215.5cm (66¼ x 84¾in.). Photo: Yigal Pardo.

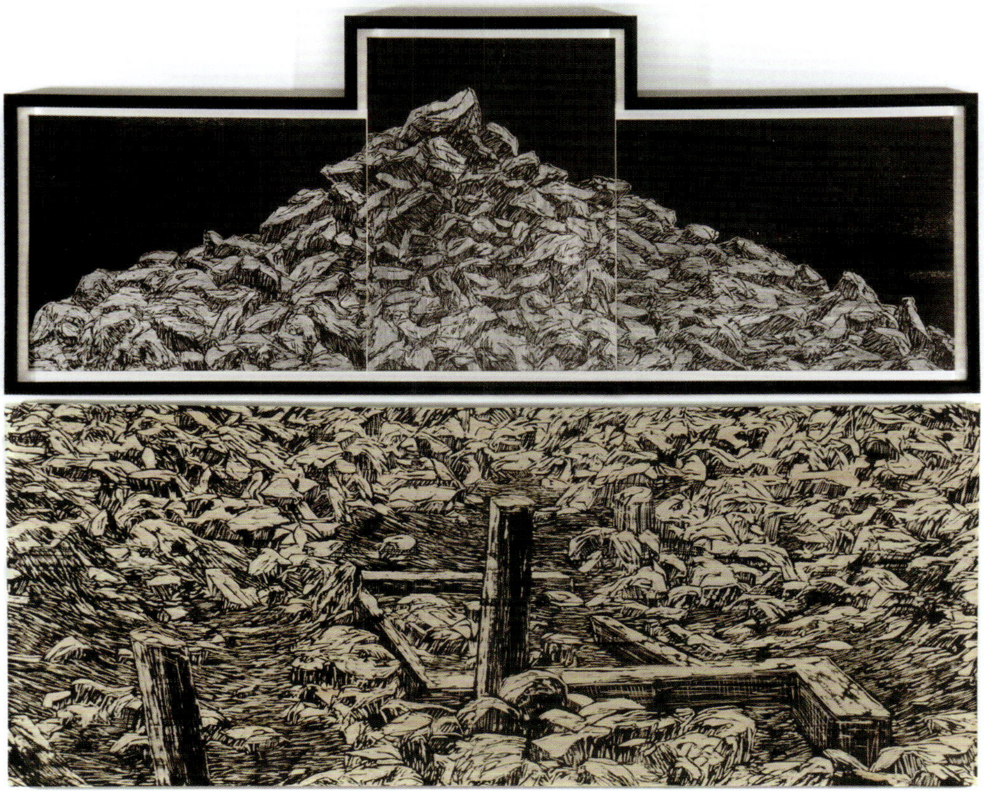

LEBANON

ALFRED TARAZI

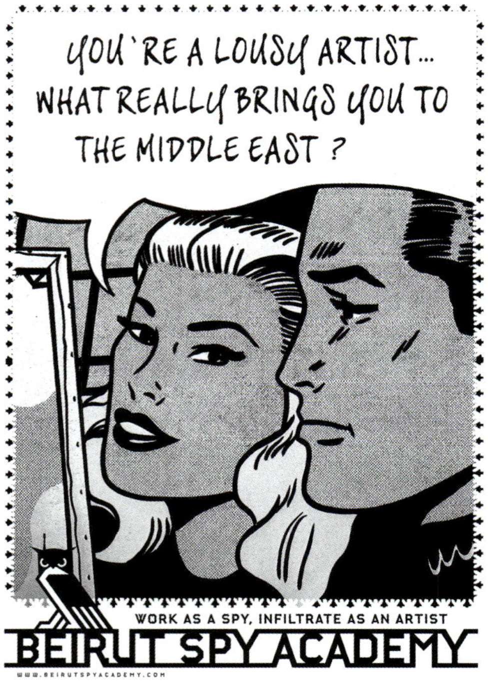

Alfred Tarazi, *Beirut Spy Academy /s6*, 2011. Giclée print, 100 x 70cm (39¼ x 27½in.).

THE HISTORY of Lebanon, from the time of the Phoenicians, through Roman occupation, the shifts of power and influence during the Crusades, and on to its subjection as part of the Ottoman Empire, followed by the years of the French mandate after the First World War, culminated in the country gaining independence in 1943, and a period of prosperity followed. Due to its geographical position the country had maintained for centuries an important position as a mercantile centre at the eastern end of the Mediterranean and as one of the terminal points of the Silk Road. As a result of its wealth the capital, Beirut, became known as 'the Paris of the East', with a sophisticated lifestyle that attracted many businesses and tourists. After those few prosperous decades Lebanon, with Israel to the south and Syria to the north and east, inevitably became consumed by the power politics of the Middle East and endured a devastating civil war from 1975 to1990.

Alfred Tarazi was born in Beirut in 1980 and went on to study engineering in the architecture and design department of the American University in Beirut, graduating in 2004. Of his early life in Lebanon, Tarazi writes, 'In 1975, what is commonly known as the Lebanese civil war started. It is said that this war ended in 1991, although the situation on the ground suggests that it is still going on.' He goes on to describe how his grandfather, before he lost his sight in 1973, had assembled an album of hand-coloured postcards in which showed the country as a picturesque tourist destination, shining in bright artificiality. With the beginning of the civil war Tarazi's father began building what his son describes as 'an impossible archive of images, books, tapes ... that would help him keep track of the events and foresee an end to the violence. He failed miserably and lost interest in this hopeless process.' This twin legacy of influences, the dreams represented by his grandfather's collection and his father's hopeless war archive, coupled with his own memories of the war as a child, provide the basis on which Tarazi has built a complex and powerful set of works. He writes, 'I did not inherit a country but images representing the dream of a country, and then, images of a country at war. I could only have a country once these images revealed their secrets, once I could find a way to lay claim to them.' Tarazi's works are, inevitably, biased and could hardly be otherwise, and they are without doubt political. But they also offer an alternative to the equally biased views presented by the Western news media. They blend fact, irony, satire, anger and a degree of dark humour in an attempt to make sense of the complex and seemingly senseless power games played out between foreign powers and internal factions, in which are entangled the lives of ordinary people.

In the series, *Beirut Spy Academy*, Tarazi uses the hard-edge techniques of Pop Art to create the cartoon frames of an apparently innocuous story, underpinned by the hard punch of the text. This form of subversion, in which a familiar, iconic style is manipulated for alternative purposes, is a strong thread through the history of political printmaking. In recent years this approach has been used as a form of agitprop, as such sharp-ended visual means can convey layers of information that require no further elucidation. The works in this series are set up as if they were advertising images for a university course in espionage, offering Beirut as an ideal ground for such an education. *A Nation's Inflation* utilises collage, another familiar method of conveying complex information, though in this case achieved electronically rather than through the time-honoured method of physical cut and paste. The sections

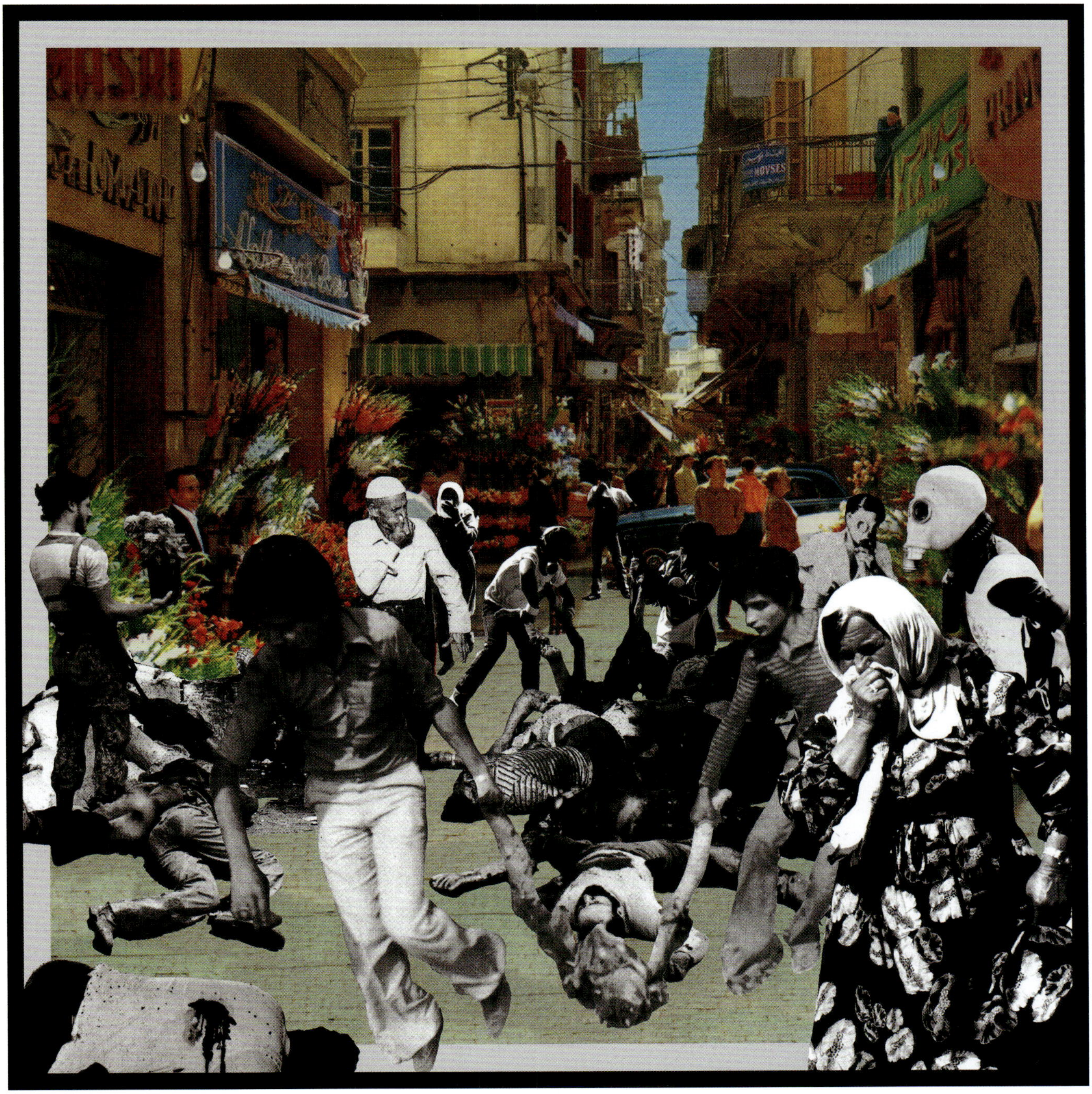

Alfred Tarazi, *The Sky Ever So Blue/Get Ready For Love*, 2011. Giclée print, 100 x 100cm (39¼ x 39¼in.).

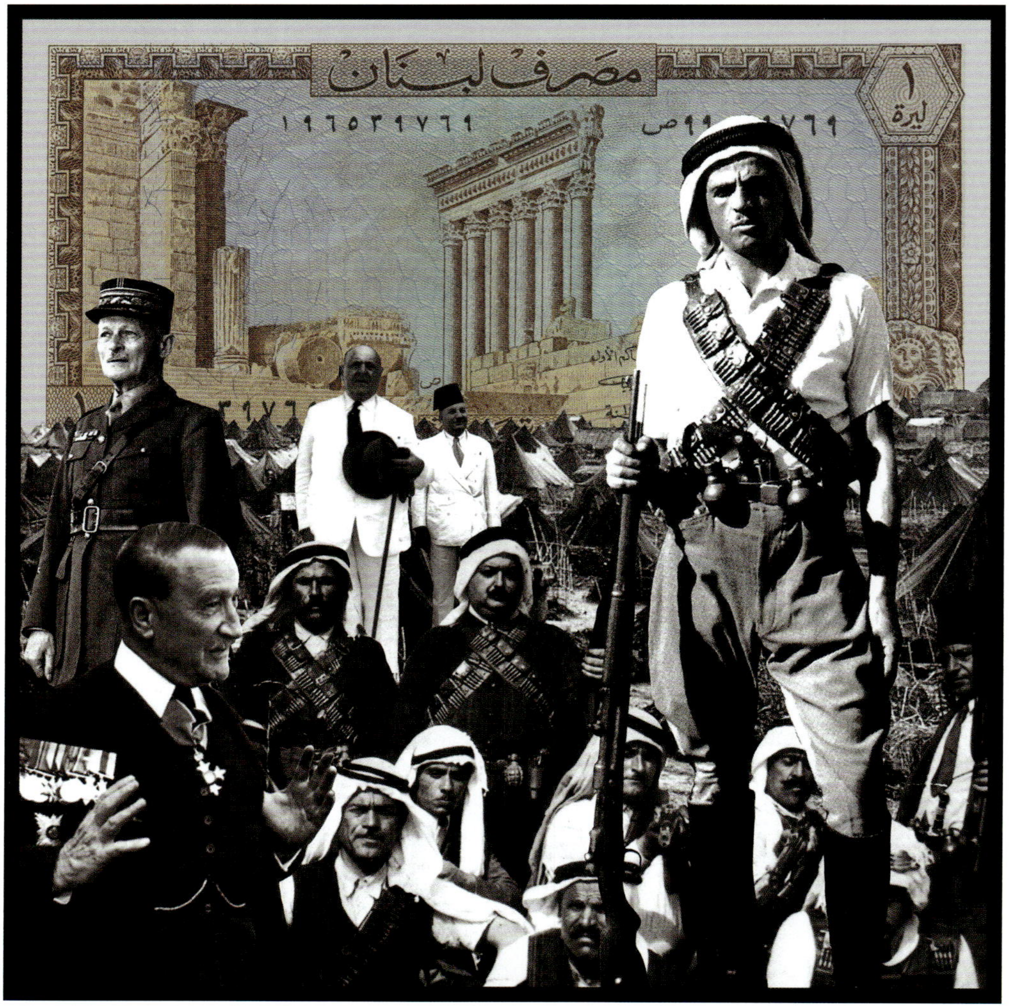

Alfred Tarazi, *A Nation's Inflation /1 Lebanese Lira (Arabic),* 2011. Giclée print, 100 x 100cm (39¼ x 39¼in.).

of Lebanese banknotes that provide the background for the works in this series are in themselves a form of appropriation, in that they depict celebrated archaeological sites such as that at Baalbek, remnants of another period in which Lebanon was under the influence of a foreign power, in this case Rome. The characters included as if in a tableau are European and Arab politicians and fighters who shaped, for good or ill, the modern state of Lebanon: depicted in front of a military camp, they position themselves in a setting that symbolises continuing conflicts which show little sign of peaceful resolution.

In the series, *The Sky Ever So Blue*, coloured images taken from his grandfather's collection of postcards form the background to collaged black and white images from the period of the civil war. The idyllic artificiality of the background, in which a photograph has been hand-coloured in an attempt to recreate the reality of the past, contrasts sharply with the foreground, in which sharply defined photographic images of terrorism, aggression and factional conflict are thrust into the viewer's face. Sadly, such images are still all too common in the everyday news material that continues to flood our media from conflicts elsewhere. In another series, *The Golden Age of American Defeats*, Tarazi positions images of comic-book superheroes in poses of defiance against newspaper photographs of events such as Pearl Harbor, the Lebanese Civil War of 1983, and the destruction of the World Trade Center – a contentious and highly political form of protest. In such ways Tarazi's work offers not only the possibility of catharsis for his own memories and those of his contemporaries, but also a symbolic and representative parallel for the experience of others elsewhere. Such clear and intelligent images state his position in unequivocal terms and place him in a long line of politically committed printmaking artists, including Rowlandson, Goya, Daumier and Posada, each of whom has since become part of the mainstream history of world art.

PALESTINE

ALEXANDRA HANDAL

'WHEN THE LANDSCAPE of your belonging is obliterated and erased so that the memory of your presence can no longer be traced, the outcome points to the power politics of imagination and the way they inform behaviour towards people and places.' Thus writes Alexandra Handal in her PhD thesis, 'Uncovering the Hidden Palestinian City of Jerusalem: Disrupting Power through Art Intervention'. The history of the Middle East is probably the most complicated and contentious of any region on earth, reaching back into biblical days and beyond, riven by national and religious wars, and subject to the impact of successive invasions. Handal's thesis addresses aspects of Jerusalem from the perspective of her, 'own sense of her place in the world … informed by a family history of intergenerational movements across disparate geographies – ones provoked by various forces whether it be war, occupation, coups d'état, and/or economic difficulties – and all of which link historically to Palestine.' Her sense of a personal geography that goes against the usual identification with a homeland has led to the development of what she refers to as her 'polyglot imagination' that relates to the many places in which she and her family have lived, and to her upbringing in a home in which Arabic, French, Creole, English and Spanish were spoken, giving her no single mother tongue. She was born in Haiti to a family with roots in Bethlehem. Her early life was in the Dominican Republic and, since her teens, has been in Europe, with regular visits to the occupied territories of Palestine. It is therefore inevitable that her sense of identity, and the creative work that springs from it, comes from the disparity of influences that shaped her growing.

In general, it is true that a work of art should communicate directly without additional documentation or explanation. It

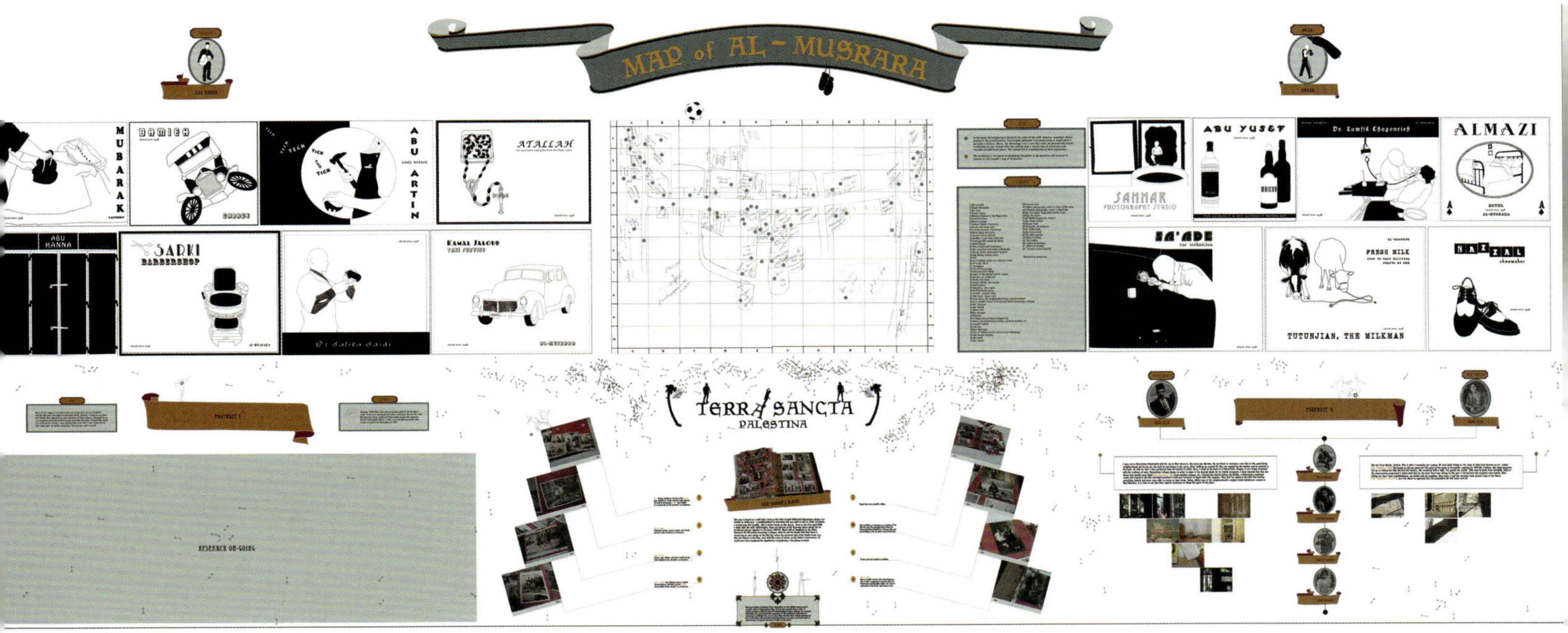

Alexandra Handal, *Vanishing Point 1*, 2008-10. Giclée print on Hahnemühle paper. 100 x 250cm (39¼ x 98½in.).

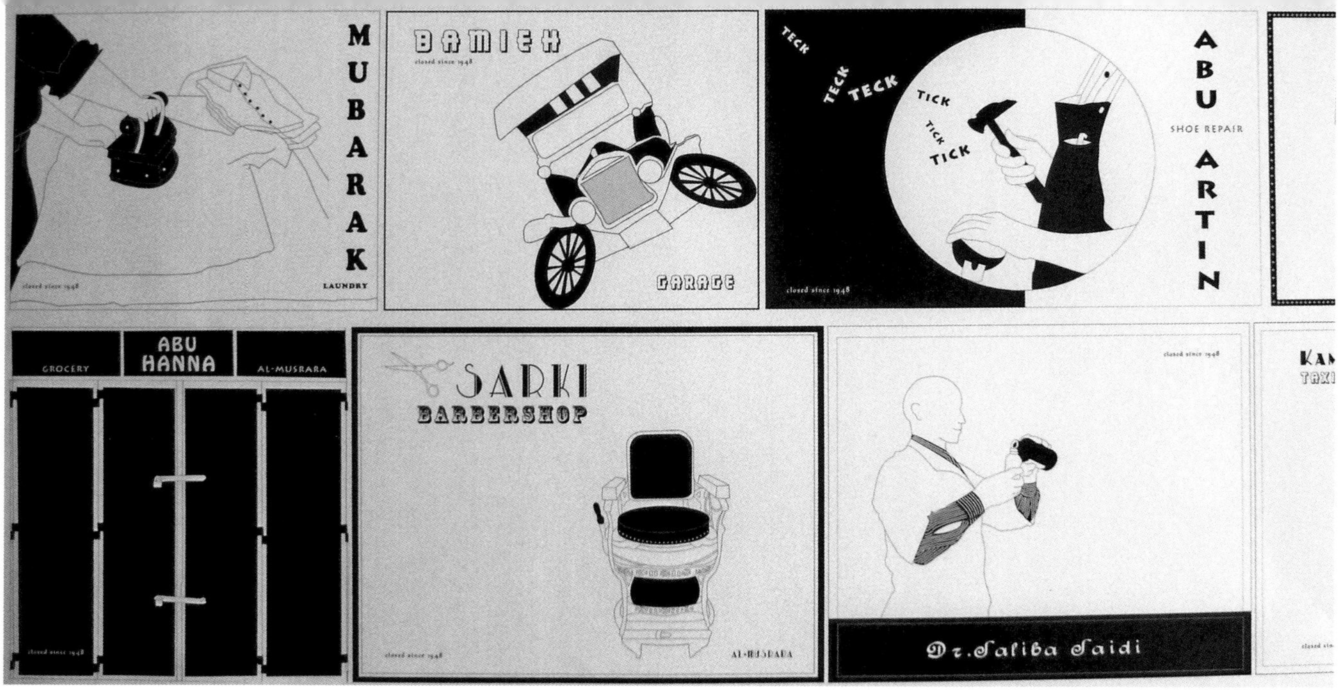

Alexandra Handal, *Vanishing Point* (detail).

is also true that understanding more of the background of the artist and the work can deepen comprehension and enhance the experience of encountering the work. There is, however, a strand of contemporary visual art that has a strongly documentary element, and benefits from a broader understanding than that given solely by a visual encounter, in which the provision of background text becomes an integral component. Handal's work comes into this category, mapping her own experience of East Jerusalem through notes, sketches and photographs, with additional contributions from the recollections, memories and photographs of others she met during research for her thesis. This form of documentary approach enables the possibility of presenting a rich visual and intellectual experience through a mixture of images and texts. Given the subject matter, and the artist's clear desire to offer the possibility of a fuller understanding of a complex situation, her work invariably straddles the realms of art, communication, social history and geography, and politics. It is very different to 'a picture to hang on a wall', and depends for its success on the willingness of the viewer to engage positively and actively with it.

Vanishing Point I is the first in what is planned to be a series of documentary art works made in response to Handal's personal history and experiences of the Palestinian parts of Jerusalem, as they once were and as they now are. Taking the form of prints, each of which will be 1.0m x 2.5m (39.4 x 98.4 in.), the series is based on personal research, on the recollections of local Palestinians of localities that are now gone and the people who once lived there, and also albums of photographs belonging to them that form a fading record of those people and the places and buildings within which they lived their lives. Handal's nomadic early life contrasts with the memories of what were once stable communities, but which have now been disrupted by conflict and by the compulsory purchase of properties as Jewish communities seek to expand throughout the city. The artist can take a view from the outside, having a wider experience of the world, but at the same time she can empathise strongly with the people she meets and their stories. Cities the world over are organic, made up of a multitude of small histories, homes and businesses, and those who lived and worked there, shifting and changing over periods of time, each with stories and mythologies of their own, and each the product of a collective imagination. As Handal writes in her thesis, 'Cities have captured the human imagination, yet it is safe to say that none has done so in such an intense and impassioned manner as Jerusalem – known in Arabic as "Al-Quds" (Holy City) and in Hebrew as "Yerushaláyim" (City of Peace).'

The prints resulting from the work Handal has done are in the form of large wall charts, with maps, diagrams, panels of text, photographs and digital images, all produced as a large single print. There is a map drawn by Issa Soudah, a local resident, a week after he took a walk with the artist in April 2008. The map depicts the streets of the former Palestinian district of Al-Masrara, which was split in half in 1948, and the individual merchants and shopkeepers who lived there, each of whom had their own tale to tell. These stories are retold by the artist, shifting them from oral history to visual form and changing them in her retelling, transforming them into a kind of archive in an imagined museum. The digital images are of fictional businesses, based on historic ones, simply drawn and lettered, each bearing the words, 'closed since 1948', the year in which the modern state of Israel gained independence and the life of the indigenous Arab and Palestinian peoples was disrupted, broken. With careful reading and thought the past regains some of its former life, albeit changed forever by the tides of history.

LEENA NAMMARI

BORN IN THE UK to a Palestinian family, her father an orthopaedic surgeon, Leena Nammari spent her first few years in Scotland before moving back with her family to live in Ramallah, on the West Bank. It was there that she graduated from school in 1988, the year of the first Intifada (uprising), whereupon she returned to Scotland with her sister to study for her higher exams. She writes, 'Unsure what to do I ended up starting nursing training in Edinburgh, right after coming back from home, and the First Gulf War, having witnessed Scud missiles sailing overhead. I finished training in 1994, and worked as a staff nurse for a couple of years. During this time I sat for my art higher exam, and later started an art and design course at Duncan of Jordanstone College of Art and Design in Dundee, graduating with a BA (Hons) Degree in Fine Art Printmaking.'

She worked in a number of jobs and artist residencies before taking a job at the highly regarded Edinburgh Printmakers in 2005, where she has since remained as studio technician. This background, briefly, has provided the basis upon which Nammari has built a strong reputation for her expertise in printmaking and for the creation of an idiosyncratic and powerful body of work. It has also given her a particular focus on the nature of the problems faced by the Palestinian people on account of the Israeli occupation of their lands, as well as the need to come to terms with belonging to one country with its numerous political and social troubles – and dealing with the range of emotions that arise from her separation from what is still her home – while living and working in another.

She has said that she has been in love with printmaking since she first encountered it during her first year at college, and that through this she 'found home artistically'. Never having been a particularly strong draughtswoman, she found that she could use photographic methods to capture and process images, though not as straightforward photographs as she has never wanted to be a photographer. Screenprinting and darkroom photography formed the backbone of her college studies, and she taught herself to use Liquid Light, which initially enabled her to produce monochromatic images, and then later, through the use of screenprinting, to add in colour; she has remained with this process and variations on it ever since.

Liquid Light is an emulsion, analogous to the light-sensitive surface of photographic printing paper, which can be applied to a wide range of surfaces, upon which images can fixed using an enlarger or projector, or by contact printing, for subsequent processing in a similar way to the production of analogue photographic prints. As such, although it is a difficult process to perfect, it provides the means for the creation of images on surfaces other than photographic paper, which can then be manipulated during the processing to create a wide range of effects. Nammari has also developed ways of using cyanotype, an analogue technique from the early days of photography that produces images in a distinct range of blues, and in addition a range of photo-etching techniques. She has a good knowledge of paper types and

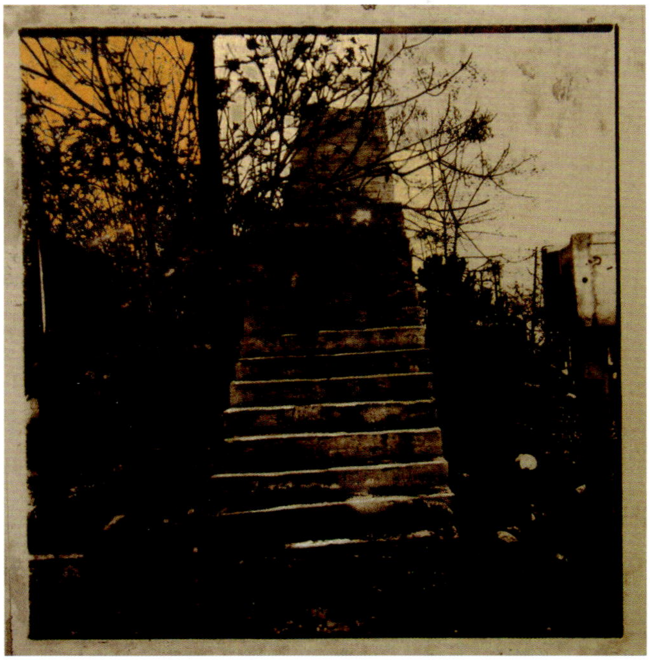

Leena Nammari, *Stairs*, 2011. Etching and gold paint, mounted on MDF, 20 x 20cm (8 x 8in.).

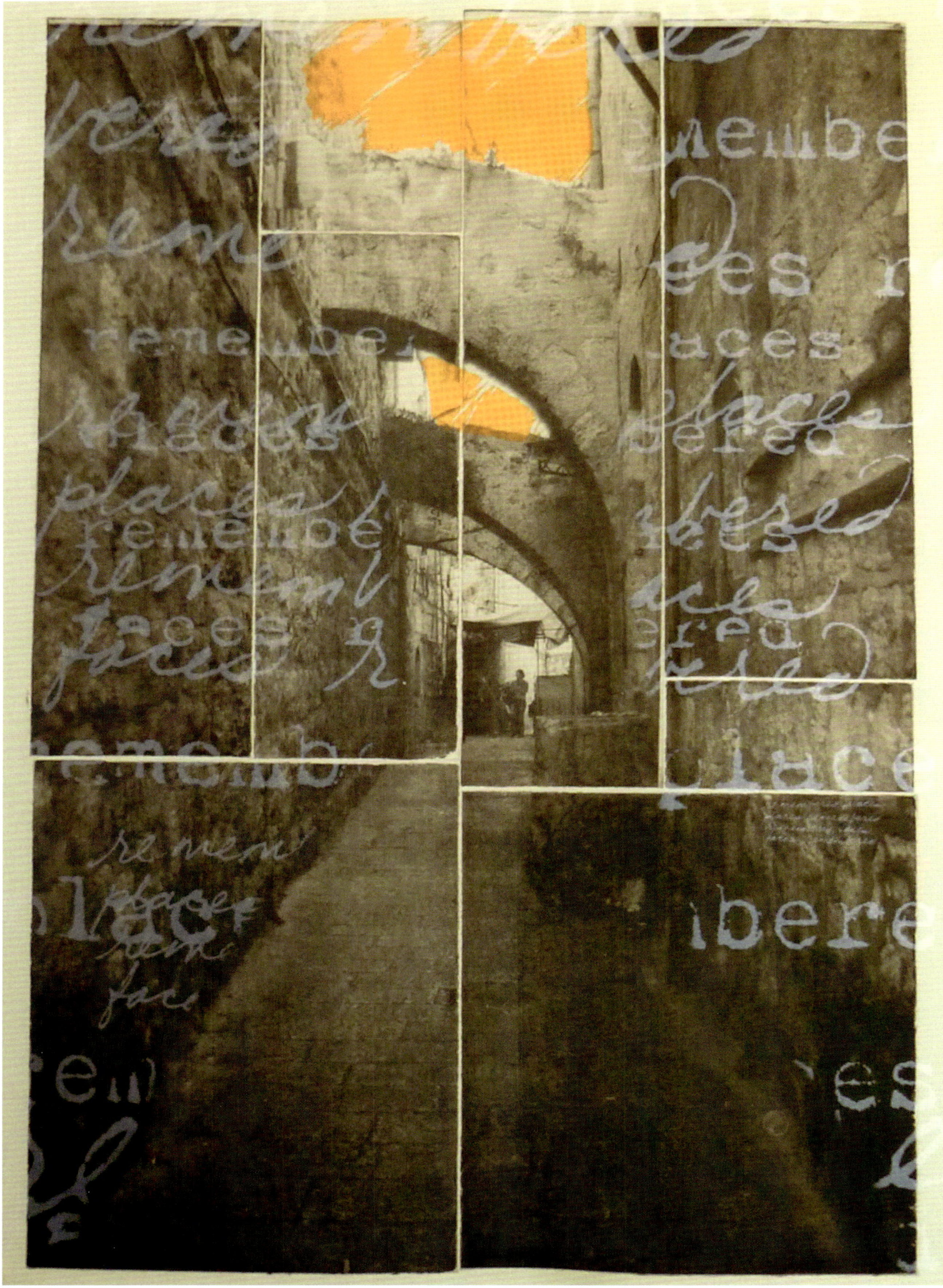

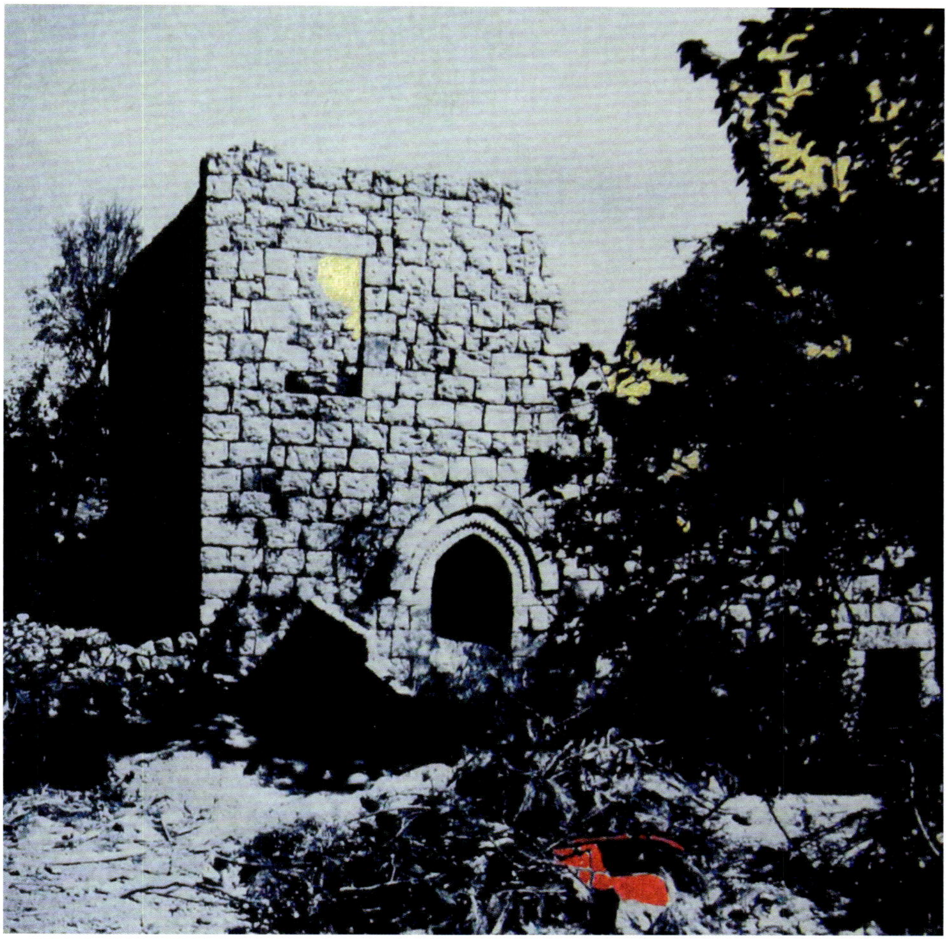

Left: Leena Nammari, *Remembered Places – Arches*, 2011. Etching, screenprinting, stitching and PVC, 70 x 50cm (27½ x 19¾in.).

Right: Leena Nammari, *Off the Beaten Track – Birzeit Ruins*, 2011. Cyanotype and gold paint, mounted on MDF, 15 x 15cm (6 x 6in.)..

surfaces, which appeals to her in that, as she has written, she has led 'a somewhat peripatetic existence, moving from one place to another quite frequently', and has found paper to be essentially a portable medium.

Printmaking appeals to her for its aesthetic qualities rather than as a medium for producing editions, something that she rarely does, and only then in small editions of four or five. The medium also appeals to her because of the flatness of the images produced and the way in which different sizes and colours can be used to control how the image appears. In addition, she enjoys printmaking as a social/communal activity and writes that 'the alchemical/science/mysterious part of the art making gives me quite a thrill', something with which many printmakers will agree.

Leena Nammari's work is usually produced to a small format, often as small as 20 x 20cm (8 x 8 in.), partly due to the limitations of her chosen processes and partly to retain the essential sense of intimacy that she wishes to convey. The images originate from photographs that she has taken in and around her childhood home in Palestine, and more rarely within her current apartment. They have a sense of being highly personal, but also have wider resonances for those who see them, creating a kinship to the places that they have seen and which remain, half-undiscovered, within memory. This gives them an air of melancholy but also a sense of quiet recording of the mutability of human habitations, which in turn becomes a requiem for those places that disappear through conflict or neglect, rendered beyond recovery except through memory or through these attempts to capture them in some form.

Stairs is a photo-etching on grey paper, mounted on painted MDF and embellished with gold acrylic paint. Nammari came across the stairs in Birzeit, a small town outside Ramallah, and notes that they were built without a house and nothing is attached to them – they are stairs leading nowhere, linking the disputed earth with the sky. *Remembered Places – Arches* is a photo-etching with screen print sewn onto PVC, one of a series based on photographs taken in the old city of Jerusalem, in places that the artist always revisits on her journeys home, to see if they are still there. *Birzeit Ruins* is a cyanotype with acrylic gold on litho paper, mounted on painted MDF, again one of a series exploring scenes from her childhood and recording their gradual degradation through enforced and involuntary neglect. These works contain a rare combination of the celebratory and elegiac, a form of visual poetry capturing fugitive images to be recollected in tranquillity.

TURKEY: ISTANBUL

THE MAJESTIC SKYLINE of the ancient quarter of Istanbul, the legendary heart of Byzantium, contains the domes and minarets of the Blue Mosque, Hagia Sophia, the Süleymaniye and other smaller mosques, and the roofscape of the Topkapi Palace, which turns into a complex series of silhouettes as the afternoon fades towards sunset. This justly renowned sight is best seen from certain hidden places on the hills of Beyoğlu, on the other side of the Golden Horn. Although I visited such buildings, as was both necessary and inevitable, I found myself drawn during my work in Istanbul to the less spectacular but infinitely more complicated streets and buildings of Beyoğlu. That is where I stayed, and where I worked on the installation of the 4th International Print Exhibition, for which I was curator, in the extraordinary building that is Tophane-i-Amire. Built as a foundry for cannon and ball by Sultan Mehmet the Conqueror, it is now used for exhibitions by the Mimar Sinan Fine Arts University. A high echoing building of stone and brick, at the foot of a steep hill above the harbour that stretches along the northern shore of the Bosphorus, where the vast cruise liners moor and disgorge their own golden hordes of tourists as they head for the tourist sites. Many of them fail to visit the excellent galleries of Istanbul Modern, one of the best museums for contemporary art in Europe, alongside which the cruise ships are moored.

Orhan Pamuk, the celebrated Turkish Nobel Prize Laureate for Literature, is from Beyoğlu and makes his home there. There, too, in 2012 he opened his 'Museum of Innocence', in which he displays the ordinary objects and everyday artefacts that play their part in his 2008 novel of the same name. In *Istanbul – Memories and the City*, he writes about the mysterious streets and concealed histories of this quarter, drawing out the character of the place and the characters who inhabit it. He writes of the melancholic aspect of Istanbul, something that can be more easily felt in this part of the city than in the tourist-filled ancient quarter, and which reveals itself in the smaller details rather than the large picture. I walked past the ruins of a small hammam, overgrown with weeds and fig trees, and came across Sufi gravestones in a tiny graveyard between two shops, each marker stone topped with a carved depiction of the headwear that marks the sect or rank of the deceased – these also are overgrown and the sunlight filters through interlaced branches.

There are countless cats everywhere, sleek and thin, heavy and dirty, clustering in family groups of similar colour and marking, looked after by old men and women who give them dried food, and put down containers of fresh water for them to drink. The midday heat of September stills the movements of the cats and a heavy silence hangs between the houses either side of the steep narrow streets that wind up the hill to Taksim Square or down to the water's edge. One sometimes catches a glimpse of the Galata Tower on the top of its hill; indeed, it is a landmark, but finding it among the maze of streets means a frustrating search as the tower disappears and reappears, and the constant twists of the streets lead to a sense of disorientation. The main street in this part of the city is Istiklal Caddesi, now largely pedestrianised between Tünel and Taksim, and here can be found all manner of goods and places to eat and drink, or to offer diversion. In the evenings and at weekends the street is the place for walking up and down looking at all the other people doing just the same thing, and dodging the few remaining historic tramcars that shuttle constantly from one end of the street to the other.

What gradually becomes apparent in wandering around this city – and wandering is the best way to see it – is that there are multiple layers of history to be explored and stories to uncover. Few tourists visit Little Hagia Sophia, a perfect small mosque that, like the famous church turned mosque turned museum that is Hagia Sophia, was designed by Mimar Sinan, and pre-dates the larger building. Not too far away is the Basilica Cistern built by Emperor Justinian in 532 CE; visitors enter through a doorway on one street and descend into a huge space of ranks of columns standing in the water, to make their way along the walkways and climb the stairs to emerge on a different street. What also becomes apparent is that, as ever, Istanbul is in a state of change, with a tangible sense of tension between the attempts to exert a stronger Islamic orthodoxy and the equally strong desire for modernity. This tension can be seen in the clothes that people wear in the street, veering from high fashion to modest traditional clothes; it can also be seen in the work of contemporary artists, and therein lies some indication of how the next stage in Istanbul's fascinating history may develop, as the tension between fundamentalism and modernity achieves some sort of resolution.

ASLI TÜRKELI

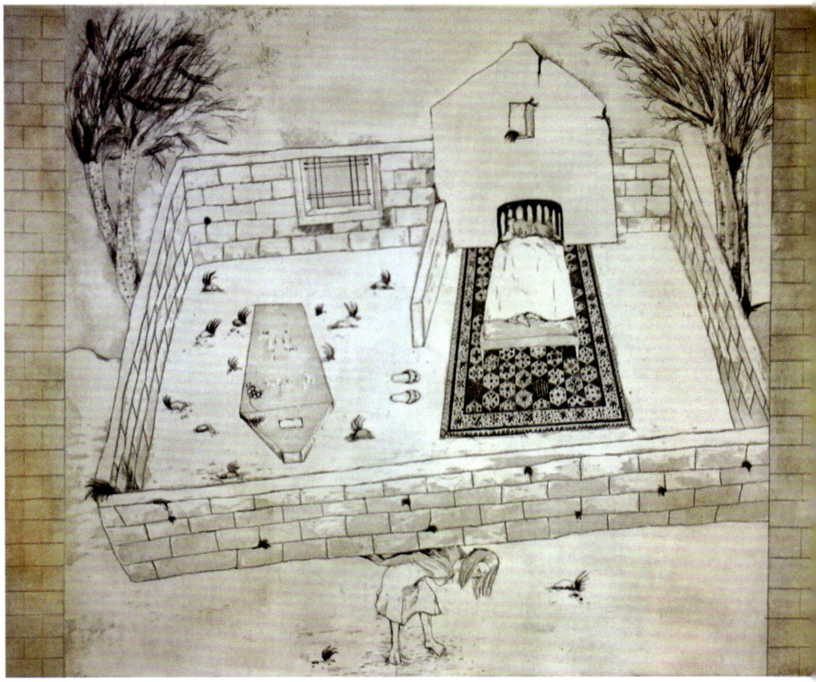

Asli Türkeli, *Quest for Privacy 4*, 2011. Etching, 45 x 60cm (17¾ x 23½in.).

BESIDE THE EASTERN end of the highway that crosses the Bosphorus on the Golden Horn Bridge there is a sign in Turkish and English that reads, 'Welcome to Asia'. This is not only geographically accurate but also a strong reminder that Turkey is now, as throughout millennia of history, a country that bridges two continents. It also signifies the unique cultural contradictions running through Turkish society, which are not immediately apparent to the casual tourist. Walking through the city one becomes aware that, discounting tourists and visitors, there are two distinct cultures clearly evident in the contrasting styles of fashions worn by younger women. One bears the hallmarks of Islamic conservatism and the other is indistinguishable from the fashionable clothing of young women in many parts of the Western world. These outward signs are linked to the twin currents in society, one that is conservative in outlook and turns towards traditional and fundamental Islamic values, the other showing a more liberal identification with the openness of European social democracy. The consequent tensions that arise affect politics and social development, and can also be identified in the contemporary Turkish arts.

Asli Türkeli was born in Istanbul in 1985 and graduated in Combined Arts in 2011 from the Yildiz Technical University. She works as an artist and designer, with painting, printmaking, typography, media art and jewellery among her activities. Her work has been exhibited in a number of local and international exhibitions since 2003, and is mainly derived from her observations and experience of her private life and the society in which she lives. Her home is in the Uskudar district – a quiet conservative and traditional suburb on the Asian side of the Bosphorus that in centuries past was deemed to be the part of Istanbul closest to Mecca, and therefore the place in which rich and pious Ottoman figures built mosques. As a young woman artist Türkeli is keenly aware of the contrasts and tensions in Istanbul society, particularly those that affect the lives of women. She describes her work as being her means of demonstrating the ways in which women have to live their lives in private and public spaces under the norms of traditional and religious society that have penetrated every aspect of life. By choosing to depict surrealist rather than actual architectural spaces within which her characters play out their lives, Türkeli aims to draw attention to man/woman relationships, 'deformed by an unfair burden that makes the woman submissive through religion and moral values, including betraying as well as being betrayed.'

She is closely aware of the double standards under which some young women live their lives – far more constrained than young men, and obliged therefore to adopt evasive and potentially deceiving strategies if they wish to pursue their right to the freedom of action that is taken for granted in more liberal societies. She writes, 'In my works I criticise the position of women in Turkish society and under Islam ... I would like that all women would like their lives, their bodies, freely, without hiding or lying.' This theme clearly has profound implications for the ways in which her work would be viewed by different communities within contemporary Istanbul society: while being appealing to many of her contemporaries it might well cause offence among older traditional communities.

In the series entitled *Quest for Privacy*, Asli Türkeli has created an alternative sense of the spaces within which her cast of anonymous figures pursue their lives and more particularly their desires. She designs the spaces as if they were stage sets, echoing the traces of past architecture but offering stages on which small dramas may be played out. Any sense of privacy is fragmentary at best in these

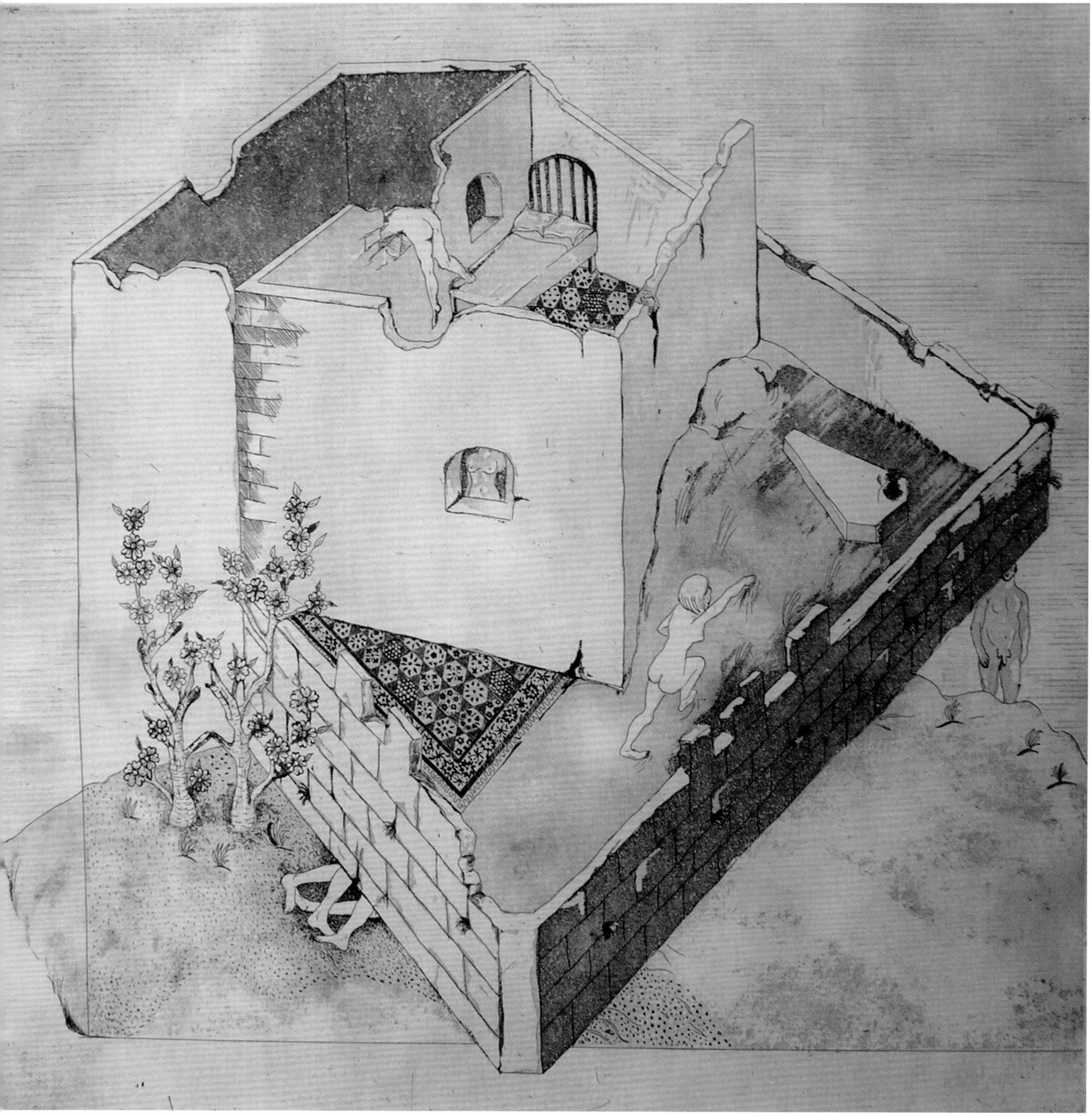

Asli Türkeli, *Quest for Privacy 2*, 2011. Etching, 55 x 45cm.

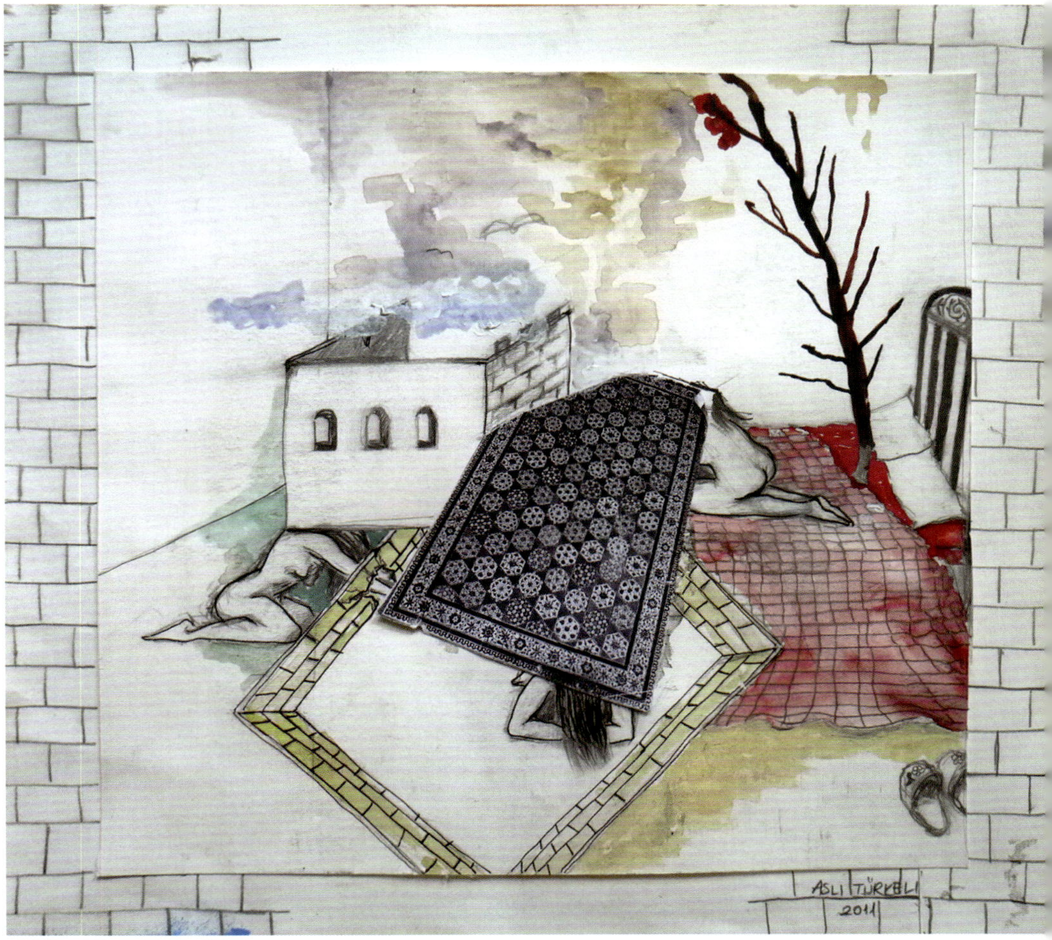

Asli Türkeli, *I Was There Too*, 2011. Sketch/collage for etching, 23 x 27cm (9 x 10¾in.).

settings, and the pervasive gaze of society and religion is suggested: any hope of escape for the protagonists is forbidden as they are trapped within the depicted spaces, and within the bounds of the print or paper. The choice of medium, whether etching or sketches for etching, is deliberate, allowing the artist to create a series of tentative spaces with the implications of societal pressure and the wrath of retribution and damnation on the male and female characters. In addition the female figures are shown as submissive, bearing – sometimes literally – the weight of responsibility for their actions in the shabby rundown places within which they attempt to pursue their affairs.

In *Quest for Privacy 4* a rectangular enclosure, reminiscent of the *hortus conclusus* paradise gardens of Islamic miniatures, contains remnants of a building, a tombstone, a neatly placed pair of slippers and an ornate carpet upon which there is a bed where a sheet covers two recumbent figures. Two trees stand outside the enclosure, which is itself lifted or supported by the bent figure of a woman. There is no visible way in to the enclosure and the window on the back wall is barred. The drama being enacted within is silent, stilled, and offers equal interpretations of desperation and sanctuary, but there is no resolution. In *Quest for Privacy 2* the architecture is more complex and the depicted drama more puzzling. Two figures lie under a wall, their limbs entangled, and a naked male watches from beyond the rocky edge. There are two naked female figures within the rectangular forms of the enclosure and a building set on top of it with a confusing perspective. As before there are carpets and an empty bed within the enclosed spaces, and trees on the outside, suggesting some sort of resolution from within the natural world, but in the drama being played out there is none, the figures are stilled and silent. A series of sketches in charcoal with colour show other scenarios in which men and women pursue their quests for privacy in a troubling world.

IREM SEVGÖR

THE LONG-STANDING distrust of traditional printmakers for digital techniques seems to have been more or less resolved, and digital techniques are now accepted in most international competitions. The position of pure photography remains in dispute, which is curious, since the world has long been used to the idea of photographic 'prints'. However, there is one area of photographic techniques that remains little known or understood, except to a few practitioners, and that is the use and modification of some of the photographic processes that pre-date the digital era. These techniques offer much to the innovative artist, and include some that do not require the possession of a fully equipped darkroom. What they do require is a willingness to experiment and to become closely involved with the chemistry and manipulation of materials. Irem Sevgör has been drawn to these alternative printing techniques, either singly or in combination. She cites as reasons their antique aesthetic, and their potential for conveying a wide range of emotional states, including an inherent sadness and melancholy, and surreal, dreamlike images. Although interested in art since childhood, she studied sciences at school and went on to study economics at university before moving on to her present master's course in media and design in the Turkish capital, Ankara, where she lives.

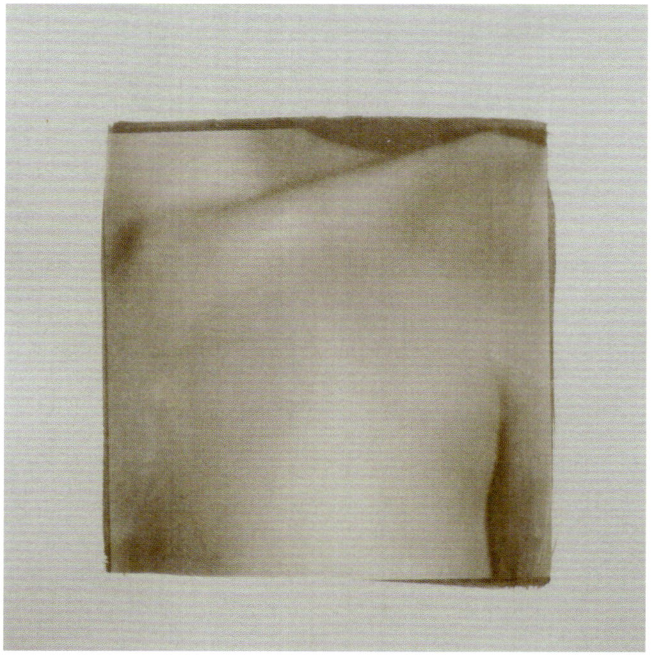

Irem Sevgör, *September 2010 – Self-Portrait* (from the *Naked* series), 2010. Vandyke Brown Sun Print on Canson paper, 23 x 30cm (9 x 11¾in.).

The attraction of working with her hands is important to this artist; she does not get on with digital techniques, which she believes lack the necessary sensitivity she seeks. What is also important for her is the potential for the unexpected or coincidental results that come from her artist's approach to her chosen methods of working. In addition, Sevgör is drawn to the possibility of exploring combinations of screenprinting, analogue photography and painting in her work. In some respects this approach makes her akin to those early pioneers of photography who began as artists using traditional mediums such as painting and drawing, before getting drawn into exploring what was at that time the cutting-edge technology of cameras, at a time before the separate discipline of photography had been established.

As Sevgör clearly realises, an artist's choice of medium depends on finding the best means for interpreting a personal vision, as well as using a technique with which she already has familiarity, in her case analogue photography. Her output of new images is small and, she writes, 'I just try to concentrate on the production and get pleasure from the process, without considering the reason or the conclusion. I produce spontaneously but slowly.' Her practice is therefore somewhat hermetic, working on her own with relatively simple techniques, to realise images that stem from an instant and individual response to visual and conceptual stimuli – 'shooting from the hip' as it were – and creating an idiosyncratic and unusual vision of the world.

Her images can be grouped into three general themes: 'Outside', 'Inside' and 'Naked'. Within each of these is a carefully conceived and made group of works that, taken together, present an individual and unusual vision of contemporary Turkey. There is a timelessness to the images,

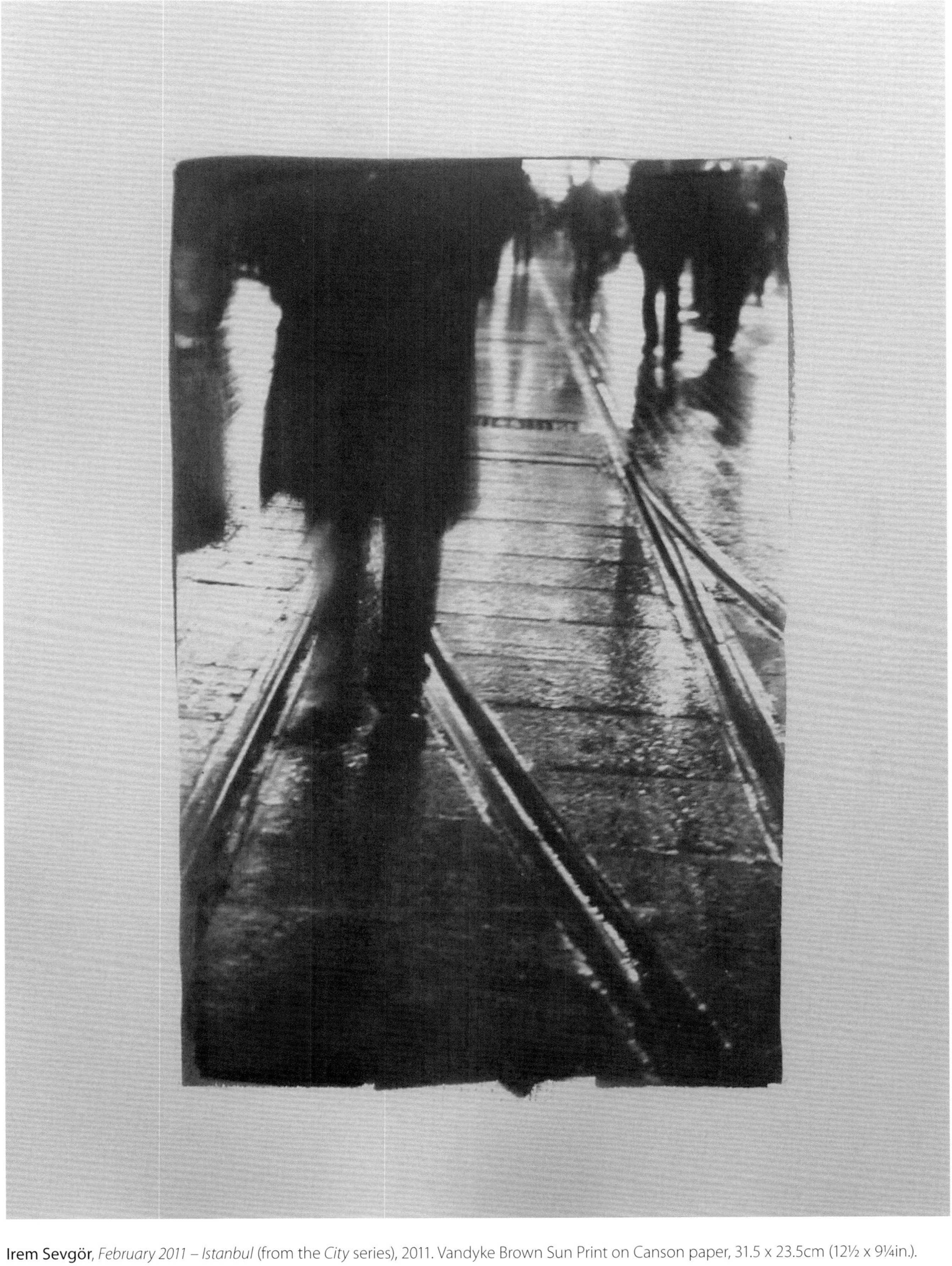

Irem Sevgör, *February 2011 – Istanbul* (from the *City* series), 2011. Vandyke Brown Sun Print on Canson paper, 31.5 x 23.5cm (12½ x 9¼in.).

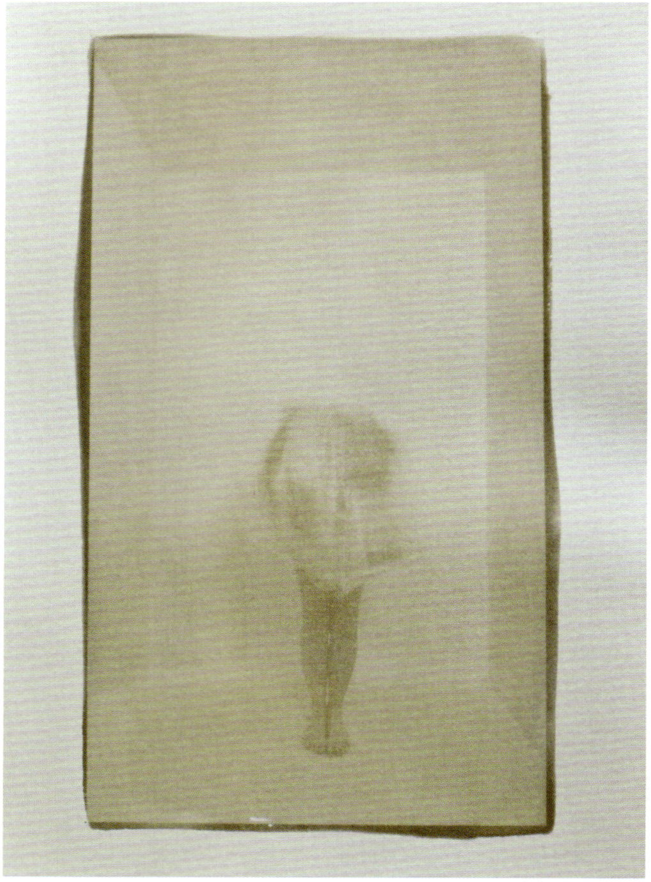

Irem Sevgör, *January 2012* – from *Ceteris Paribus – Abracadabra*, 2012. Vandyke Brown Sun Print on paper, 34.5 x 22.6cm (13½ x 9in.).

partly due to the manner in which they are made, and partly due to their inherent sense of poetry and melancholy mystery. The prints that she makes from the images are for the most part small, giving an intimacy and provoking a need to approach her work closely in order to reach some form of understanding and rapport. The 'Outside' images are mostly taken in Ankara or Istanbul, often at night, with wet streets and reflections, movement-blurred people and cars, feelings of loneliness and alienation, noise, images of rushing without clear purpose, the pursuit of a living, or profit, consuming and being consumed – all of which can be found in any city on earth.

Such images therefore transcend specific references to place and become instead symbolic of the urban world, upon which viewers may place their own recollections and experiences. The 'Inside' images are narrative, imagined and created by Sevgör. A single figure and sometimes a chair, is placed centrally within a confined space – a cell perhaps. Other than the limits of the cell no part of these images is clearly resolved, the figure is transitory, his or her identity is not revealed, nor is their purpose within the space. The figures are blurred, as if fading or appearing, and while such images might in other hands take on a sinister message, in this artist's hands they become puzzling, contradictory and captured in a moment of stillness. The world in which the figures are placed is Kafkaesque, hinting at the depersonalisation of the individual in contemporary society.

The 'Naked' images are, by their nature, intimate and personal. In common with a number of other artists Irem Sevgör uses her own body as both the subject and object of the images, being both artist and model. She can therefore retain close control of the image, framing and cropping it to create an abstraction that is both revealing and concealing, retaining a gentle eroticism and celebration of the human form. Through these depictions of herself the artist is also opening out the possibility of representing a generic form, celebrating the humanity of nakedness in much the same way as classical sculpture.

Although Sevgör's work is made in Turkey by a Turkish artist it does not make demands on the viewer to regard it as being location-specific. It is more abstract and the space in which the images are made is more generalised. Her images are of a world with which she is both intimately connected and yet from which she can maintain a strong sense of separation, of being the dispassionate observer, the eye looking steadily on the world, capturing it and then re-presenting it for the gaze of others. Placed somewhere between photography and printmaking her work offers a calmly critical and poetic vision.

ROMANIA: BUCHAREST

BUCHAREST, the capital of Romania, lies towards the southern border of a large but sparsely inhabited country, and before the Second World War was described as 'the Paris of the East'. Over the following decades, the country became increasingly little known, a remote place behind the Iron Curtain where few travellers ventured. That was until the tumultuous last days of the repressive dictatorship under Nicolae Ceaușescu in December 1989, when Romania was thrust into the global limelight. In the 23 years since then the changes have been considerable, especially since the accession of the country as a full member of the EU at the beginning of 2007.

I was prepared to encounter a crowded city with traffic congestion and the omnipresent traces of Ceaușescu's regime among the destruction of parts of the city centre. In that respect I was not disappointed, but I was not so prepared to see an up-to-date European city with elegant parks among the eclectic architectural styles of the past – an intriguing palimpsest of past cultures. Neither did I expect to encounter a cosmopolitan lifestyle with a vibrant café culture in the heart of the old part of the centre. Within this mixture of cultures and lifestyles there is a strong contemporary arts community, with numerous private galleries complementing a rich variety of state museums and art galleries. I was not able to travel more widely in the country due to my research commitments, so an exploration of the culturally rich cities of Timisoara and Cluj-Napoca, as well as the renowned natural environment of Transylvania and the north, will have to wait for another time. What I did manage was to accumulate some snapshot impressions of an intriguing city.

Herăstrău Park is huge, containing wooded walks and a large lake, beside which is the National Village Museum, an open-air display of conserved historic buildings relocated there from villages throughout the country. One of Europe's oldest open-air museums, it allows the beginnings of an understanding of the richness of the country's vernacular architecture, mostly of wooden construction. Another smaller park, the Cișmigiu Gardens, has an aviary with pure white peacocks. Many of the roads in this part of north Bucharest are wide boulevards lined with elegant villas dating from the 19th century. By contrast the area around the Palace of Parliament bears witness to the egotistical ambitions of Ceaușescu, who ordered the destruction of a vast area of the old city for the construction of what has been described in the Lonely Planet guide to Romania as 'the crassest and craziest tribute to dictatorial megalomania'. The Palace of Parliament is the second biggest building in the world, after the Pentagon in Washington, D.C. The result is a structure of unbelievable bulk, containing the upper house of the parliament, as well as the cold and unwelcoming National Museum of Contemporary Art, and countless empty rooms.

I was taken by friends to meet Ethel and Silviu Baiaș, two artists and printmakers whose remarkable works were celebrated in the 1970s and 80s, both in Romania and abroad, with exhibitions throughout their native country and also in Europe and Japan; between them they won many awards. Ethel Baiaș was renowned for her *Rhinoceros* series of woodcuts in which the tyrannical Ceaușescu is depicted as a blundering rhinoceros. That these prints were shown in Romania during the dictatorship is remarkable, and their power is undiminished even in more enlightened times. Silviu Baiaș, also a highly regarded illustrator of children's books, achieved equal acclaim for his woodcuts on environmental themes, many of which can now be seen to have been prophetic. Sadly, their work is almost completely ignored in present-day Romania, but deserves to be seen more widely, both there and abroad, where the work would resonate powerfully.

One final snapshot: the press launch for the 5th International Experimental Engraving Biennial, to be staged from December 2012 to Spring 2013, was held at the A-Club in the heart of the old city. The club was down two flights of stairs from the narrow street, painted black, the walls covered with posters, with a small bar, a stage for rock bands, and very smoky. I was reminded of some of the clubs in Liverpool in the early 1970s. After the press launch we climbed back to street level to find crowded bars and restaurants, with terraces beneath bright umbrellas in the heat of the spring evening, making Bucharest feel Mediterranean. I was left with the distinct feeling that there is much more to discover, both in the city and elsewhere, in a fascinating country that is an ideal destination for the culturally inquisitive.

CIPRIAN CIUCLEA

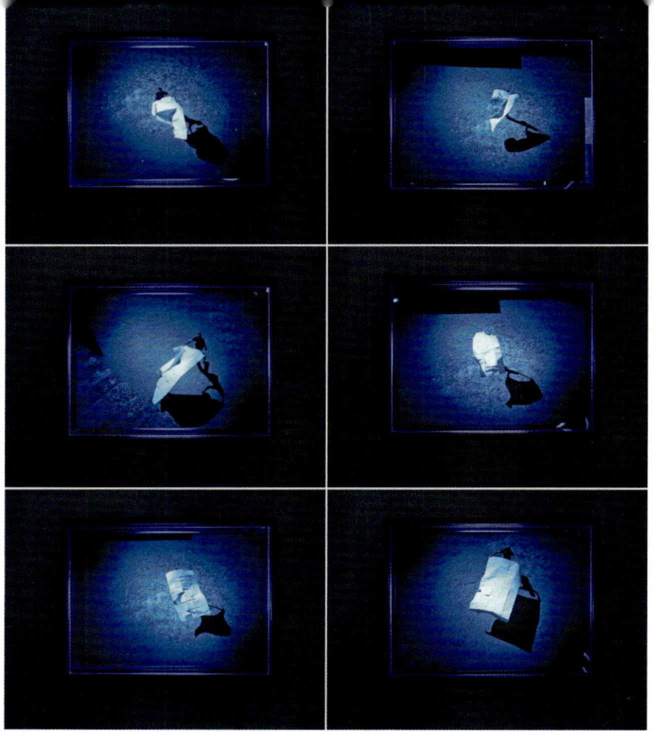

Ciprian Ciuclea, *Apparent Silence, Movement 1–6*, 2011. Ultra-giclée on acetate, six light boxes, each 24 x 35 x 10cm (9½ x 13¾ x 4in.).

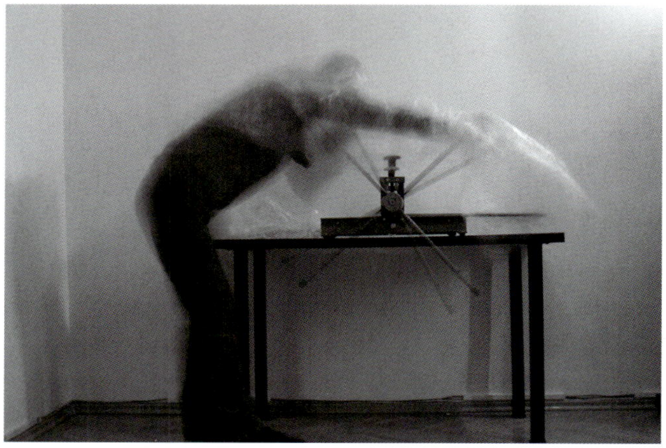

Ciprian Ciuclea, *Process, Sequence B*, 2011. Ultra-giclée on smooth paper, 61 x 76cm (24 x 30in.).

PRINTMAKING TECHNIQUES, as with all art techniques, whether traditional or electronic, take time; they require knowledge, experience and concentration. Looking at art, and actually seeing art, also takes time; coming to an understanding of the artist's intentions takes even longer. All these activities also require practice and concentration. Attempts at creating 'fast art', analogous to creating and consuming 'fast food', inevitably fall short of bringing satisfaction. In an increasingly internationalised society in which it is rare to encounter anyone actually taking time to achieve the best outcome in any activity, time and its passing remain difficult concepts for artists to portray. In the 20th century, the Futurists and, rarely, photographers such as Jacques Lartigue and Harold Edgerton, went some way towards capturing in still form the passing of time. Time is perhaps the most difficult of human concepts to capture and portray in visual form, outside the medium of time-lapse photography, and yet time remains a fascination for many people, artists and viewers alike.

Ciprian Ciuclea, born in Timisoara, a city noted for its part in initiating the revolution that overthrew Ceaușescu and Communism in Romania, graduated from the Western University in the city in 2006. He now lives in Bucharest, where he practises as an artist and designer, and is Director of the International Experimental Engraving Biennial, staged in the Romanian capital. His work has been shown in many national and international solo and group exhibitions, and he has been the recipient of a number of awards. His work is described by the Romanian critic, Adrian Guţă, as being 'inscribed in the area of conceptual-art avatars' with 'A hard economy of means vs. maximum of effect'. Much of it is largely concerned with capturing and portraying time while also dealing with a complex set of other concerns, all based on his perception of his own sensory experience, presented by Ciuclea for contemplation and consideration through a series of installations, images and objects.

Ciuclea's subject matter is drawn from his own experience of sensing the world around him, but also from the disciplines of science, psychology and medicine. He therefore operates between the realms of pure artistic creation and hard empirical research, a sometimes contentious territory that runs the risk of being neither one thing nor another, but which provides a rich point of origin for his work. What remains central to that work is his concentration on the human body, particularly his own, as being the place in which sensory phenomena are registered and processed, and from which his works are then created. Some of those works include him as the subject and also the object, shown performing actions that could be described as rituals, or otherwise being subjected to experiments from which he derives images and further inspiration.

The iconic Vitruvian Man of da Vinci shows Man as the measure of all things; Ciuclea takes this further to the extent that he closes the gap between the artist and the art work, between aesthetic theory and actuality, between art and life. In so doing he presents opportunities for those who encounter it to

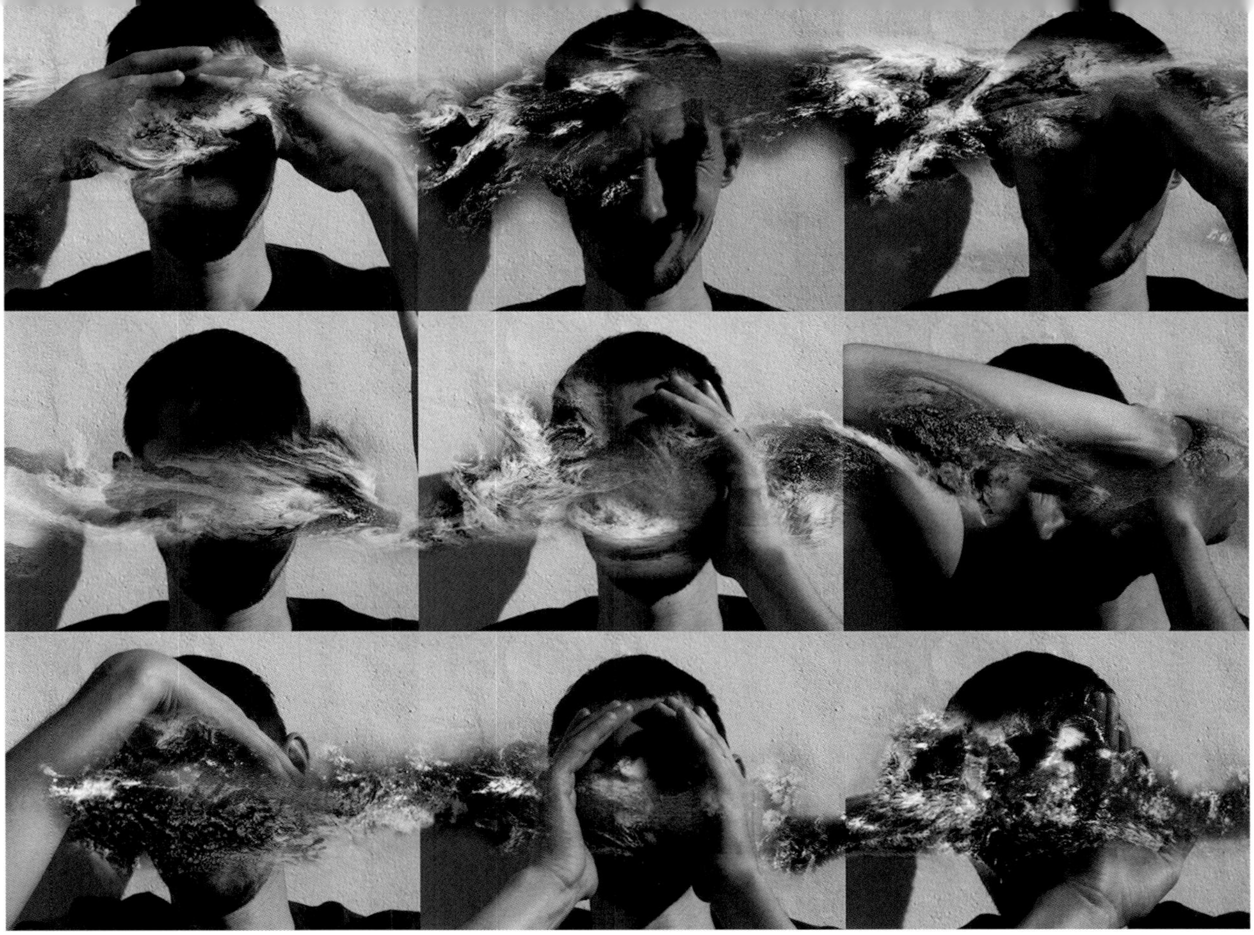

Ciprian Ciuclea, *Auto-Protection 1*, 2009. Ultra-giclée on smooth paper, 75 x 100cm (29½ x 39¼in.).

consider or reconsider their own experience of, or reactions to, sensory phenomena. Much of his work is presented in the form of photographically based prints or video, two current forms of printmaking that serve to bridge another gap – between the work of printmakers and the contemporary art galleries that would, in the past, have found the showing of conventional prints to be outside their interest or remit.

In *Apparent Silence – Movement* the artist is photographed from a high point looking directly down as he attempts to open a large sheet of paper that has been folded and folded again into an ever smaller piece, lit by strong light that forms sharp shadows, while all the time the paper is blown about by the wind. Each of the six images, tinted blue, is built into a light box, so that its illumination comes from within. The six images suggest the movement, while the title suggests that there was the noise of the paper being blown by the wind, but all that remains for the viewer are the six still and silent images, held within the work as they existed, momentarily, when the photographs were taken. The imagination of the viewer is called upon to fill the gap between the images and the deeper meaning of the title.

A similar degree of mystery exists in *Auto-Protection*, a grid of nine sequential photographs of the artist standing against a wall in strong sunlight, moving his hands to shield his eyes. Across and between the space of his eyes and the protective hands are superimposed images of rough water flowing fast. The hands, from the evidence of the photographs, succeed in keeping much of the strong sunlight from the eyes, but fail to protect the eyes from the fast-flowing water. These nine images contain verification of actual hand gestures of protecting the subject from real light, yet offer only symbolic protection from the superimposed images of a torrential flow of water, or rather the illusion of this created by the making of the images using computer software. Illusion and reality are called equally into question.

The title of the third selected image, *Process – Sequence B*, suggests that there were other sequences, but seen alone the image answers no such enquiry. The artist is shown leaning across a table on which there is a small printmaking press, turning the handles of the rollers, as if in the process of creating a print. There is no evidence of which print, if any, was being made, or whether the action had any outcome other than the photographic images taken in a sequence and then selectively superimposed to create an illusion of movement. Once again, nothing is certain, beyond the concrete reality of the printed image.

ORTANSA MORARU

AS WELL AS BEING a natural material, wood is also an eloquent one for those who are able to understand and work with it. The slow pace of growth in a tree is in close correspondence with the climate in which it develops, and, when it is felled and rendered into timber, the knowing eye can find evidence of good and bad growing seasons from the growth rings and the grain. Dendrochronologists are able to analyse a sample drilled from a wooden beam in an old house to determine the age of the building. Trees not only have a crucial role in world ecology and a central part in mythology, but also deep cultural significance in many countries. For all these reasons wood is an entirely appropriate material for artists to use as a matrix in printmaking. Working with wood requires sharp tools and a sharpened mind that understands the nature of the material with the intuition born of experience, together with the stamina needed to work on the matrix over an extended period. In addition the artist has to appreciate the intrinsic challenges offered in both the surface and the deeper grain, and the physical strength required to cut into the wood in order to interpret the drawing and render it as a print. It is perhaps little wonder that many woodcut artists use this medium to produce prints that are narrative in nature: regardless of whether the resulting images are figurative or abstract, or somewhere in between, there is always a story to be told.

Ortansa Moraru grew up in Craiova in Romania and gained her MFA from the fine arts department of Western University in Timisoara, where she is now a PhD candidate. She emigrated to Toronto, Canada in 2002. She has a considerable record of solo and group exhibitions on both sides of the Atlantic, and has received a number of awards. In a statement about her work she writes, 'Printmaking has always been a special medium to me. I have found inspiration in my surroundings. I also enjoy drawing, which strongly influences the two techniques involved when I dream compositions, envision spaces and feel surfaces: woodcut and lithography. Woodcut is the technique through which I have reinvented myself, maybe because of the urge to wrestle something – working against the grain being a dialogue, miraculously balanced by the spectacular results in the quality and accuracy of the cut.' This statement, and her experience of living and working in two contrasting countries with sophisticated and deep-rooted cultures, one deep inside the Southeastern European heartland and the other in North America, provide much of the basis of her work. The process of moving from a natural homeland to an adopted home carries with it a mixture of excitement and difficulties; having to learn to live in a country with a different language is in itself a challenge even before the cultural changes can be assimilated. Moraru writes that she found that, '... all things around me were either too colourful, too big, too many ... quite intimidating sometimes'.

Given her personal story, it is not surprising that the prints she made in the first few years after arriving in Canada were in two series, *Nests* (2006) and *Roots* (2009), with all the resonances and evocations that these words contain. Moraru had come across a supply of cedar boards with rounded corners, and used these to build up larger matrices by combining them in various grids. While being born of expedience, this element remained part of her work for the two series of works, though translated into formed MDF for the *Roots* series. The matrix of *Nest V* comprises six such cedar boards, with the surface grain being incorporated into the deeply cut central motif, a swirling dynamic series of interlaced curves echoing not only the form of natural nests but also the sense of implosion, of being sucked into a new place. This theme is present in all six prints in the series, settling into a near stasis in the final image.

The *Roots* series reflects a different stage in the artist's assimilation of her adopted country, from which she has been able to explore the nature of her relationship with her home culture, as well as her place within the Romanian community in Toronto, and beyond that within the multicultural mix of that city. With matrices built up from multiple sheets of MDF – being a dense, virtually grainless and very stable manmade material that allows for both large deep cuts and intricate detail – the artist has made a series of works of considerably greater complexity. There are two parts to the series of six; within each part the first print is in black and white, while in the second there are

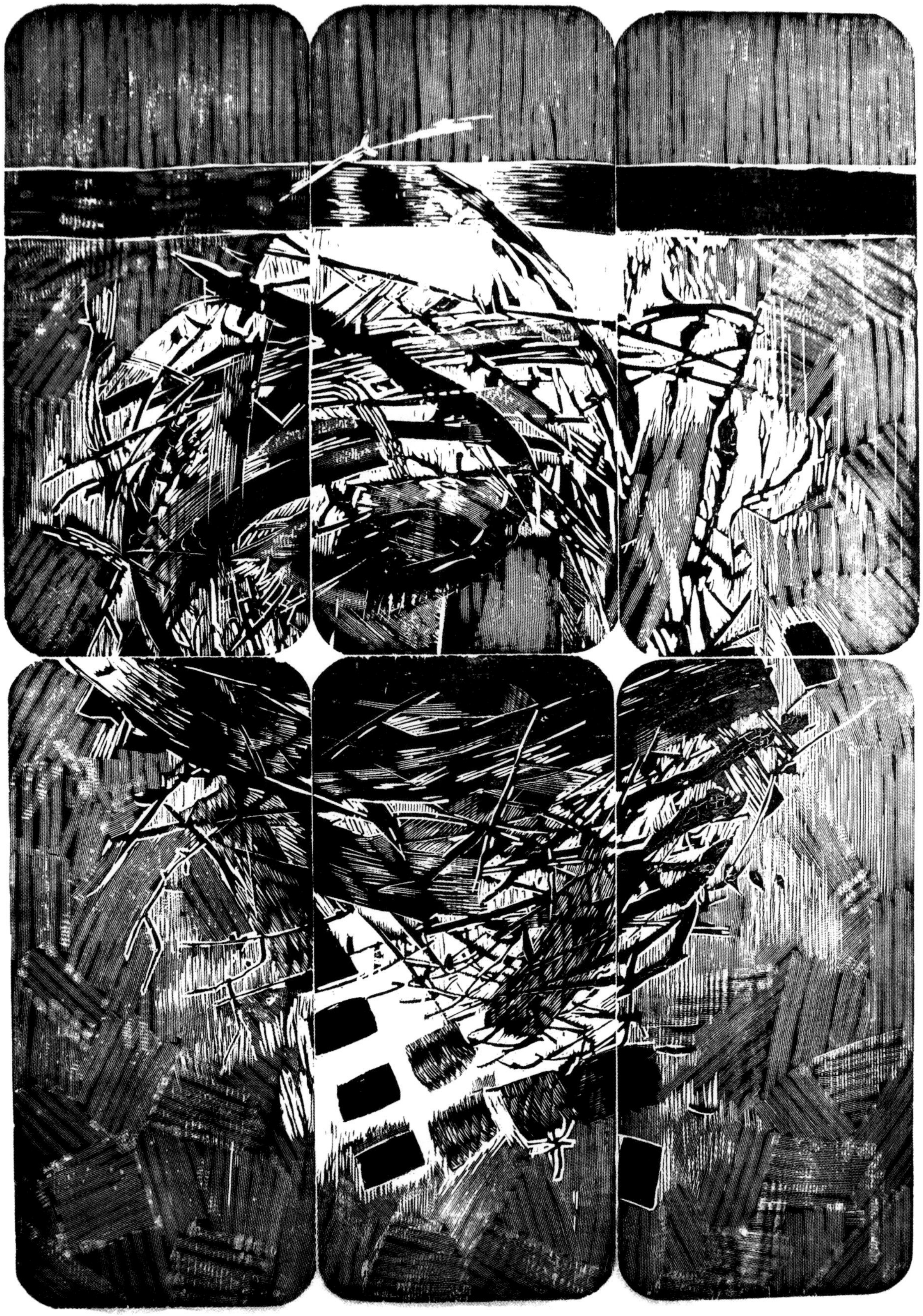

Ortansa Moraru, *Nest V*, 2006. Woodcut, hand-printed from cedar blocks, etching ink on Japanese washi, 75 x 52cm (29½ x 20½in.). Collection: Dr Delia Curea, Toronto. Photo: Alexandru Moraru.

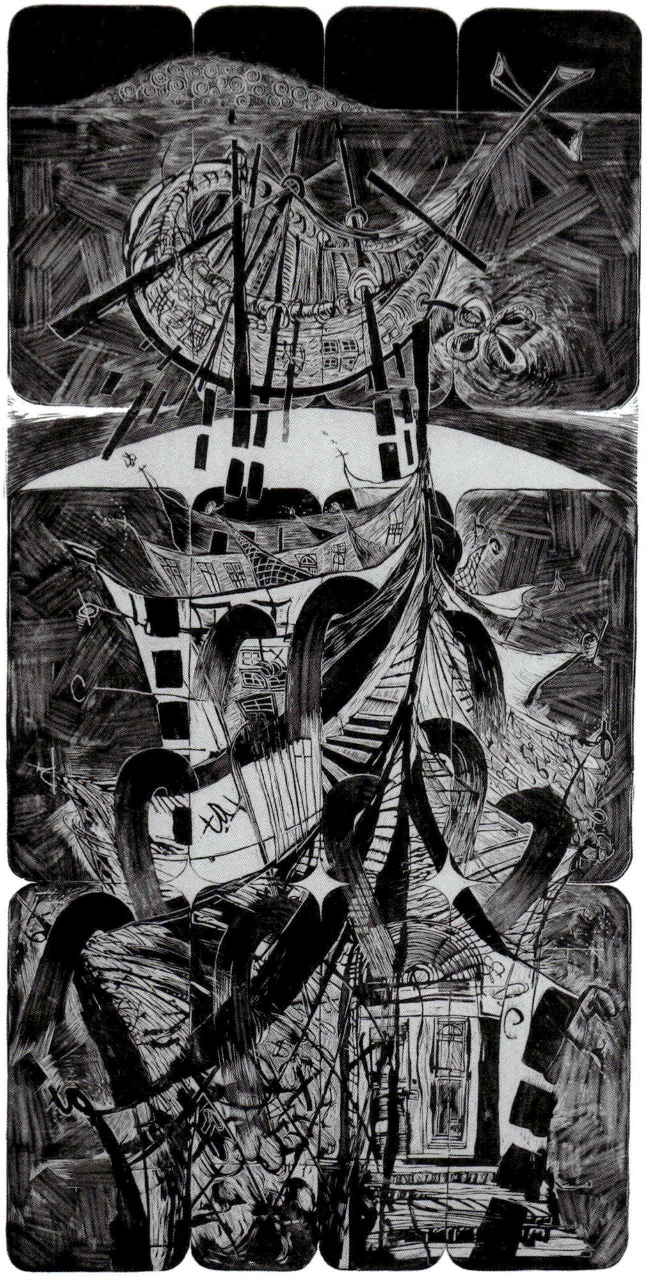

Ortansa Moraru, *Roots I*, 2009. Woodcut, hand-printed from MDF block, etching ink on Japanese washi, 122 x 61cm (48 x 24in.). Photo: Alexandru Moraru.

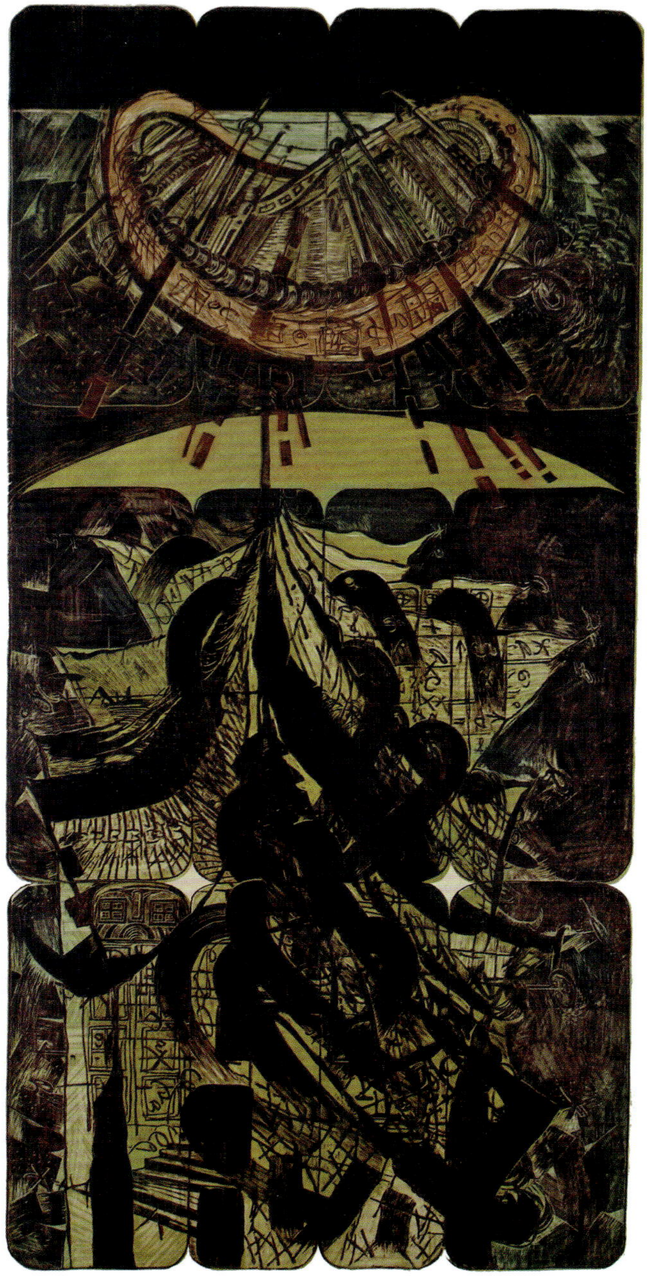

Ortansa Moraru, *Roots VI*, 2009. Woodcut, hand-printed from MDF block, etching ink and Pearl Ex pigment on Japanese washi, 122 x 61cm (48 x 24in.). Photo: Alexandru Moraru.

variations of colour. This has allowed the artist to explore further not only the nature of the landscapes of memory and the connections between them, and the transition from one culture and country to another (to which the images refer), but also the technical challenges of colour, and the ways in which variations can allow an accumulating series of impressions.

Inspired by a return to her homeland in 2010 at the start of her PhD studies, Moraru created a large-scale print installation, *Down the Danube*, in which she traces the course of the lower part of that major European river from the fabled Iron Gates to the broad delta on the Black Sea coast. The prints, large and small scale, with a variety of inks and colour and metallic pigments on Japanese paper, trace the course of the river through a varied landscape which has been shaped by its long history. This installation indicates a further direction for an artist whose consideration of roots and destinations is at the core of her work.

SUZANA FÂNTANÂRIU

THE WOODCUT TECHNIQUE for producing relief prints has a very long history, and includes the masterworks of traditional Japanese artists such as Hokusai and Hiroshige, and the European tradition including the likes of Dürer, the German Expressionists and Frans Masereel. Woodcut provided the means for editions of books and individual prints that could be made at a relatively low cost, and played a major part in the dissemination of ideas, including the influential introduction of Japanese art into Europe during the Impressionist period. More recently, woodcut has gained a major position in contemporary art through prints at large or very large scale, often drawn, cut and printed by the artist; the American artist, Tom Huck, and the German artist, Thomas Kilpper, are among those at the forefront of this renaissance.

The common thread among all woodcut artists is the use of a natural material as the matrix: in some cases solid wood with its variable and sometimes unpredictable grain; in others plywood, often with a birch surface that allows consistently fine detail. In all cases the time-consuming work of cutting the matrix requires strength and accuracy. Prints can be produced either using a press, often entailing very large machines, or by hand, in which case the block is inked and the paper is laid over it so that the image can be transferred onto the paper using a traditional baren or the back of a wooden spoon. In this latter case the labour is intensive but allows the artist to check on the progress of the transfer of the image and to adjust the pressure should this be required; as a consequence, editions made in this way tend to be limited to a just few prints.

Suzana Fântanâriu is a Romanian artist whose prints have taken the woodcut traditions of her country into new territory through a series of major exhibitions of her work. While woodcut and printmaking have remained central to her work, her concerns have extended into many other areas of the visual arts, with prints, installations, and sculptural forms incorporating print techniques. Born in Baia-Fălticeni, she graduated from the Institute of Visual Arts in Cluj-Napoca, and is currently a professor at the Faculty of Fine Arts of the Western University in Timisoara. She has a long history of national and international solo and group exhibitions, and has been the recipient of numerous prestigious awards. Her earlier work, as in the 1975 piece *I-Feminism*, was comparatively conventional and in line with the post-Pop Art trends of that period, combining a number of different elements within one print. Nonetheless, even at this stage there are indications within the print of her desire to explore not only the techniques of woodcut, including the method of rendering the face in the upper section of the print, but also the language of mark-making to create a wide variety of textural effects within the strict grid lines and subverting these with areas of freeform mark-making.

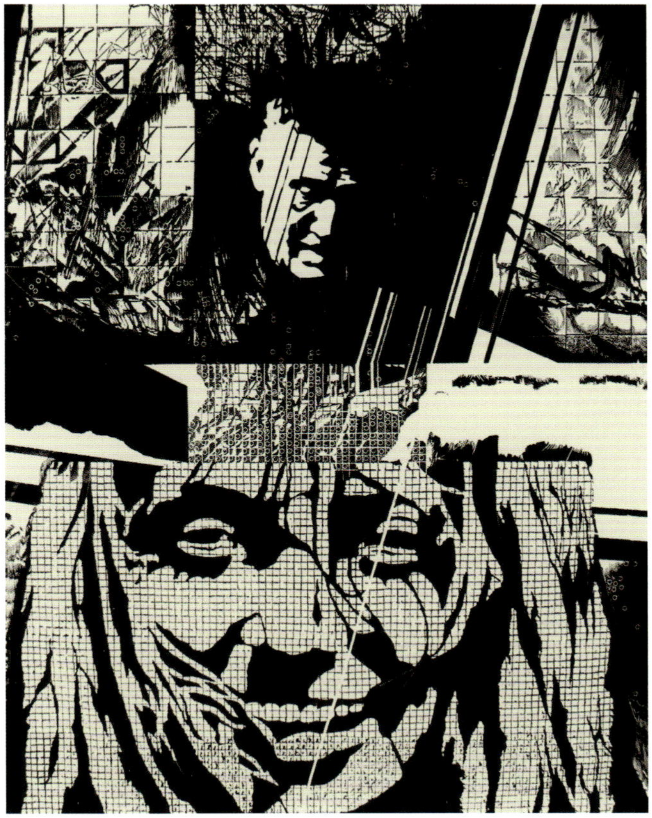

Suzana Fântanâriu, *I-Feminism*, 1975. Woodcut handprinted on Japanese paper, 125 x 100cm (49¼ x 30½in.). Private collection.

Even this early in her career, Fântanâriu was already showing indications of the directions in which her work would progress, with a breadth of approaches to the making of art. Towards the end of the 1980s her work in print became increasingly abstract, exploring the nature of mark-making on the surface of the wood matrix and deepening her quest for understanding the relationship between chaos and order. By cutting the matrix, and producing the small editions of each print by hand-rubbing, she was able to achieve large-size prints of great sensitivity which reveal the closeness of the relationship between the material, the artist's work and the final result.

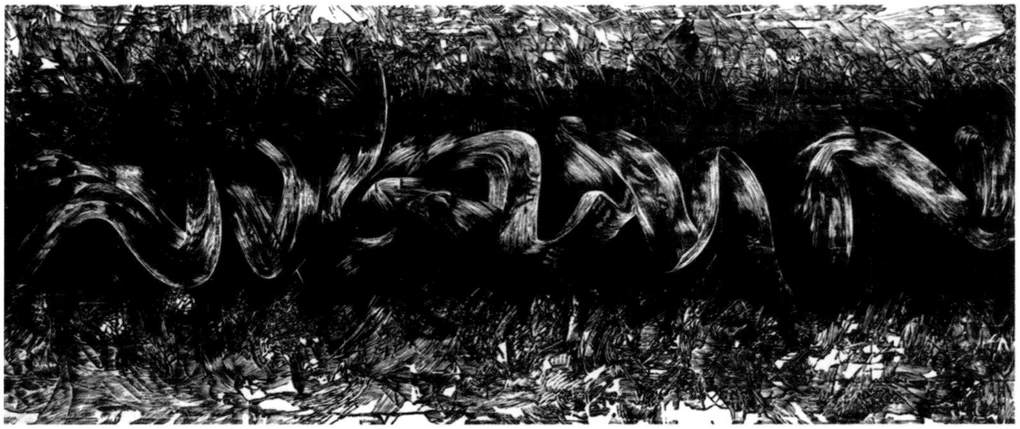

Suzana Fântanâriu, *Dragon H*, 2001. Woodcut handprinted on Japanese paper, 100 x 300cm (39½ x 118in.).

Dragon H (2001) exemplifies this period in her work, in which the nature of the surface of the wood and the subtle range of her cuts creates a dynamic image of sweeping lines, reminiscent of brushstrokes, which emerge from the deep black area across the centre. A complementary series, *Palimpsestus*, made during the same period, explored further the nature of communication through written language. Just as the ink writing on a piece of vellum could be scraped away to allow the material to be reused, with traces of the earlier marks still remaining visible, so too in her cutting into the surface of the wood the artist allows the inner nature of the wood a continuing presence that becomes integral to the image. Works such as these continue to be of importance to Fântanâriu, sometimes installed in exhibitions as long narrow combinations of prints extending down the gallery wall and across the floor, and in some cases incorporating the limited use of colour. In other related works such images are wrapped around tall thin cylinders, to be installed as a series of columns between which exhibition viewers can pass. In another series, *Wrappings for my Soul*, the artist has taken flat prints with the same title, shaping them into sculptural forms resembling ancient sarcophagi. Shown together as an installation, the prints and sculptures create a haunting evocation of relics from an unknowable past.

The artist's interest in exploring works in three dimensions has also resulted in a series of objects that relate to European Surrealism and Dada, in that they place together disparate objects with no immediate sense of relationship, but which result in forms with their own idiosyncratic logic. Some of these works incorporate print along with household objects and fragments of wood and metal – the detritus of the past given new associations and new potential. During her residency at the Cité Internationale des Arts in Paris in 2006, as a recipient of the Constantin Brâncuşi bursary, she created an exhibition of just such coalesced fragments found in the streets and flea markets, and also participated in the event called Eurotic, in which music created by the jazz pianist Mircea Tiberian accompanied a collection of images made by Fântanâriu.

Right: Suzana Fântanâriu, *The Shadow of the Book*, 2003. Object, wood, paper, acrylic, 30 x 21 x 17cm (11¾ x 8¼ x 6¾in.). Private collection.

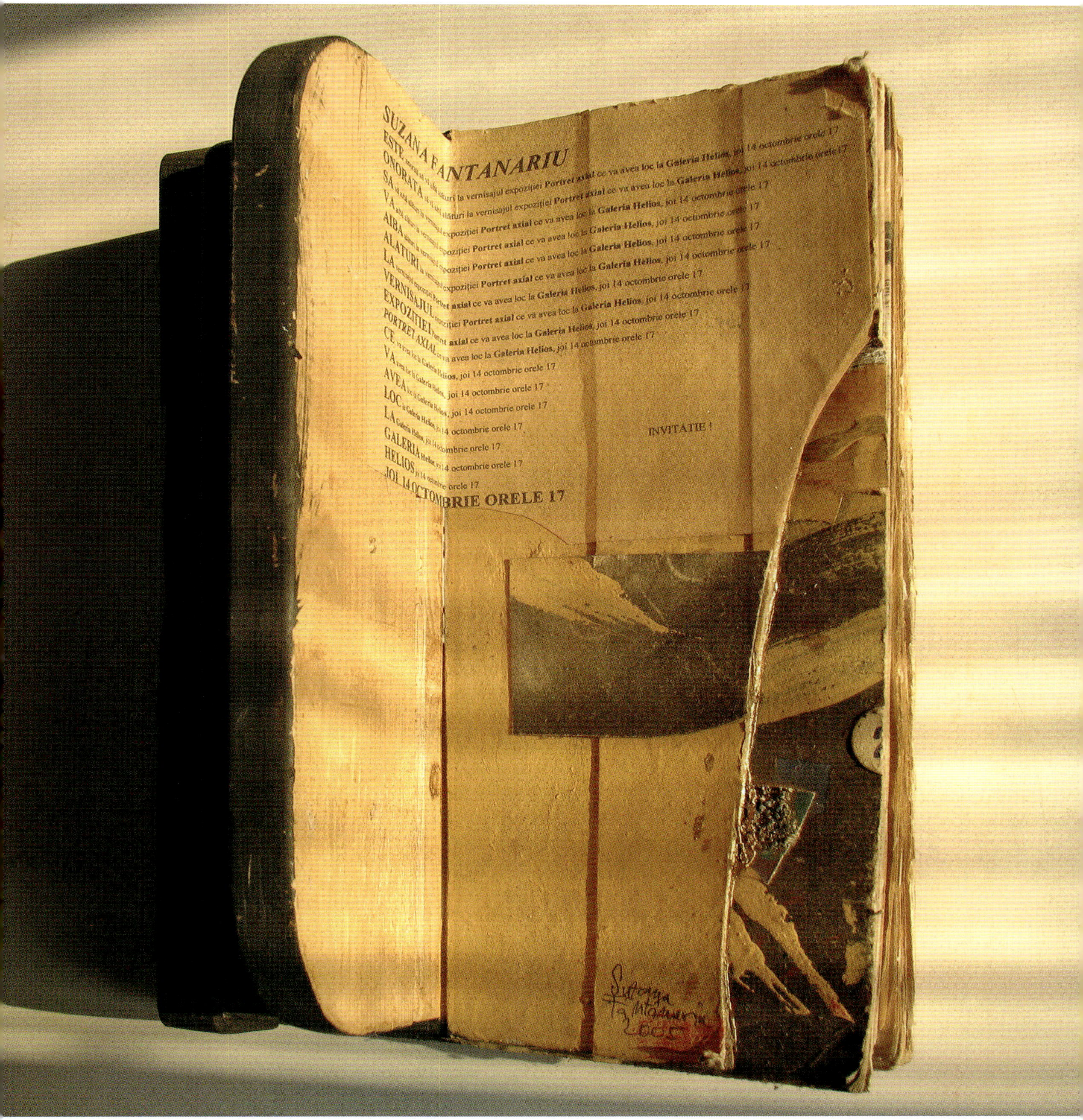
SUZANA FANTANARIU
ESTE ONORATA SA VA AIBA ALATURI LA VERNISAJUL EXPOZITIEI PORTRET AXIAL CE VA AVEA LOC LA GALERIA HELIOS
JOI 14 OCTOMBRIE ORELE 17
INVITATIE !

VALERIU SCHIAU

MOLDOVA is an independent, landlocked country sandwiched between Romania and Ukraine, and includes the disputed breakaway territory of Transnistria on its eastern border. Because of its geographically strategic position on the route between Asia and Europe, Moldova has had a complex and troubled history of invasions and occupations ever since late antiquity, with shifting borders and the control of the country passing between successive foreign powers and regimes. The Ottoman Empire and Tsarist Russia played their roles in the country's development, and in the early half of the 20th century it became a pawn in the political machinations between Communist Russia and the Axis powers before becoming a Soviet Socialist Republic. The country suffered greatly in the Stalinist period and, although declaring independence in 1991, was led by Communist parties until 2009. Since 2010 it has been led by the Alliance for European Integration coalition, under whose guidance, despite the country having a poor civil-rights record, moves towards joining the European Union continue.

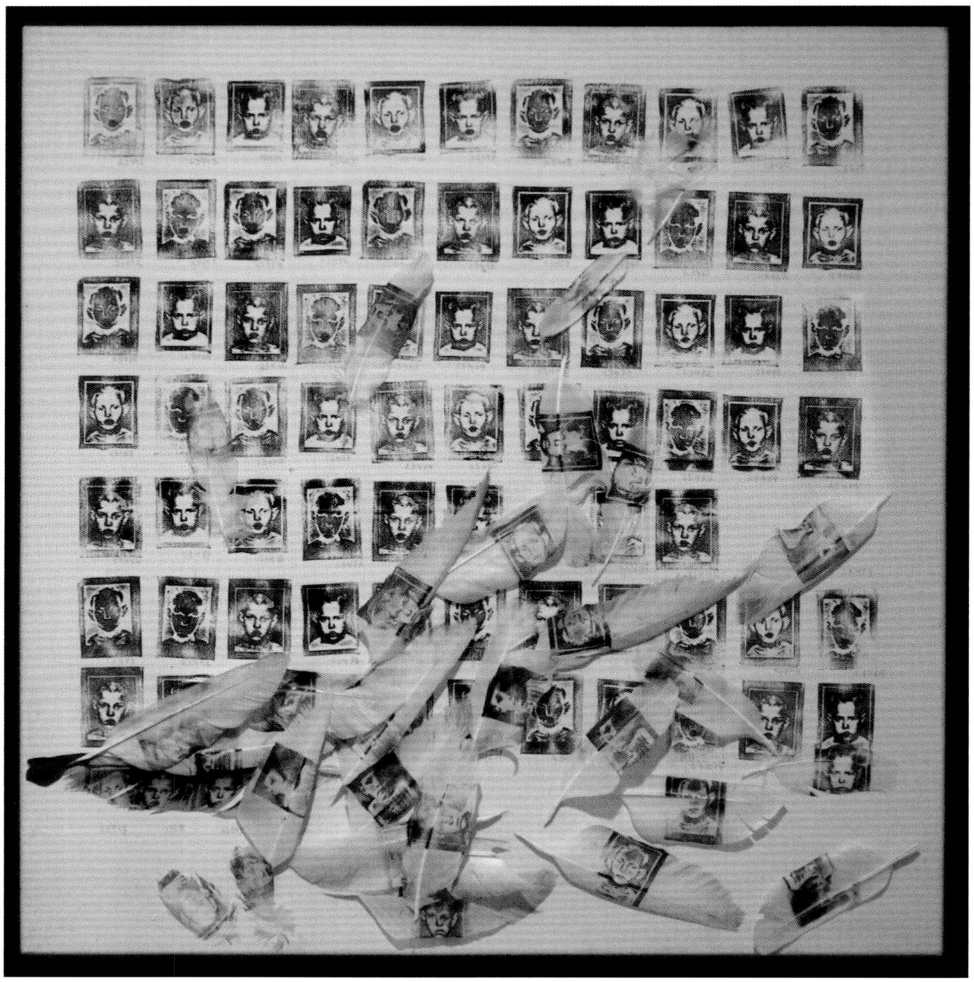

Valeriu Schiau, *Born in the USSR*, 2009. Linocut on feathers and canvas in metal box frame, 50 x 50cm (19¾ x 19¾in.).

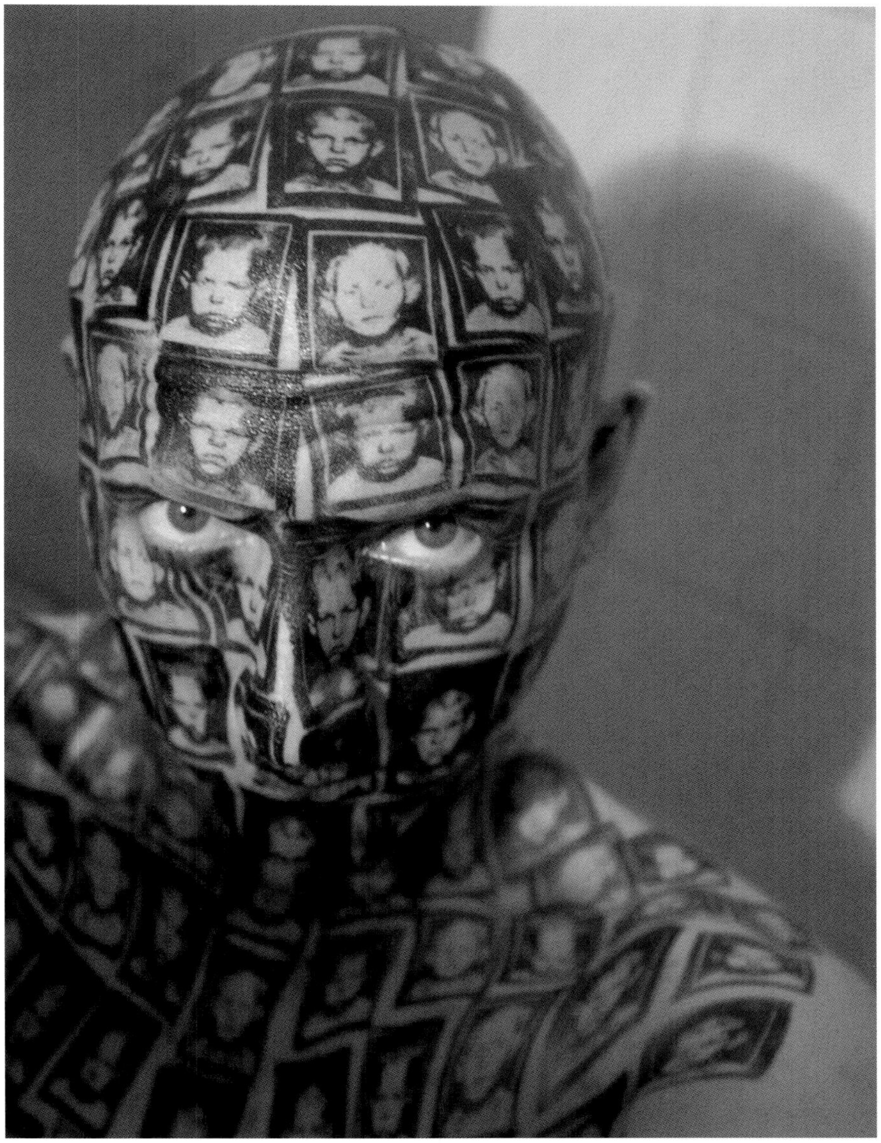

Valeriu Schiau, *Born in the USSR*, 2008. Still from video performance, linocut on body, 10m 07s.

The history of Moldova, and in particular from the mid-20th century onwards, is the main driving force behind the work of Valeriu Schiau. He was born in Colibaşi in the Republic of Moldova in 1969, and was educated at the Fine Arts High School in the capital, Chisiniau. His compulsory military service from 1987 to 1989 was served under harsh conditions in Siberia. In 1990 he left Moldova with a scholarship from the Romanian government to study at the National University of the Arts in Bucharest, graduating in 1997. He now lives and works in Bucharest, and has a record of solo and group exhibitions in Romania and Germany.

In a brief statement about his work, Schiau writes, 'For me, experimenting is one of the most important aspects of artistic creation. This is the engine behind artistic evolution. My themes are connected to personal issues and everything reflected by the environment I live in. The image of children in my work represents a personal relationship with my own history, as a person living in a totalitarian regime before 1989, and as a father.' Schiau has a studio in the curious circular concrete tower building on a corner of central Bucharest opposite the national bank. The building is a warren of artists' studios, small in size but very varied in nature. In the shared space outside his studio Schiau has stored huge parts – a head and an arm – of what will become the sculpture of a giant baby built from plaster over a wood and polystyrene armature. The sculpture will form the centrepiece of a major installation. Many babies and small children perished during the dark days of Moldovan history under Stalin, particularly

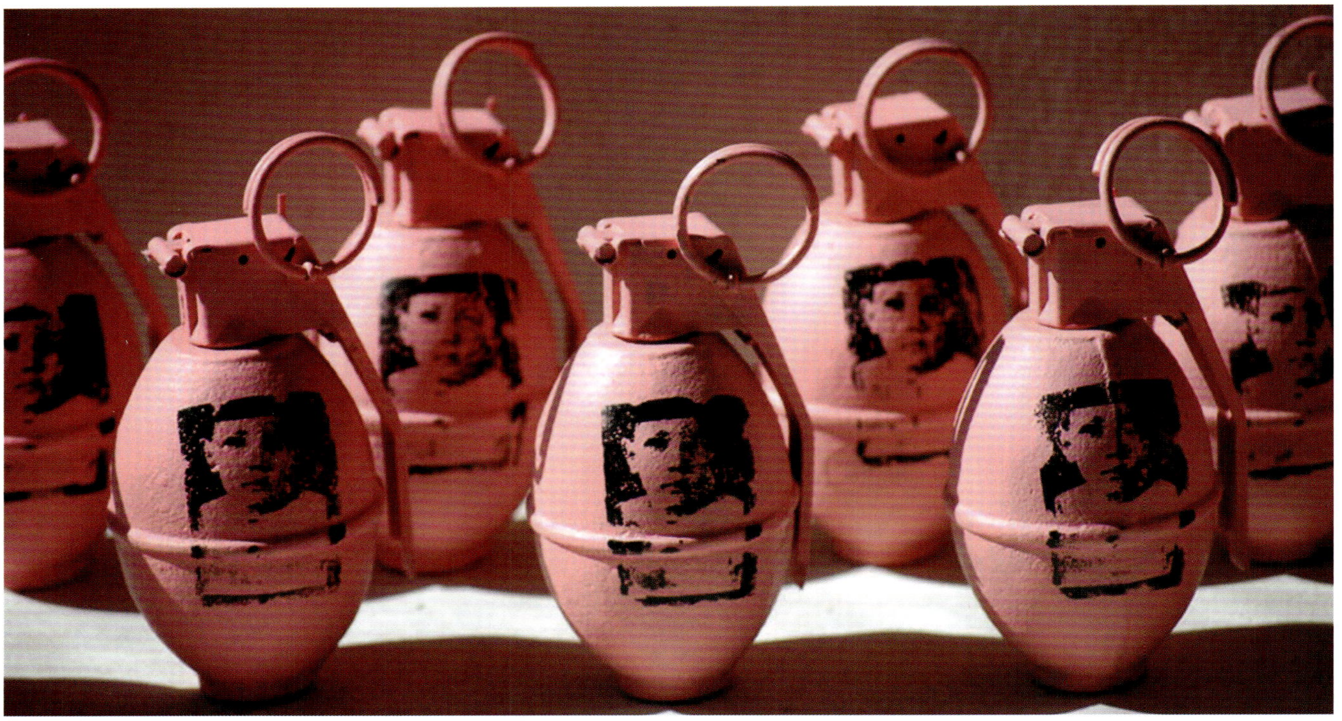

Valeriu Schiau, *Big Bang*, 2010. Linocut on grenades/installation, variable dimensions.

as a result of the famine of 1946–7 when almost a quarter of a million Moldovans died, followed by others in the subsequent years of hardship. The artist has addressed this painful issue in a major series of works in various mediums, including linocut, entitled *Born in the USSR*.

Linocut is, in essence, a simple and straightforward technique, more usually seen with the relief image printed onto paper. A number of artists have found the means for transferring such images to other surfaces, including three-dimensional ones such as ceramics, using a flexible matrix. In Schiau's case this has included transferring images of children's faces onto his own head, chest, shoulders and arms, documenting this process in a video performance (see: http://www.youtube.com/watch?v=P9lNwL5LIGw) that was part of his 2011 solo exhibition at the Brancovan Palace Cultural Centre in Mogosoaia. Following the painstaking application of many small images to his skin, the artist methodically wiped his hands over the images, obliterating them until all that was left was his blackened skin. In applying the images to himself Schiau subsumed in symbolic fashion his own identity beneath theirs, briefly joining their history with his own, and continuing their existence within another framework.

A number of works in the same series were framed behind glass in metal box frames, incorporating on white feathers printed images of children that the artist had collected in his homeland and taken to Romania, in some of them with red circles superimposed over their mouths, again with the images taking on symbolic resonances through the links with innocence, flight and the angels' wings of Medieval and Renaissance painting. In another work, *Big Bang*, from 2010, the images of children were transferred to defused hand grenades, painted pink, and exhibited in groups – in one case arranged in a cardboard egg tray painted the same pink – while in *The Dream*, a related later work from 2012, a grid of identical images of a child's face is printed on the back of a large sheet of Plexiglas, the centre of which has been blow-moulded into the three-dimensional form of a larger-than-life baby's head.

Schiau has also produced paintings and assemblages, on the same or linked themes, as well as performances. In one of the performances, *Personal Issues* (2011), he made large-scale drawings of babies on cardboard, using butane fluid as a substitute for pencil or paint, and then set fire to them, burning the images into the board to create drawings that were subsequently exhibited in a gallery. The use of a volatile flammable liquid that, if not burned, evaporates into the air, is a powerful medium to add to those normally used to make drawings, and lends a considerable poetic weight to the work.

The extended metaphors within the printmaking and related work of Valeriu Schiau further raise the profile of an intentionally disturbing aspect of contemporary art in recent years, through which artists with powerful motivation are seeking forms of catharsis for social and political events that lead to the mistreatment and death of children. These contrast radically with the saccharine images of suffering children that typify much late 19th-century genre painting, which could not be further from the emotional world of Valeriu Schiau.

BULGARIA

I VISITED BULGARIA in the spring of 2012, staying in Sofia but also making short visits to Plovdiv and Samokov. Although Bulgaria did not become a full member of the EU until January 2007, and as a consequence lags some way behind other former Iron Curtain countries such as Poland and the Czech Republic (which joined three years earlier), it nevertheless became clear during my stay that the country is making rapid progress towards becoming a modern European state, and one that retains a strong cultural and national identity.

Sofia provides a range of contrasts, with the city centre offering designer label shops, glittering new office buildings and historic buildings and parks from many eras. This makes a strong contrast with the endless and dispiriting concrete housing developments on the outskirts dating from the Communist era. I was welcomed with typically warm Bulgarian hospitality by Robert Baramov and Nevena Valcheva in their apartment in one such area. There is a tangible energy in the city centre, the result of some positive developments, among which is the development by the National Art Gallery of what promises to be an excellent gallery dedicated to contemporary art, the Sofia Arsenal Museum for Contemporary Art (SAMCA), due to open fully in 2014. This will add to the wide variety of museums and galleries, both private and state-owned, that celebrate the diversity of Bulgarian culture stretching back from contemporary art through five centuries of rule under the Ottoman Empire, and even further back to the riches of ancient Thrace.

A two-day visit to Plovdiv, 94 miles (152 km) to the south-east of Sofia offered a complete contrast, a less hectic pace and some fascinating architecture. The city, Bulgaria's second largest, dates back to around 5000 BCE when it was a major centre of Thracian culture, and offers a fascinating series of explorations for anyone interested in architecture and culture. For example, the Centre for Contemporary Art, set in an ancient hammam (bathhouse), is run by Emil Mirazchiev and provides a unique and atmospheric setting for cutting-edge sculpture, video and installation. It is situated near the Old Town, an area of steep cobbled streets winding between a unique style of painted wooden houses, courtyards and churches, leading up to a well-preserved Roman amphitheatre that is still used for performances. Many of the houses are now museums dedicated to various artists and an eclectic mixture of collections that repay the time given them by the curious visitor. A major archaeological site in the city centre is revealing an extensive Roman urban complex, and there are also remains of buildings from the Byzantine and Ottoman periods, with more yet to be discovered. The whole atmosphere of Plovdiv is very different to that of Sofia, the result of its long development through some of the most important epochs of European history. Little wonder that it is one of the major centres for contemporary art in Southeast Europe.

I travelled to Samokov with Onnik Karanfilian to visit the Print Centre there, which played an important part in the development of printmaking in Bulgaria from the 1960s onwards. The road from Sofia leads south through a silent forested and hilly landscape, passing rivers and lakes and rising over 1000m (more than 3000 ft) towards the Rila Mountains. Samokov is only 35 miles (55 km) from the capital, but such is the difference in character that it seems much further than that. The Print Centre is dedicated primarily to lithography and is situated in an old single-storey wooden house with carved wooden ceilings which contribute to an atmosphere of quiet concentration. There I met Geno Genev, a master lithographer who has now retired after working at the Print Centre with the most celebrated artists in the country. We crossed the road to visit the Orthodox Church, dedicated to the Dormition of the Mother of God, with a justly celebrated wooden interior and a beautifully conserved iconostasis. Later, Geno Genev took us to his apartment, where he maintains what must be one of the finest collections anywhere of mid-20th century Bulgarian printmaking. In the evening, Onnik Karanfilian drove me back to Sofia and showed me a collection of his own work in his home and also in his impressive new studio at the top of a concrete apartment block in the city centre. The contrast with the Print Centre could not be more different, but the vitality and high quality of Karanfilian's work shows him to be a clear successor to the artists whose work I was shown in Samokov.

A short and intensive visit will never allow more than a first glimpse of a culture so rich in experiences, but the abiding impression is of a country with a long and deep history that is poised to become an even more interesting place to visit, with a vibrant contemporary art scene that deserves to be discovered.

ONNIK KARANFILIAN

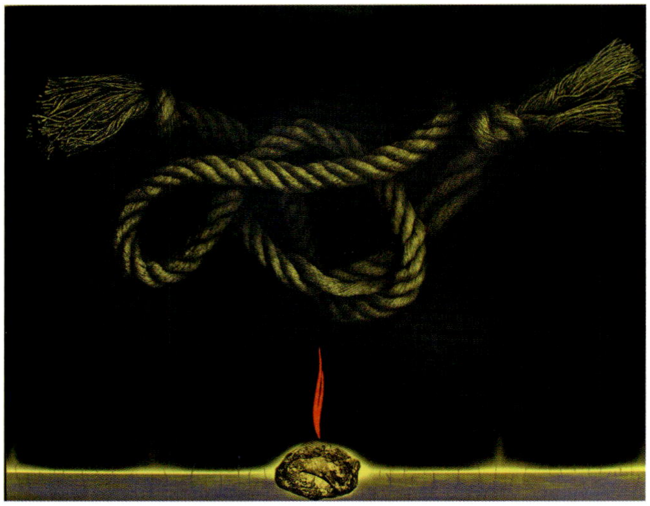

Onnik Karanfilian, *Beginning and End V*, 2006.Litho offset, etching, drypoint, stencil, 73 x 100cm (28¾ x 39¼in.). Collection: Kochi Triennial, Japan.

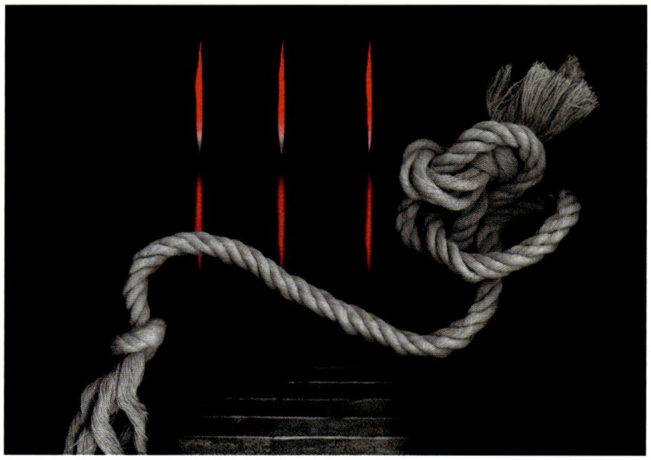

Onnik Karanfilian, *Cutout Remembrances from the Seaside*, 2008. Litho offset, drypoint, collagraphy. 73 x 100cm (28¾ x 39¼in.). Collection: RHMD Museum, Istanbul.

ONNIK KARANFILIAN, was born in Sliven, Bulgaria in 1963, and has been active as a printmaker and painter since graduating from the National Academy of Fine Arts in Sofia in 1994. He has exhibited in Bulgaria and internationally since 1985, including representation in many of the important international biennials and triennials, and has been the recipient of many prestigious awards; his work is included in numerous public and private collections throughout the world. In addition he has taught computer design at the National Academy of Fine Arts in Sofia, and has conducted classes elsewhere in Europe. His personal work covers a wide range of fields, from graphic design for a number of major publications, book illustration, painting and drawing, and printmaking in a number of traditional and digital techniques, and in ex-libris prints. His activity in this latter field has also led him to founding the Ex Libris Biennial in Bulgaria and to the establishment and editing of the first Bulgarian journal for this medium. This latter form – of creating personally dedicated small editions of bookplate-sized prints in traditional techniques – is more widely practised in Eastern than Western Europe, and has developed a specific language of styles and approaches that have rendered it eminently suitable for small-scale specialist collections.

The countries in Eastern Europe were somewhat isolated from the rest of the world during their years in the Soviet Bloc, and the evolution of printmaking in those countries during that period is too little known and appreciated in the wider world; knowledge of printmaking arts in the pre-Communist period is also a somewhat specialist subject. With the ending of Communist Party dominance in 1989, and increasingly during the period between then and the accession of many of those countries into the European Union, more has became known of what had been developing.

It is clear that the work made since 1945 developed through a unique range of styles and approaches based on national art histories, linked to the tangled social and political histories of Eastern European. Even given this unexpectedly rich tradition, the range of Karanfilian's work is impressive, both technically and conceptually. He is equally adept working with traditional techniques such as etching, aquatint and lithography as he is with digital technology; and he can also handle a number of scales, from small ex-libris prints to those in excess of 100cm (39in) wide. This range allows him the flexibility to choose medium and scale to suit the concept of the works he has in his mind, many of which are produced in series. He reads widely and has studied not only world art history but also mythology and history, in particular the evolution of symbols and language.

In 1995 the artist produced what is claimed to be the first Bulgarian print made entirely with the use of a computer, following his first steps towards such use in his MFA diploma project. The print, *Adam and Eve*, is a contemporary interpretation of the 1507 work by Albrecht Dürer, updated with the tools and detritus of the 20th century. Made in the same year, *Dance in the Street* combines a computer-generated image of a crushed

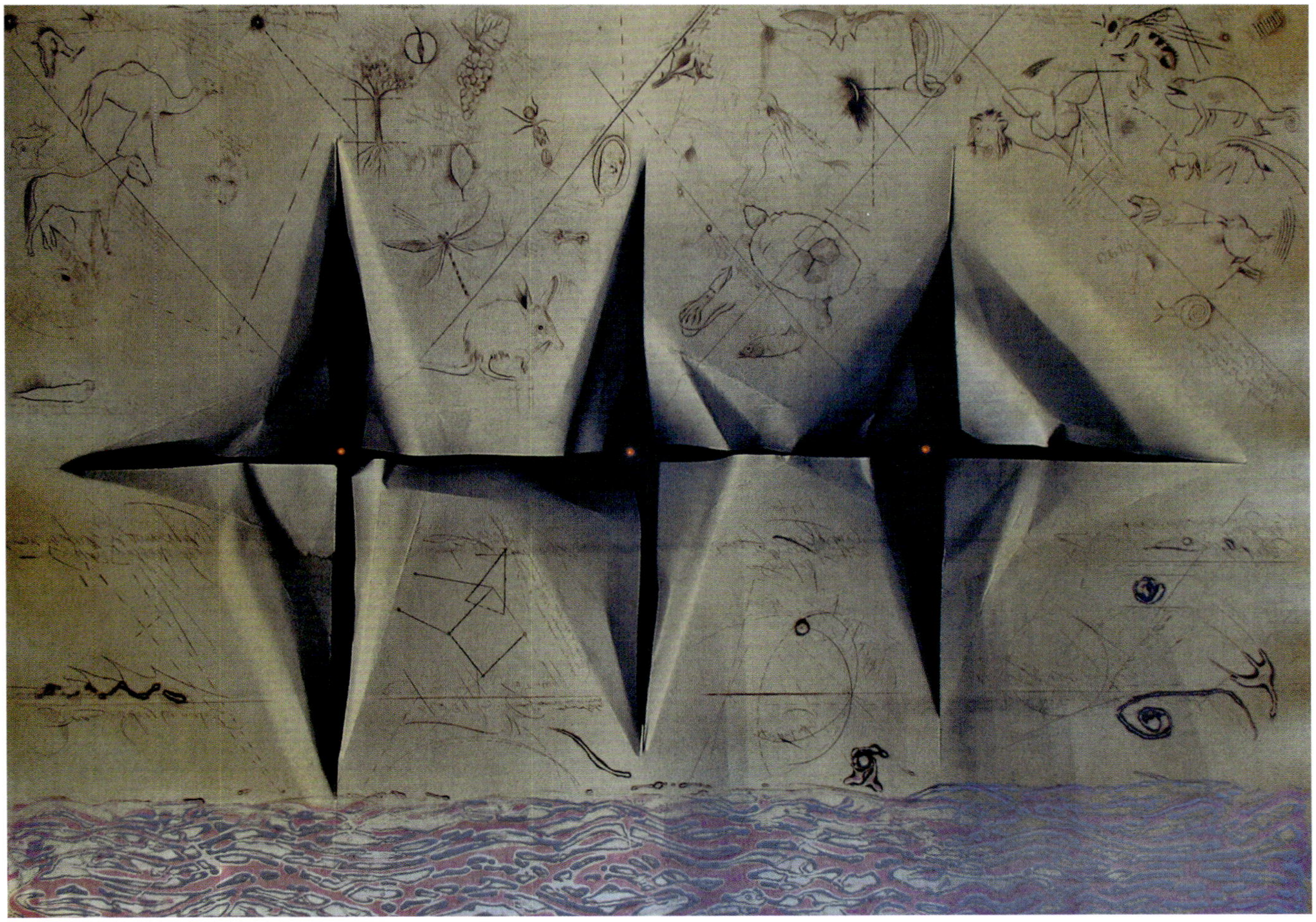

Onnik Karanfilian, *Other Side I*, 2008. Litho offset, drypoint, collagraphy, 73 x 100cm (28¾ x 39¼in.). Collection: Bangkok Triennial of Print and Drawing.

Pepsi can and cigarette ends with a finely detailed etching of a crowded urban street in perspective. The combination of many small images within a larger whole is a recurrent theme in the artist's work, a means of establishing a non-hierarchical narrative that is open to personal interpretation.

Since 2001 a recurrent theme has been a length of thick rope, knotted in various configurations and frayed at the ends; a length of such rope lies on the floor of his studio. In the *Beginning & End* series the rope is positioned against a black background in the upper part of the print, with red strokes like cuts (or perhaps symbolic lambent flames) revealing the colour behind, and with a narrow band at the bottom in the form of a predella revealing a faintly drawn row of figures or vehicles or a landscape of dead trees, this content varying from one print to another. As before, the works in this series offer no easy and immediate answer to the question of meaning, and nor indeed should this be sought. They operate in the mind as a form of poetry that can be appreciated for its immediate appearance or otherwise contemplated in the quest for an interpretation of its meaning. In any event the works are of the highest technical accomplishment.

Other Side I, a mixed-technique work in drypoint and collagraphy, presents a densely packed series of images of geometry, animals and insects – details, as if drawn from sketchbooks, on a *trompe l'oeil* surface of cut and folded paper, revealing a black background in which three small red spots gleam above a narrow band of what could be polluted water. Once again, the meaning is open to personal interpretation. A second print, *Other Side II*, relies on a similar technique, but the images of the natural world are replaced by images from the technological and engineering world. Taken together, the mystery of the imagery is increased.

Cutout Remembrances from the Seaside is one of a linked series of works of entirely digital origination, of greater simplicity but open to deeper metaphysical interpretation. The complexity of the imagery has been pared down to a few essentials: a length of rope, red strokes with possible reflections against an inky blackness, out of which what may be steps emerge towards the foreground at the bottom of the print. Like other works from the same series, this is a print of great subtlety and intelligence, suggesting that the future work of Onnik Karanfilian will be well worth seeing.

PETER LAZAROV

'MY SECOND BIRTH as a citizen was in 1990 when I settled in Holland and where my home is now and where, apparently, I am the last (active) wood engraver.' So writes Peter Lazarov in his text, 'Talking about Art is always talking about traditions and personalities'. Born in Plovdiv, Bulgaria in 1958, his story and his career as an artist span two contrasting eras, that of his childhood, education and early career in a Communist satellite state of the Soviet Union, and subsequent to the fall of Communism as a citizen of a liberal democracy with a long tradition of art, including printmaking. In the same text he writes of his dual experience, 'Building an image of the West based on the negation of the political system in Eastern Europe of the '70s and '80s proved to be as false as any notion based on negativism. To know one side of a coin doesn't mean that one can create the other by just an 'opposite' image'; and, in relation to the question of the freedom of the arts and artists anywhere, 'I believe Art should be an intrinsic part of Culture and Society, fulfilling essential spiritual need, reflecting people's hopes, doubts and dreams, and not mere commodity or an excess.' Lazarov's position, and his views, encapsulate the dilemma of the East/West discussions that have to be continued in order to create a synthesis within which all the various aspects of pan-European culture can be accommodated and accorded equal respect.

Lazarov is a prolific and highly skilled printmaker, using woodcut, wood engraving, lithography and other techniques, and working at scales from ex-libris to very large, to explore and present his view of the world: he has had a long and remarkable record of exhibitions, residencies and awards, and has travelled widely. His work is figurative, based on the traditional and classical academic basis of his art education in Bulgaria, in which life drawing, largely from the nude, was the core activity. His printmaking training was in intaglio techniques – etching, drypoint, aquatint and mezzotint – using zinc plates, as access to more costly matrices such as wood or copper was not possible.

As a young artist, coming from a long Christian tradition, Lazarov chose not to join the Bulgarian Artists' Association, which at that time was run by Communists. Unable therefore to use their studios or to obtain materials from their store, he was instead reliant on the help of friends to get his working materials. But the motivation to develop his skills as an artist was strong; his mother is an artist and she and her friends inspired him as a child to follow in their footsteps. One artist advised him to concentrate on the graphic arts, and this combined with his discovery of the works of Dürer and Escher, inspiring him with the combination of social content and imaginative image making. His introduction to wood as a matrix came through one of his professors, who gave him three woodblocks. This began his close connection with wood engraving (in which the end grain of the block is used) and woodcut (using the face of the block). As he and other artists using these techniques have remarked, such techniques are hard, requiring sharp tools and, as mistakes cannot be corrected, equally sharp minds, and also lengthy periods of time in the carving. What they do not immediately require is much working space, as prints can be made from the finished matrix using just the back of a wooden spoon.

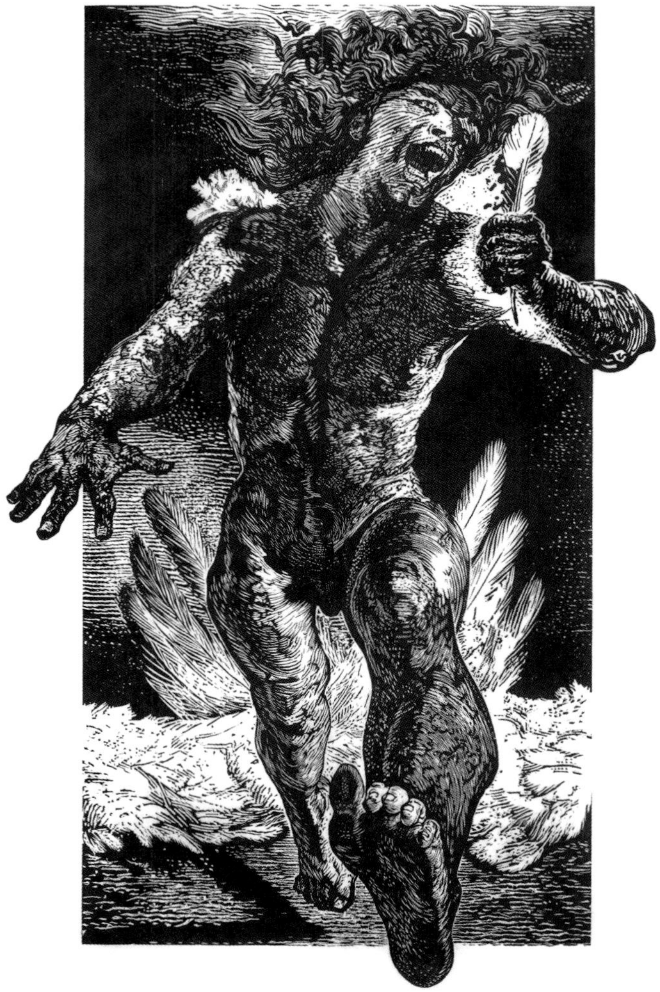

Peter Lazarov, *Angel*, 2010. Woodcut, 120 x 62cm (47¼ x 24½in.). Printed at Guanlan Printbase, Shenzhen, China. Photo: Sijtze Veldema.

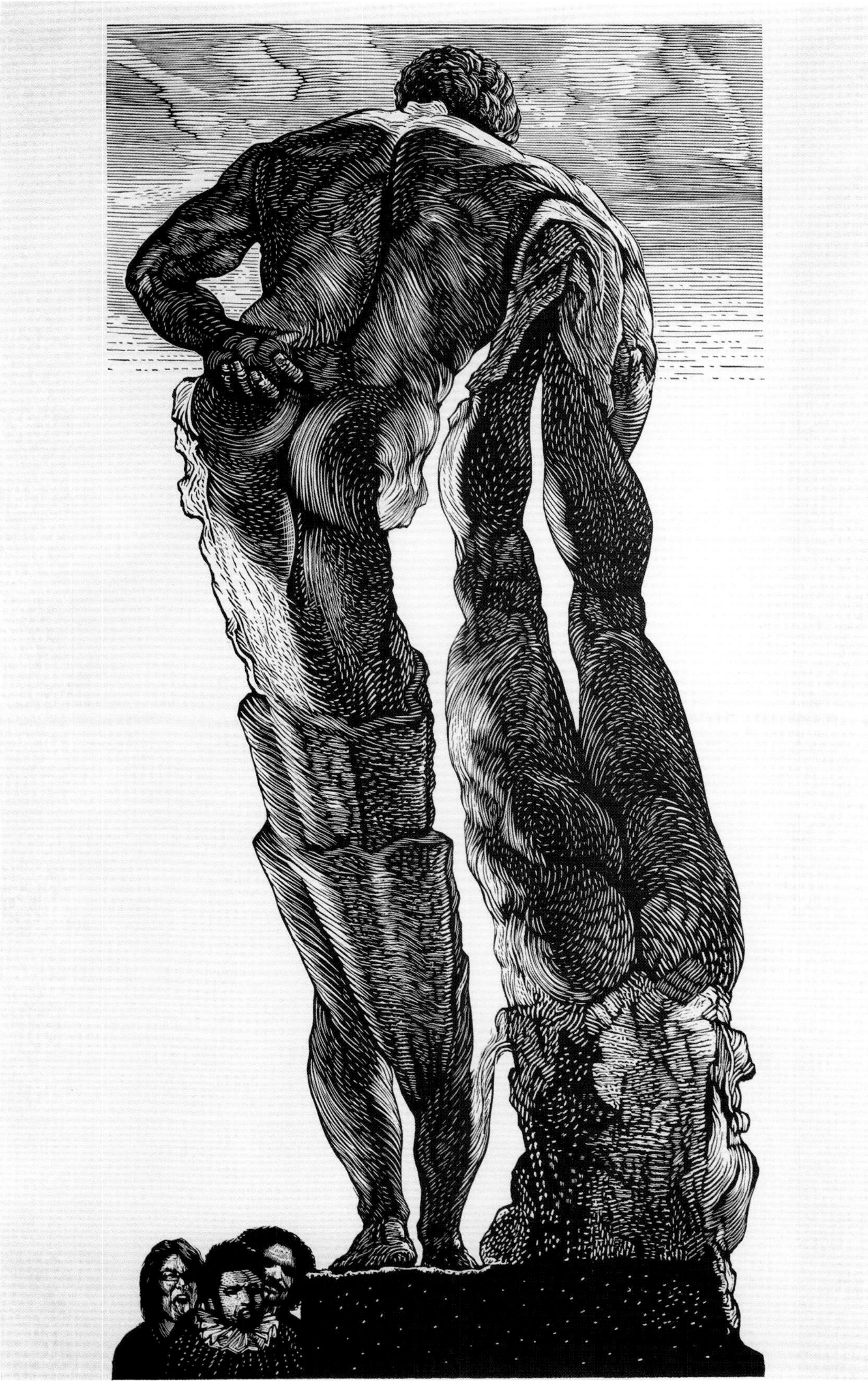

Peter Lazarov, *Goltzius Revisited*, 2009. Engraving on MDF, 120 x 60cm (47¼ x 23½in.). Collection: Rijksmuseum, Amsterdam. Printed at Guanlan Printbase, Shenzhen, China. Photo: Sijtze Veldema.

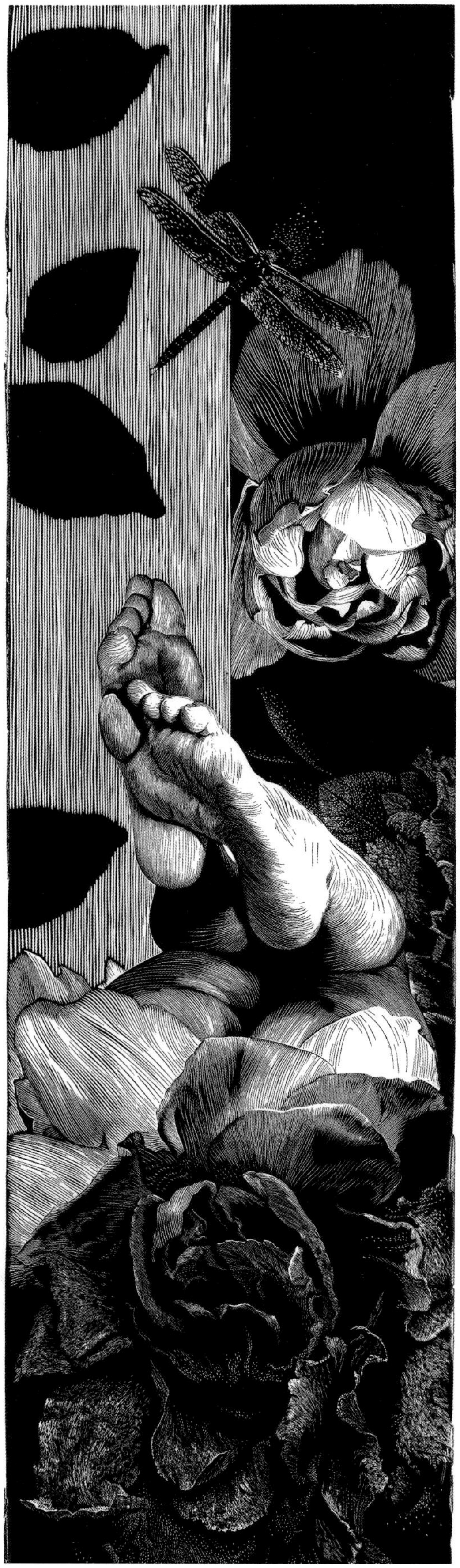

Peter Lazarov, *Hakka Dragonfly*, 2010. Engraving on Plexiglas acrylic board 67.7 x 22cm (26¾ x 8¾in.). Printed at Guanlan Printbase, Shenzhen, China. Photo: Sijtze Veldema.

Another crucial part of the development Lazarov's career has been his involvement with travel to Japan and China. He was invited to participate in a workshop in the *moku hanga* (water-based printmaking) technique in Japan in 2000, an experience which widened his horizons not only through what he describes as a 'charmingly intimate technique' but also through other aspects of Japanese culture. Further invitations to participate in the residency programme of the celebrated Guanlan printmaking centre in Sichuan, China each year from 2009 to 2012 have provided him with further inspiration and experience of working within a millennia-old living printmaking tradition.

The three selected images demonstrate Peter Lazarov's technique and imagination, and also his willingness to explore the use of less conventional matrices. In *Goltzius Revisited* he pays homage to Hendrik Goltzius (1558–1617), the Dutch printmaker and painter whose skills were said to rival those of Dürer, with a large-scale print of a monumental figure at the foot of which are three small portraits, including the subject and Lazarov himself. The print is a demonstration of Lazarov's extraordinary technique and also of the lightness of touch, or even a sense of levity, that he can bring to his work. This work justifiably places him within the long continuum of art in his adopted country.

Hakka Dragonfly is inspired by his time in Sichuan, home to many Hakka people, a Chinese minority with a distinct variant Chinese language and cuisine, noted also for their communal defensive architecture in the circular 'tulou' style. The print shows the legs and feet of a reclining nude figure amongst flowers with a dragonfly, a lyrical evocation of the heat and luxuriance of summer and a demonstration of the clarity of line that can be gained with the use of a plastic matrix. The third image, *Angel*, is a very large tour-de-force woodcut that shows Lazarov's mastery of the technique, and also the relevance of his classical training in Bulgaria. A dynamic nude male figure emerges from the background in which lie discarded wings, clutching a single feather and shouting silently as he emerges not only from the background but also from the conventional rectangle of the block, beyond the picture plane and into the realm of the viewer, creating an immediate bond between artist and viewer that cannot be ignored.

ROBERT BARAMOV

ROBERT BARAMOV was born in 1966 in Tolbukhin, a town in eastern Bulgaria roughly equidistant from the Black Sea city of Varna and the Romanian border. In 1990 the town's name was restored to Dobrich, having been previously renamed during the Communist era. For artists of his generation, the transition from their early years under a totalitarian regime to the considerably different circumstance of the post-1989 period, and more recently to changes following the accession of the country as a member of the European Union, created tensions, the resolution of which is not yet complete. Baramov has written, 'The balance between social life and striving for development, no matter what the established conventions, political situation, education and environment are, raised my potential needs of a different space, the consequence of which is my desire to organize it and feel comfortable in it.' This statement is key to gaining an understanding of his work, which can be termed visionary, iconoclastic, subversive and, most of all, surrealist.

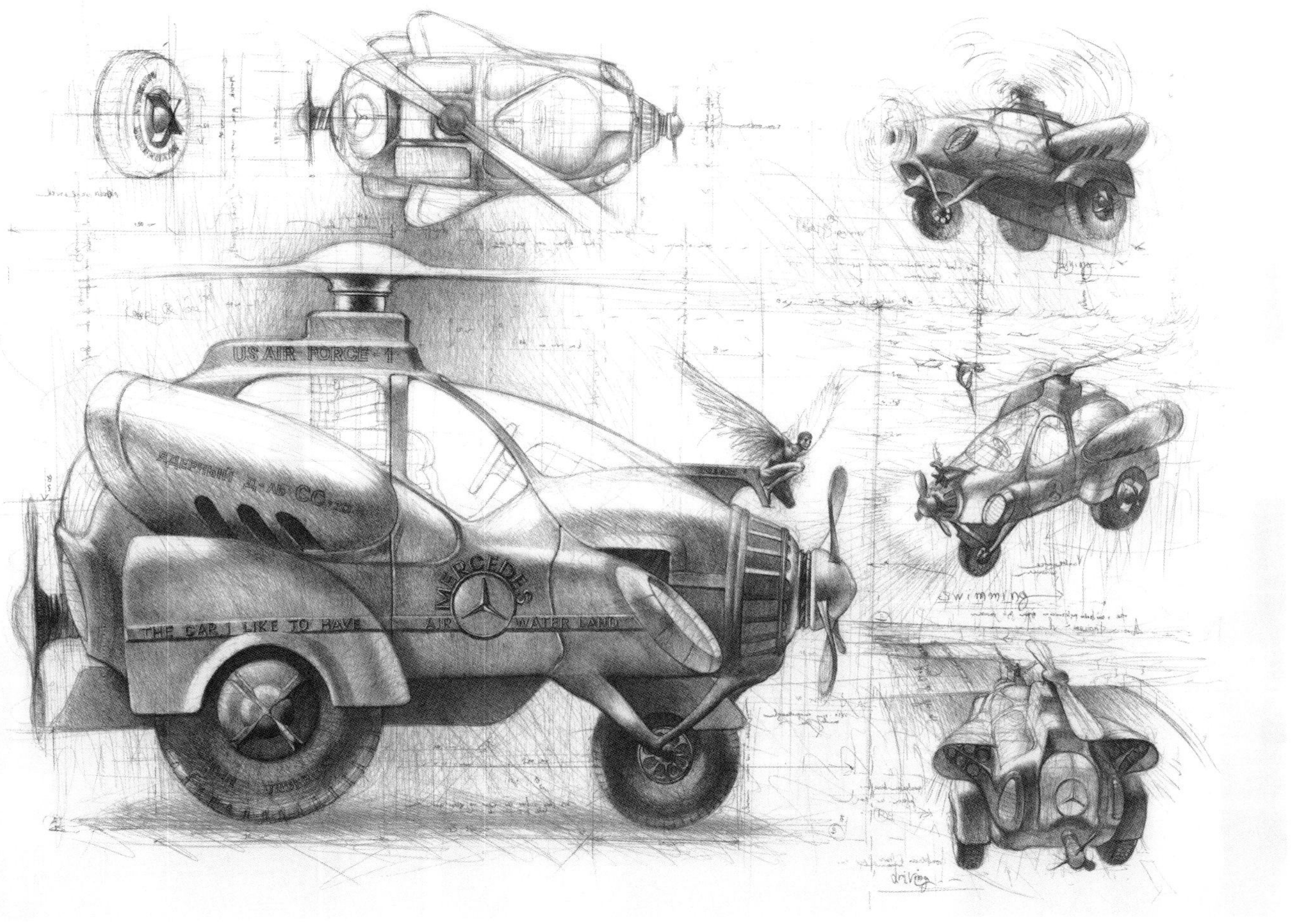

Robert Baramov, *Object, Air, Water, Land*, 2002. Stone lithograph, 78 x 116cm (30¾ x 45¾in.).

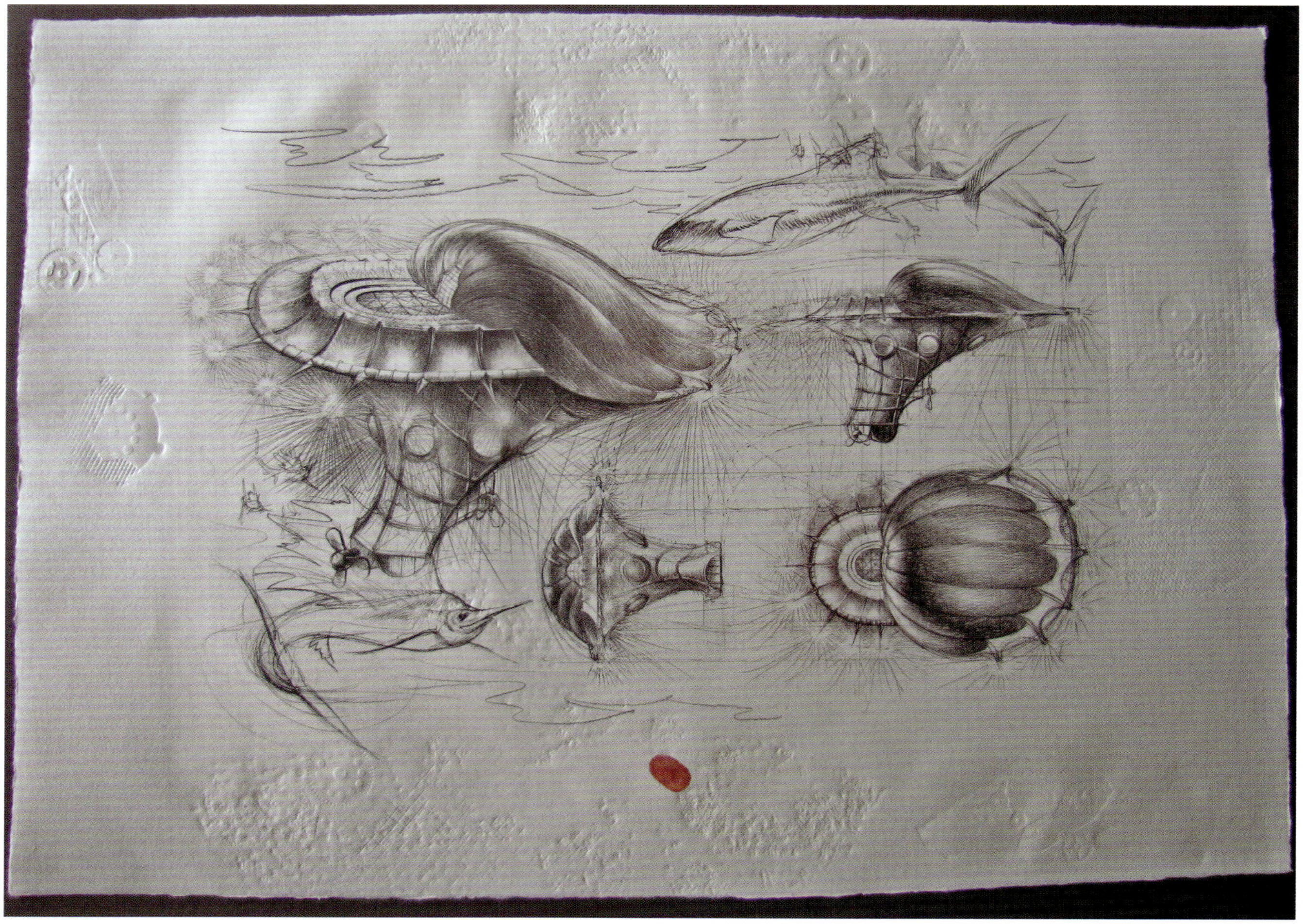

Robert Baramov, *Underwater Architecture*, 2008. Alugraphy, 53 x 78cm (20¾ x 30¾in.).

Like many artists of his generation who wish to work in that profession full time without the support of a teaching job or other work, the need for autonomy comes at the price of having to pursue two parallel strands of work: one tending towards the commercial market, the other towards the relative purity of personally oriented work. Baramov's work encompasses painting, printmaking and video, with occasional performance works: in 2012 he was appointed curator of exhibitions at the Natural History Museum in Sofia. He has exhibited his work extensively in Bulgaria and also in international exhibitions and competitions.

In the central theme of his lithographs Baramov explores the notion of improbable dualities, blending elements of the natural and built environments with engineering and technological solutions to problems that have not necessarily yet been posed. His drawing skills are clearly evident, as is his ability to conceive in minute detail the machinery and buildings that emerge from his imagination. The world he depicts hovers somewhere between dream, fantasy and science fiction, elements more usually found in visual form in film and television presentations. In such forms the large scale is created in a filmed reality or implied through the increasingly sophisticated use of computer graphics that has replaced the finely detailed models that preceded this technology. By contrast, Baramov draws his imagined worlds in fine detail and often at very small scale on the matrix, building up images of buildings or vehicles, alone or in combination, resulting in prints that are modest in scale but grandiose in intent. These works draw the eye immediately through their initial strangeness, then draw it in still further as details emerge to the attentive viewer. There is a logic in the worlds created and yet, at the same time, a crazy illogic that argues against the initial impression but does not prevail. Adding further to the images are blind-embossed details of textures and components, and his signature red thumbprint, and sometimes titles and signatures in expansive script. A suite of oil paintings entitled *arTchitecture* follows similar themes, using bright colour and an equal attention to detail and structure.

In a linked series Robert Baramov presents his ideas in the form of project sheets, in which he illustrates and details *The house I was born in and the house I want to live in*, which

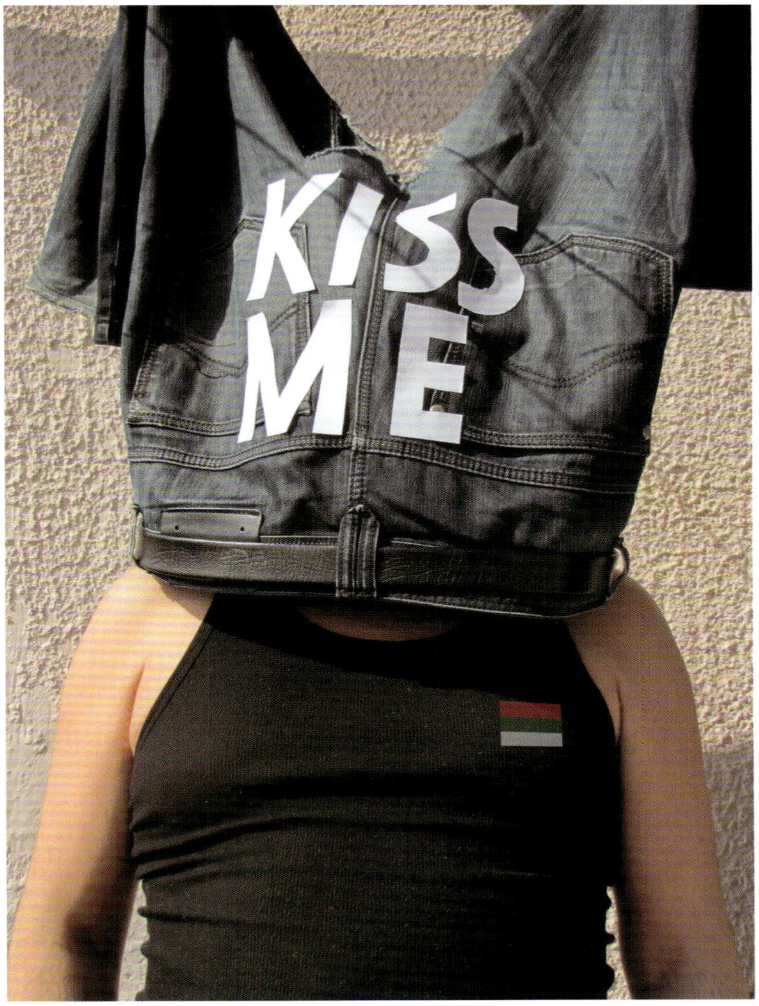

Robert Baramov, *Very Important Announcement*, 2012.
Photography, variable dimensions.

includes photographs and a plan of his birthplace and his 'dream' house (which is partly in the form of a horse within which are rooms and windows); *A project I tried to realise – the Noah's Ark*, a 50-metre long construction that he hoped to build in Germany in 1994; and *A project I want to realise*, which shows his 'dream' car, a Mercedes that will travel with equal ease on land, sea and in the air. The projects are presented in full detail, using a range of mediums, and demonstrate an imagination running at full tilt while also containing elements that suggest dissatisfaction with the Bulgarian social and political situations at the time when they were conceived. Baramov's art is not always as straightforward as it at first appears.

Another dimension to his work comes with the way in which he has taken his lithography and used it as the source for computer animation. The resulting videos show elements similar to those in his lithographs on paper, which after an interval of stillness are animated to incorporate movement, at first subtle then frenetic. Parts of the land/sea/air vehicle begin to move, vehicles come and go across the surface of the images and between the buildings, while the undersea buildings begin to move and ripples cross the image. All these movements are accompanied by loud inchoate sound, suggesting the movement of some vast machinery. The effect can be unsettling, such as when the video works were shown in a room in the ancient hammam baths in Plovdiv, which have since become a centre for contemporary art. The contrast between the textures and colours of the vaulted room and the powerful impact of the projected video could not have been more extreme.

Printmaking is this artist's primary medium, but he also explores ways to convey his ideas, and is often critical of and angry about the society and the art world in which he lives. In his *KISS* project he envisages a graphic presentation for Bulgaria in the Venice Biennale, in which an announcement is made to the effect that, 'The Republic of Bulgaria declares war on contemporary art by refusing to present Bulgarian artists in 2013'. An accompanying image shows the artist with a pair of jeans over his head, with a strong and graphic message on the seat. Baramov's intention could not be clearer, and would find resonance in a number of countries whose choice of artists for Venice can be controversial.

SERBIA & MONTENEGRO

DANA TOSIĆ

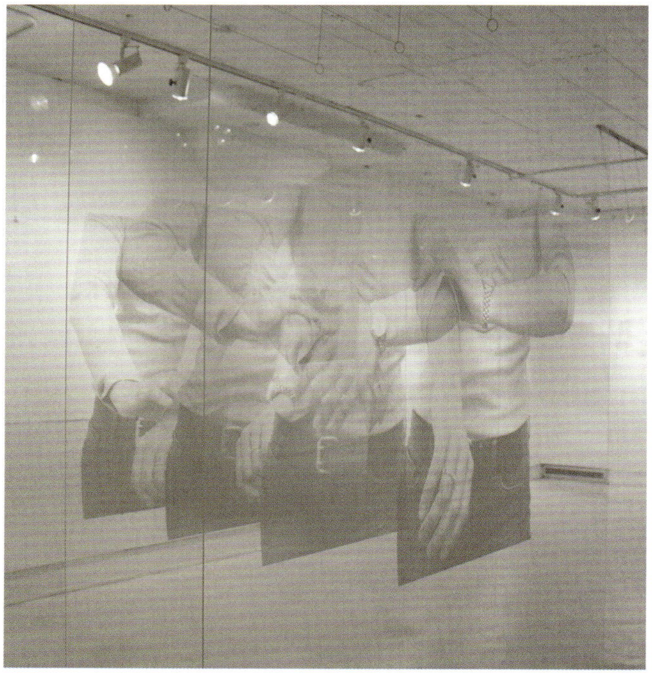

Dana Tosić, *Moments between Moments 3*, 2011. Screenprint on Plexiglas, 183 x 122cm (72 x 48in.) (each of four) x 60cm (23½in.) apart.

THE ROUTE TAKEN by Dana Tosić into printmaking was unusual, but mirrors both her family and her personal history, reflecting some crucial aspects of late 20th-century history and technological development. Born in Canada to parents who came from Serbia and Montenegro respectively, she was raised with a strong connection to her Balkan heritage, Serbo-Croat being her first language. Her summers were spent visiting relatives in what was then still known as Yugoslavia, and also in Nuremberg and Rome. In addition, she relates that she was raised in a house full of prints, many by the Belgrade artist Veljko Mihajlović, and that staying in Nuremberg included annual visits to Albrecht Dürer's house, all of which meant that she grew up very much aware of the history and techniques of printmaking. The conflict in the Balkans in the 1990s had a profound effect on her, in particular through the a sense of disillusion and alienation from her cultural heritage due to the very different attitudes of the new wave of immigrants, and the friction between her former identification with Yugoslavia and the aggressive nationalism of the incomers.

Before studying for a BFA in Printmaking she spent a year with her extended family in Rome, which stimulated further her interest in art and architecture, and in languages. She was fortunate in her BFA studies in that the professors in the printmaking department of Queen's University in Kingston, Ontario, encouraged an open and experimental approach to the subject, and a fluid movement between printmaking techniques and other art disciplines. Following her BFA she lived in Japan for three years, teaching English, but also studying Japanese, calligraphy and Kendo – the latter giving her a profound insight into, as she writes, 'practised movements, simultaneous absorption/disengagement of the mind, the experience of the body in relation to the space around it, and communication (verbal, non-verbal and the intrinsic relationship between the two), and these ideas, combined with my interest in performance, phenomenology, time, memory and trace, formed the basis of my MFA thesis.'

Following her time in Japan she lived first in Toronto and then in London (UK), working in administration in architectural practices, which initiated her interest and experience in digital technologies. On returning to Canada she began thinking more deeply about the relationship between printmaking and the digital world, a preoccupation that developed extensively during her MFA studies at the University of Calgary; this included a period as an exchange student at the Royal College of Art in London that brought her into close contact with 3D scanners and rapid prototyping, all of which fed into her MFA studies and thesis, and has informed her personal work since then. The interweaving of her heritage, her personal history and education, and her experience of a number of world cultures has encouraged her broad and unusual approach to printmaking. This experience has coincided with a distinct evolution in the connections between technology and the arts, in which the rich possibilities of digital creation have broadened the potential for greater interactivity between 'professionals'. in both fields. At the

Right: Dana Tosić, *Moments between Moments 3* (detail).

Bottom right: Dana Tosić, *Forgetful Gestures 3*, 2011. Digital print on Archival paper, 168 x 112cm (66¼ x 44in.).

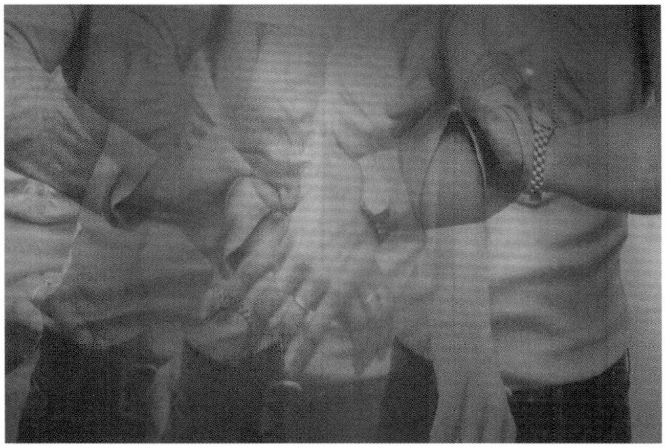

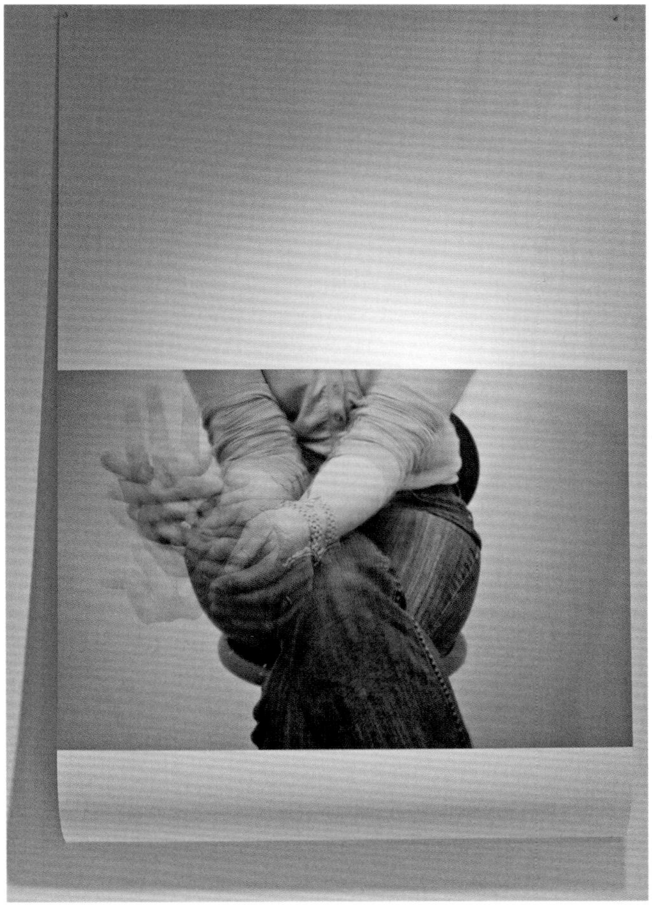

same time there has been an understandable friction between those practising traditional techniques and those becoming involved with digital technology, although digital printmaking is increasingly being accepted as being 'just another technique'.

In her earlier work, Tosić has used traditional techniques such as lithography but has always been willing to push those techniques to the limit, breaking the rules to achieve new outcomes. In particular her work has been concerned with reducing the image towards invisibility and finding ways of recording movement – and thereby the passage of time – within a single image or a series. More recently, she has made extensive use of technologies developed in the first place for industrial and medical applications. She sees this as being a logical extension of the appropriation of commercial print techniques for artistic use (or vice versa) that has been a central characteristic of printmaking for centuries. She has therefore explored new developments in 3D scanning, rapid prototyping (or 3D printing, seen as being the next big area for consumer technology) and in haptic devices – that is, those devices using the sense of touch or tactile feedback in the interfaces between the user and the computer. But, while reliance on such technology might perhaps imply a diminution of the deeper aesthetics of printmaking, this is not the case in the work of Tosić. Instead, by combining her experience of different cultures and a range of approaches to making art, she is creating works that contain the sense of mystery and depth that typifies memorable art in any medium.

In her series, *Everyday Ephemera*, she captures the movements that we use and see in others in normal life, encapsulating them in permanent form. These prints are made using 3D scanning, which in medical applications requires the subject to remain motionless so that clear images can be obtained for diagnosis. By moving while the scanning is in progress a multiple image is obtained, not through photographic and computer processes that combine disparate images by layering and combination, but as a single image that captures motion in time. The resulting prints are in washed-out colour, heightening the viewer's sense of witnessing something that is essentially evanescent. In a major installation, *Moments between Moments*, Tosić takes the process a step further by printing single monochrome images obtained from 3D scanning on perspex sheets that are then suspended in close proximity from the ceiling of the gallery, enabling the viewer to experience them from many angles and to see the images in conjunction with each other in ways that replicate the motion captured in the process. While conveying the human presence in a way that is greatly different to that used by Dürer, Tosić's outcomes are nevertheless as much a reflection of our times as the master of Nuremberg's were of his.

SERBIA

ANA MILOSAVLJEVIĆ

JUST AS the physical matrix is the intermediary between the artist's ideas and the finished print, so too can the chosen technique become the intermediary between the artist's vision and conceptual thinking, and its interpretation and expression in the form of the finished work of art. This duality, in which a broader definition of the matrix links idea with practice and outcome, is true for all printmakers' work and all printmaking techniques, whether traditional or electronic mediums, or variations and combinations of them. It is, however, a particularly potent duality in a technique such as collagraphy, in which the artist is able to manipulate the surface of the matrix (usually cardboard or wood) by adding and deducting material, gluing and cutting, resulting in a plate that can then be inked for printing as either a relief or intaglio plate, or as a combination of the two. An extremely flexible technique that is highly suited to an exploratory approach, as compared with the refinement and precision of, for example, mezzotint or digital techniques, collagraphy has been defined as the only printmaking process to be developed strictly as a fine art medium, in that it does not have a counterpart in the commercial printing world.

Ana Milosavljević was born in Sokobanja in Serbia and lives and works in Belgrade. She graduated from the Academy of Arts in Novi Sad in 2004 and completed her postgraduate studies there in 2008. She has had several solo exhibitions in Serbia and has participated in numerous national and international group exhibitions, winning a number of awards. Her work is based on the notion of the city and relates closely to her own visual experience. Belgrade, the Serbian capital, and Novi Sad, the second city, have an eclectic blend of buildings, from the medieval to the contemporary, with many sites of historical significance as well as buildings that were damaged during the NATO bombing strikes in 1999. Belgrade has a distinct place in the history of the region in the late 20th and early 21st centuries, but it also has ancient roots, being at the meeting point of several important trade routes.

While this historical and contemporary reality is part of the visual inspiration for this artist's work, she is also

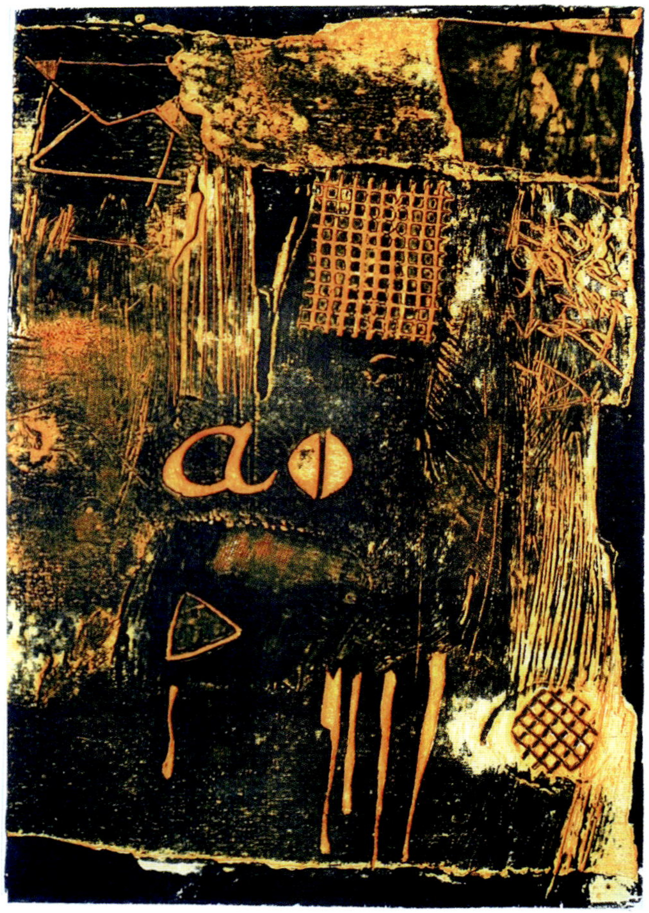

Ana Milosavljević, *Deo dvadesetdevet (Of Twenty Nine)*, 2010. Collagraphy, 32 x 22cm (12½ x 8¾in.).

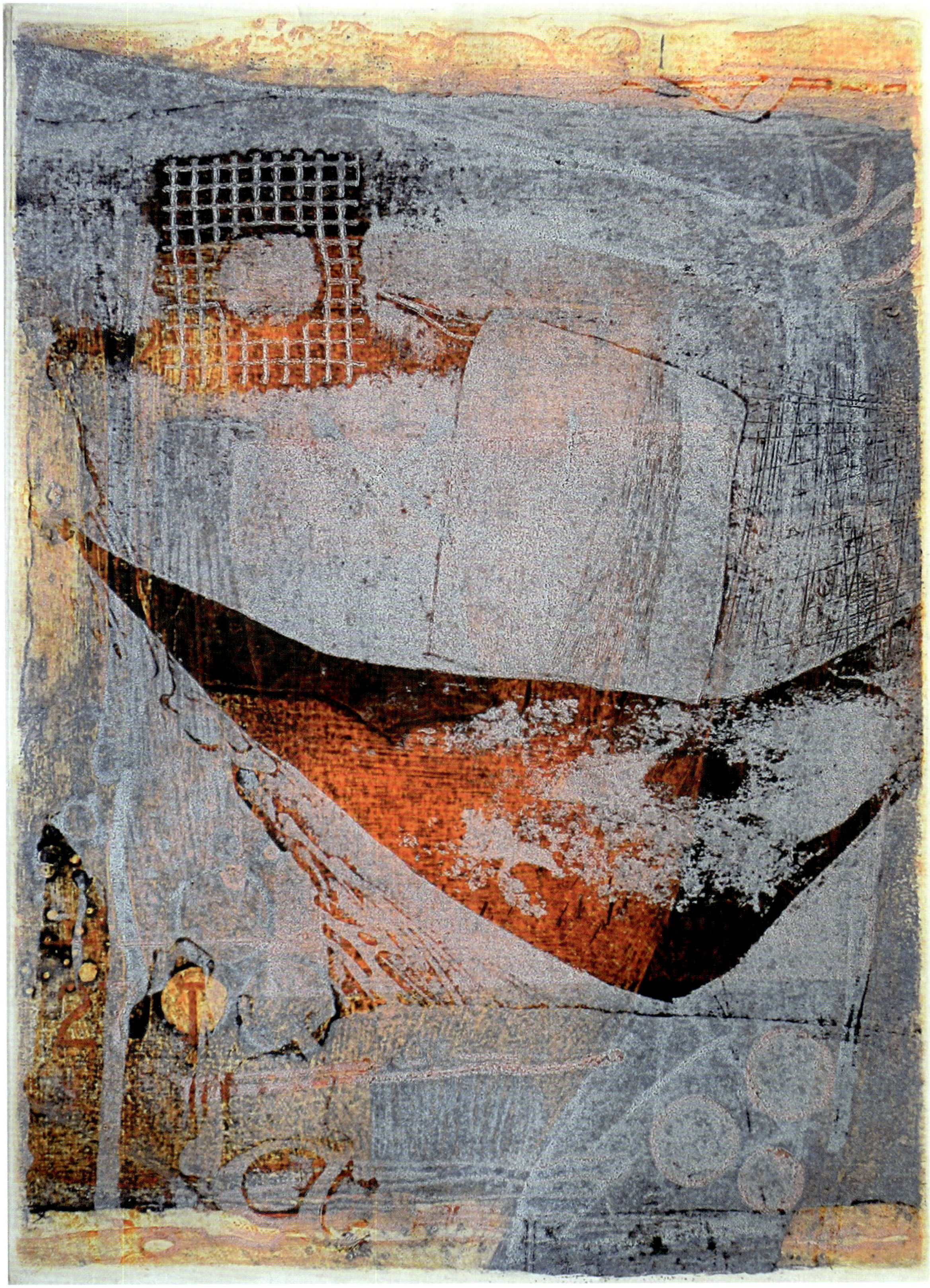

Ana Milosavljević, *Mistična Reka (Mystic River)*, 2010. Collagraphy, 32 x 22cm (12½ x 8¾in.).

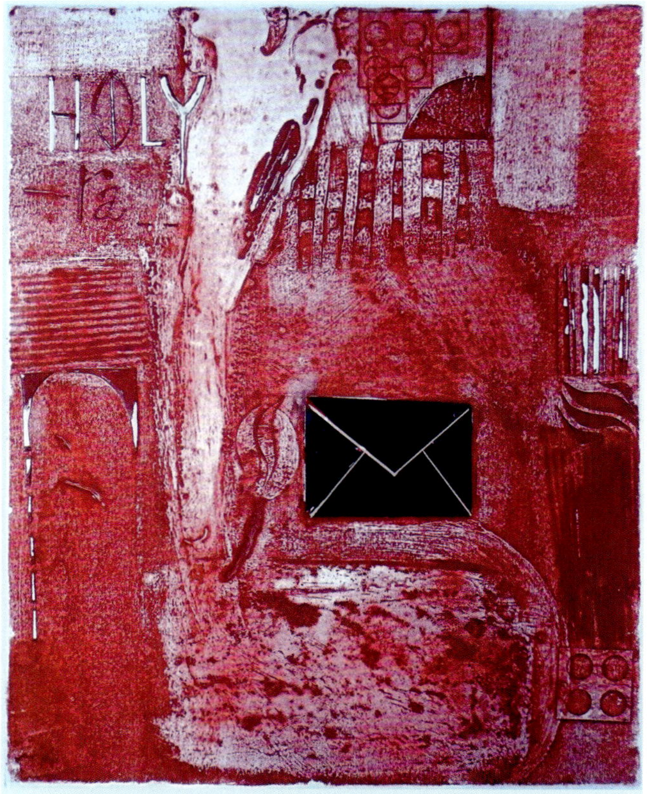

Ana Milosavljević, *Monopol (Monopoly)*, 2012. Collagraphy, 43.5 x 35.5cm (17¼ x 14in.).

interested in the notion of 'cities' in general and the balance between chaos and order that such places have. In this she shares the approaches of many artists and writers since the beginning of the 20th century, for whom the city is not simply a daily reality but also the inspiration for the cities of the imagination, such as the London of Conrad, the Barcelona of Zafón and the Istanbul of Pamuk. She writes, 'My visual experience starts by perception, real shapes are connecting, saturating and transforming into completely abstract shapes, into one abstract system of organisation'; and, 'Looking at everything that is around me, nature inspires me, instigates me to fancy, to dream with open eyes.' In her working process she seeks ways to open out her own perception and experience to others through the wider field of her prints, seeking the essence of her visual experience through formal means – line, form, texture and colour – describing this as, 'a need to announce some experience'.

In work that is essentially non-figurative, Milosavljević nonetheless finds inspiration from the details of the urban streetscape and incorporates these into her works – letters, road signs, symbols, the textures and colours of surfaces, the complex play of light and shadow, grime and decay against pristine surfaces, all surrounded by constant movement – with all those elements combining to create a visual mélange of the city that is also a visceral experience. Her work has been likened to the new expressionist style of visual arts that emerged, particularly in Central and Eastern Europe, in the 1980s, which has left a legacy that still inspires a new generation of young artists. But it is more than that, and the links can be traced back to the early developments in Pop Art and its precursors, bearing some similarity with the works of the American artist Stuart Davies in the 1920s, who incorporated fragments of signs and letters into his paintings. There are also indications of the impossible cities of the imagination, a whole world of science-fiction creations, the inchoate chaos of *Bladerunner* and *Mad Max*. For all that, this artist's prints are still and quiet, fragments captured in a moment of resolution and organised into balanced and chromatically harmonious compositions to create prints that bear repeated viewing and contemplation, giving individual viewers, perhaps, the possibility of considering their own impressions, visions and emotions.

These works are abstract in that they are abstractions from reality, not that they are derived from or devoted to 'pure art'. They contain elements of the spiritual – not the spirituality of formalised religion but rather the deeper feelings that arise, for example, when a certain intensity and colour of light falls across the deep textures of an old wall, or on the surface of a wet city street; those brief moments of incandescent clarity that can come when moving through a crowded urban scene. They combine a seriousness of intent and concentration during the making process with a quality of spontaneous joy that can emerge when the prints are studied and allowed to penetrate the open mind of the viewer – to resonate, perhaps, or otherwise to be remembered later. Milosavljević's use of colour – orange and gold in *Deo dvadesetdevet* ('Of twenty-nine'), limpid blue and the colours of sunset in, *Mistična reka* ('Mystic River'), and strident pinks in *Monopol* ('Monopoly') – carries much weight in the quiet assurance of her technique, providing an harmonious balance with the driving force of the original ideas and inspiration, through the studied concentration of the preparation of the plate, to the production of the final print.

ALEKSANDAR MLADENOVIĆ LEKA

THE PUNK ROCK period in late 20th-century culture started in the USA, the UK and Australia and then spread to other countries. Aside from the pared-down style of music and lyrics, the well-documented, anti-establishment punk subculture also included a distinctive style in graphics for posters and other materials, as well as fashions in clothing and body adornment. While fashions inevitably move on, elements of punk are still very much alive and well in some quarters of world culture and show no sign of disappearing. In addition, there are periodic phases of punk revival as new generations discover for themselves the vital energy of the punk approach to music-making and to style, reinterpreting it in different contexts. It is also a factor in the contemporary arts, particularly in graphics, and has made its presence felt in printmaking through the work of artists such as Aleksandar Mladenović Leka, for whom the style offers both inspiration and a formal methodology.

Mladenović was born in Belgrade and studied at the University of the Arts, completing his postgraduate studies in 1994; he is currently studying for a doctorate at the same institution. He has taught in the printmaking department of the university since 1999 and is currently an assistant professor. With a long record of solo and group exhibitions in Serbia and internationally, he is represented in a number of public collections and has received many awards in Europe. He describes his attitude as, '... to have "serious fun". As a paradox, I'm a hard worker. My work is influenced by the visual art heritage, but I find a great source of inspiration in film, photography, music, literature, cultural history and especially the punk and post-punk do-it-yourself ethos.' The paradox is continued in that he is well-versed in the traditional techniques of printmaking, and also digital technologies, moving between them and combining them as required for the work he has in hand. This approach to combining materials from a range of disparate sources using different mediums is something that he likens to the approach of a DJ, citing Nicholas Bourriaud, who (in *Postproduction*, 2002) describes the contemporary artist as a 'compiler'.

In 2005 the artist produced a large (40 x 100cm, 15¾ x 39½in.) etching with aquatint, entitled *The Last Traditional*

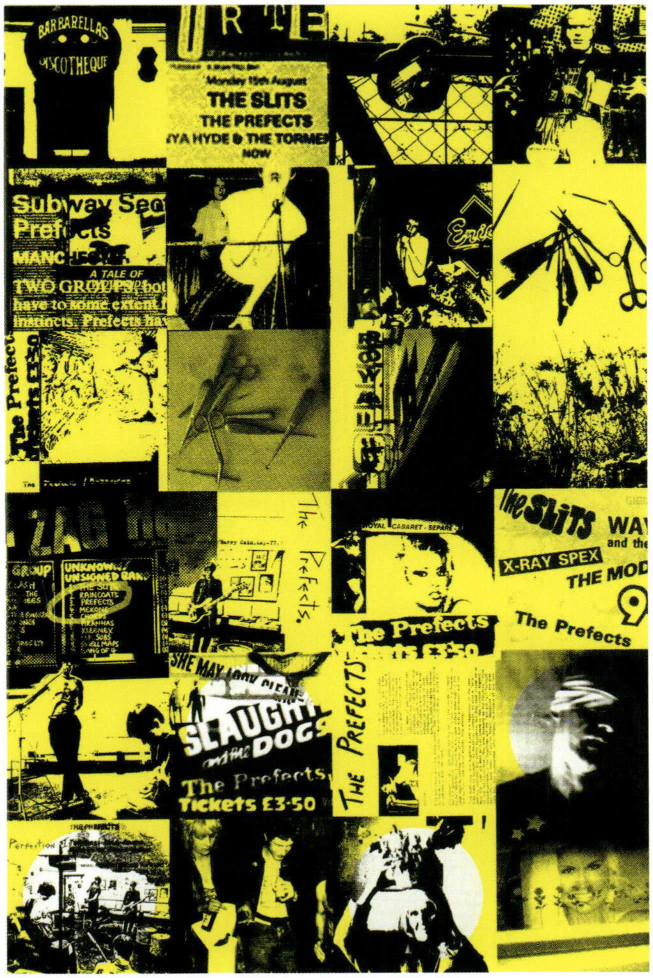

Aleksandar Mladenović Leka, *The Prefects – VD, riff E7 A5-E5 A3, 3/10 Day-Glo yellow*, 2012. Acrylic and silkscreen on canvas, 144 x 96cm (56¾ x 37¾in.). *The Prefects'* photographs by Brendan Jackson, from *Bombsite Fanzine* 1977.

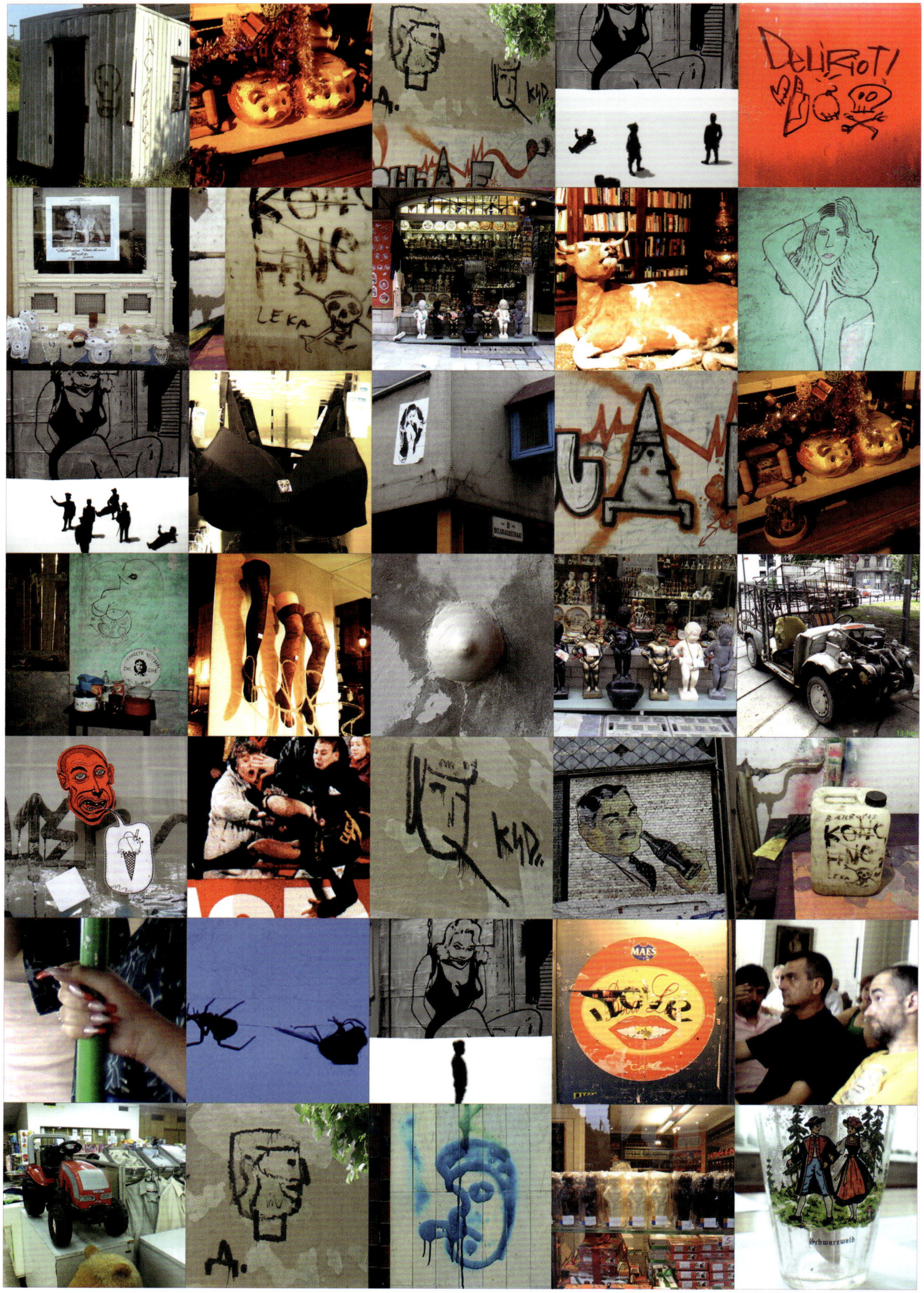
DELIRIOT!
LEKA
MAES
Schwarzwald

Left: Aleksandar Mladenović Leka, *F2*, 2008. Digital inkjet print, 98 x 70cm (38½ x 27½in.).

Right: Aleksandar Mladenović Leka, *Prince Mihailo Obrenović the 3rd*, 2011. Etching and aquatint, 65 x 50cm (25½ x 19¾in.) (plate).

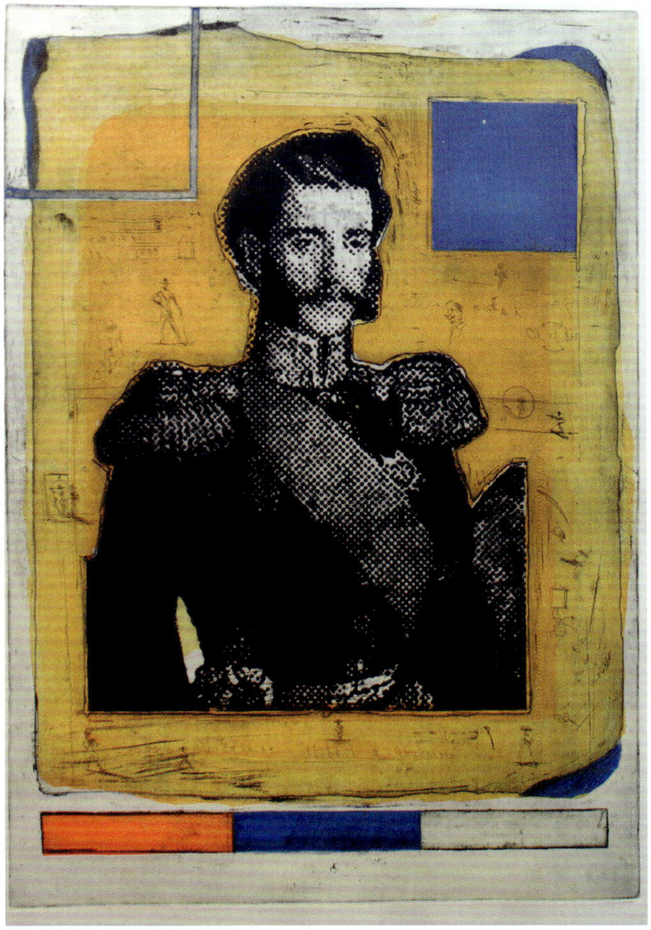

Print in the World, Ever, a masterly and somewhat surreal print reminiscent of de Chirico. The ironic title implies not ending but continuation, for printmaking in general and for this artist in particular, in that he continues to make prints using traditional mediums that can be placed comfortably within the long history of printmaking. However, most of his recent work is in mixed digital techniques. His approach is aligned not only with punk, but also in some degree with Pop Art, the two genres being linked through an emphasis on the appropriation of imagery from the worlds of commerce and advertising, which in turn appropriate some elements from the do-it-yourself imagery of youth culture – a process of circular self-referencing in which everything influences everything else, a cultural maelstrom of immediacy. It is within this nexus of possibilities that Mladenović is working and from which the selected images are taken.

F2 is a large digital print comprising a grid of 35 seemingly random square visual elements arranged in a strict grid. While most people are used to the idea of reading text from one side to the other, and to being subjected to a welter of imagery through the news and entertainment media (and doing so in a world in which it is said that the average attention span of a human being in the industrial world is decreasing), the presentation of imagery in this chosen form is, to say the least, a challenge. Reading such works requires an ability to go beyond *seeing* – namely, an ability to read them in much the same way as one reads a succession of words that make up a text: scanning sequentially from one side to the other and from top to bottom or, alternatively looking at is as a whole and then allowing images to impinge on one's consciousness, and connections to be made. The print challenges conventional ways of looking and presents all manner of potential visual subtexts through which a fuller appreciation of the artist's intent becomes possible.

The other two pictures are, curiously, linked by a quirk of history. *The Prefects-VD, Riff E7 A5-E5, 3-10, Day-Glo Yellow* is one of a series of large hybrid print/paintings in acrylic and silkscreen on canvas, and relates to a recording by the punk rock band, The Prefects. The artist uses a similar technique to that in *F2*, with square units of photographic and text images arranged in a grid. The text images relate to the cheap photocopying and printing that was used on flyers for appearances by such bands, while the photographic images are of the band, some places where they played, and various surgical instruments, combined together to echo the anarchist attitudes adopted by punk rock bands and many of their fans. *Prince Mihailo Obrenović the 3rd* is based on a portrait of a 19th-century prince, seen as a creator of modern Serbia, whose stand against the Ottoman Empire that ruled the country at the time was based on a disruptive manipulation of politics and economics, intentionally using corruption as a means to an end – as Mladenović writes, 'subversive and very "punk"'. The artist relates that Obrenović also had great counsellors in the Italian revolutionaries Garibaldi and Mazzini, who were linked to the anarchist movement. The artist's next exhibition is entitled *Monanarchiste*, blending monarchist and anarchist in a neat play on words and ideas. Given the quality of the work he has already produced on these themes, it is one to look forward to.

LIDIJA BOGDANOVIĆ

BORN IN 1978 in Požarevac in Serbia, Lidija Bogdanović graduated from the graphic department of the Faculty of Fine Arts in Belgrade in 2006, and is currently completing her PhD studies. She has had numerous solo exhibitions in Serbia and has participated in international group exhibitions. In addition she has been involved in numerous art and humanitarian projects and workshops in Serbia. Her personal work includes painting and drawing, printmaking, photography and mixed-media works, including the use of new technology. The philosophical background to Bogdanović's work is based on Chinese and Japanese sources, including the poetry of Matsuo Bashō. The contrast with European and particularly Balkan sources is considerable, and something that has offered her the freedom to explore beyond the usual frameworks of Serbian graphic art. She writes, 'I seek to penetrate beyond the appearance of background "reality", by recasting things in terms of searching for aesthetic expression and spatial "silence", viewing this in a phenomenal world clean of all the excess names, descriptions and functions by which Man explains the world around him – coating over the matter; I seek to break the mirror of life, so that I can look existence in the face.'

The artist's work in the middle part of the first decade of this century was mainly in the form of prints using algraphy, an offset technique related to lithography but using an aluminium plate instead of a stone. These works are characterised by areas of flat colour, beneath or on top of which are hand-drawn lines and forms. These lines establish a dialogue with the areas of colour, so that the prints can be seen as being in the long tradition of abstract printmaking in the Balkans. However, there are already present in these earlier works indications that the artist was developing in a tangential direction, breaking away from the strict purity shown in some of her predecessors' abstract work. In the more recent prints using aquatint and etching, the lines coalesce into square forms around another square of a contrasting colour to the main colour field. The smaller square operates in a way that's akin to an opening or window, setting up a spatial dialogue that apparently penetrates the picture plane. The artist writes, 'The square as a sign, a present absence, a two-dimensional surface, which divides the real and unreal. The symbol of cosmic and metaphysical illusion of space beyond our daily existence as a symbol of initiation, transcendence – the liberation of limited physical existence ... the path of transformation is the way of substantial knowledge. My art becomes a transformative process in which multiple values are reached, bringing together and not separating ...'

In conversations with the artist it became clear that, by developing her knowledge and understanding of East Asian philosophies in her work, she finds a form of absolution from the tensions she experiences through contemporary developments in Serbian society and politics. She is able to locate and delineate a sensitivity towards the eternal within the ephemeral pressures of 21st-century life in a country that is still emerging from a totalitarian past and developing into a modern European nation. In finding this solution she is not unique in world terms, as many other artists in the past have found solace and inspiration in alternative philosophies, but her work positions her as somewhat unusual in strictly local national terms.

Lidija Bogdanović's PhD exhibition project had the title, *Walkers – Touch through a transcultural dialogue.* The works that were shown are based on the manner in which much international dialogue is now conducted, through the medium of the internet and in particular through the use of Skype. Such technologies have the paradoxical duality of enabling face-to-face conversations in real time but simultaneously emphasising the physicality of the distances that separate the participants. The computer screen has become the interface through which much communication takes place, with the imperfection of web cameras and the occasional instability of internet services combining to create what can in effect become a barrier rather than an aid to human communication. The meetings that occur through such technology are not real but exist in a virtual world. Any recorded sound and grabbed screen images or video are at best fragmentary records and serve as more little more than a limited form of recollection. Echoing this reality, the records that the artist has made are fragmentary, snatched images of the participants – the artist in Belgrade and her counterpart in Syria – taken at different times and under varying lighting conditions, and of a low technical standard that is typical of the technological context. The participants, the 'walkers', play out a scenario in which they meet via their computers. The rules of

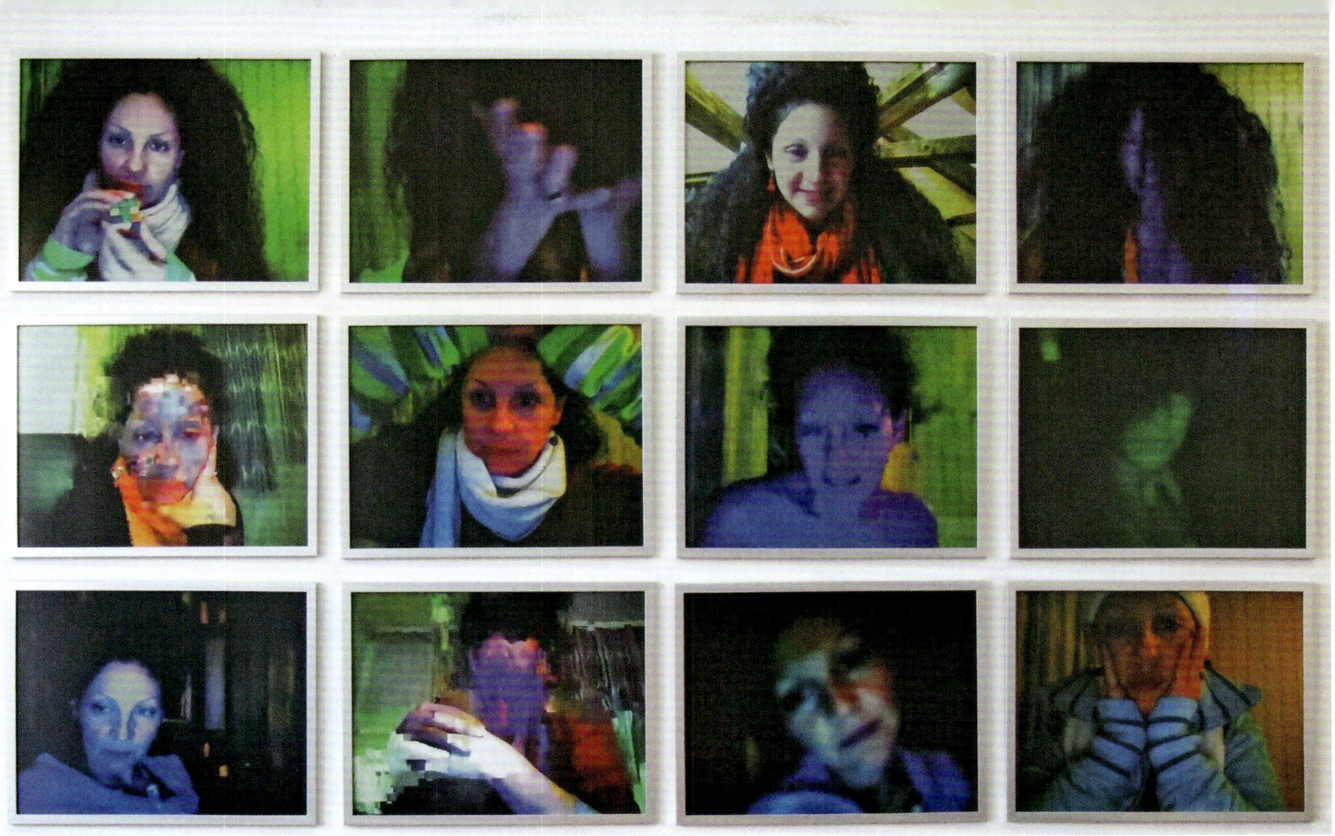

Lidija Bogdanović, *Walker* (part of installation), 2011. Digital prints on Fabriano Rosaspina paper, each image 46 x 62cm (18 x 24½in.).

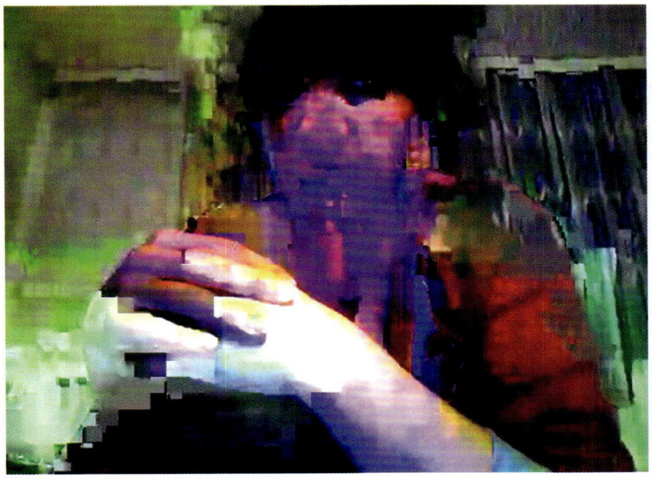

Lidija Bogdanović, *Walker L8-10*, 2011. Digital print on Fabriano Rosaspina paper, 46 x 62cm (18 x 24½in.).

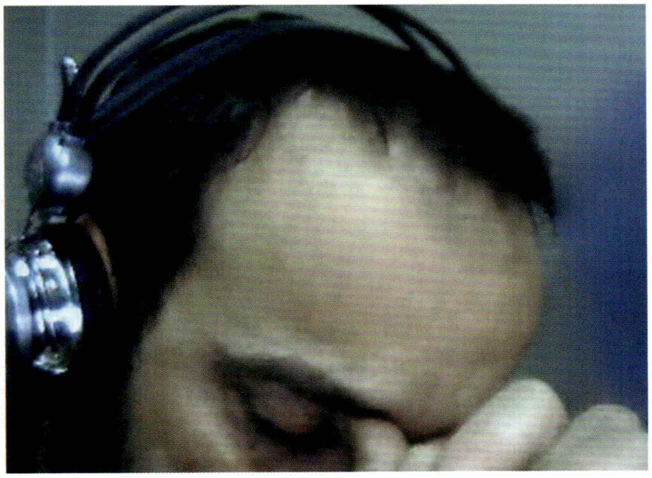

Lidija Bogdanović, *Walker W1-12*, 2011. Digital print on Fabriano Rosaspina paper, 46 x 62cm (18 x 24½in.).

the game, such as they exist, mean that either participant can initiate or terminate the program, and can choose whether or not to enable the video link as well as the aural link. Neither participant can be certain what type of record, if any, is being made of any of their conversations, nor can either be certain that they are not witnessed by other, silent and invisible, persons at the other end of the internet link. It becomes a sort of game, the creation of a temporary and alternative reality within which forms of communication exist. Selected visual remnants, in still and video images, formed the gallery exhibition.

As we come to rely increasingly on computer technology within our lives, this project by Bogdanović seems to take on an important relevance. The fragmentation of society and the deracination and cultural dislocation that come from the uncertainty in many people's lives are factors that disrupt the apparent security of traditional society. We are in danger of losing touch with ourselves, and internet communication offers little more than a partial solution. The resolution of this, set against the artist's personal philosophy, will no doubt lead to further explorations.

ZELJKO SKRIBIĆ

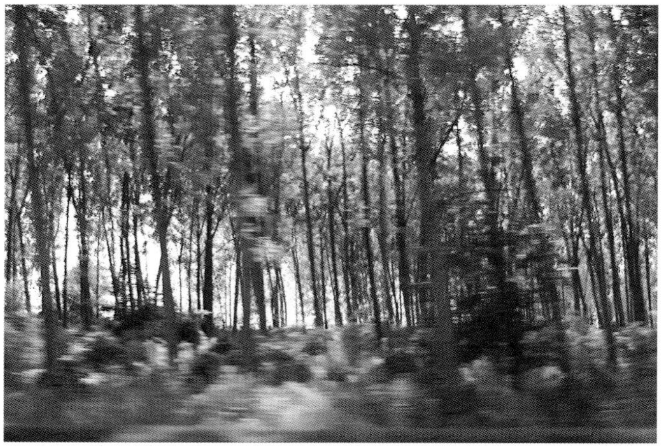

Zeljko Skribić, *Dilemma 5* (from the *Where Is It Better To Live?* series), 2010. Analogue black and white photographic print, 30 x 20cm (11¾ x 7¾in.).

THE TRADITIONAL ARGUMENT against photography – that it isn't an art form – dates back to the birth of the medium and has been resuscitated on numerous occasions since then. That it isn't an acceptable part of printmaking is also a long-running argument, to which there seems to be no final resolution. From its inception, photography (literally 'light drawing') was intended to be an art form and was presented as such in regular salon exhibitions. What is seldom admitted by traditionalists in either the fine art or printmaking fields is that photography, by virtue of its accessibility and openness to experimentation, has been successful in infiltrating both fields. Works by many photographers are now highly collectible, with prices to match for prints from limited editions – as evidenced by many photographers now considered artistic greats. At the same time, photographic techniques have become integral to many forms of printmaking, such as screenprinting, photogravure and lithography, becoming a crucial element in the creation of limited-edition prints. The arguments against photography as either a fine art or a printmaking technique have long ago been lost.

Zeljko Skribić was born in Novi Sad, the second largest city in Serbia, where he still lives and works. He originally graduated in physical sciences, in which he holds a doctorate, and in which he taught as Professor of Physics at the University of Novi Sad's Faculty of Science. For more than 30 years he has pursued a parallel career in photography, and in 2005 he moved to the Academy of Arts in Novi Sad to teach photography, becoming a professor in 2009. His primary interest was and remains in analogue photography, using film and the laboratory processes of the darkroom, and in the totality of the process by which the initial inspiration of the subject can be maintained with integrity through the staging and taking of the photograph, the laboratory processes of development and enlargement, and thence in the form of a print to the exhibition space. He also uses digital techniques for projects in which the immediacy offered by this form is appropriate, or when speed of access to the image is important. By using both analogue and digital techniques, according to the demands of the project, and with either source resulting in the production of prints, he believes that his work can legitimately be considered as a form of printmaking.

With the ubiquity of digital photography comes a different set of problems. The witnessing of an event (and the 2012 London Olympics proved this emphatically) usually produces endless examples of people, whether or not they are professional photographers, viewing the event via the screen of a digital camera or smartphone, taking shots and then immediately viewing the image to check its success or otherwise, with many posting the results almost instantly on the social-media networks of the internet, adding to the digital soup in which most of us are immersed. Skribić is aware of the risks and possibilities inherent in digital photographic technology and, while he does not denigrate it, feels strongly drawn back to using analogue techniques when seeking to make images of the world he sees around him, in order to produce thoughtful, meditative visual responses to it.

The three selected examples illustrate some aspects of the manner in which this artist works. The *Free Themes* series comprises photographs that are not linked to specific concepts but are taken for personal reasons when he is out walking, a partial record of the vision of a 'flâneur', the stroller who observes the world around him and records it in words or images. In reviewing the images that result from such expeditions he selects those that convey a 'clean image' – that is, one that does not 'talk' a lot. There may be a metaphorical sense that emerges from such essentially graphic images, but this follows as the result of the purified approach that he takes towards the creation of images built from the play of light and shadow. In the given example the landscape is reduced to near abstraction, broken only by the presence of the white building reflecting the light of the sun; human presence is implied through the building and by extension through the manner in which the land has been worked.

The *Dilemma* series is more complex in that it produces images in the form of diptychs. At their simplest these pairs of photographs contrast the human presence, through figures and buildings, with the natural, often wild, world. Beneath the simple contrast a range of further possibilities lies open to the viewer's imagination and analysis. The paired images operate as a form of visual poetry, as the presentation of abstract ideas to which the eye is drawn and to which it may return for further consideration. In choosing to use the notion of 'dilemma' for this series Skribić is intentionally offering the viewer the opportunity to look at the images and then to form their own responses according to the choices they have made about the environment in which they live.

The *Nightmares* series is unusual in that it was conceived for the use of digital photography, as the artist wanted to get an instant feedback on the success or failure of the images. The theme is of 'one sleepless night and a difficult young girl who dreams unfulfilled erotic dreams'. Taking a somewhat different approach than the more convention idea of a nightmare as being some sort of Gothic horror story, Skribić has instead positioned his nude model with a white sheet in a white studio space, and using a long exposure (around five seconds) has captured impressions of her movements with tenderness, modesty and a subtle eroticism. The results provide a counterpoint to his work in other genres, though in everything he does his photographic prints are of a high order.

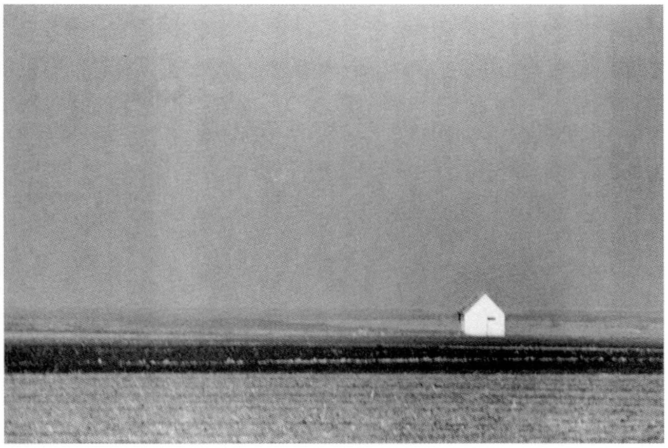

Zeljko Skribić, *My Dream 6.9*, 2011. Analogue black and white photographic print, 20 x 30cm (7¾ x 11¾n.).

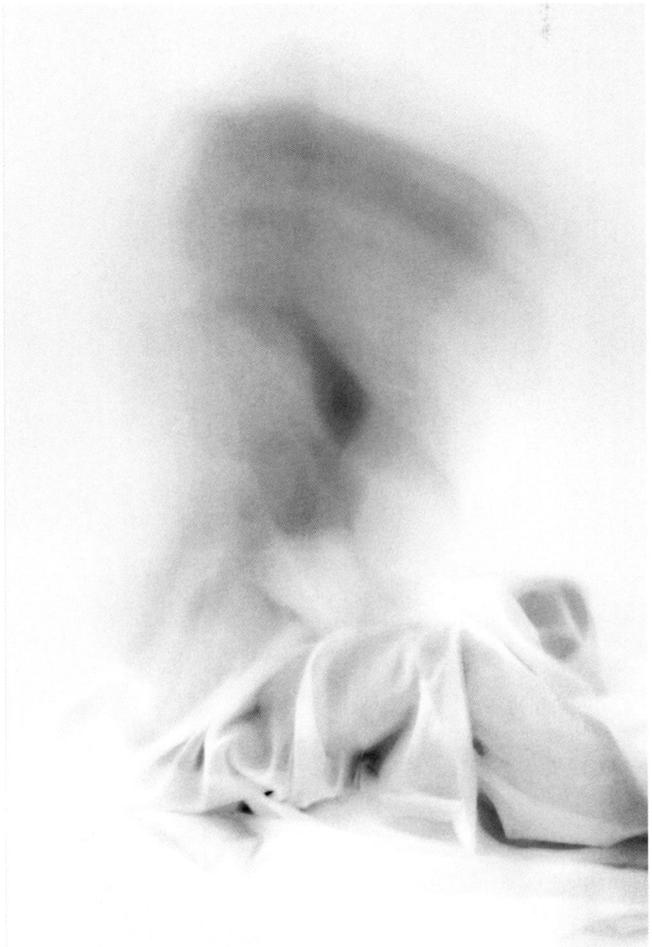

Zeljko Skribić, *Insomnia 3.1* (from the *Insomnia* series), 2012. Digital photographic print, 30 x 20cm (11¾ x 7¾in.).

ZORAN TODOVIĆ

SOME OF THE high-rise blocks of Novi Beograd have an unexpected feature on the top floor – namely, compact studios for artists, each with a terrace giving views across the new and old parts of Belgrade and into the surrounding countryside. One such, occupied by Zoran Todović, contains a considerable accumulation of his previous work from which some idea of his artistic development can be gained. Born in 1958 in Gornji Milanovac, and educated at the Faculties for Applied Arts and Fine Arts in Belgrade, obtaining his PhD in 1985, he is currently a professor at the Academy of Arts at the University in Novi Sad. He has a long history of solo and group exhibitions in the former Yugoslavia, latterly in Serbia, and internationally.

Among the list of exhibitions is the major solo exhibition, 'Speak Serbian so that the Whole World Can Understand You', staged at the art pavilion in Kalemegdan Park in Belgrade in 2006, where a large selection of his major works filled the spaces of that important building. The catalogue contains an interview between Todović and Ljiljana Ćinkul, Director of the Galerija Grafički Kolektiv, the Belgrade gallery dedicated to the graphic arts, which celebrated its 60th anniversary in 2009. The interview reveals some of the thinking behind the artist's work and in particular his view of printmaking as being an integral part of the contemporary visual arts and not a detached autonomous discipline. Many of the works were in the same style as those seen on visiting the artist's studio: essentially comprising a mosaic-like grid formed from stacks of paper squares about 8 x 8cm (3 x 3in.) and 5cm (2in.) thick, set out on large baseboards. The outermost surfaces of each square varied according to the subject of the work – in one piece fragments of funeral announcements, in another fragments of images from art history – and the artist then painted over parts of these images. Questioned about the connection of such works to his former preoccupation with more traditional graphic forms Todović says, 'I could not overlook the fact that newspaper sheets are prints in the broadest sense of the word ... one should consciously accept that the deconstructed, disintegrated system of everyday life is built into a new form.'

Further into the interview there is a discussion of the role of sign and symbol in the artist's work and also of the concept of language: Todović speaks of how a 'single language was converted into multiple languages by means of administrative political decisions'. In the context of the 20th-century history of what was formerly Yugoslavia and has become a multiplicity of countries, some with boundaries that are still not completely resolved, this remains a strong factor. Ćinkul refers to the way in which the exhibition, '... underlies the reflection and self-reflection of alienated individuals, ethnics of a country with a flexible name and territory'. The longer history of the Balkans is characterised by the way in which the constituent countries changed their names and boundaries again and again as political and social alliances were made and then broken; and also by the influence exerted by foreign powers, putting significant pressure on ethnic and religious traditions, leading to the disastrous regional conflicts of the last decade of the 20th century, whose resolution is still uncertain. These thoughts, coupled with Todović's summary of intellectuals – 'some talk out of fear, some fear to talk' – give a good sense of this artist's work.

One of the constituent parts of the major exhibition was a series of self-portrait photographs in which the artist adopted disguises using different clothes, hats and moustaches, creating images of himself as some of the archetypes of men in Serbian society over recent decades. In this work Todović becomes a sort of Everyman, staring straight into the camera, shifting his appearance to comply with the expectations among various parts of the Serbian population, not fearing to portray the diversity of attitudes among the society in which he lives. This personalised and closely focused use of self-portraiture is repeated in a recent series of prints in which he combines a digital photographic portrait of himself with a digital reproduction of portraits of well-known artists, blending the two images using editing software. The self-portrait part of each image remains the same, and in itself replicates the celebrated photograph of Einstein that was taken as he was being driven to an awards ceremony, sticking his tongue out at the photographer, Arthur Sasse. The series of Todović images, a dozen so far, runs the gamut from Leonardo da Vinci to Marina Abramović, and taking in the likes of Dürer, Schiele and Beckmann along the way.

The titles refer to certain of the characteristics by which each artist is often remembered. Thus he portrays himself as Van Gogh, *An artist can be mad*, Beuys, *Anyone can be an artist*, and Gauguin, *An artist can be free*. The combined images vary, as some blend almost seamlessly, others with a degree of friction.

In the hands of a lesser artist a series such as this might be interpreted as coming close to narcissism, or even as being too light-hearted. While there is an element of levity in the images there is also a profoundly serious provocation to reconsider the ways in which the contemporary media treat artists – sometimes as archetypes, sometimes as heroes or villains, but increasingly as commodities. Given the fitful and difficult transition of Serbia from a troubled state towards becoming a member of the European Union, the complex and provocative work of Zoran Todović provides a fascinating insight into the way in which one Serbian artist is facing up to his own history and that of his country, as well as to the position and function of the visual arts in international society.

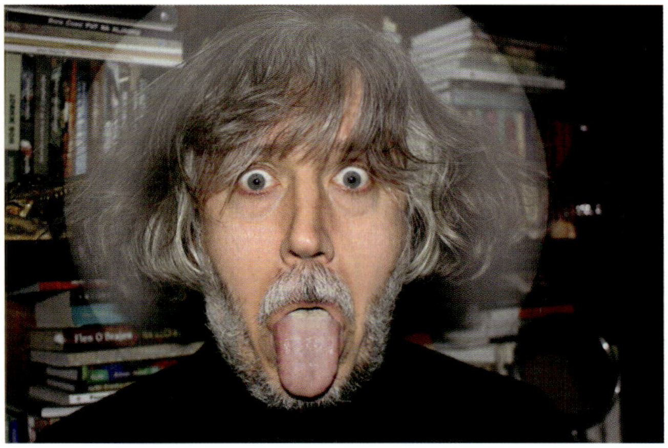

Zoran Todović, *The Artist Can Be…*, 2012. Digital print on Fabriano paper, 50 x 70cm (19¾ x 27½in.) (image).

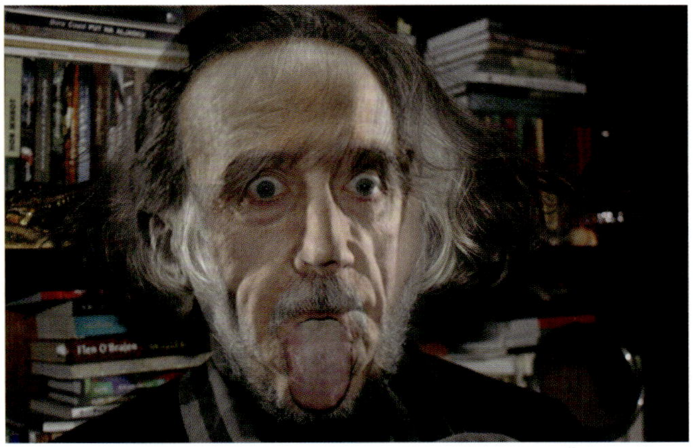

Zoran Duchamp, *The Artist Can Be a Flowerpot*, 2012. Digital print on Fabriano paper. 50 x 70cm (19¾ x 27½in.) (image).

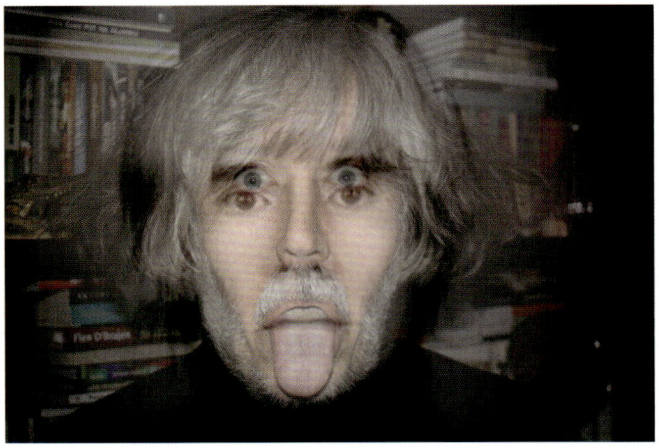

Zoran Warhol, *The Artist Can Be Famous*, 2012. Digital print on Fabriano paper, 50 x 70cm (19¾ x 27½in.) (image).

BOSNIA & HERZEGOVINA

ENDI POSKOVIC

ENDI POSKOVIC is well-known internationally for a style that marks his prints as both instantly recognisable and continually intriguing. His large and colourful woodcuts, with a powerful graphic style and a caption that is frequently at odds with the image, have been highly successful for a number of years, being shown in a large number of solo and group exhibitions both within the United States and internationally. He has been the recipient of numerous prizes, study and travel awards. The artist was born in Sarajevo, Bosnia and Herzegovina, where he developed a deep interest in both music and art during his time at primary school. Inspired, among other things, by reproductions in a Serbo-Croat grammar textbook of works by modernist painters such as Rothko, de Kooning and Klee, he decided to pursue a career in art at high school before going on to study for a degree. He graduated from the Academy of Fine Arts of the University of Sarajevo in 1990, specialising in printmaking, following which he travelled first to Norway and then settled in the USA, where he gained his MFA at the State University of New York, Buffalo, in 1993. He has developed both a significant academic career and a strong parallel career as an artist. Poskovic is currently Associate Professor of Art and Design at the School of Art and Design of the University of Michigan at Ann Arbor, where he has worked on the development of a unique programme of cross-disciplinary studies. In 2011 he was awarded a fellowship by the John Simon Guggenheim Memorial Foundation, allowing him to develop an entirely new project, *Crossing*, which marks a departure for him in terms of the medium used and its application.

In an interview for the Guggenheim newsletter of June 2012, Poskovic relates how he was drawn towards woodblock, having previously made large photo-based intaglio and lithographic prints. Having accepted a teaching post at Ball State University in Muncie, Indiana, he found he had no access to a printmaking studio, and on the advice of an artist friend began to explore hand-cut and hand-printed relief as a printmaking medium. While his work is generically related to the traditional Japanese *moku hanga* technique, familiar to many through the celebrated *ukiyo-e* prints by artists such as Hiroshige, Utamaro and Hokusai, he takes the process to very different, and much larger, ends. He says, 'Once I realised I could make prints without a press, I decided to make them as big as the largest sheet of paper available on the market, Okawara washi, 99 x 182cm (39 x 72in.), would allow. Over the course of a year, I began to employ classic *ukiyo-e* tradition with visual strategies of European travel and political propaganda posters.'

The artist's roots are in what at the time was still Yugoslavia and in a city that played a tragic part in 20th-century European and world history. This, together with his experience from a distance of the violent conflict of the 1990s in his country, and its subsequent breakup into separate nations, has been a major part of the context within which he works. He speaks of how his work has 'evolved into an amalgam of hybridised narratives and treacherous scenarios' from the position of being 'neither here nor there, an immigrant and an outsider for whom constant adaptation is the norm'.

This attitude to adaptation evidences itself in the *Crossing* project, in which Poskovic has made a radical shift in both his working practices and the contextual material from which he works. As part of his research for the work he travelled for the first time to the rugged southeastern part of Herzegovina to explore the deeply rural, mountainous character of the region, with remote hamlets pre-dating the Ottoman colonisation that began in 1463. The theme of this work is a story, said to be true, originating from 1943, when the Axis powers launched their attack on the Yugoslav People's Liberation Army, led by Josip Broz Tito, resulting in many deaths before the Yugoslav Army defeated their enemy. When the remains of one of the dead, Ibro, were returned to his mother, she noticed that both legs were left legs and, not knowing which was the real one, decided to bury them both with the rest of the body. They were laid to rest near Silver Rock, a burial place for many victims; but that same night Silver Rock disintegrated mysteriously, and the following day two new rocks stood in its place. The story is based on the account of Ibro's sister, Emina, who was nine years old at the time.

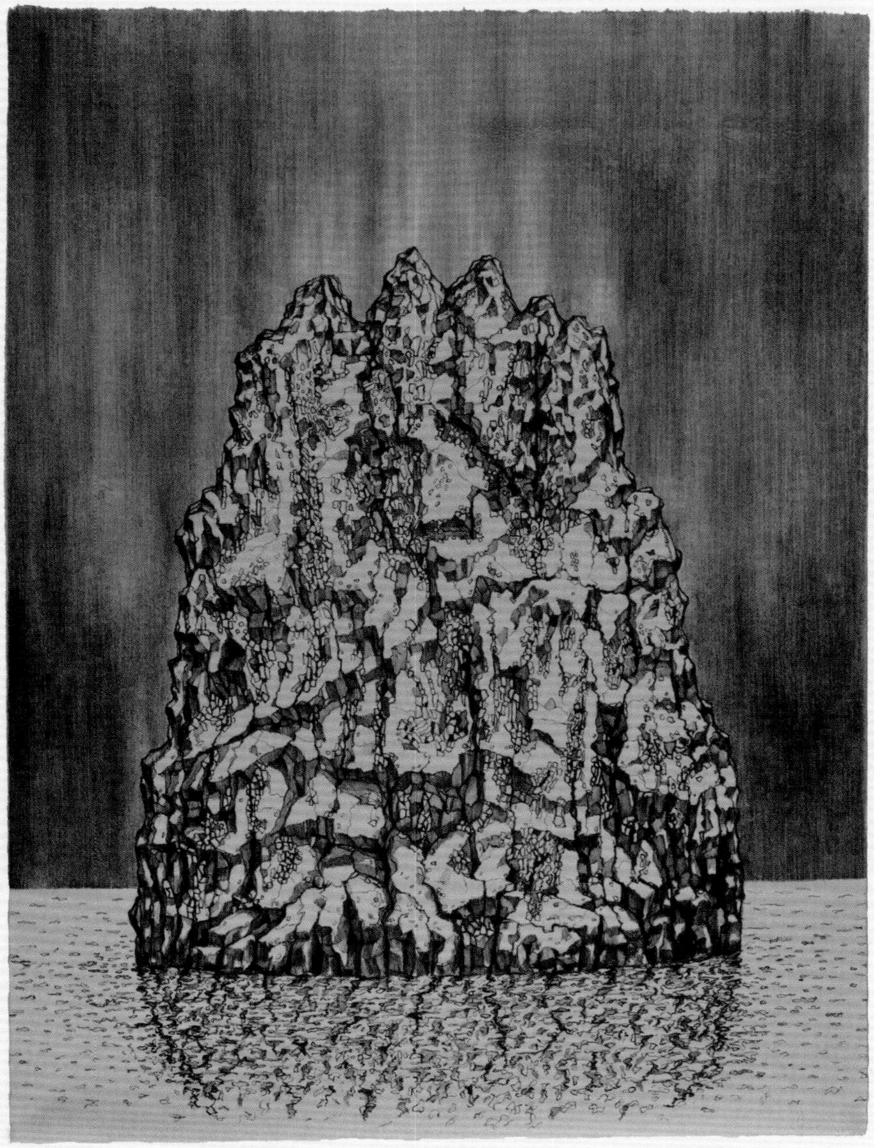

Endi Poskovic, *Silverberg I*, 2011. Stone lithograph on Kozo Okawara washi, 51 x 66cm (20 x 26in.). Printed by Jill Graham. Collection: Open Studio, Toronto. Photo: Peter Leix.

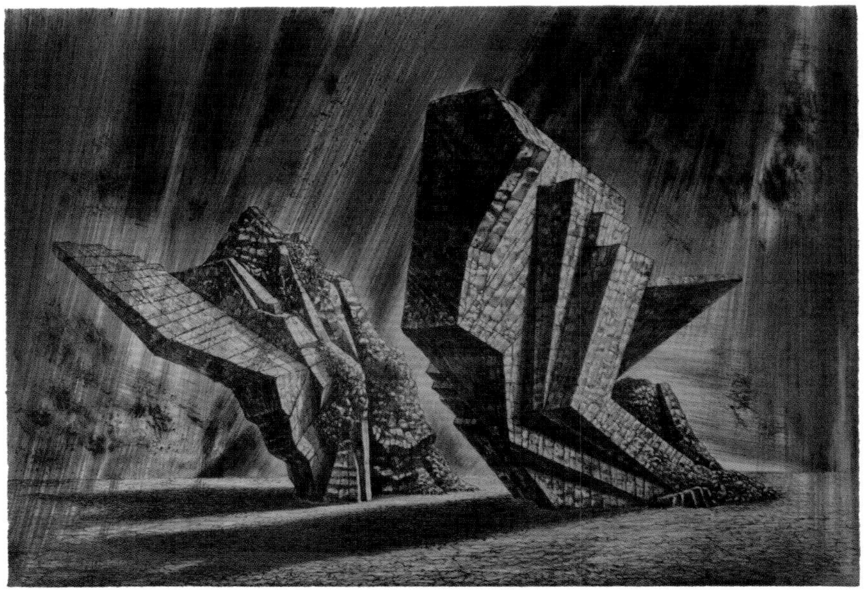

Endi Poskovic, *Spomenberg II*, 2011. Stone lithograph on Kozo Okawara washi, 61 x 91.5cm (24 x 36in.). Printed by Jill Graham. Collection: Open Studio, Toronto. Photo: Endi Poskovic and Peter Leix.

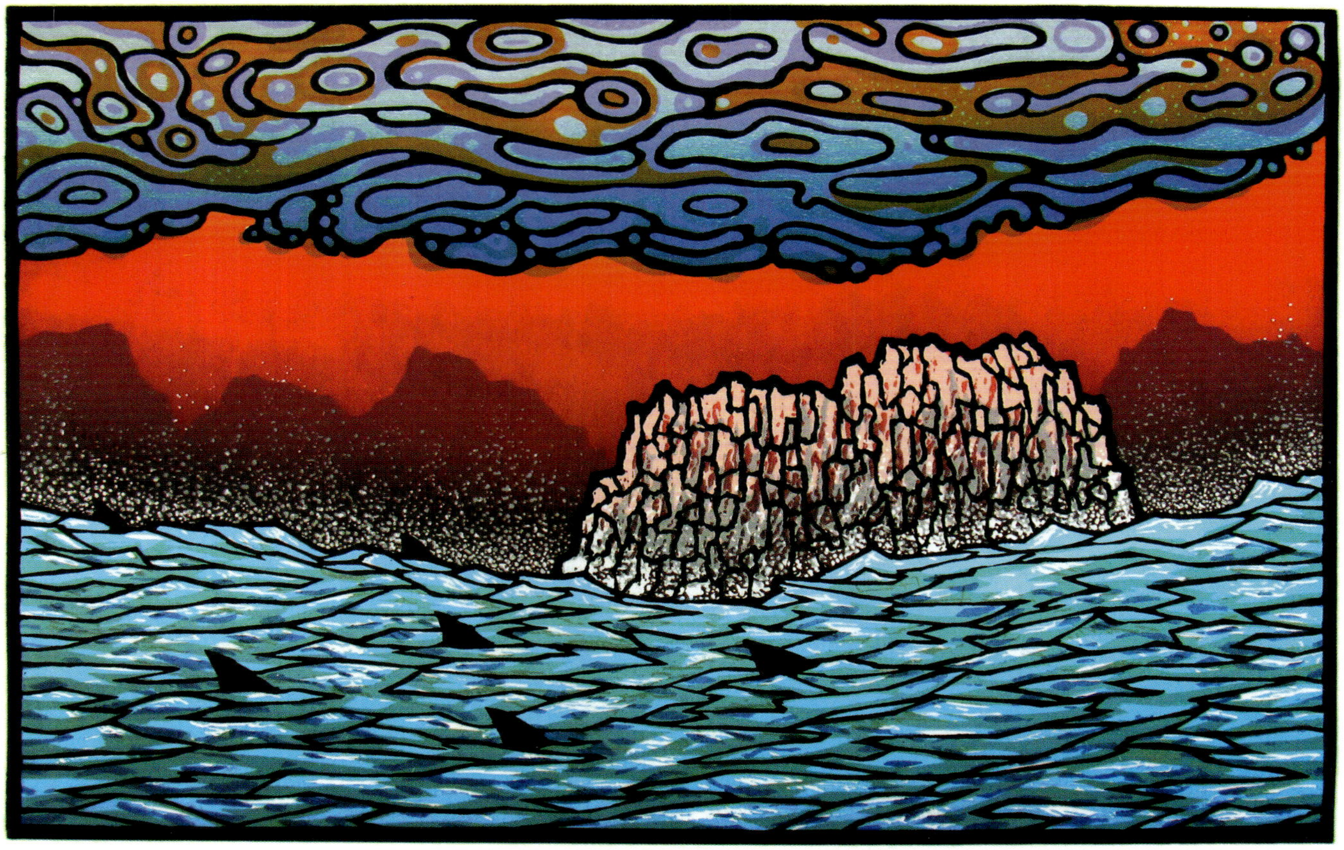

Endi Poskovic, *Night Watch with Small Mound in Pink and Large Cloud in Grey*, 2012. Colour woodblock, 12 colours, 34 blocks on Kozo Okawara washi 33 x 48.5cm (13 x 19in.). Printed by the artist for the portfolio, Hell or High Water, presented at Southern Graphics Council International conference, New Orleans, 2012. Collection: University of Louisiana at Lafayette. Photograph: Endi Poskovic and Peter Leix.

Poskovic decided to relate this tale through a series of more than a dozen large stone lithographic prints, produced in collaboration with Jill Graham, Tamarind Master Printer at the Open Studio in Toronto, and to use the resulting prints to create an animated film. Each print is derived from an extensive number of sources, including sketchbooks, drawings, collages and digital montage, among others. But whatever the source, the artist is adamant that his draughtsmanship remains the critical unifying force behind the prints, based on his own perceptual and physical activity. In addition, he stresses that the project is a highly collaborative one, working not only with Graham and her Toronto colleagues but also with colleagues and students at Ann Arbor on the task of utilising the lithographs as the starting point for the film animation. The animation is still in progress at the time of writing but, on the evidence of the trailers I have seen, will be dramatic, with a soundtrack of traditional music from Bosnia & Herzegovina.

Each artist who, by choice or necessity, seeks exile from their roots will have their own memories and their own stories to tell, and the methods and mediums they use will be different. Poskovic has chosen his own unique way.

JELENA MILESIĆ

CHILDHOOD and young adulthood are formative periods in the life of any person, and in the case of an artist can shape the way in which her or his art develops for a considerable period of time. For young children to be taken from the familiar surroundings in which they have grown up is a particular cause of feelings of deracination and disconnection from the familiar culture that has informed all the circumstances and stimulus of a young life. For the whole of the 20th century, and on into the 21st, there have been great shifts of parts of European communities, caused by conflict, religious friction and political dissent, and wars caused by the clash of cultural and religious beliefs. The full impact of such shifts is still not clear, and may take many years to assess. Nevertheless, there is evidence to be found within the work of artists who have been forced into exile, or have sought it, as a result of the conflicts in Europe over the past century or more. The visual arts can offer a path toward catharsis, but equally can help to illuminate the thinking of those whose young lives have been relatively untroubled, and who look upon the experience of artists in exile as though they were encountering something strange.

The breakup of the former Yugoslavia has resulted in continuing tensions in some parts of that region, but also a widespread dispersal of populations, part of the realignment of national communities that is helping to redefine what it means to belong to a certain group or nation, and equally leading towards an increasing growth of internationalism. (Indeed, it may well be that in the future this period of change will be seen as something of a watershed in human

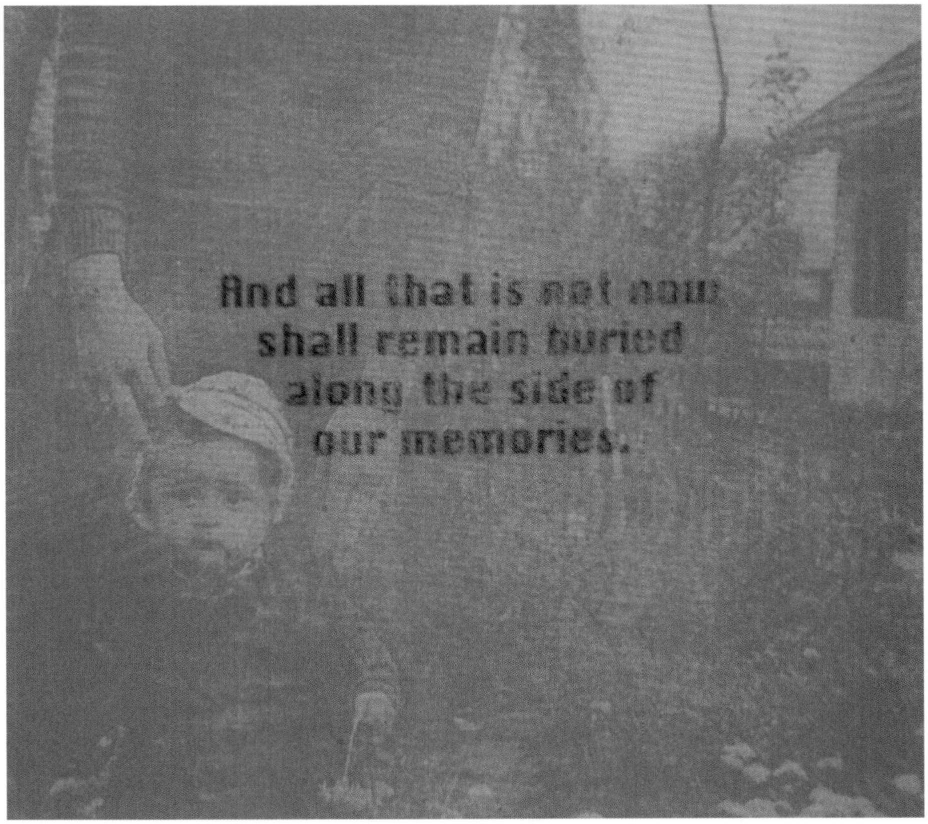

Jelena Milesić, *Untitled (And All that is Not Now . . .)*, 2012. Etching, digital print, 35 x 28cm (13¾ x 11in.).

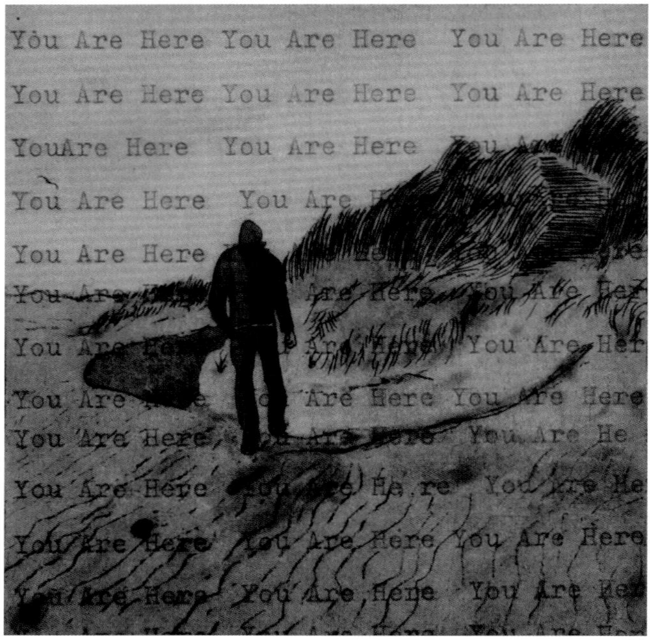

Jelena Milesić, *Untitled (This Moment . . .)*, 2012. Linocut, digital print, 28 x 35cm (11 x 13¾in.).

relations.) Jelena Milesić writes of her experience: 'Because of the war in Bosnia I had to leave my place of birth, and it wasn't by choice. Not having been given proper guidance as to what was happening had left many unanswered questions and confusions in my head. My confusion and loneliness only grew when I moved to the United States as I was soon discovering that I didn't fit in. How I learned to understand life prior to moving to the United States was soon proving not to be the "right way". My old values, morals and ethics were now up against new values, morals and ethics that were different – that, at the time, I had found hard to accept. What do social morals mean when they vary from culture to culture? Who's right and who's wrong? The truth is, we make up rules and we invest so much of our faith in these made-up rules that we make them seem important. But most of the rules were here before we were even born; therefore, we didn't even have an option to make a choice. We invest so much of our faith in these made-up rules that we kill each other over them.'

Currently a student at the University of Arizona, Milesić is still developing her mature style, but already there are indications of an acute sensibility, and an ability to use essentially simple approaches to create prints that speak not only of the nostalgia that she understandably feels for the country of her birth but also of moves towards images that chime with the experience of other dispossessed people. Asked about her experience of a workshop led by the First Nations artist, Randy Kemp, and whether she had noticed any similarities between her work and his, she replied that she hadn't thought about it but that she and Randy had enjoyed a long conversation about their growing up and how they now build their lives around such memories, and added, 'I guess we both use our art as an instrument to keep our culture alive and close to us.'

This certainly is true for her earlier work in linocut, in which there is a deceptive simplicity – an initial experience of 'what you see is what you get'. However, something else comes through, perhaps the echo of a lost time, a nostalgia for a broken childhood that can never be regained. The images have certain similarities with those seen in traditional cross-stitch samplers, and depict objects familiar in a household, a self-portrait in traditional costume, a portrait of her grandfather, and formalised images of plants and objects, some with names added in Cyrillic script. Deceptive in their simplicity, they bear a freight of memories and associations that will be deeply personal to Milesić and her family, which to outsiders will remain mysterious, detached from their own personal experience and beyond the possibility of full comprehension.

Her work from 2011 onwards marks a change not only in its substance but also in the changing attitude it reveals. This derives from her decision to come to terms with her identity as a young woman who remembers her past in a country, Yugoslavia, that no longer exists in name, and who now lives in the United States. She writes, 'Why do I have to consider myself either or? What does it all mean? And why does it matter? It's just another stupid label that doesn't mean anything. A label that makes us feel that we are different from other human beings. A label that we might kill for, or be killed for.' With this changed viewpoint she has embarked on work of a very different nature, which still has links with the past but also a different style and sensibility that are very much of the present. She combines typewritten texts that offer clues, with images from the distant past in etching, linocut or digital print, and sometimes mixing techniques. This is taken further in prints that relate to more recent memories of her life in America, indicating a new trajectory in her work.

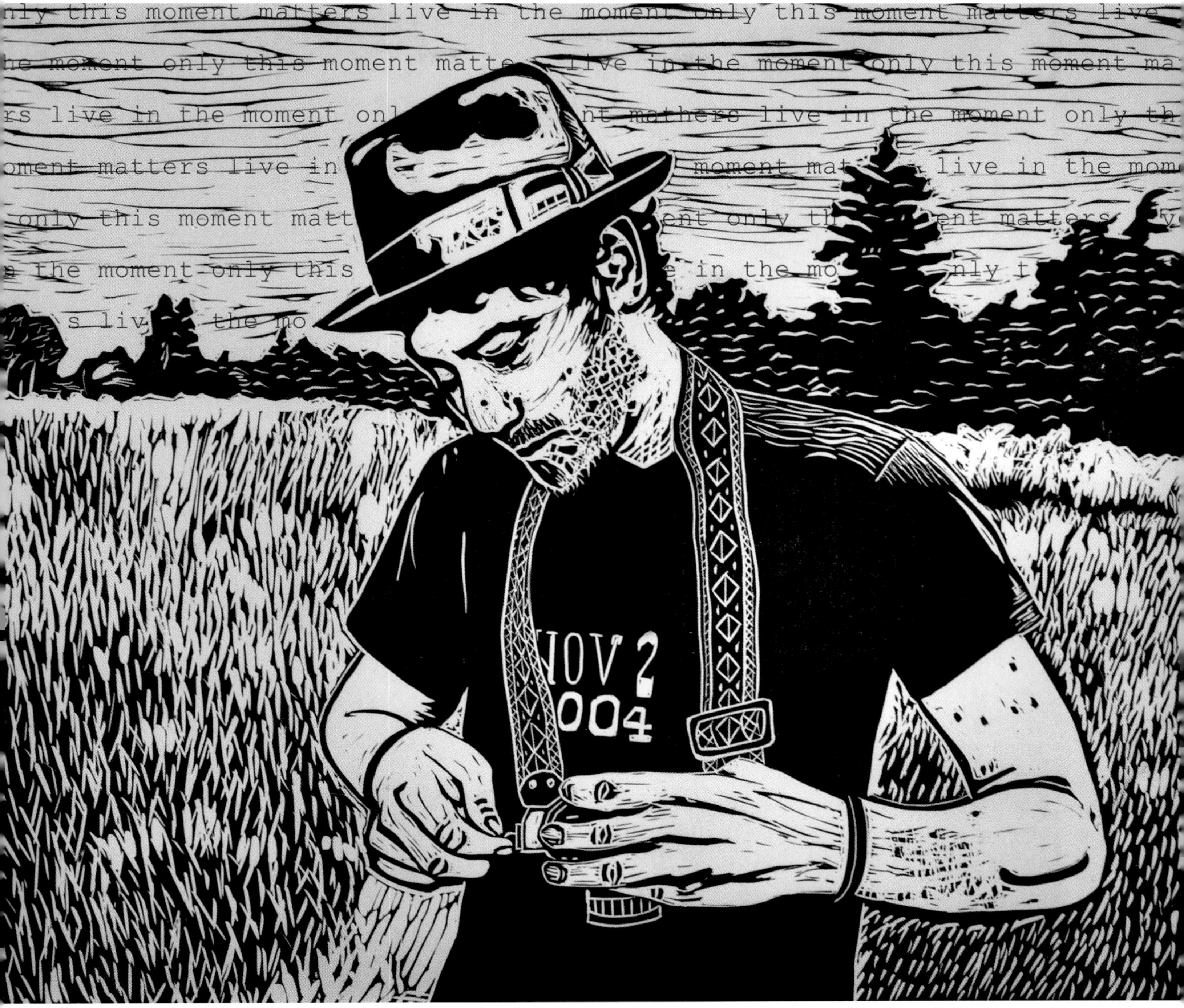

Jelena Milesić, *Untitled (The Road Always Leads to Here . . .)*, 2011.
Etching, typewriter, 35 x 28cm (13¾ x 11in.).

CROATIA

KAREN OREMUŠ

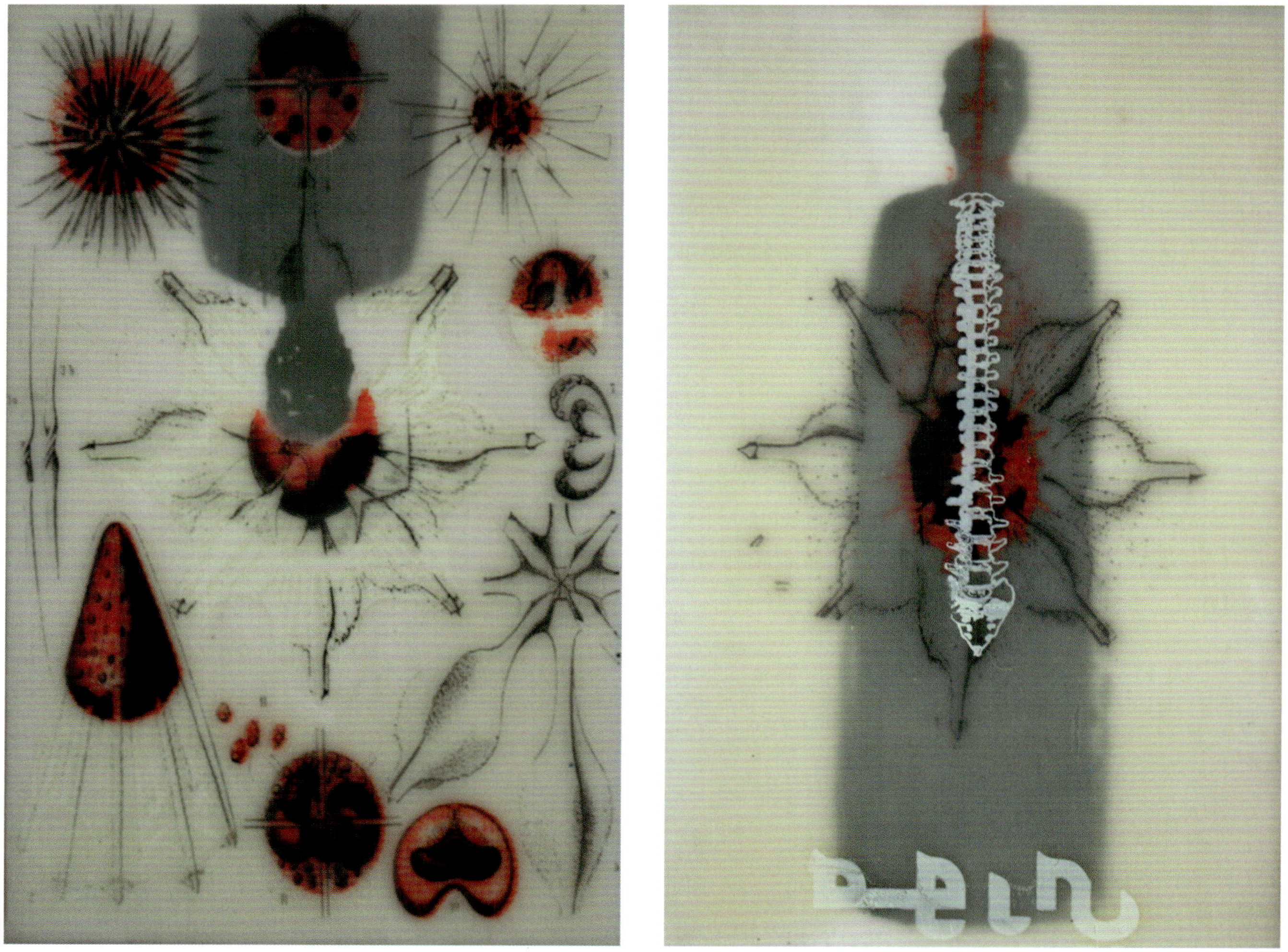

Karen Oremuš, *Ascension (Diptych)*, 2010. Etching, screenprinting on wax, wood, each 35.6 x 25.4cm (14 x 10in.).

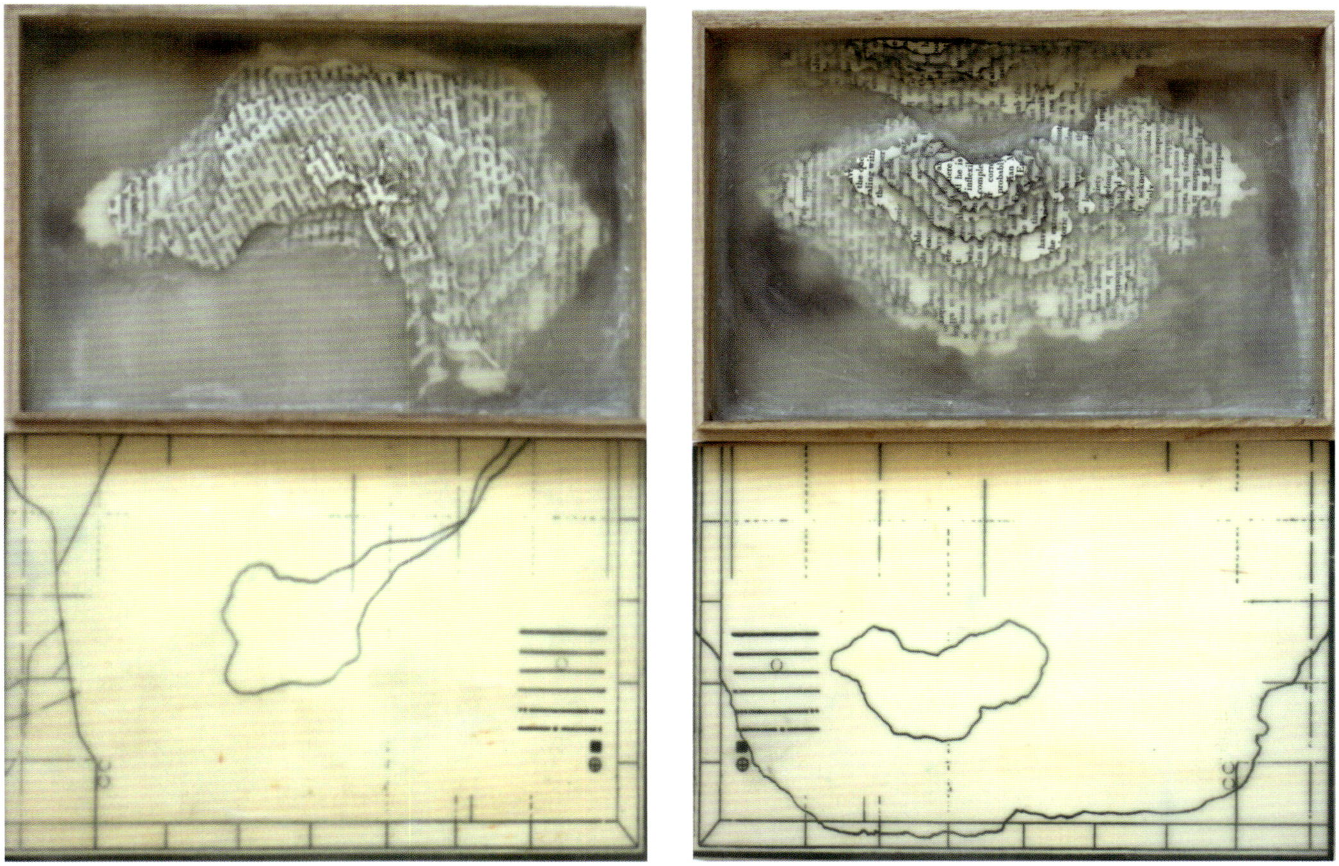

Karen Oremuš, *Deconstruction/Reconstruction (Diptych)*, 2010. Deconstructed antique book encased in wax in a wood frame, screenprinting on wood, each one 25.4 x 35.6cm (10 x 14in.).

KAREN OREMUŠ has an unusual profile and range of experience which has informed a body of work based on printmaking, but encompassing other mediums and approaches that give it a distinct signature. A first-generation Canadian, born in Montreal to a Croatian father and a German/Slovakian mother, she holds a BFA in Fine Art (Printmaking) with a minor in Roman Archaeology from Concordia University in Montreal, and an MFA in Printmaking from Tyler School of Art at Temple University in Philadelphia, as well as qualifications in painting from the Accademia di Belli Arte in Rome and in field archaeology from Warwick University in England. She has worked in many countries in archaeology and as an artist and educator. Since 2003 she has been a professor in the department of art and design at Zayed University in the United Arab Emirates, where she teaches printmaking and drawing, and was responsible for establishing the first printmaking studio in Abu Dhabi. She is currently Chair of the College of the Arts and Creative Enterprises at the university. Her work has been shown in numerous solo and group exhibitions around the world, and is included in several public and private international collections. In addition, she has worked intensively to establish indigenous printmaker/artists in the UAE through exhibitions that she has curated or co-curated in the emirate states and further afield.

Much has been made in recent years of the nature of palimpsest in the contemporary visual arts, especially in printmaking where the reliance on a matrix is a primary concern. In the case of Oremuš the combination of deep experience, both of archaeological excavations and the creation of visual art, offers a rich seam of palimpsest, in which the evidence of the past informs the present, leading either to academic cataloguing of artefacts and remains, or to personally focused work derived from her own, and her family's, memories. In her art, as in archaeology, there is the evidence of the careful uncovering of layers and the contemplation of meaning and significance. She writes, 'Human memory is encoded in river sediment, the earth's strata and urban decay. As an archaeologist, uncovering this history served (and still continues to serve today) as a grand forum of inspiration for my art work. Excavating civilisation upon civilisation was an eye-opening experience for me, and I started to question the fragility of the world in which we live.'

Her family history, particularly with reference to Croatia, a country injured many times, and with that the injury experienced by her family, led her to working on restoration

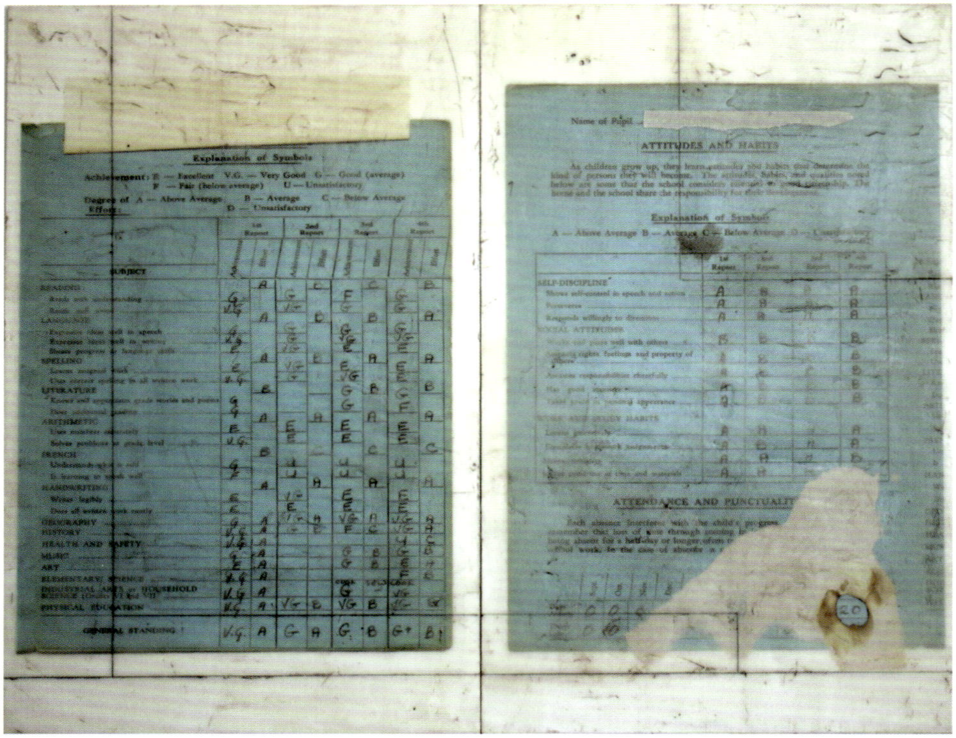

Karen Oremuš, *Relic VIII – Report*, 2008. Digital print on Concord rag paper, etched wax on wood, 61 x 91.4cm (24 x 36in.).

and rebuilding projects after the recent war. She speaks of feeling 'the sorrow in the structures of the land', and how this led eventually to her decision to take the art path rather than the archaeology path in her future work: 'While I am no longer excavating, my work is still motivated by place, family, heritage, memory and history.'

The diagnosis of Alzheimer's disease in her mother and her death eight years later brought into focus for Oremuš the need to capture the memories contained in an object, a fragmented recollection or a family heirloom, and to attempt to preserve them by encasing them in wax, as in the artist's later works. She writes, 'This later work explores matter, energy, mind and spirit and their interplay immersed in the experience of the ephemeral.'

In addition to working from her personal experience of archaeology as a process of rediscovery and of seeking to understand the past, and also from the development of her own art practice across many years, the recent work of this artist also depends on *wabi-sabi*, a Zen Buddhist philosophical and aesthetic principle that is embedded within her work. The belief enshrined in *wabi-sabi* is that all truth depends on the observation of nature, that nothing is permanent or complete, that all things are imperfect and that change – a state of metamorphosis – is the constant factor in life, and that all things eventually disappear into nothingness; the aesthetic is one of great beauty being found in the ephemeral and the passing moment. For Oremuš this tenet is behind her attempts to come to terms with the unpredictability of life and the impermanence of everything. It is evidenced by the highly finished quality of the works, despite their initial appearance of being temporary and haphazard collisions of apparently disparate elements. Such contradictions and paradoxes are encountered not only in Zen Buddhism, but also in the ways in which we accumulate memories and objects in our lives, holding on to them as we grow older until they cease to make sense to others and become dispersed. Fragility and strength are entwined in these print works, made with care so that they will last, and encapsulating the fading impermanence of things within prints of a high archival permanence.

Oremuš approaches the making of these works in a careful, scientific manner. She uses nitric acid on etching plates, a process with a less-than-predictable outcome, leading to deterioration of the matrix in unplanned ways. She incorporates digital photographs of fading and decaying remnants and documents of her and her family's past, manipulated and deteriorated through the use of computer software. In some works antique books are used as material for her work, to be cut and torn and then carefully restored. Such initial elements are then brought together and rebuilt to restore the art work printed from the plate or digital printer, and subsequently veiled with thin layers of paint, or in some works encased in wax to prevent further deterioration: the artist refers to her admiration of the Fayyum portraits from the Roman period in Egypt, in which, using the wax encaustic technique, realistic portraits of the deceased were painted on their coffins. Time and memory are melded together in the mysterious and haunting works of Karen Oremuš.

MELINDA KOSTELAC

SITUATED AT the head of a bay on the Adriatic, with the Dalmatian Islands stretching away to the south, Rijeka has long been settled, invaded and fought over by a succession of peoples, reaching back to the Celtic settlement of Tarsatica and its subsequent rebuilding by the Romans. The sense of history runs deep in the region and has had an influential role in the works of many contemporary artists. The printmaking of Melinda Kostelac has been concerned with more recent history since the Croatian war of independence of 1991–95, coinciding with her first degree studies. That period, one among the series of conflicts that ripped through the region that had once been Yugoslavia, set ethnic and religious groups against each other and left in its wake social and economic disruption on a large scale. The processes of reconciliation and recovery will take some time, but in the meantime the cultural resurgence, including in the visual arts, is going a long way towards healing some of the deep wounds.

Kostelac was born in Rijeka and graduated from the university in that city in 1996, following this with a Master's degree in Printmaking from the Academy of Fine Arts in Ljubljana in 2005. She is currently studying for her PhD at the Academy of Fine Arts in Zagreb, and lives in Opatija close to Rijeka, where she teaches printmaking at the Academy of Applied Arts, and also leads the Erasmus programme, the student exchange project established by the European Union. The history of places, entwined with the histories of those who inhabited them, provides much of the background and inspiration of this artist's work. In addition to her art practice, she also writes books on the history of Opatija, and received an award for this from the municipality in 2011. Her work has been seen in a number of exhibitions, both locally and internationally.

The majority of this work over the past 20 years was made using non-toxic techniques, and has included a number of experiments with photographic transfer, allowing her to incorporate archive materials from her family's history in her prints. In addition to her work in printmaking she has also made site-specific environmental projects within the local community, including *12*, made for the *Day of Planet Earth* in 2003, which consisted of an installation of helium-filled balloons along the course of the Rječina River in the urban centre.

In an ongoing project entitled *Hortikultura Stanja* (State's Horticulture) Kostelac is exploring memories of her childhood through a series of large prints (100 x 69cm/39 x 27in.), largely made using aquatint and collagraphy. The individual prints in the series incorporate handwritten text, drawing and photographic images, layered together and printed in a restricted palette of colours. Among the incidents she portrays are lying awake unable to sleep and watching the three cypress trees in front of the house until their silence washes over her; climbing a fence and cutting her hand on a rusty wire, then watching her blood flow in red drops on green-painted concrete; and dreaming when

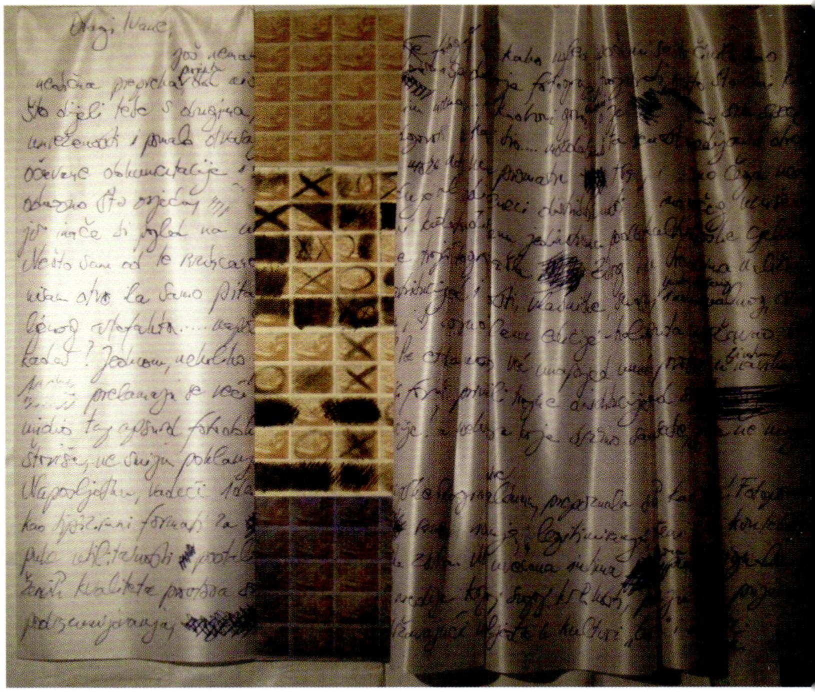

Melinda Kostelac, *Letter to Ivan*, 2009. Print installation: digital silk print, offset, drypoint, on silk sheets and Fabriano paper, 300 x 210cm (118 x 82¾in.).

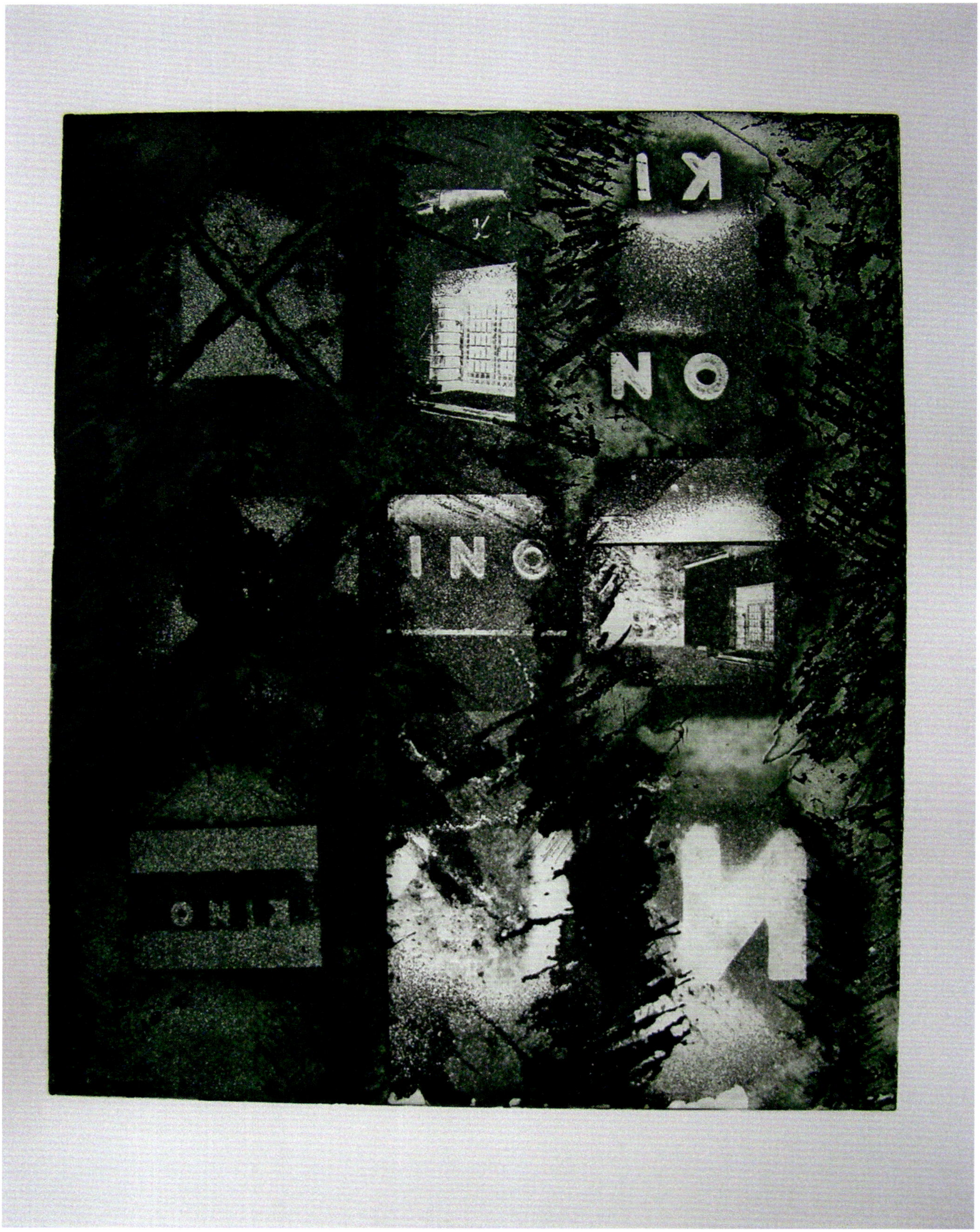
NO
INO

Left: **Melinda Kostelac**, *War in Opatija – Cinepatia*, 2010. Aquatint, sugar-lift etching, etching on Fabriano paper, 70 x 50cm (27½ x 19¾in.).

Right: **Melinda Kostelac**, *5 Minutes of Memory*, 2012. Aquatint on Hahnemühle paper, 39 x 29cm (15¼ x 11½in.).

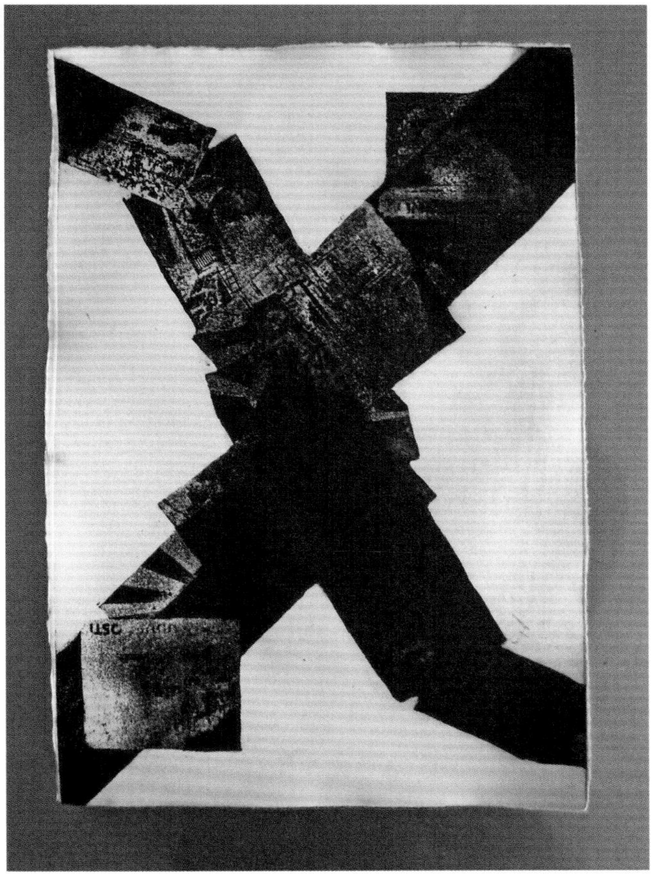

she was four years old of a giant butterfly landing on her, and the effect this had on her. These micro-histories are approached in the same way as other parts of her work, and demonstrate her fascination with memories and her need to find a visual language to use when retelling them through the medium of printmaking.

In *Letter to Ivan* (2008) she created an installation of 16 prints arranged in a 4 x 4 grid, each in turn with a grid of identical printed images, derived from an early photograph of her grandfather, who owned a photography studio in Opatija at the beginning of the 20th century. Some of the images are partially obliterated and overlaid with colour, and together they convey the sense of repetition and thereby the passage of time. The prints are displayed behind silk curtains printed with enlargements of an intimate letter to her grandfather that reveals her thoughts about family – using artefacts and photography as a symbol of divided and lost identity, attribution and ownership.

War in Opatija – Cinepatia is the artist's account of the complex history of the cinema that was once at the heart of the artist's home town. With the shifts in fashion over time, the building fell into disuse and became a ruin, not as an effect of the war of independence but rather as a result of what she calls, '... the recklessness and political games that made this building a metaphor for the state of society in the whole country. The real war consequences are seen now ...'. It is estimated that up to 25% of Croatia's economy was destroyed in the war, and Rijeka is itself now undergoing an uncertain transition from its former status as a manufacturing base to that of a service economy largely dependent on tourism. The print, with its emphasis on the word 'NO' spelled out in the reversed image, coupled with the layering of images and textures, becomes symbolic of both the inevitability of history and the melancholic remembrance that this brings.

The third image, *5 Minutes of Memory*, deals with both individual and collective memory, collaging old photographs and facsimiles of newspaper pages into an 'X' form, and then almost destroying the subtleties of the originals through an intensive etching process until only fragments of the original detail remain. The technique is at the same time both destructive and creative in that it erodes the sense of history in the original images, just as the process of time and conflict has destroyed much else, while at the same time creating a new form, an emphatic 'X' that both marks the spot and prohibits further action. All three images, when taken together, present a quiet meditation on the past history of a country undergoing change.

UKRAINE

KONSTANTIN KALYNOVYCH

THE BIOGRAPHICAL circumstances of artists' lives, while not essential in gaining an appreciation of their work, add deeper levels of understanding and a fuller sense of the journeys they have travelled. It is inevitable that artists living in countries with histories more volatile than those of stable countries are likely to have a different, and often more politically-charged, range of influences. This can be particularly the case in the countries that comprise Eastern Europe and the western parts of what was formerly the USSR, and even more so given the history of such regions in the 20th and 21st centuries, in which political turbulence and conflict have combined with the long cultural traditions of the wider European continent to offer a rich ferment of possibilities.

Konstantin Kalynovych was born in 1959 in the industrial city of Novokuznetsk in the Kemerovo region of Southern Siberia. He studied at the Ukrainian Academy of Printing in Lviv, graduating in 1992. This city, formerly Lvov when part of pre-WWII Poland and with a distinct culture of its own, would have given the artist an environment that contrasted strongly with that of his childhood. In the same year as his graduation, and already having gained an international reputation for his distinct style of printmaking, he was elected an Associate of the Royal Society of Painter-Printmakers in London.

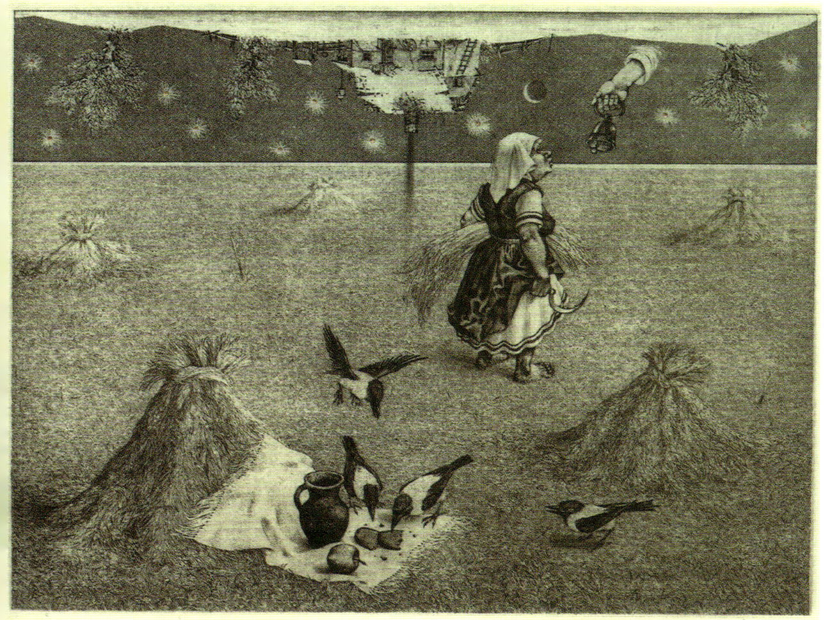

Konstantin Kalynovych, *Lunch Time*, 2010. Etching, drypoint, coloured 13 x 18cm (5 x 7in.). Photo: Alexej Kalynovych.

Since then Kalynovych's international exhibiting record has extended into many parts of the world and he has gained many important prizes. He now lives in Lugansk in southeast Ukraine. This city developed from the metal-working factory founded there in 1795 by the Englishman, Charles Gascoigne, and is now the location of a major locomotive-building company. Given this brief biography, it is not surprising to find in the artist's work many threads that link it to the cultural evidence of an older Europe, in which borders, inasmuch as they existed, were more open than they became in the middle years of the 20th century. There are echoes of Eastern European folklore, and a world that in many works seems to have been frozen in a 17th-century Dutch or German winter. There is a sense of the melancholy in them, of the difficulties of survival in the harsh winters of that period, but also a deep sense of humanity.

Unusually, a watercolour of 2012, *One More Summer*, depicts a scampering dog leading a young girl, followed by an old woman, across a sunlit grassy hillside. But even in this example, thanks to the title, there is an underlying sense of melancholy. As with the paintings, so with the prints: the pervasive chill of winter weather runs through many of the etchings, some with drypoint, and wood engravings, which demonstrate this artist's remarkably assured skills of imagination, composition and execution. While there are strong resemblances with the humanist approach of 17th- and 18th-century artists such as Bruegel and Vermeer – and there is the sense that such artists would identify with Kalynovych's works – these pieces are not merely imitation. Rather they are intellectually sound progressions from the

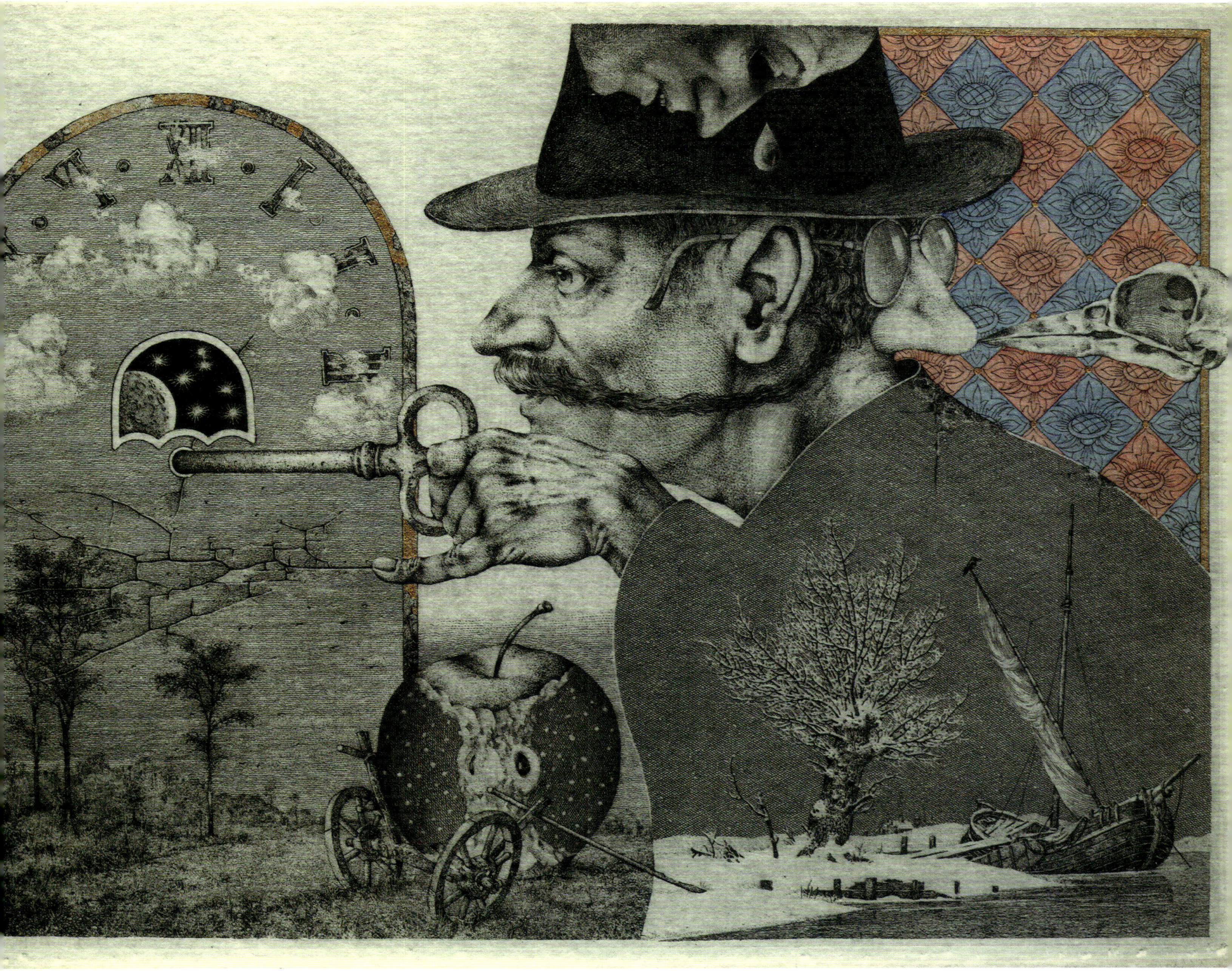

Konstantin Kalynovych, *The Big Watchmaker*, 2011. Etching, drypoint, colour, 12 x 16cm (4¾ x 6¼in.). Photo: Alexej Kalynovych.

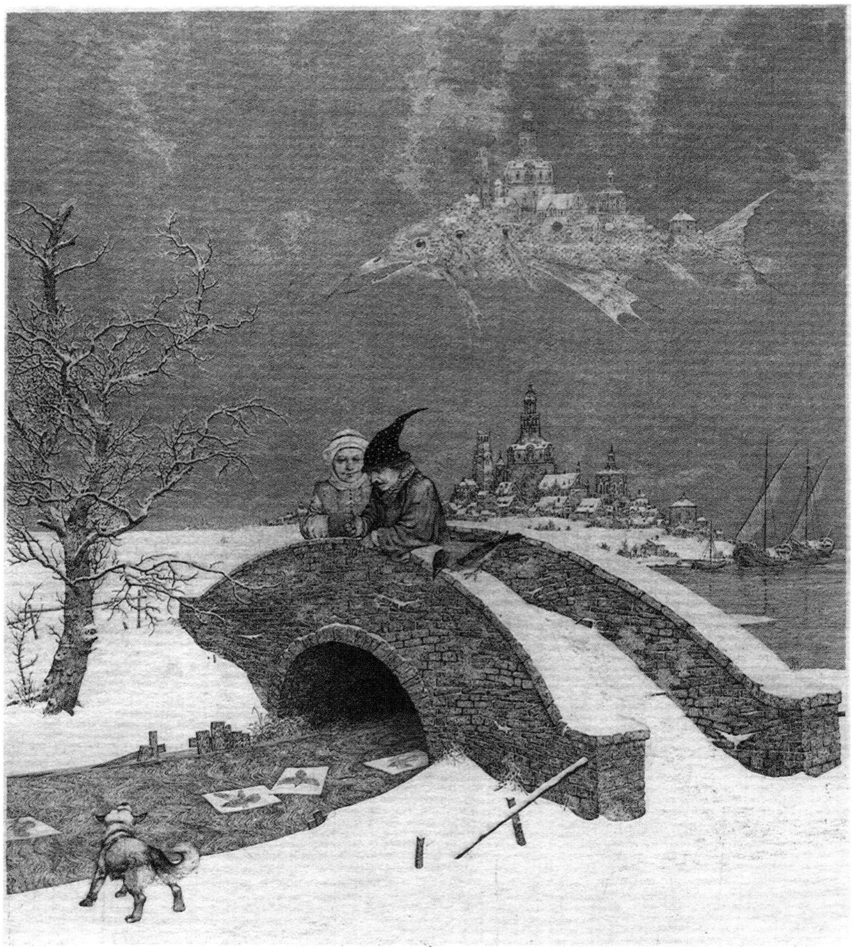

Konstantin Kalynovych, *Birds of My Heart*, 2011. Etching, drypoint, 17 x 15cm (6¾ x 6in.). Photo: Alexej Kalynovych.

art of those centuries that reveal a deep understanding of the continuing function of art as a means to inform, entertain and provoke, to seek echoes of contemporary life within images, and to experience through this process the desirability of a taking a humanitarian approach to life. These concerns come together with technical virtuosity in *The Big Watchmaker*, in which the disparate parts of this small print are composed with a rigorous sense of balance to produce an image that intrigues and holds the eye, but which is almost impossible to decode in such a way that the artist's full personal intent becomes clear. Instead, the viewer is left with the possibility of reading the image as if it were music, and considering it as if it were poetry. In other prints there is an element of the surreal, but that of the works of Bosch rather than those of Dalí; significantly, this too positions the work of Kalynovych closer to humanism than to psychoanalysis.

In addition to his work with paintings and editioned prints, including ex-libris prints, Konstantin Kalynovych also works in the more unusual medium of book-making. In 1994 he produced a single handwritten book of *The Song of Songs*, measuring 15 x 12cm (6 x 4¾in.), in which the text of perhaps the most sensual book in the Bible was written in calligraphy in several colours, together with full-page illustrations in watercolour and gouache, with a cover made with silk, leather, boxwood, ivory and amber. He followed this in the same year with a single handwritten edition in Finnish of the *Kalevala*, 21 x 16cm (8¼ x 6¼in.), using coloured inks for the calligraphy and etchings for the illustrations, inside a cover made from leather, brass, and oil with engraving; and in 2003 with a single handwritten edition of *The Revelation*, 25 x 16cm (10 x 6¼in.), using coloured calligraphy and hand-drawn marginal illustrations for the text, along with full-page illustrations in watercolour, gouache, ink and bronze. Combined in the making of these unique books are craftsmanship and artistry in the noble traditions of the scriptorium, honouring the purity of the text with work of the highest order, and resulting in books that are also fine art.

In early autumn 2012 another book work by the artist was published by Nevsky Tower under the direction of Kirill Avelev. This edition of 33 copies of *The Book of Ecclesiastes*, the best-loved book in the Apocrypha of the Bible, and with a text that is much quoted in non-religious contexts, included reproductions of the calligraphy text and illustrations in etching. Together with the other work by Kalynovych, these books demonstrate the skill of an artist whose output creates a bridge between past and future.

OLEG DENYSENKO

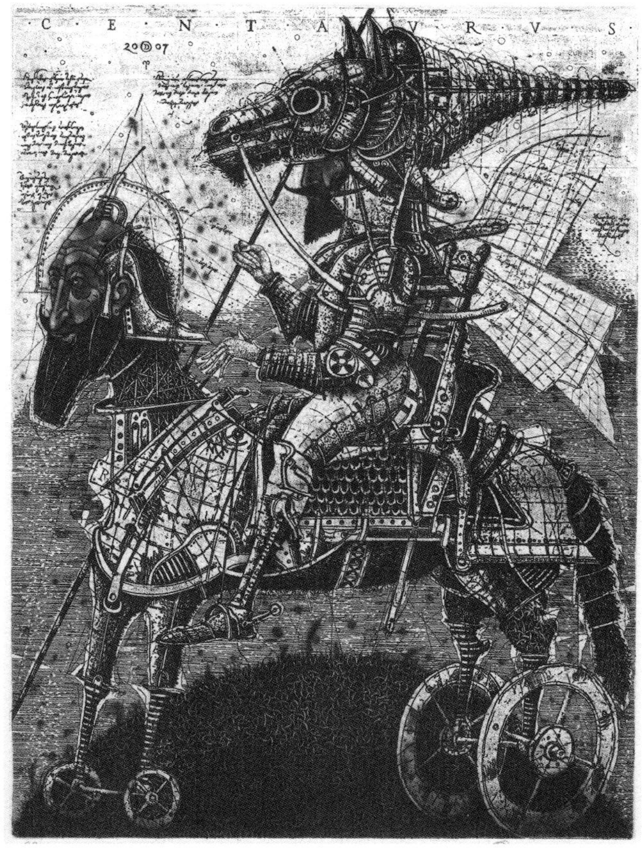

Oleg Denysenko, *Centaurus*, 2007. Intaglio, 24 x 18cm (9½ x 7in.).

UKRAINE is a large country in Southeastern Europe, bordered by the Black Sea, Russia, Belarus, Poland, Romania and Moldova. The country, whose name means 'borderland', including the major cities of Lviv and Kiev, together with places such as Odessa and Yalta, has a long and tumultuous history stretching back more than 3000 years. Always at the crossroads of invasion and trade routes, it was settled by the Scythians from Central Asia in the 7th century BCE, and subsequently by other nomadic invaders. In the 9th century CE the might of Kievan Rus established an empire that extended to much of what is now European Russia. The character of the country developed through successive centuries, with invasions, wars and shifting boundaries, as the country's fortunes rose and fell. Harsh times during the Soviet period and WWII, then later the nuclear disaster at Chernobyl in 1986 and independence in 1991 following the fall of Communism, have all left their mark on the country. Since then the changing and somewhat unstable political situation has been accompanied by a dynamic growth in business and tourism, in conjunction with the country's ambitions to play a fuller part of the wider European community. In this regard, strides forward have been made: in 2005 Ukraine hosted the Eurovision contest and in 2012 co-hosted (with Poland) the European Football Championships.

Oleg Denysenko was born in Lviv in 1961 and graduated from the Ukrainian Academy of Printing, specialising in graphics. His work, in the fields of printmaking, painting and sculpture, has led to a successful international exhibition history, to numerous major international prizes, and his inclusion in many major international private and museum collections. In an international printmaking community that is evolving rapidly, with a multifaceted and highly diverse range of mediums and stylistic approaches, it is encouraging to encounter a number of artists for whom the traditional techniques and genres continue to provide inspiration and the continual opportunity for diversification.

Denysenko is one such, an artist whose work can be placed in a direct lineage stretching from artists such as da Vinci and Dürer to the present day. But what this work does not do is to simply reiterate what has gone before: the same consummate skills can be discerned, the result of years of effort and many hours of painstaking work on each new matrix, and there is ample evidence of a sensibility that is equally aware of the past and the present, through which a synthesis of forms and images can be presented. His virtuoso skill in intaglio printmaking, primarily in traditional etching, is coupled with his interests in literature, myth and history, archaeology, psychology, walking in the mountains and international travel. Through all these he absorbs a welter of impressions and information that become part of his working vocabulary.

Denysenko considers that modern Man is confused by globalisation, and the way TV and the internet have captured space, and further that people have stopped analysing, thinking creatively or reading books, with a consequent reduction in their interest in classical manifestations of culture. His central concern is that of 'the hero', the man with problems and ideas whose image comes through art, and the role of true artists who are engaged in the creation myth. Of his general theme he is quoted, in an unattributed interview, as saying, 'Art in general is itself a myth, a fiction ... a huge bubble. After all,

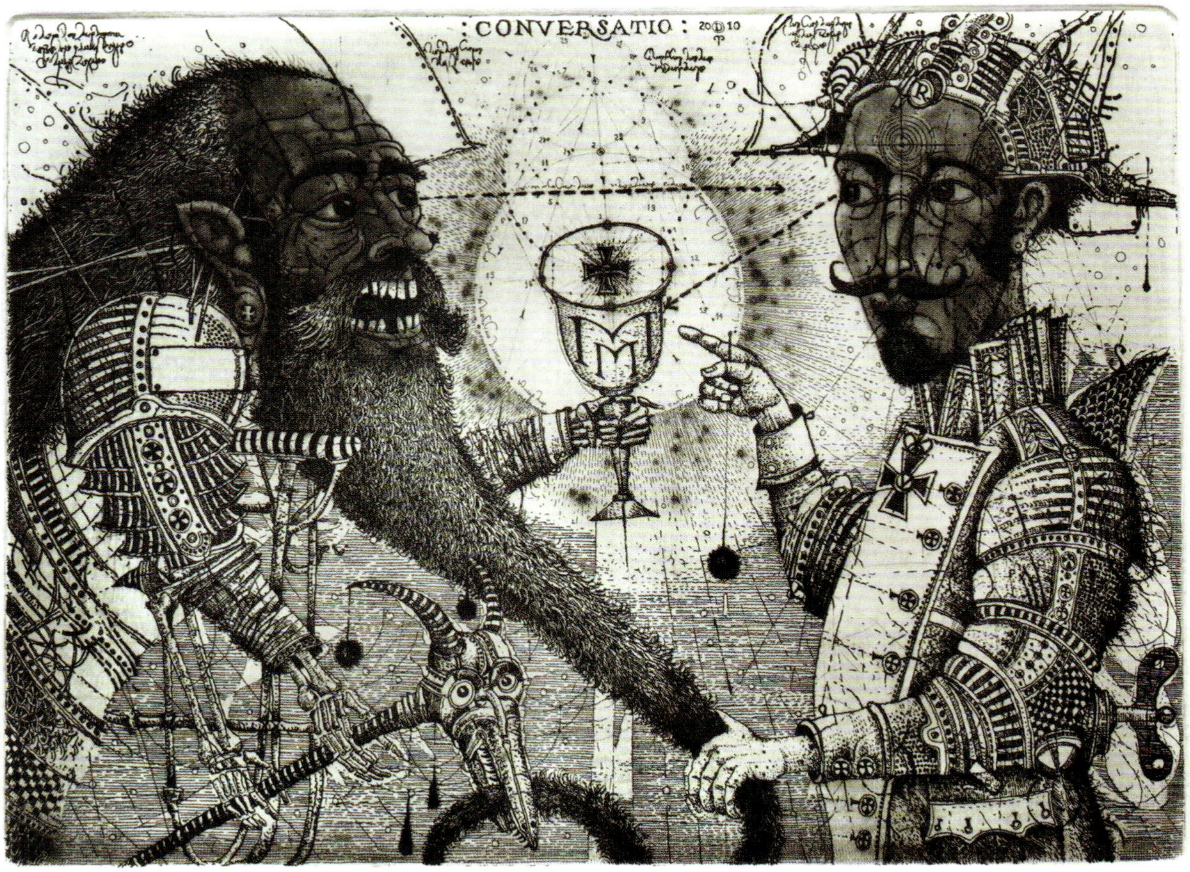

Oleg Denysenko, *Conversation*, 2010. Intaglio, 13 x 18cm (5 x 7in.).

Right: Oleg Denysenko, *Looking for Balance*, 2009. Intaglio, 25 x 16cm (9¾ x 6¼in.).

a man takes a board, a piece of cloth or paper and by some means (paint, pencil) creates something. And it's inspiring, it affects many people. This is a myth, a hoax, no clear magic. Therefore all artists are the creators of myths.'

In the same interview he expresses the view that there are only a couple of dozen people involved in etching in Ukraine, and that only the strong can afford to work in the technique, adding that, 'It is easier to take a canvas, bright colours, a brush, make a few strokes – and the image will be there.' Significantly, he also produces paintings, but using the time-consuming and highly technical method of working in layers of thin glaze applied to gesso on wood, another deeply traditional technique that produces jewel-like results. Oleg Sidorov-Gibelynda describes Denysenko as an 'artist-philosopher who fears philosophical definitions as the devil fears incense – which, in short, makes him all the more philosophical.' He also writes, 'Denysenko's heroes live among continuous windmills … they are out to please.' This is particularly apt, since the heroes shown in his etchings are much closer in spirit to Don Quixote than to the mounted figure in Dürer's 1513 etching, *Knight, Death and the Devil*.

The etchings depict, in astonishing and finely drawn detail, a world in which the illogical evidently becomes possible, and in which a high-flying imagination is combined with a sure and certain technical skill in drawing, in following the precise stages of etching and finally in producing the print. The resulting images of the artist's world have a mythic resonance and a sly sense of humour. It becomes entirely credible, in *Centaurus*, to witness a heavily armed knight on horseback, in which the knight resembles a carefully crafted robotic figure rather than a man; especially given that his head is covered with a metal horse mask and that the horse, complete with a face mask that resembles that of the artist, is mounted on wheels. Such fantastical images defy logic, belonging instead in that same sphere of the universe from where come myths and fairytales. They may, certainly, be taken for themselves, as superlative works by a master etcher, and further than this they may be viewed against the contextual background of the artist's clear sense of the function and place of art in the 21st century.

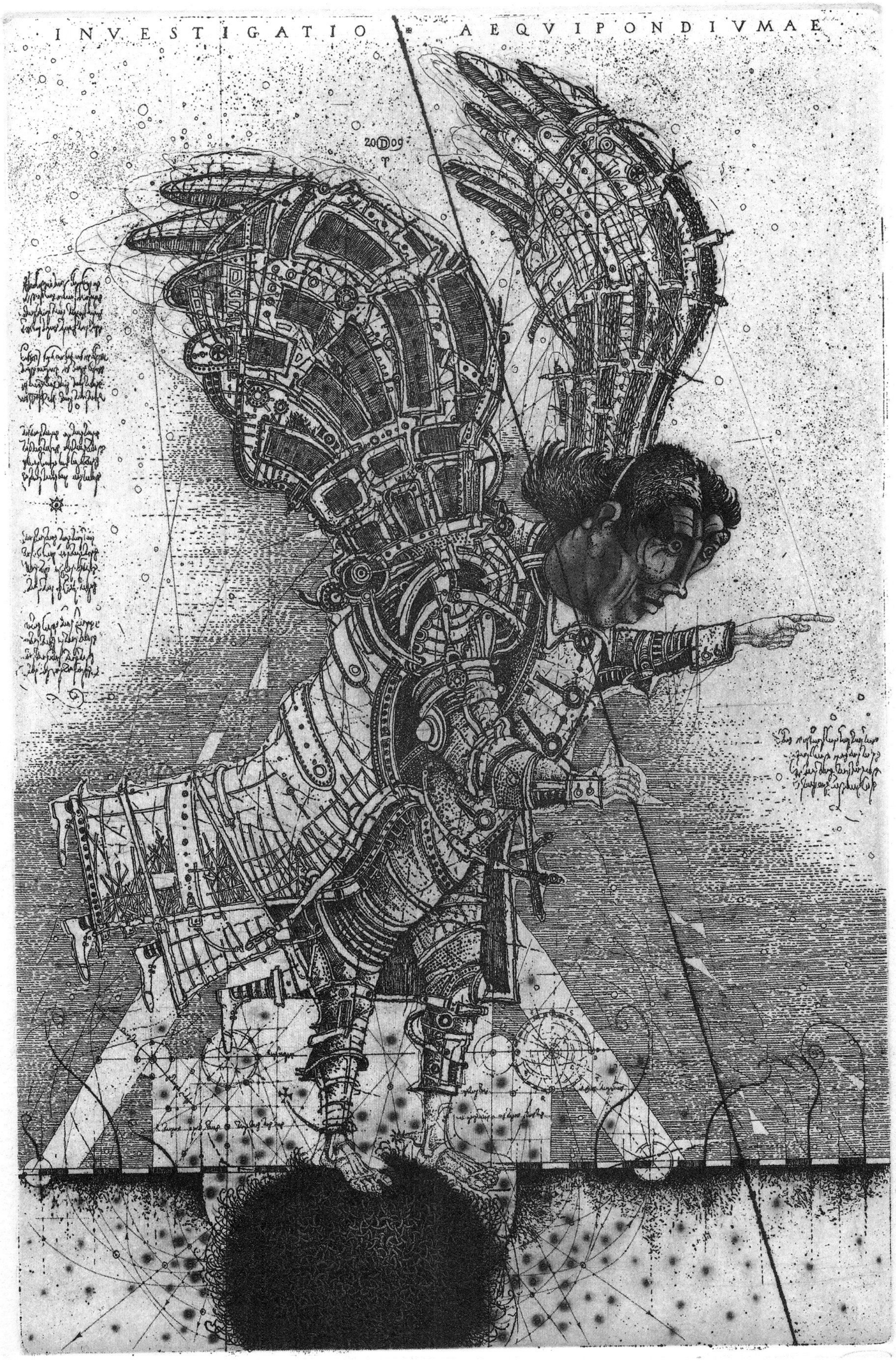
INVESTIGATIO AEQVIPONDIVMAE

BELARUS

ALEXANDR GRIGORIEV

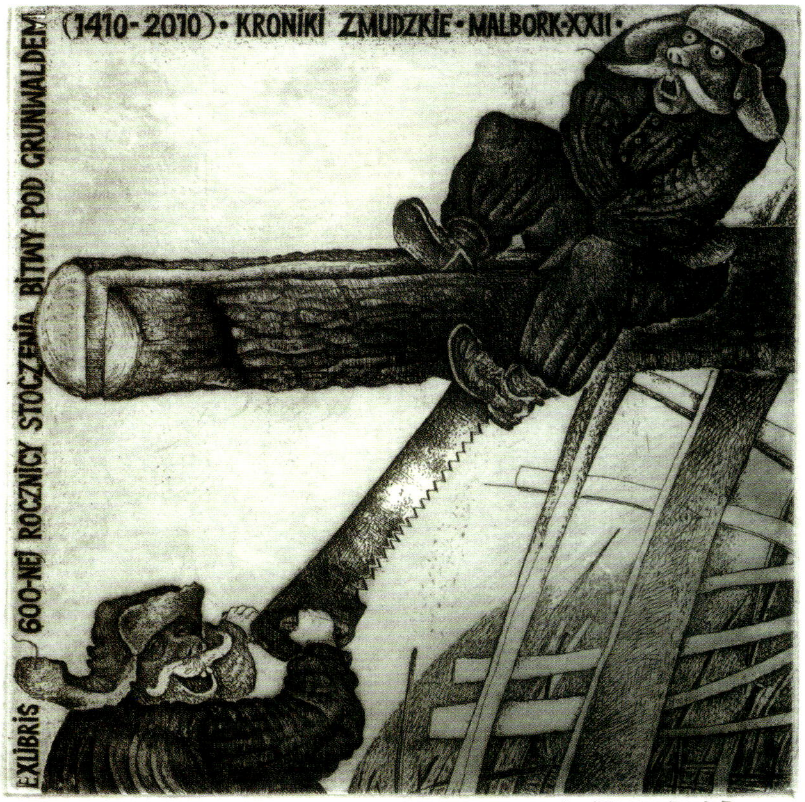

Alexandr Grigoriev, *Cheerful Gossip*, 2008. Etching, 15 x 15cm (6 x 6in.).

BELARUS, described by some as the last dictatorship in Europe, remains little known and often criticised for its lack of democratic freedoms and the authoritarian rule, since 1994, of President Lukashenko. The position of the country, between the eastern borders of Poland and the western borders of Russia, has for many centuries placed it at the crossroads of much historical change, resulting in an historical culture that has many influences and a richness that is little known in the Western world. It is often overlooked that a number of influential 20th-century artists had their origins in Belarus, among them being Kasimir Malevich, Chaim Soutine, Ossip Zadkine, El Lissitzky and, most notably, Marc Chagall, all of whom drew inspiration from their national cultural history. The upheavals in Europe after 1918 led to many artists seeking exile in France and other Western countries. The journey I made to Vitebsk in eastern Belarus, the birthplace of Chagall, gave me a clear insight into the roots of that remarkable artist as I walked around the old town and recognised the sources of fragments of his paintings. An appreciation of the contemporary arts of Belarus is less easy to gain than in other European countries, but there is an active visual arts life and a willingness among artists to engage in wider dialogues with artists elsewhere. The problems arising from the perception of the country by governments and media in the West, and the need for visas, act as a restraint on travel, a matter for regret.

Alexandr Grigoriev (born 1955) is a printmaker, painter, scenographer, puppet maker and exhibition curator who lives and works in Brest, on the historic Bug river that separates Belarus from Poland, and also on a major railway line between Europe and Russia. He has an extensive record of international and national exhibitions, having gained a number of awards, and his work, particularly in ex-libris prints, is collected in many countries. He is a prolific printmaker and works mainly with the traditional techniques of etching and aquatint in

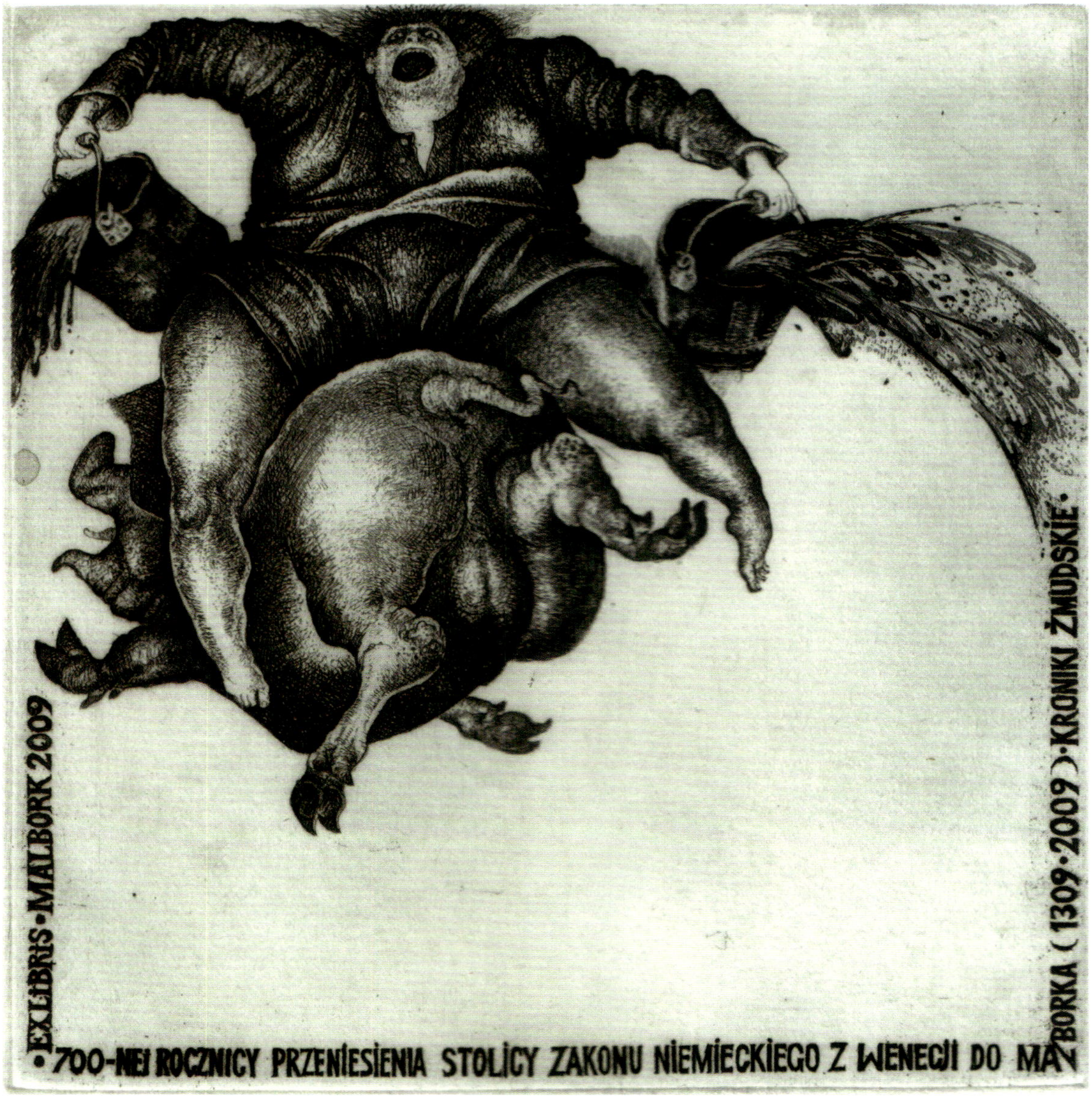

Alexandr Grigoriev, *The Pig*, 2008. Etching, 15 x 15cm (6 x 6in.).

traditional figurative genres but always with his distinctive personal style. As with many parts of Eastern Europe, the heritage of folk tales remains strong in Belarus, with the familiar figures of heroes and villains playing their part. Many Belarusians follow Eastern Orthodox Christianity, but the characters of the folk tales are not forgotten. With this in mind, Grigoriev describes his activity as, 'developing a conceptual project in the style of tragic farce … characterised by an allegorical way of thinking, understanding life and living contemporaries.'

The historical culture of the country, based on ideals of kindness and humanity that personify the soul of the nation, remains at the core of Grigoriev's work. At the same time his work contains its own idiosyncratic nuances and a rich vein of visual humour that belies the seriousness with which he approaches his work, and indeed the national background of his daily life. Living in an historical city at the crossings of international borders and transport routes gives him a unique opportunity to relate his work back to his deep cultural roots while at the same time having the opportunity to look westwards across the river to connect with a wider European culture. As such he can be said to occupy a unique position from which to pursue his art.

The techniques used by Grigoriev – namely, etching and aquatint – demand great skill and fine control not only in the stage of drawing on the plate but also in the preparation of the plate and its subsequent printing. The size of his prints, usually 15 x 15cm (6 x 6in.), makes even greater demands given the degree of detail that the images contain. The drawing skill shows clearly the academic traditions of his

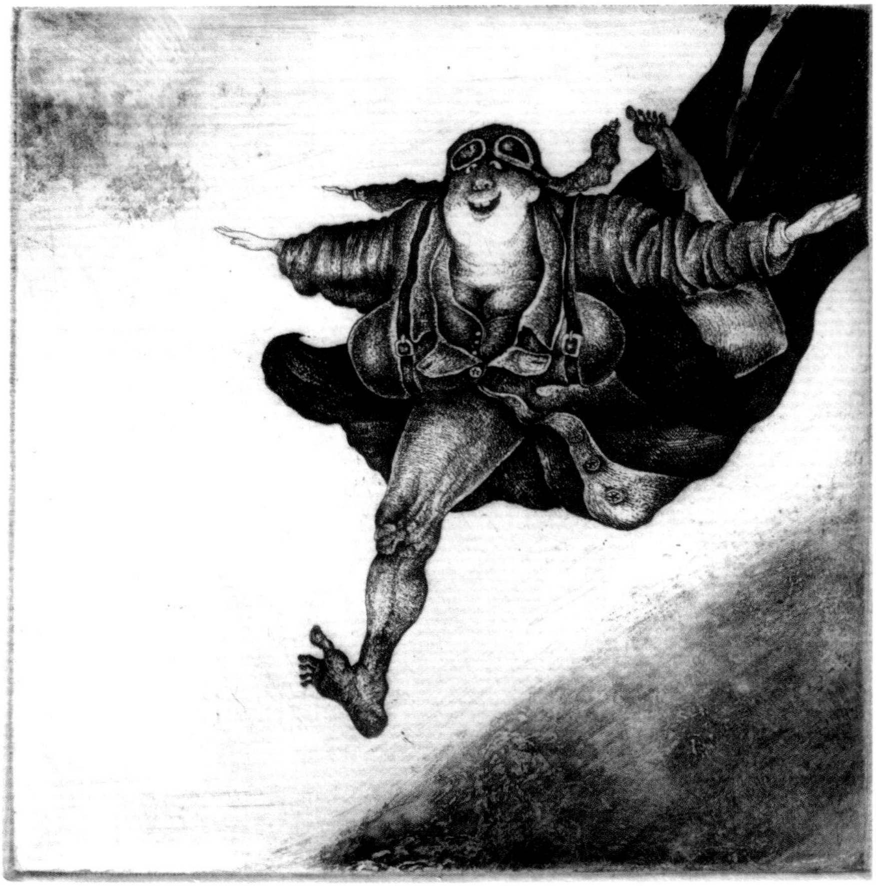

Alexandr Grigoriev, *The B52 Flyer*, 2011. Etching and aquatint, 15 x 15cm (6 x 6in.).

education, in which drawing skills are seen as paramount and central to all further art techniques. Sadly, such skills are not always taught in Western European academies. The fine detail, the combinations of marks that build up to create a full range of textures, and the assured understanding of the use of form and perspective, all provide a firm foundation upon which Grigoriev can build his images, with their rich vein of humour stemming from his warm personality and his accurate eye for absurdity and the signs of human frailty.

Pig illustrates a bizarre situation in which a large woman carries two buckets on a pig moving at high speed through the air, her mouth open in a silent shout. The moment in between the past of the story and its future is frozen in this image, and the story cannot be deciphered. Nonsense perhaps, absurdity for certain, and possibly an agricultural parable: viewers can appreciate the image and perhaps make up their own story or parable. *Cheerful Gossip* depicts a scene of bucolic amusement for one of the characters in the image and profound discomfort for the other as two sawyers attempt to cut a plank from a tree trunk on a building site. The amusement is cruel, but with a sense of *schadenfreude* viewers can choose whether to align themselves with the laughing 'bottom sawyer' or otherwise empathise with the injured 'top sawyer', who, traditionally, was considered to be the fortunate one of the pair. Both of these prints were made for the XXII International Biennial of Modern Ex Libris, held in the historic Polish city of Malbork in 2009. *The B52 Flyer* shows a different sort of fantasy, one shared by many small children as they pretend to be aircraft: a large woman – perhaps the same character as in *Pig* – runs barefoot wearing a long coat and a flying helmet, her arms outstretched as she attempts, foolishly, to fly while knowing (but not caring) that she will fail. A symbol perhaps of the desire for freedom, still a political dream for many Belorussians?

JURI JAKOVENKO

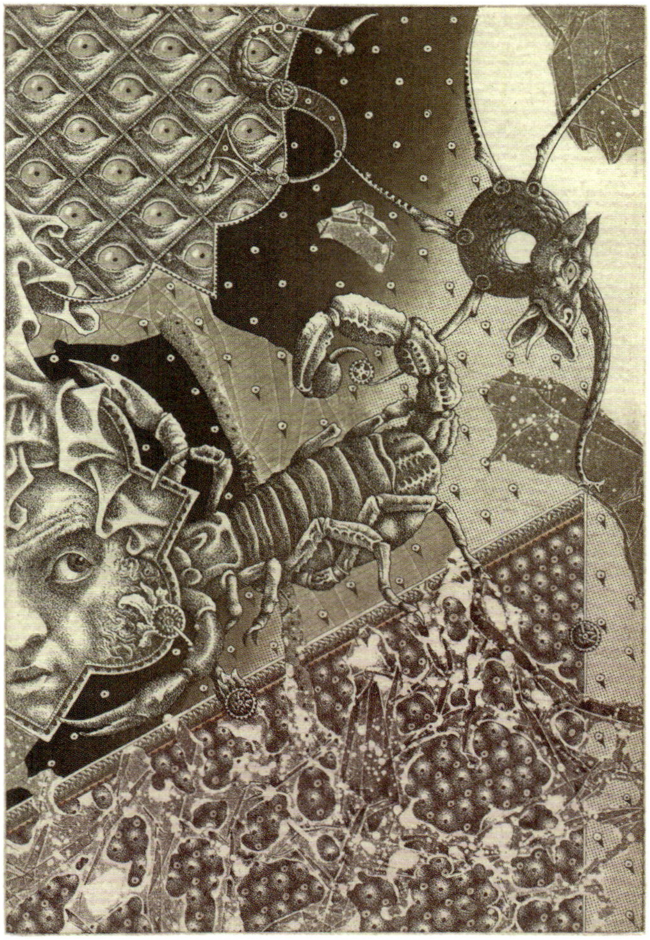

Juri Jakovenko, *S*, 2010. Etching, 17.5 x 12cm (7 x 4¾in.).

THE PARADOX in the work of Juri Jakovenko is that his inspiration and the origination of his imagery lie in Belarus and the cultural and historic context of that country, and yet the restrictions placed on the citizens of his birthplace, in particular the requirement for visas before contemplating any travel to Western Europe, prevent him from participating as fully as he would wish as an artist in the wider European context. He acknowledges that there are negative views of Belarus in the West, but questions how many of these are the product of propaganda from unsuccessful politicians, and result from the difference of perspective from inside and outside the country. This view points to the need for an improvement in democratic conditions within the country that would in turn lead to an increase in pan-European cooperation and a greater openness; the politics of this dilemma may yet take years to resolve.

Jakovenko was born in Grodno in Belarus in 1965, as he writes, as 'a coincidence of the destiny of my parents, my Ukrainian father and Russian mother'; as such, he feels a strong attachment to his native land despite the problems that he sees around him. He graduated in 1992 from the Academy of Art in Minsk, with a strongly traditional art education behind him, and since then has gained a strong reputation in international graphic art circles, being the recipient of numerous awards at exhibitions and in competitions; since 2001 he has taught at the Academy. Despite the restrictions that he feels limit his full freedom of movement, he has succeeded in building an enviable record as an artist whose work reaches out to a discerning public through the distinctive mediums of prints, including ex libris, and also through the production of limited-edition fine books.

Jakovenko's printmaking work, primarily in etching, is mostly at small scale, and produced in editions of around 50, aligning it with traditional print practices. He writes that the sources of his inspiration lie in the Middle Ages, a period of strength and artistic excellence in the countries in Eastern Europe. He stresses that this does not make him a representative of the Russian school, as his influences spread throughout the Czech, Slovak, Polish and Bulgarian traditions of drawing and graphic excellence. All these countries, he notes, have strong academic drawing traditions: he comments that he feels that the majority of artists in Western Europe lack ability in academic drawing. His work is highly detailed, and enlargements of his prints reveal the extraordinary precision with which he creates detail and texture. This technique allows him to explore and present images that are surreal, with hints of the occult, the grotesque, and hermetic knowledge, fantastical with layers of interpretation, and akin to some of the imagery of Bosch or the wilder excesses of Bruegel, whose work depicts a more generic notion of Europe rather than specific places. The images in Jakovenko's work do not allude to particular incidents or stories and are not readily decoded, as they contain layers of possible meanings and interpretations, a richness such as would have been familiar to educated people in the Middle Ages, a time in which superstition and religion exerted equal and often opposing influences, when the potential for damnation or salvation as a result of actions taken was a palpable and widely held fear.

Comparisons may be drawn between this artist's work and the work of other artists, periods and traditions: its originality is based on a deep understanding and appreciation

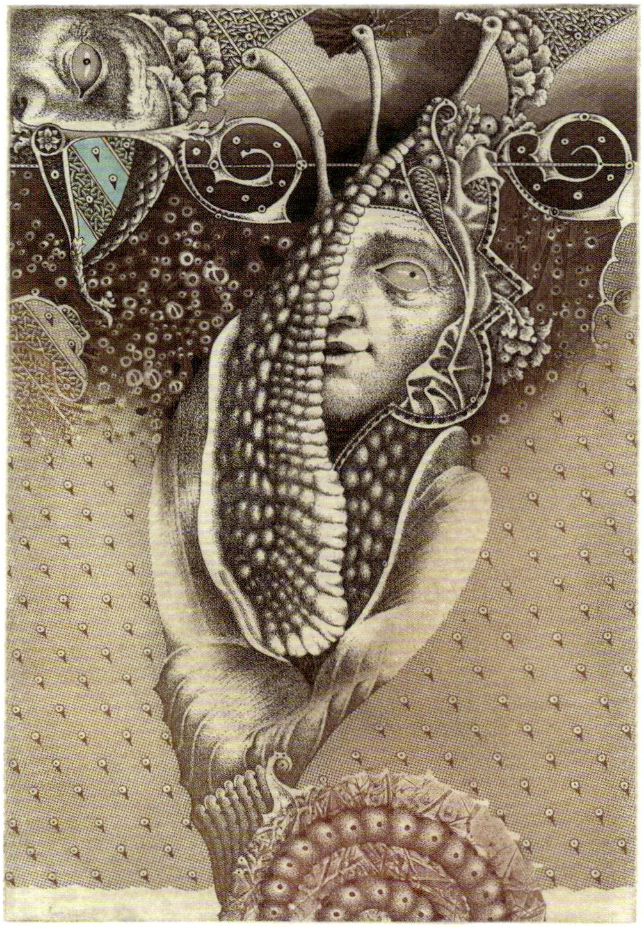

Juri Jakovenko, *V*, 2010. Etching, 17.5 x 12cm (7 x 4¾in.).

of the long history of European culture. Jakovenko's classical art education provided a strong foundation upon which his long fascination with drawing could be developed to make him one of the foremost European artists in etching, aquatint and mezzotint. All these techniques require great skill and attention to detail, and a sound understanding of the processes involved. In the making of the fine books he works in close conjunction with master printers and bookbinders in the Italian city of San Benedetto del Tronto. There is a time-honoured tradition for such cooperation in printmaking, which for many years has been one of its central strengths. The fusion on the one hand of the artist's imagination and skills in producing the visual language of the images, and on the other hand the experience and knowledge of master craftsmen in the techniques of printing and selection of materials, produces limited-edition works of great beauty and lasting worth.

One such book is *The Song about a Bison*, based on the masterpiece by the 15th-century poet and diplomat from the Grand Duchy of Lithuania, Mikalai Gusuoski. The poem is printed in its original Latin in fine letterpress typography on handmade watermarked paper with etchings by Jakovenko, the whole being bound in a cream leather hardback book. The etchings are circular, echoing the fashion of the Renaissance, and take key moments in the poem and the life of the poet, creating finely detailed, intricately researched images. The central theme of the poem concerns the need for harmonic relationships between man, nation and society, based on historical and cultural legacy – something that the artist believes still applies in the present day. The artist's most recent book project is an interpretation of *The Song of Songs of King Solomon*, to be produced with his Italian publisher in an edition of 150 copies. Given this artist's dedication to the pursuit of excellence in printmaking and book production, it is certain that this new work will follow the extraordinary standard of previous works. It also clearly evident that this artist's work deserves to be far more widely recognised outside his own country, and in this regard it is to be hoped that a more open relationship between Belarus and the West and beyond will one day make this possible.

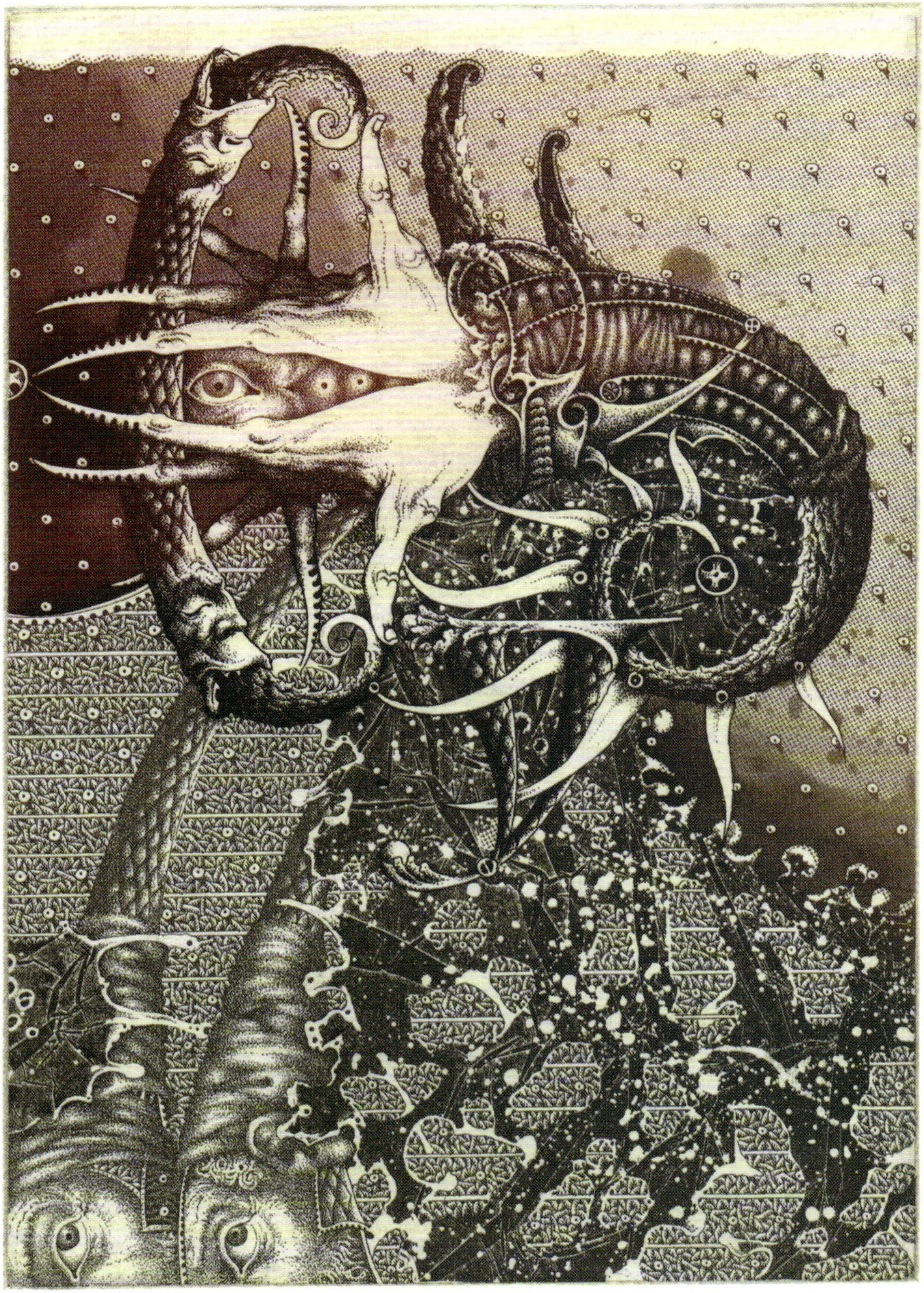

Juri Jakovenko, *Y*, 2010. Etching, 17.5 x 12cm (7 x 4¾in.).

RUSSIA

ANNA CEEH

THERE IS A strong element of anarchy in the work of Anna Ceeh, not so much a willful disobedience or destruction, but rather a controlled and premeditated disordering of convention and the technological matrix of much urban living. There is also a sense of playfulness, not so much for its own sake as for the manner in which such gestures can illuminate and question much that is taken for granted in Western society.

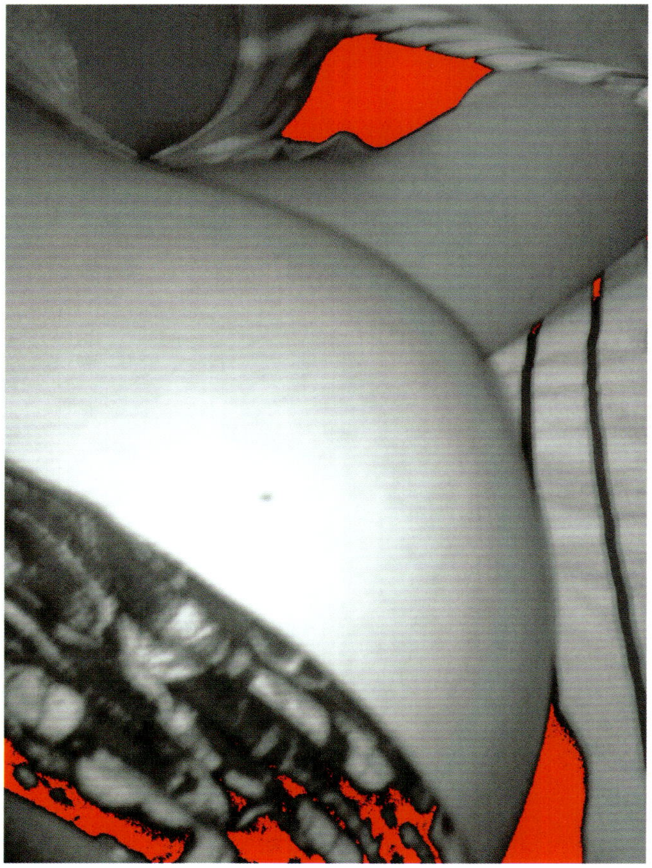

Anna Ceeh, *Mother_Phrenia_Antenatal_2*, 2011–12. DIY inkjet print, 22.5 x 30cm (8¾ x 11¾in.). Photo by courtesy of Charim Gallery.

Born in what was then Leningrad in 1974, since around 2002 Anna has been active in the international multimedia arts scene and in Vienna where she now lives. Her activity encompasses electronic music, sound environments, video and photography and the interrelationships between these disciplines. She writes that, 'The vocabulary of my activities reflects my biography and examines the dimensions of the real and the virtual in the context of the relationship between human being, object and space.' Her work in multimedia genres has been seen widely throughout Europe, in North and South America and in Japan. Her work in the medium of electronic music and sound involves cooperation with other exponents in this field, including some who remain in Russia whose work is published largely on the internet. A selection of her work (made in conjunction with F. Pomassl) was awarded an Honorary Mention in the 2011 Prix Ars Electronica, and her work (with Perry Bard) on the global remake of *Man with a Movie Camera* received both a similar award in 2008 and Le Prix des Nouveaux Média in the Digital Communities category at the Centre Pompidou in Paris in 2010.

The multiplicity of forms through which Anna Ceeh pursues her investigations into her history, her identity and her evolving position within the social, environmental and technological dimensions of the world in which she lives, also encompasses her explorations of analogue and digital photography, in much of which she operates not only as the photographer, but also as the model and as the observer of the resulting work in a structured and analytical performance. Along with a growing number of artists for whom this conscious form of personal exploration through self-portraiture, the artist's body becomes subject and object, a form of closed loop, to be recorded and mediated through the use of digital technology. In Ceeh's case she sees this a sort of performance, and takes this mediation forward by subverting the technology concealed within conventional inkjet printers, cracking the software, ignoring the machine's demands for fresh ink cartridges and running some colour cartridges empty or by switching the order in which they are

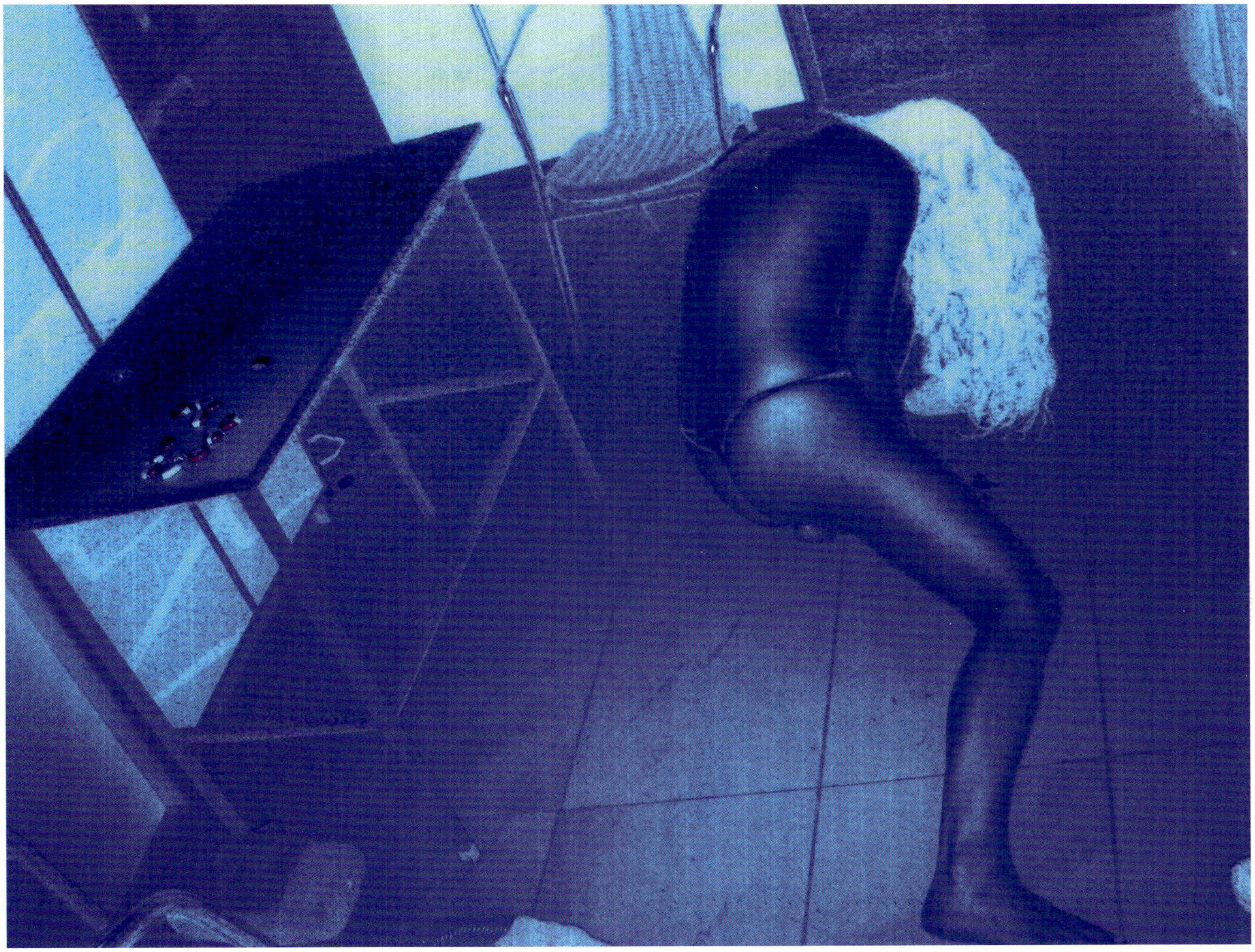

Anna Ceeh, *Self-Portrait.Peng!4*, 2011–12. DIY inkjet print 20.5 x 26.9cm (8 x 10½in.). Photo by courtesy of Charim Gallery.

inserted into the printer. On a superficial level this is a form of play, but in a deeper sense it is intended, as she puts it, to 'expand my photography to the next dimension of reality, that of crazy shifted reality.' There has been a long-running strand through the avant-garde arts since the early 20th century in which alternative means of photographic reproduction are harnessed in the service of the visual arts (Moholy-Nagy and Man Ray, for example, are two artists who followed this path) and a concurrent strand in which chance elements have been allowed to play an integral part in the creative process (in the work of Duchamp and Cage, for example).

While much of the development of digital photography and printmaking has been predicated on the increasingly sophisticated technology of cameras, postproduction software and printers designed to replicate 'reality' as closely as possible, there is a growing trend to use such equipment and software as tools or servants of the creative process, rather than as masters to be obeyed, and to break the rules rather than to follow them. This seriously playful approach, an adoption of creative anarchy, has had the interesting effect of recreating the distance between photography and traditional art mediums, adding an interesting tangent to the old assertion that photography would lead to the death of painting, and also to the claims of photography as a fine-art medium.

In the *Peng* series, created for the Austrian publication of the same name, Anna Ceeh set up wordless scenarios in which she positioned her near nude body in often extreme poses within a domestic environment, seeking to create tension and contrast between herself and the rooms she inhabits, together with elements carried over from her upbringing in the Soviet Union. Following the making of the initial image within the camera came the method, described above, through which

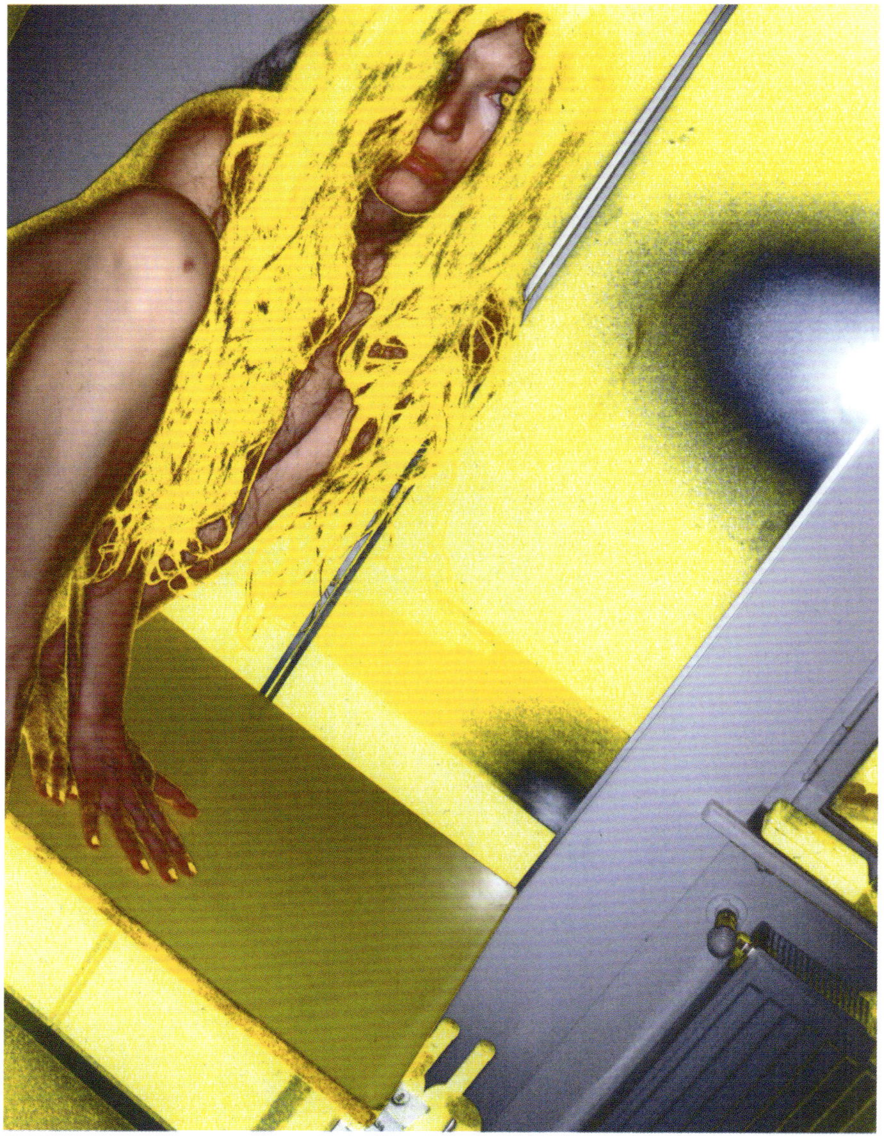

Anna Ceeh, *Self-Portrait. Peng!19*, 2011–12. DIY inkjet print, 20.4 x 26.4cm (8 x 10½in.). Photo by courtesy of Charim Gallery.

the final, one-off, unrepeatable prints could be produced. The subversion is considerable, and stands in direct contrast to the commercial use of the giclée method of reproducing a painting in limitless editions. In the case of Ceeh's work, reproduction is only possible through a subsequent process in which a digital file is transmitted across the internet or otherwise rendered into printed form in a magazine. This disruptive process is central to Ceeh's work and to others of her generation who have seized on the readily available digital sound and image technologies as a means of creating their own highly idiosyncratic responses to the world in which they live.

In a current (summer 2012) series of works, entitled *Mother-phrenia*, Ceeh is documenting her second pregnancy through the use of the digital camera built into her phone, not staged or premeditated in the way that the *Peng* images were, but instead in the more direct form of a private and personal record to be printed out using similar means and for subsequent sharing. While being different in both concept and content, the images occupy a similar territory, offering a privileged insight into a personal world, while at the same time offering us the chance of identifying with one of the most common and profound physical experiences. In a world in which digital technology enables all manner of personal explorations, this is a bold step, but one that will undoubtedly produce further fascinating insights into what it means to be a human subject in a technological world.

FINLAND

ANNU VERTANEN

ALTHOUGH she travels internationally to exhibit her work, and as a visiting lecturer within her country and elsewhere in Europe, Annu Vertanen chooses to live and work in her studio in Imatra. This small town in eastern Finland is closer to St Petersburg than it is to the Finnish capital, Helsinki; her family roots are there, she was born there, and the character of this borderland has been part of her thinking for a long time. The border between Finland and Russia shifted after WWII – her father was born further to the east in what is now Russia – and a degree of tension remains. It is an area of forests and lakes, and it is among this natural beauty that Vertanen finds the space to digest the impressions and influences of her travels. As she writes, 'The atmosphere and quietness are important, the possibility to concentrate on my own ideas, not to get disturbed. Nature is important for my mind and thinking, but I have never been interested in including nature as itself in my art, even if some of my pictures are some sort of landscape.'

Finding stimulation in cities (New York, London, Stockholm) remains important to this artist, as she finds a different kind of energy in such places, but it is in Imatra that she is better able to work. She writes, 'This area where I live is my land, I could not imagine living in another remote place in Finland. While being able to look this place from distance, I started to realise the special value that the place has for me. I think these kinds of frontiers always have special character and atmosphere.'

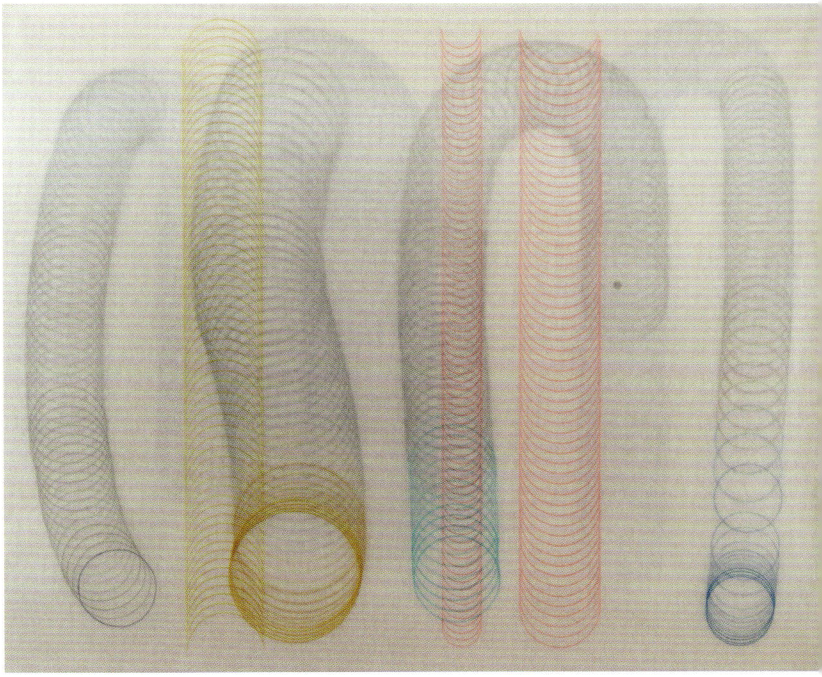

Annu Vertanen, *Transition II*, 2012. Woodcut, 100 x 125cm (39¼ x 49¼in.). Collection: State of Finland Art Collection. Photo: Tommi Kahara.

Annu Vertanen was born in 1960 and originally studied painting – in Lahti and later in Helsinki. After graduation she found that graphic art became a growing interest, and her work developed to the point at which she could abandon the use of brushes and canvas and instead place her painter's personality perfectly within her chosen medium of woodcut. With the international revival of woodcut as a printmaking medium in the 1980s she found that she could embark on the development of her idiosyncratic style without preconceived attitudes rooted in the traditions of wood engraving, but instead could treat the technique in unorthodox ways, working with the conventions of making and showing prints, and yet imposing her own approach to matrix, colour and material. In essence, her work has combined figuration and abstraction – she cites the influence of the 20th-century minimalism of artists such as Agnes Martin and Yayoi Kusama – and in her more recent work an evolution towards pure abstraction. In absorbing the traditional methodology of printmaking she has been able subsequently to refine her own visual and conceptual approach, focusing, in her words, 'on the points of intersection between two-dimensional print and spatial analysis'.

There are elements of Vertanen's work that are immediately reminiscent of the Japanese traditions of woodcut,

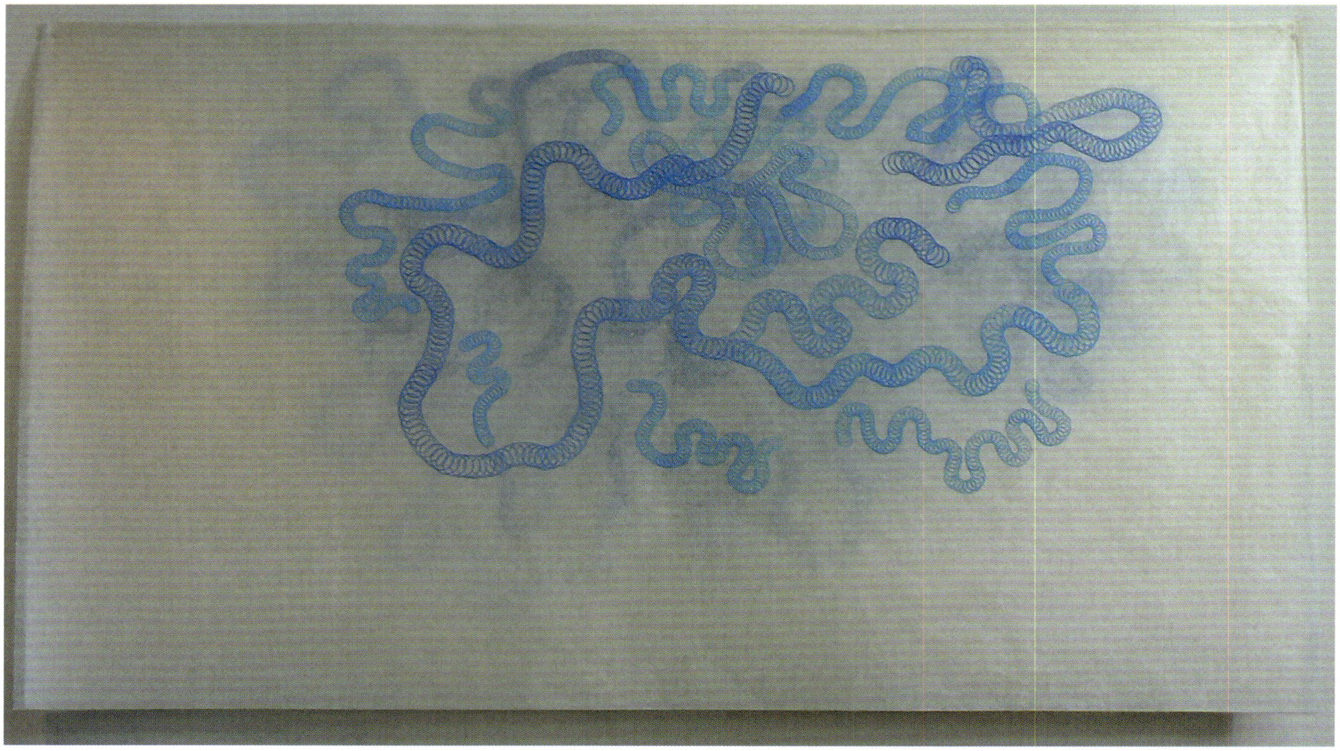

Annu Vertanen, *Love Clouds*, 2011. Woodcut, 100 x 180cm (39¼ x 70¾in.).

Right: **Annu Vertanen**, *Position Charts: Inhaling*, 2011. Woodcut, 92 x 61cm (36¼ x 24in.). Collection: Kiasma. Photo: Tommi Kahara.

in particular her choice of papers and her limpid palette of colours, but throughout there is a strongly individual core which infuses the natural environment of her homeland with a deeply metaphysical sense of presence that melds the sensibilities of Finland and Japan. On the face of it the contrast between the two countries could not be more extreme, but in fact there are strong similarities. Both countries are on the fringes of the great land mass of what is now Russia – one a group of islands, the other a frontier land of forests – with all that goes with living on or beyond the edge; the peoples of both countries have a strong identification with nature and the natural environment; both countries have a blend of traditional folk cultures on the one hand and modern technological society on the other; and both have unique languages. With all these similarities in mind, and her fascination with woodcut, it is no surprise that Annu Vertanen spent a long period in Japan in 1997 and has been back there since that time. She readily admits the continuing influence of Japanese culture and of Buddhism on her work, and has said that this provided her with all the answers to her early questions concerning art.

The synergy between this artist's heritage and that of Japan becomes evident when considering her work across a period of years. Whether working at a relatively small scale or making installations and wall-sized arrays of prints, she creates an initial impression of meditative calm and introspection. With deeper consideration the viewer is led into the subtleties of texture and colour within and on the surface of the paper – or in many instances the layers of paper – that she utilises in the creation of many of her works. Preferring not to frame them behind glass, which would both flatten the works and create an unwanted layer of reflection, she allows the lightweight paper to float away from the surface of the wall, responding to air currents, adding a further dimension to the work. The transience of all things, a central tenet of Buddhism, is embedded within the concept and appearance of the works, and the gentle motion of the sheets of paper becomes akin to breathing. At the same time the inherent strength of the Japanese papers and the permanence of the pigments that she uses give the works a positive strength, creating a balance between the senses of 'there-ness' and 'not-there-ness'. In *Love Clouds*, for example, the eye of the viewer is drawn first to the apparent simplicity of the repetition of snaking lines of overlapping circles, and then through to the underlying layers fading into the depths. The impression is similar to that created by the images of passing clouds reflected in still water rippled suddenly by a passing breeze. A close observation of the cycle of transience in nature continues, and is contained, in the work of this artist.

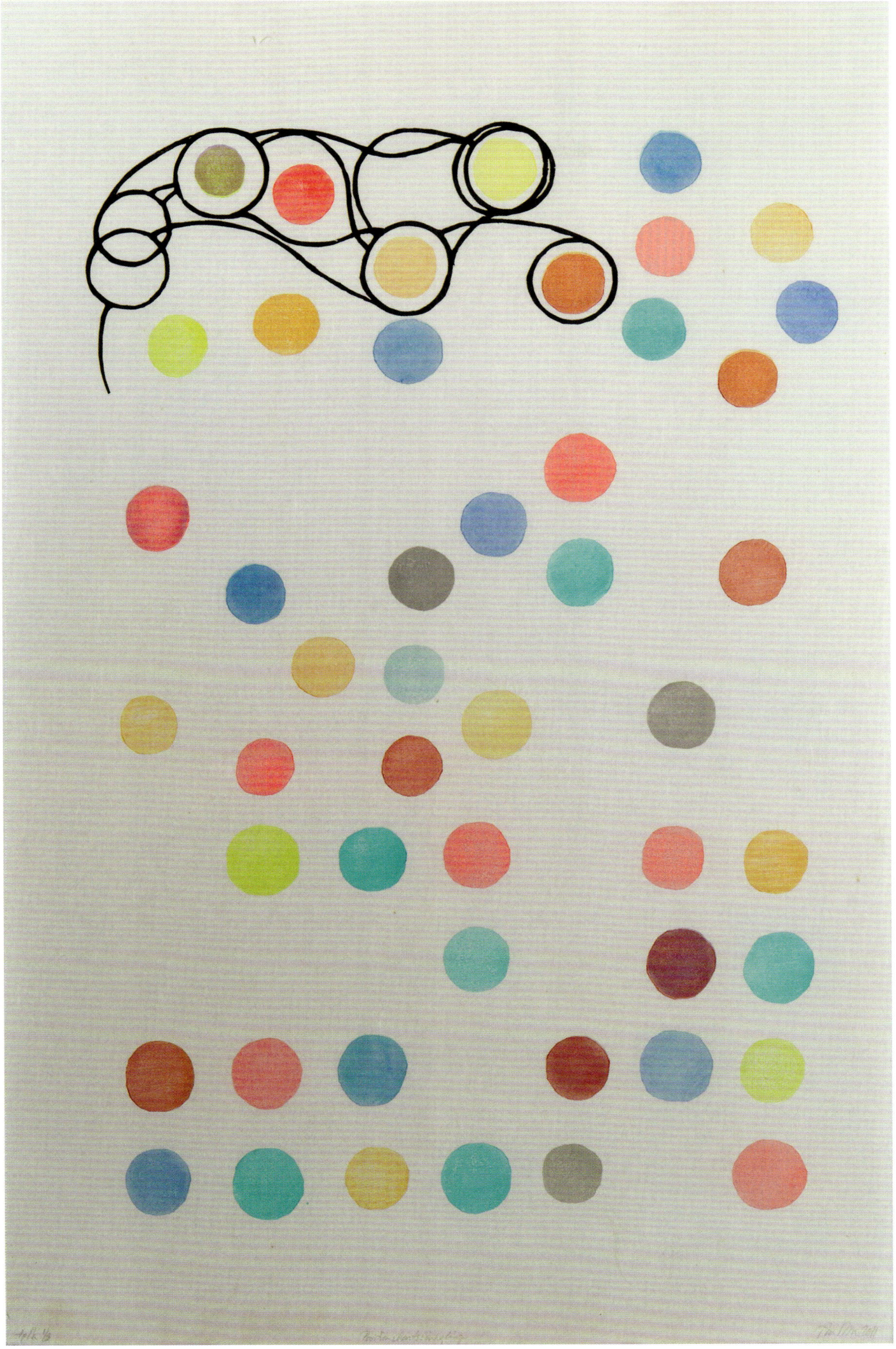

VENEZUELA

IRENE FURLAN

IRENE FURLAN was born in Venezuela to a family of painters and recalls starting to draw and paint at an early age, and growing up thinking 'that there was nothing amazing, nothing special in knowing how to draw ... drawing was just a skill I was born with.' However, this did not motivate her towards seeking a career in art and she went on to study chemistry at university and then spent several years working as a chemist before turning to making art, initially as a painter before later becoming involved with printmaking. She has an extensive record of exhibitions both in Venezuela and internationally. She comments that, 'When you are painting, what you do is what you see and what you get. When you are printing, what you get is not necessarily what you thought you would get. And you either love that image or embark on the sometimes very long journey of trying to get on paper what you have in mind. The chemist in me enjoys the process, enjoys preparing the plate, changing methods, improving results … I love printmaking because of its versatility, because its results are unique and, believe it or not, because it is not easy.' Furlan says she enjoys the challenge of producing a work of art through processes that balance artistic sensibility and scientific ingenuity.

Venezuela, on the northeast coast of South America, is noted for its biodiversity and the extensive range of its habitats, from the high Andes to the Amazonian rainforest (including the highest waterfall in the world: the Angel Falls), to a broad central plain and the Caribbean coast, on the edge of which Caracas is situated. First colonised by the Spanish in 1522, the country has developed rapidly since the discovery of oil in the early 20th century, and the capital reflects the relative prosperity that has come from the exploitation of this natural resource. The recent regime of Hugo Chavez was highly controversial, and accounts of injustice and the suppression of opposition were rife. The city has the reputation of being one of the most crime-ridden and corrupt capitals in the world, and yet, despite this, has a cultural life that includes two internationally renowned universities and, since 1974, a contemporary art museum. The

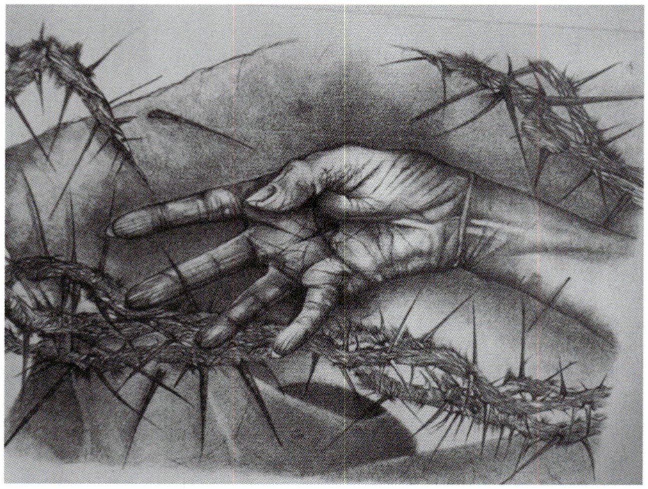

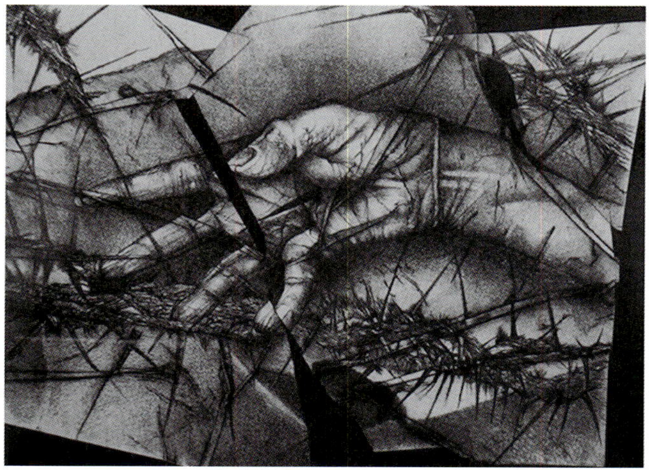

Irene Furlan, *Cilicio*, 2005. Wrinkled intaglio from two copperplates, 89 x 58cm (35 x 22¾in.).

Right: Irene Furlan, *Eve*, 2010. Intaglio from copperplates, 120 x 80cm (47¼ x 31½in.).

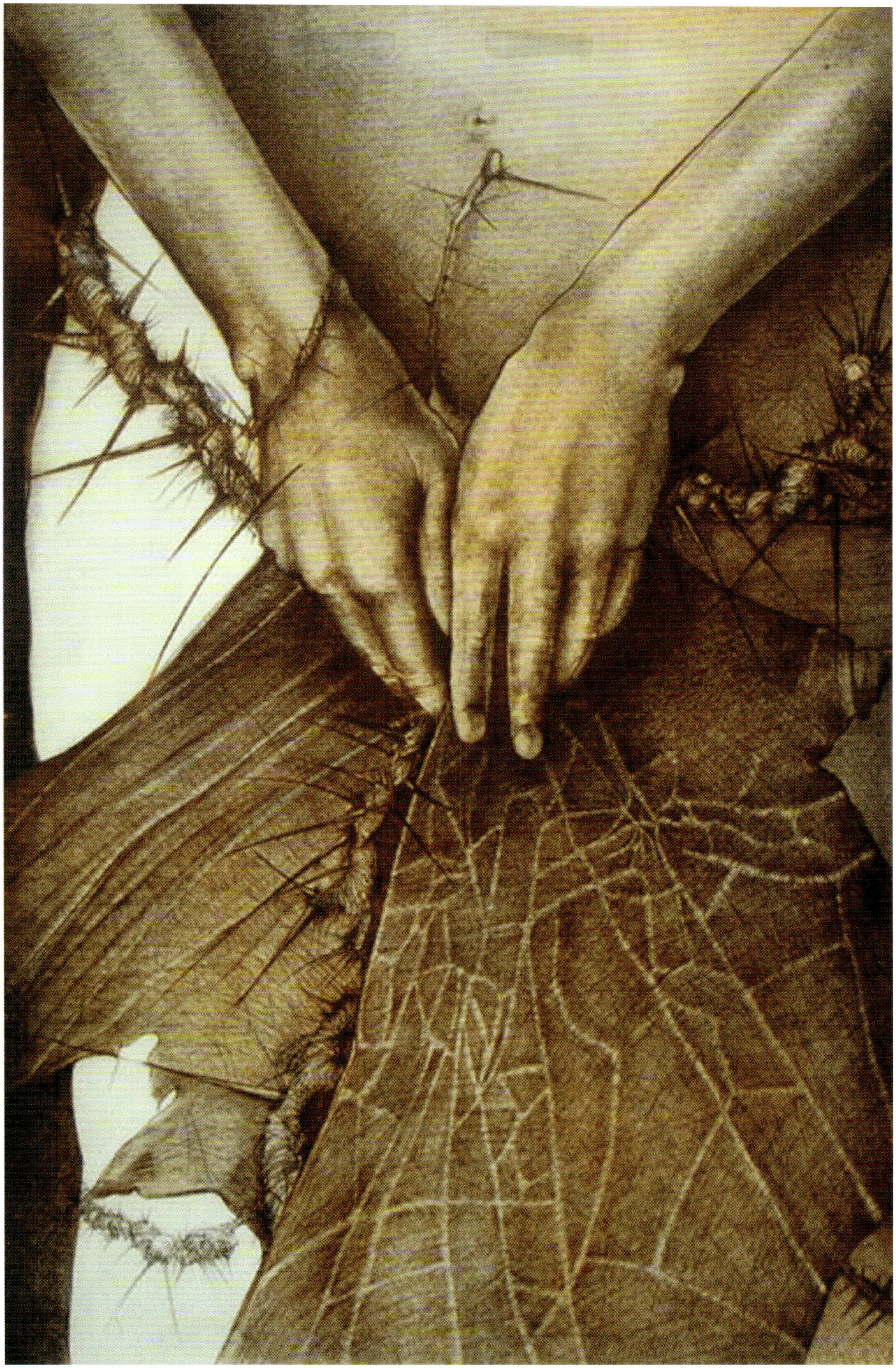

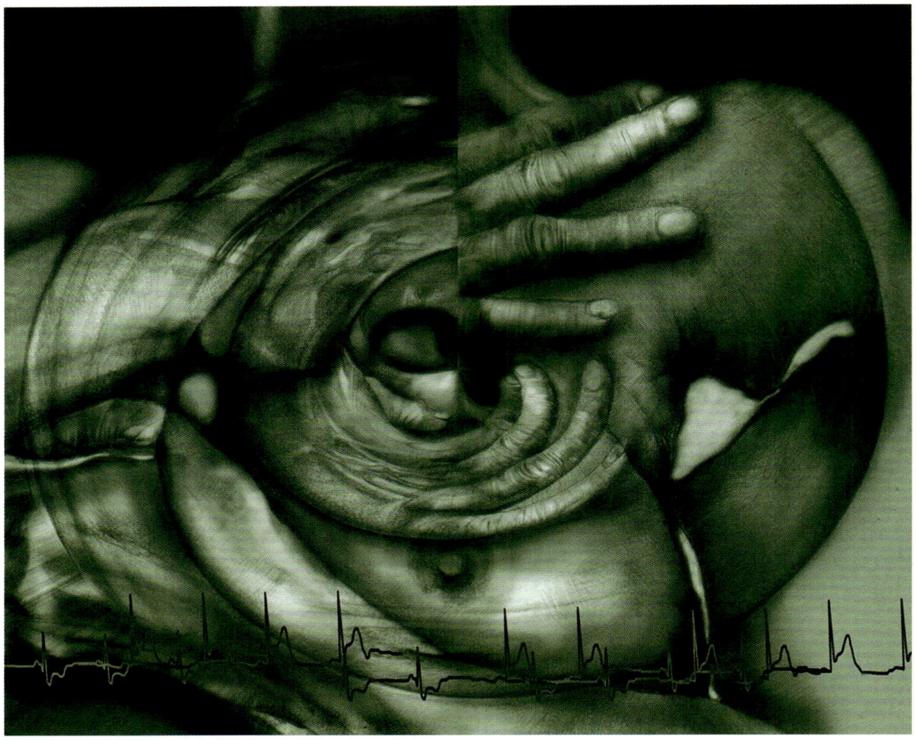

Irene Furlan, *Pliers of Anxiety*, 2004.
Intaglio from copperplate, 62 x 82cm (24½ x 32¼in.).

continuing instability of the country has initiated a growing unease, especially among young professionals, and this situation looks unlikely to change in the near future. Furlan currently lives in Caracas and the circumstances in which she lives inevitably affect the work of this sensitised artist: while her work has a strongly autobiographical element, reflecting not only her immediate worries, traumas and doubts, it also reflects (even if not explicitly) the more extensive problems of daily life in Venezuela, and also the feeling of being torn between wanting to remain in the country to which she feels a powerful attachment and wanting to leave to seek better conditions elsewhere.

While her earlier paintings were largely abstract and at times are the result of what she readily admits is 'playing with colour', her prints tend towards monochrome, or at most a limited range of colours, and are usually large in scale. Most of her earlier prints are made in intaglio techniques from one or more copper plates, although she has more recently turned to using photopolymer and solar plates. *In My Diary*, dating from 2000, a self-portrait of the artist stares out at the viewer from a plate that is fractured and fissured, suggesting a cracked mirror. The expression is tense, apprehensive and wary, an unsettling image for the new millennium in her life and country. In 2004, Furlan produced *Pliers of Anxiety*: prompted by health concerns, the image contains elements produced through the manipulation and distortion of photographs, accompanied by the trace of a cardiogram, and is printed in a livid green that conveys a cold despair. While being derived from a personal experience this image also speaks metaphorically of the disease within Venezuelan society, taking the symbolism of the hand and breast into deeper regions of interpretation. In a similar way, *Cilicio* (2005) is associated with her husband's serious health diagnosis and subsequent successful treatment, a very difficult period for the artist which resulted in anxiety bordering on depression; the anguish depicted can also be seen to represent the sentiments felt by many others in the country. A more recent work, *Eve* (2010), is a large print produced from three copper plates with a style of drawing that relates back to Renaissance images of Eve, and forward into the present, creating a continuum in which the suffering of a society in crisis can be seen as being symbolically portrayed.

About the current development in her work, Irene Furlan writes, 'I have been working on a series of drawings but I have not made them into prints yet. They are inspired by the diaspora that this country is living: people are able to cope with bad salaries, inflation, unemployment, poverty, pollution, traffic, bad public services, all that; but if you add insane levels of delinquency and insecurity, people will start to flee. Venezuela was a country of immigrants, they'd find here plenty of opportunities and friendly people with open arms. Venezuelans never even thought of considering going away. Now, our younger, better-educated people are leaving at amazingly high rates. We have ended up being a country of divided families, broken hearts and lost resources. A real diaspora. I hope I will be able to express in my art work the deep feelings I have about this situation.'

ALASKA, USA

ALLIE HIGH

THE CANON OF Western art is derived from a long evolution of styles and forms derived largely from, or in reaction to, the inspiration of the Judeo-Christian ethical and religious framework, and more recently that of Islam; so-called native art is derived from very different belief systems and ways of making art. During the past century or so, as international trade and travel have increased and the worldwide web has become truly global, the world is becoming rapidly ever more connected and the distinctions between cultural frameworks that existed previously are to a large extent dissolving. For example, the long history of the invasion, colonisation and exploitation of North America by European nations has brought about the fading of some traditions and the dilution of others, resulting in the loss of many of the practices and processes that helped to sustain the former strength and distinction of individual tribal cultures. However, as a reaction to such effects, partly influenced by the ways in which tribal societies sought to increase their income by the production of items for the burgeoning tourist trade, and partly due to the international movements for the reassertion of tribal identities, there has been considerable progress in the re-establishment of traditional ways of working, and with this have come changes in the ways in which artefacts and art works are produced. As the members of those societies have become integrated with society in general, learning from them while maintaining traditions, using different art forms and materials to strengthen their art, so in the process stronger sociopolitical identities have been developed.

Allie High was born in Ketchikan, Alaska, to a family in which her grandparents were from the Raven and Killer Whale clans of the Tsimpshian people. Her early life was influenced by listening to them speaking their native language and by their use of traditional herbal medicines, as well as by their obvious connections with the land and their experiences with nature, in short the natural rhythm of their lives. She relates how, at the age of 12, she attended her first masked performance in Haines, Alaska, and how this drew her into learning more of her culture. With a first degree in art education from the University of Oregon, she worked for some time as an art therapist in Louisiana before attending the University of Texas at Tyler to study for an MA in Interdisciplinary Studies, including art, theatre and sociology. Since returning to Alaska she has received a number of grants enabling her to expand her knowledge and practice of traditional art forms, and her work has been shown in numerous exhibitions across the United States. She currently lives in Eagle River, Alaska. The trajectory of her varied career therefore typifies that of many First Nations artists who have come through an individual series of experiences to value and reassess their traditional cultural background and to find their own ways of interpreting it in a contemporary manner.

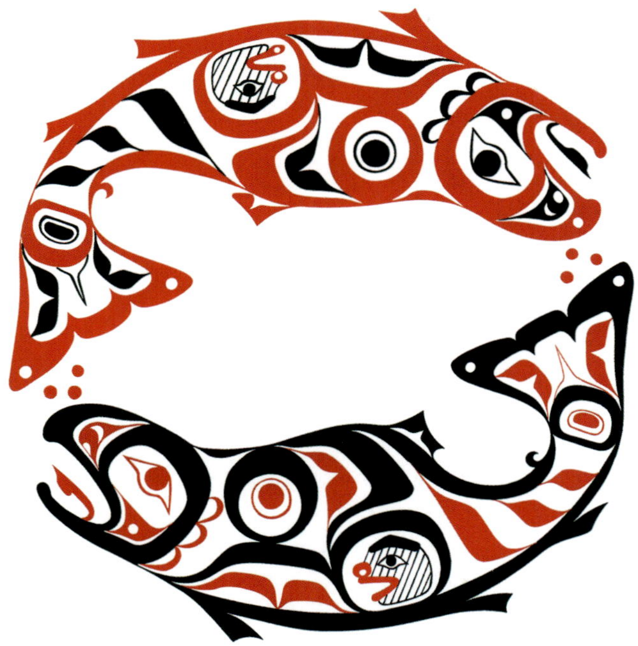

Allie High, *Salmon Cycle*, undated. Silkscreen on Arches paper, 40.6 x 38cm (16 x 15in.) Printed by Chris Nowicki.

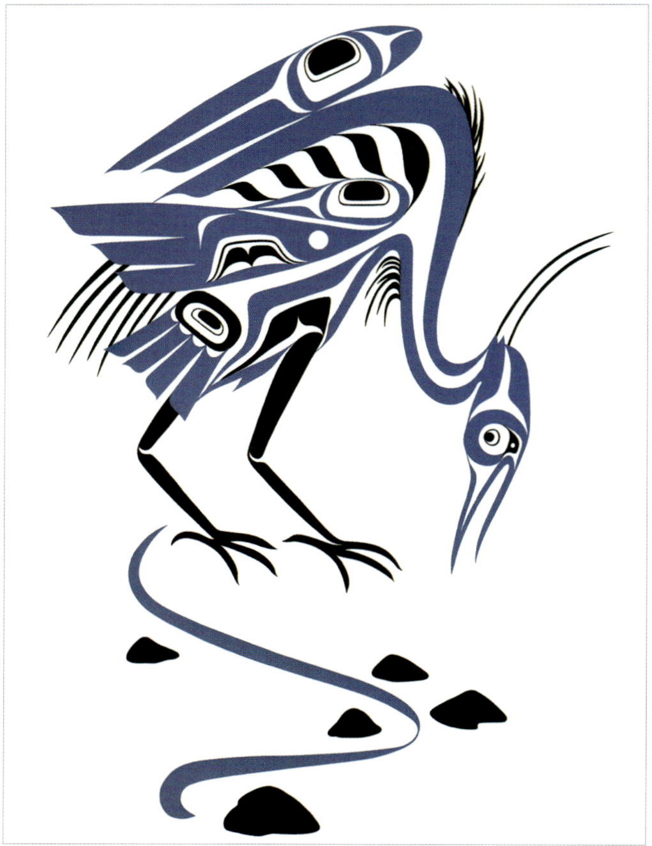

Allie High, *Blue Heron*, 2009. Silkscreen on Arches paper, 75.6 x 55.8cm (29¾ x 22in.). Printed by Chris Nowicki.

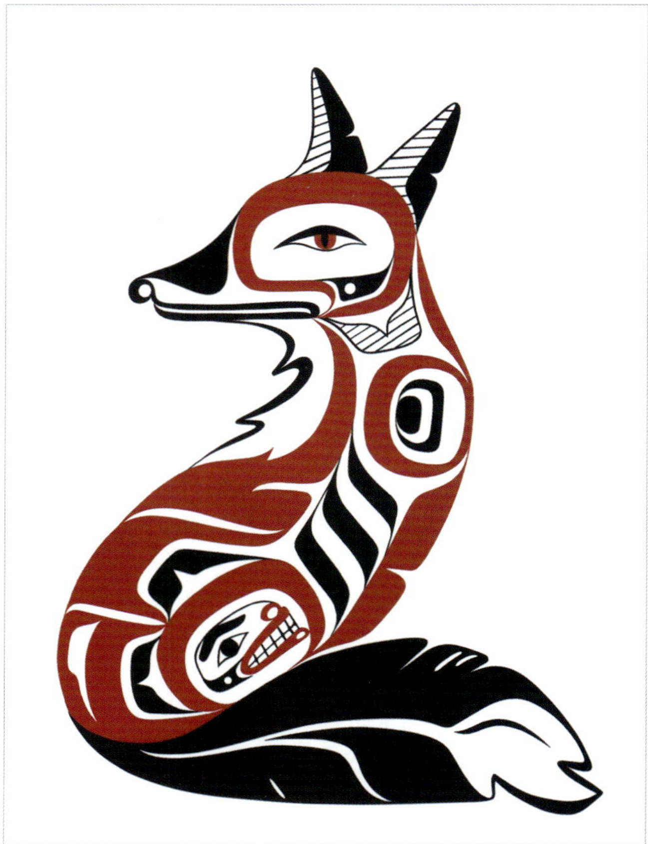

Allie High, *Foxy*, 2011. Silkscreen on Arches paper, 50.8 x 38cm (20 x 15in.). Printed by Chris Nowicki.

Each of the selected images has a background and contains a narrative element. In *Salmon Cycle*, there is the dual use of yin–yang symbolism, in the forms and in the reversal of dark and light, with the egg forms representing the next generation. The whole form represents the cycle of life upon which her father's career as a salmon fisherman relied in order for him to be able to provide for his family in a sustainable way. The design was made originally for a drum to commemorate her father's retirement from fishing, but it has been adapted for use as a screen print. High describes how she enjoys the challenges of working within a round shape, in which the curvilinear forms add to the sense of movement. By contrast, *Blue Heron* is a print that the artist found daunting to make. It does not follow the traditional use of red and black on a white background, and neither does it abide by the traditional method of bilateral symmetry. Instead it is printed in blue and black and is asymmetric, seeming to her to be more closely related to Eastern rather than Western forms. She writes of how the work relates to her efforts to assist a student with a drum design on which she was working some years before, and how she was able later to help to refine that design to make a less cumbersome and more balanced form. Through observing a blue heron in front of her house, where rivulets made their way from the hillside behind her towards the sea, she noticed the way in which the bird would pick its way among the rocks. By spending time cutting out varying shapes and arranging them on a sheet of paper to create the design, Allie High was able to come up with the resulting design that she subsequently transferred to the screen from which this unusual print is made.

Foxy began with the artist's encounter with a female fox sitting beside the road between Anchorage and Fairbanks one winter. The fox was turned into the wind, a position of strength, with what she describes as 'a haughty, elegant look'. Foxes are not normally seen much beside the coast and so do not generally figure in the art of the Northwest Coast. The striking form that has resulted in this print, adopting a curvilinear S-shape yet stylised to exclude direct references to the legs, captures much of the essence of the fox and its universally recognised attributes of cunning and devotion to family. While the art of Allie High is thoroughly contemporary it relates back to the traditional beliefs of kinship with animals and the transformative power of mythology. As she writes, 'To do less than feel these things is not to experience the subject, and certainly a work of art that is void of this substance cannot have life.'

ALASKA, USA & POLAND

CHRISTOPHER NOWICKI

THE PRINT DISCIPLINES of mezzotint and screenprinting contrast greatly, but come together in the career of Christopher Nowicki. He first discovered the world of printmaking through screenprinting, learning the techniques at high school, and taking an evening job printing commercial signs. During his BFA course at the School of Art and Design of the Toledo Museum of Art, he studied a wide range of print techniques with an emphasis on etching, which continued during his MFA course at Washington University in Seattle, from which he graduated in 1977. Following the award of his MFA, Nowicki taught at the Pratt Fine Arts Centre in Seattle, covering screen techniques and also lithography. While there he pursued the development of his own work in both screenprinting and mezzotint, and also methods for combining them in a single print. Then in the early 1980s he was asked to produce a suite of limited-edition prints for the First Nations artist, John Goodwin, of the Makah tribe. This in turn led to working with other artists from tribes in the Seattle area and through this he developed a deep interest in the traditions of Northwest Coast styles that has remained with him. After showing his work in a number of galleries in the USA he was invited in 1989 to have an exhibition at what was then the DESA gallery in Wrocław in Poland. Having Polish grandparents and a curiosity about the country, he went to Poland for the opening of the exhibition. He writes, 'I had always heard that printmaking in Poland was very high quality and some of the best in the world, so I decided to go. I was not disappointed; I met wonderful people and was amazed by the prints. Nothing could have prepared me for this.'

This turning point led him to visit Poland again in 1992, and on his return to the US he decided to move to Poland for a few years to develop his aesthetic skills and philosophy. Before he could do this he was invited by Lee Heinmiller, Director of Alaska Indian Arts in Haines, to spend some time working there to produce limited-edition screen prints with local artists. His enjoyment of this experience has led to him returning to work in Haines every summer since.

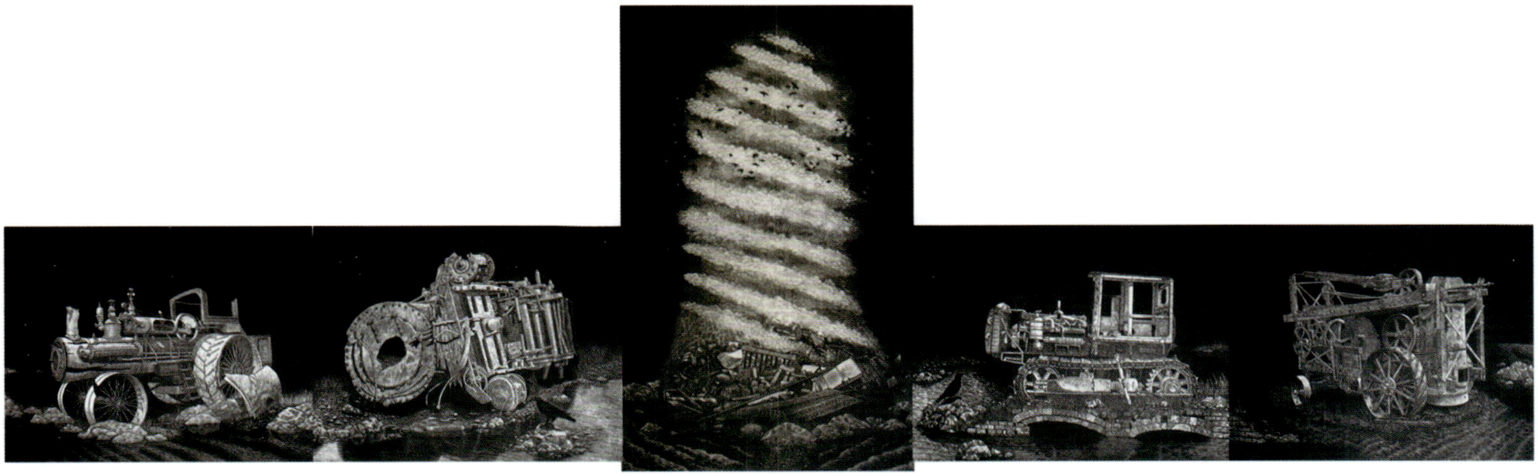

Christopher Nowicki, *Entropy* (entire series), 2001–10. Mezzotint from copperplate, 45.7 x 325cm (18 x 128in.).

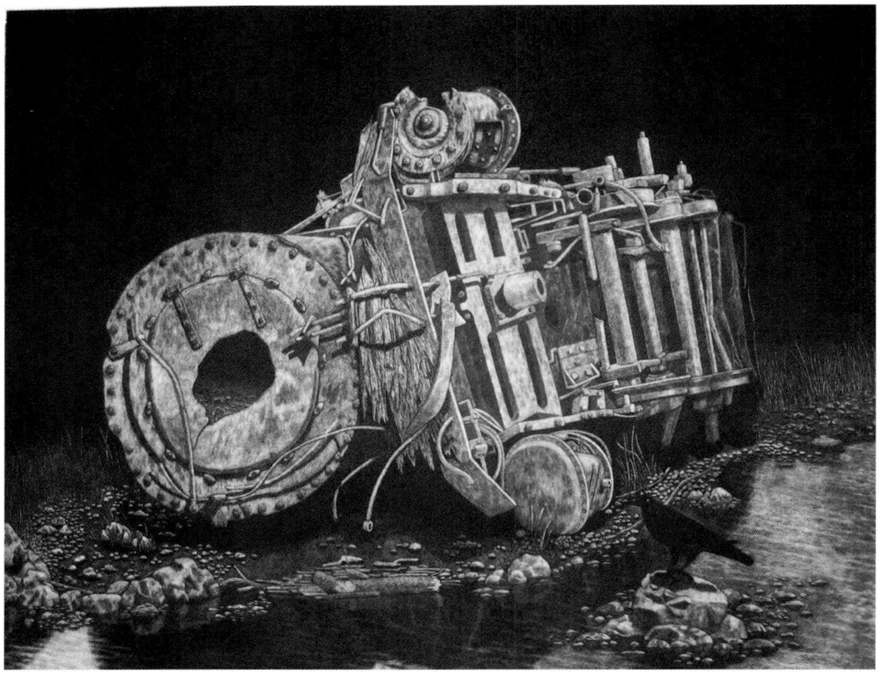

Christopher Nowicki, *Entropy (Locomotive)*, 2001. Mezzotint from copperplate, 45.7 x 60.9cm (18 x 24in.).

Of the experience he writes, 'At first I wasn't attracted to this complicated art form. I didn't understand it. But as my awareness grew my appreciation grew also. I have the utmost respect for these artists, this art form, and this culture. It is fascinating.' He moved to Poland in 1993, and in 1996 was appointed senior lecturer at the Academy of Fine Arts in Wrocław, gaining his PhD from the same institution in 2001 and being promoted, most recently in 2006, to Professor of Printmaking. Notably, this academy now offers a printmaking degree, taught in English, and under Nowicki's curatorship has created a major exhibition of Polish printmaking that is travelling the world, including visits to China and India.

In Poland Nowicki has concentrated on working with mezzotint, a demanding technique that in essence requires a metal plate to be given a finely textured surface either by machine or through the use of a handheld rocker, upon which the artist works with fine tools to burnish sections to varying degrees, resulting in the production of a print with deep velvety blacks and delicate details varying through a range of greys to pure white, producing, literally, light from darkness. Nowicki writes, 'The most important aspects of my mezzotints are technique and symbolism. I choose the mezzotint technique because it allows me the most freedom with the way I want to present my ideas. It is possibly the most difficult technique but because of this it gives me the most satisfaction.' Through his interest in symbolism, the philosophy of literature, and Eastern thought, links can be found between his personal work and teaching in Poland, and the parallel world of his involvement with First Nations art in Alaska.

In his *Entropy* series of mezzotints Nowicki has produced one of the most notable and haunting sets of images of recent years. The term 'entropy' comes from the science of thermodynamics, but is more generally applied to the decay of the universe from order into chaos. The full series of five prints has at its centre a whirling spiral of cloud or dust rising from a furrowed field littered with the detritus of human habitations, while to either side there are images of machinery standing motionless against the darkness in the wasteland of a field: a locomotive is beyond use, lying on its side, observed by a raven, while a bulldozer is stranded helplessly at the end of a broken bridge surrounded by water, observed by two ravens. The other images are of vintage farm machines: a steam drill and a tractor, rendered equally beyond use by neglect, rejection or some unnamed disaster. This set of prints, produced during his time in Poland, represents a disturbing vision of a time out of joint with history. Layers of meaning exist, or can be imagined, within these prints: are they symbolic of all human decay of which, as T.S. Eliot writes (in *Four Quartets*), 'the parched eviscerate soil / gapes at the vanity of toil', or are they concerned with the degradation of industrial society in the face of technology, or, even further, symbolic of the decay of Western society as a whole? Whichever way they are interpreted, these prints are masterly in conception and execution.

Christopher Nowicki's career, with a distinguished record of exhibitions and awards, has resulted from a number of interlinked and unexpected opportunities that have combined to lead him off his own particular beaten track into creating unique bridges between his Polish heritage and his present Polish home, and between his classical approach to mezzotint and his devotion to First Nations art in Alaska. His fascinating journey continues.

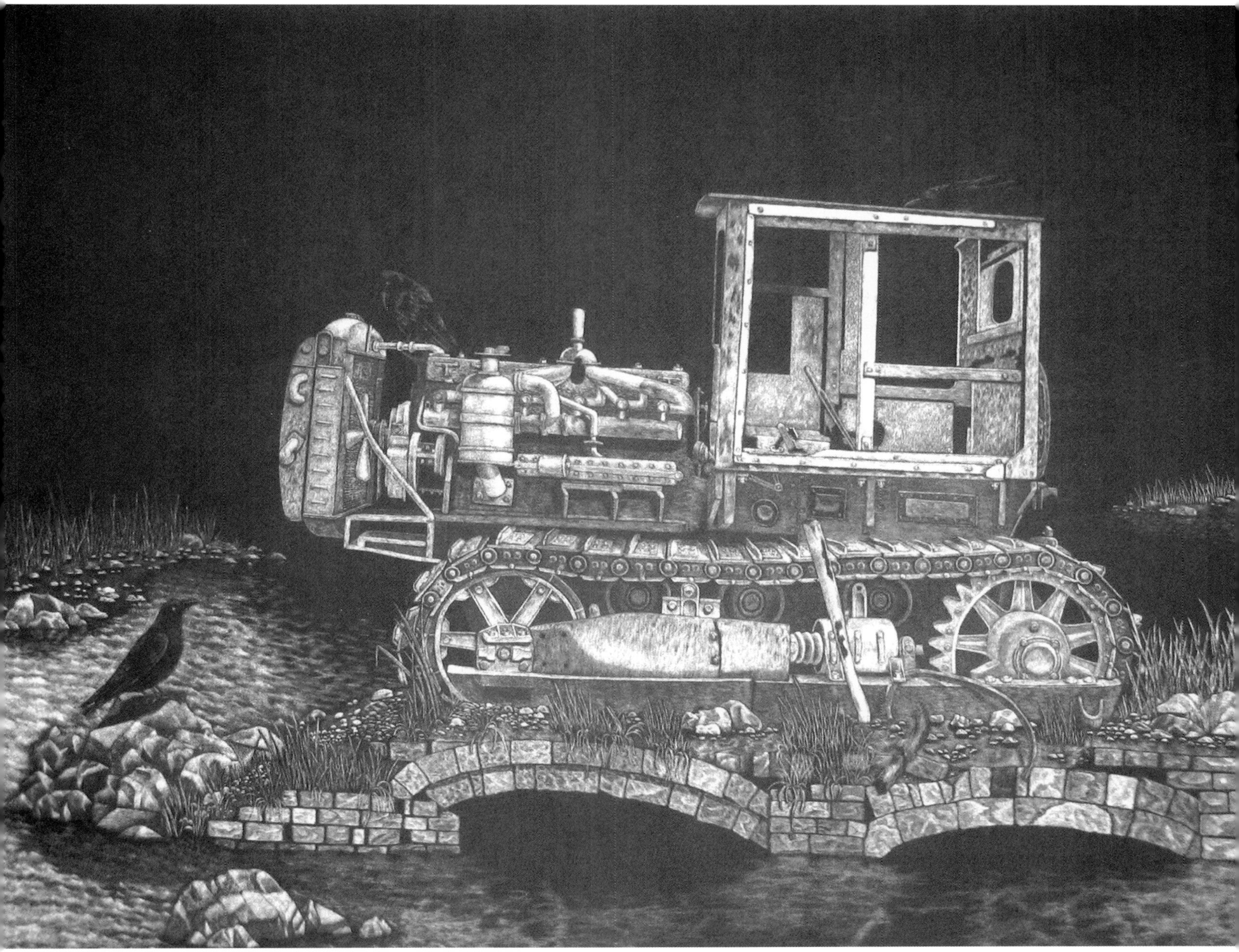

Christopher Nowicki, *Entropy (Bulldozer)*, 2003. Mezzotint from copperplate, 45.7 x 60.9cm (18 x 24in).

JAPAN

YOKO HATTORI

THE PATH ALONG which each person's life leads presents a succession of images and challenges. The imperatives that drive each life are different, but for an artist can include the need to capture by whatever means they choose those fleeting moments that seem to be most important. Traditional forms of printmaking, being labour-intensive and process-driven, are time-consuming in a similar way to traditional painting and academic drawing. With the development of digital photography and film has come the ability to seize the fleeting impression of a moment in time and to re-present it within a work of art. In turn, through the persuasive eye of an artist, these two modes of working can intersect, offering new hybrids of making. While still being in the early part of her career, Yoko Hattori has found ways of interpreting her experience at the intersection of two different cultures. Born in Hiroshima, she received her BFA in Design from the University of Hawaii before moving to Minnesota State University to complete her MA in Design and Printmaking and thence to the University of Wisconsin, Milwaukee, where she is completing her MFA degree in printmaking and multimedia. Although based in the USA she retains strong links with her family and roots in Japan, returning when she is able.

In a statement about her work Hattori writes, 'My work is about memory and transition between places, time and people. My ideas stream from exploration of my own memory and thoughts where repressed consciousness finds expression. I think that visual art bridges the gap between here and there, now and then, self and other, and as an artist I stand in between, creating that bridge.' The culture in which she grew up, with its blend of philosophies and religions, remains central to her work in printmaking and multimedia installations, as do her memories of growing up in a place whose name has attained a mythic resonance around the world. She recalls playing hide and seek in an underground room beneath a vegetable garden, only finding out later that it was a bomb shelter. She remembers, 'seeing a big black imprint of shadows on a wall in the city of Hiroshima' and learning that 'it was the shadow of a person or object as they were the very moment the bomb hit'. Her grandfather went through World War II and came back alive: he would not tell her about his experience, except that it was hard to live with the memories that kept haunting him. When she moved to Hawaii to study she lived with a Japanese-American family and learned about their internment and the hardships they endured as being neither fully American nor fully Japanese. After moving to the mainland of the US she became increasingly interested in understanding how personal experience and reported experience can be processed as part of memory and can influence thought.

In her earlier work this artist produced conventional prints of a rare delicacy, combining digital and traditional techniques on traditional papers. She also made books that enabled her to convey a narrative of experiences and memories of her life in Japan, including her childhood friendships, and her later experiences in Hawaii (itself both a fully-fledged US state and yet something of an interim space with a distinct heritage and culture of its own) and then on the mainland of the USA. But while these works gained considerable success and demonstrated beyond question the strength of her imagination and skills, she found herself searching for a fuller means to develop her ideas. These means arose during her MFA studies in Milwaukee, as part of an innovative cross-disciplinary program, through which she developed a new approach to the use of installation, combining structure, print and video to create a delicate and powerful hybrid form. In *Reminiscence*, a video projection on folded hanging fabric moves freely with air currents, with printed images and shadows of suspended cut-out forms creating constant and subtly changing forms and impressions.

In a major installation, *49 Days*, Yoko Hattori presents a meditation on the death of her grandfather, combined with her feelings about other events in Japan, piecing together memories, thoughts and dreams to represent her understanding of being away from home in 'the world of the in-betweens'. In the Buddhist tradition the first forty-nine days following a person's death is the intermediate stage

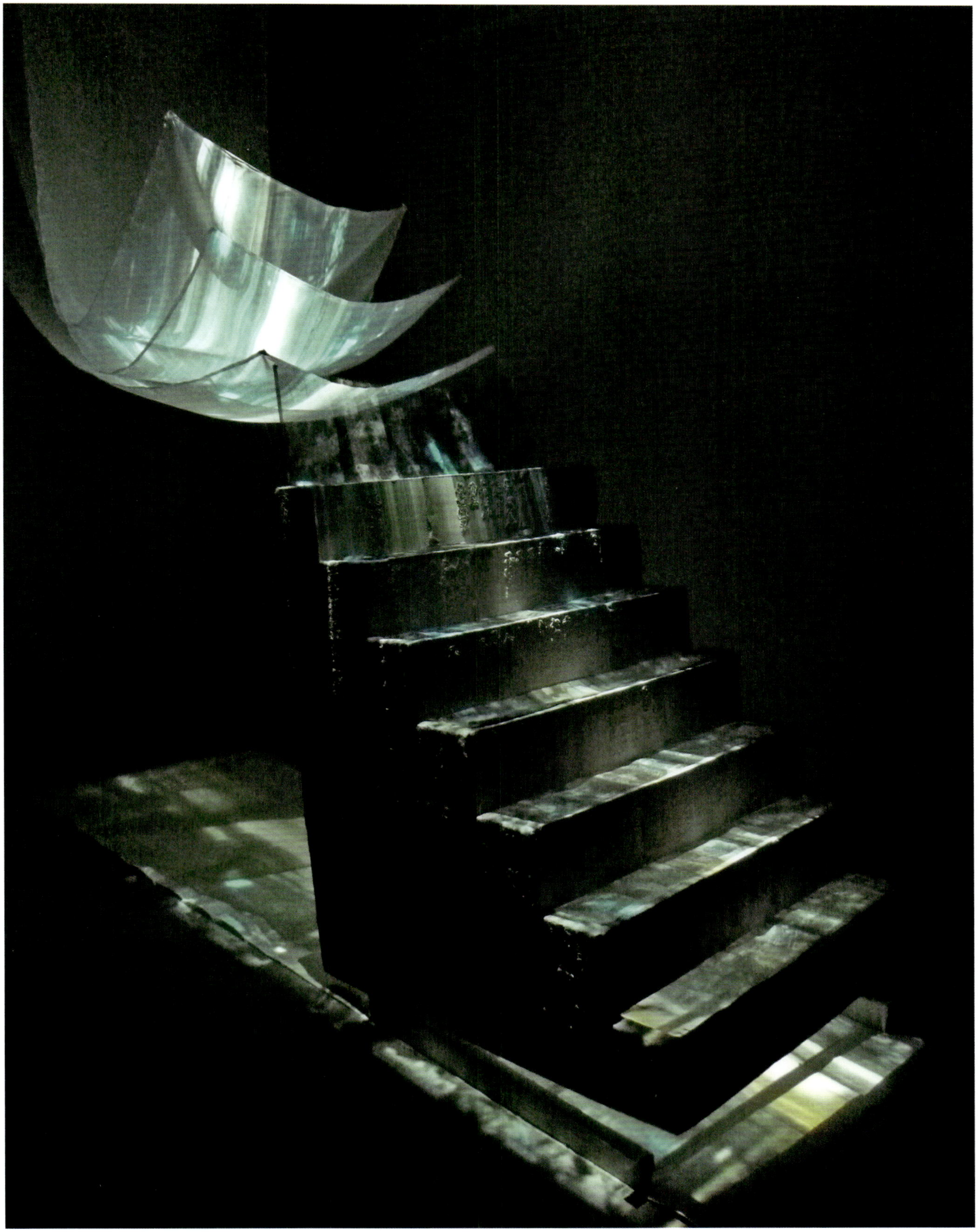

Yoko Hattori, *49 Days*, 2012. Installation, cement, digitally printed silk organza, polyester, relief prints, fusible interface, video projection, variable dimensions.

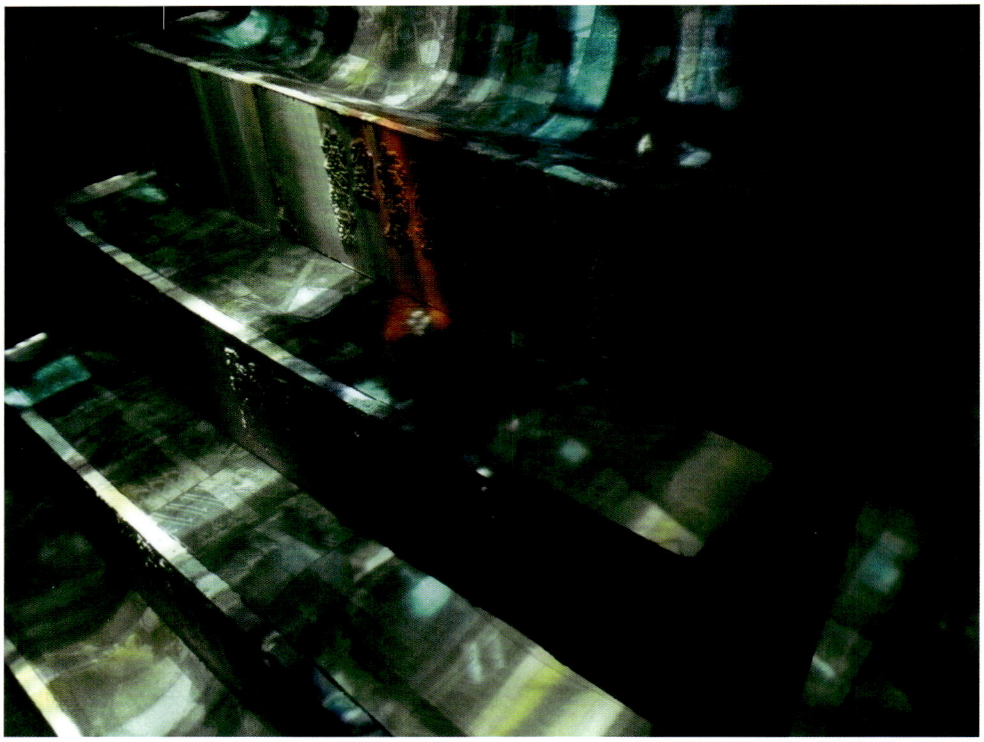

Yoko Hattori, *49 Days*, 2012. Installation, cement, digitally printed silk organza, polyester, relief prints, fusible interface, video projection, variable dimensions.

between death and rebirth, the soul passing through seven stages, each lasting seven days, a mourning period known as Shijukunichi. During the Buddhist funeral ceremony the *Heart Sutra*, the essence of Buddha's teaching on the Dharma, is chanted and this is often repeated during the forty-nine day mourning period. The *Heart Sutra* is at the core of Hattori's installation, being carved by her into blocks that were then cast to form the tiles that face the risers of the seven treads of the stairway, and subsequently used as relief blocks to make prints on Japanese calligraphy paper. These were then fused onto a fabric interface and sewn together to make the floor piece. The video that is projected onto the installation is of travellers on a moving pathway in an airport, for Hattori, 'a transitional space, crossroads and gateways of entry and exit points that connect two different places.' She considers airports to be a non-space existing between cultures, neither here nor there.

The visual strength of the installation comes from the poetic integrity with which this artist has invested it. It demonstrates beyond question that, given the rigorous approach through which this work has been conceived and made, the combination of different cultures and different visual art mediums can achieve a resonance that transcends those cultures and mediums. This powerful piece, *49 Days*, is a work of, and for, the 21st century, and indicates the clear direction of an artist with considerable promise.

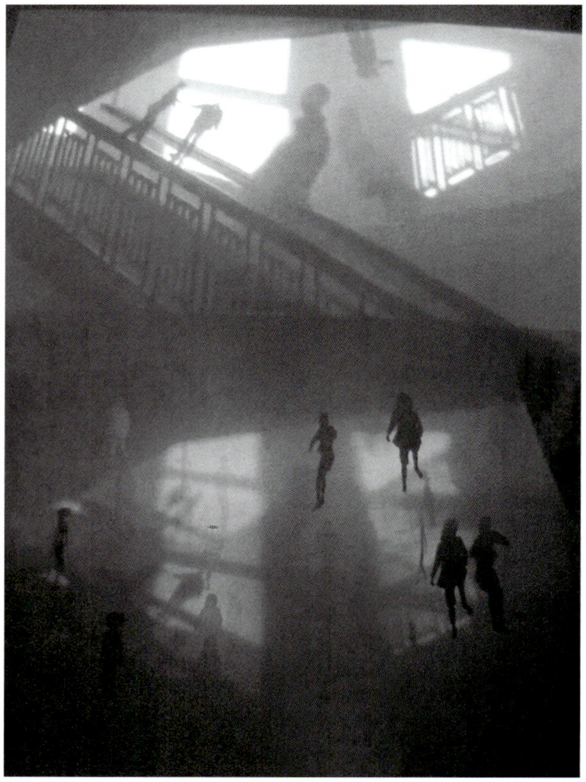

Yoko Hattori, *Reminiscence*, 2011. Print image from installation – photo-etching, 26.7 x 35.6cm (10½ x 14in.).

INDEX